With Compliments

Contact details are on the reverse of this document.

RICHARD VOGLER
DEPT OF CENTRE FOR LEGAL STUDI
UNIVERSITY OF SUSSEX
FALMER
BRIGHTON
BN1 9QH,UNITED KINGDOM

Reference no 51696363 HGI
Please quote when enquiring 2012384189
Customer account no 10373136

Date 12-11-2001
KCT
Page no 1 Inside

FREE EXAMINATION COPY - the enclosed title(s) has been requested by you or is being sent by your local Pearson Education representative for you to consider for course adoption. Please could you indicate below whether you are adopting the title(s)* and provide full course details where appropriate. Please include the type of recommendation* and the names of any colleagues teaching the course.

1 X 0 582 29966 7 LCRS.Bowling:Racism, Crime and J_p   *Adopted/Not Adopted

Module Code: Module Name: Start Date:

Adoption Type: *essential/recommended/background reading
No of Students: Current Text: Other Lecturers:

Comments:

The bookshop/supplier I will inform of the adoption is: _____
My contact details are: Tel: _____ E-mail _____

Please e-mail adoption details to your local representative or send to: Academic Information Dept. HE, PEARSON EDUCATION, FREEPOST ANG2666, Harlow, CM20 2YH, UK. Fax: +44 (0)1279 623862. For online resources visit www.booksites.net, or for further information on our titles please visit www.pearsoneduc.com or contact your local rep: Faye Upfield
Tel: 07909 974738 E-mail: faye.upfield@pearsoned-ema.com

Items now available, as ordered 08-DEC-2000 , our ref 40347494

GROS
15817/829
10373136

(024)
GSS 65802

51696363

All goods are supplied subject to Pearson Education's standard terms and conditions as printed overleaf.

Pearson Education Limited
Registered office Edinburgh Gate,
Harlow, Essex, CM20 2JE
Registered number 872828
Registered in England and Wales

Racism, crime and justice

Longman Criminology Series

Series Editor: Tim Newburn

Titles in the series:

Peter Ainsworth, *Psychology and Crime: Myths and Reality*
Ian Brownlee, *Community Punishment: A Critical Introduction*
Adam Crawford, *Crime Prevention and Community Safety: Politics, Policies and Practices*
Les Johnston, *Policing Britain: Risk, Security and Governance*
Philip Rawlings, *Crime and Power: A History of Criminal Justice 1688–1998*
Gary Slapper and Steve Tombs, *Corporate Crime*
Claire Valier, *Theories of Crime and Punishment*

Racism, Crime and Justice

Ben Bowling and Coretta Phillips

An imprint of **Pearson Education**

Harlow, England · London · New York · Reading, Massachusetts · San Francisco
Toronto · Don Mills, Ontario · Sydney · Tokyo · Singapore · Hong Kong · Seoul
Taipei · Cape Town · Madrid · Mexico City · Amsterdam · Munich · Paris · Milan

Pearson Education Limited
Edinburgh Gate
Harlow
Essex CM20 2JE

and Associated Companies throughout the world

Visit us on the World Wide Web at:
www.pearsoneduc.com

First published 2002

© Pearson Education Limited 2002

The rights of Ben Bowling and Coretta Phillips to be identified as authors of this work have been asserted by the authors in accordance with the Copyright, Designs and Patents Act 1988.

All rights reserved. No part of this publication may be reproduced, stored in a retrieval system, or transmitted in any form or by any means, electronic, mechanical, photocopying, recording or otherwise, without either the prior written permission of the publisher or a licence permitting restricted copying in the United Kingdom issued by the Copyright Licensing Agency Ltd, 90 Tottenham Court Road, London W1P 0LP.

ISBN 0582 29966 7

British Library Cataloguing-in-Publication Data
A catalogue record for this book is available from the British Library

10 9 8 7 6 5 4 3 2 1
05 04 03 02

Typeset in 10/12 New Baskerville by Fakenham Photosetting Ltd, Fakenham, Norfolk
Printed in Great Britian by Henry Ling Ltd at the Dorset Press, Dorchester, Dorset

Contents

Series Editor's Preface	ix
Acknowledgements	xi
Introduction	xiii
From pre-Scarman to post-Lawrence: racism, crime and justice 1979–2001	xv
Organisation of the book	xvii

1 History — 1
- The origins of the 'race' idea — 1
- Race and migration in Britain — 5
- Changing perceptions of ethnic minority communities as disorderly — 7
- Changing perceptions of minority communities as vulnerable to attack — 12
- The Lawrence Inquiry: towards a new agenda — 14
- The post-Lawrence era: from bad apples to root and branch reform — 17
- Conclusion — 18

2 Concepts — 19
- 'Race' relations — 19
- Racism — 20
- 'Race' without racism — 23
- Ethnicity — 24
- 'Race' and 'ethnic' categorisation — 33
- Prejudice, attitudes and stereotyping — 36
- Discrimination — 38
- Institutional racism — 40
- Contextual discrimination — 41
- Equal treatment, equal opportunity or equal outcome? — 43
- Disadvantage — 44
- Anti-discrimination law — 51
- Conclusion — 54

3 Criminological theory — 55
- Classical and control theories — 56
- Biological and psychological theories — 57

	Cultural theories	60
	Structural theories	64
	Conclusion	74
4	**Offending and victimisation**	76
	The social construction of ethnicity and criminality	77
	Defining crime	82
	Official statistics on ethnicity and offending	83
	Self-report studies	98
	Controlling for demographic and social factors	104
	Conclusion: searching for a chimera?	106
5	**Racist violence**	108
	The extent and nature of racist victimisation	109
	Racist offending: from profiling to explanation	114
	Responses to racist violence	119
	England and Wales after the Lawrence Inquiry	124
	Conclusion	125
6	**Policing**	128
	Police deployment and targeting	128
	Immigration policing	130
	Police violence and deaths in custody	131
	Attitudes towards the police	135
	Stop and search	138
	Arrest	148
	Outcomes following arrest	149
	Police processing of juveniles	152
	Police remand	154
	Explaining discrimination in policing	155
	Police governance	163
	Conclusion	166
7	**Prosecution and sentencing**	168
	The decision to terminate or prosecute cases	168
	Bail and remand decisions	169
	The prosecution	172
	Acquittals	172
	The sentencing process	172
	Sentencing in the magistrates' court	176
	Committals	180
	Outcomes at the Crown Court	181
	Juries	187
	Youth justice	188
	Conclusion	190
8	**Prison and probation**	192
	Ethnic monitoring of the prison population	192

	The historical and policy context	199
	Racism in prison	200
	Parole	206
	Foreign nationals	207
	Immigration detainees and asylum seekers	208
	Brutality and deaths in custody	208
	The probation service	209
	'Race' and racism in probation practice	210
	Conclusion	211
9	**Practitioners**	213
	Ethnic minority police officers	214
	Ethnic minorities as prosecution and court staff	220
	Ethnic minority prison officers and staff	223
	Ethnic minority probation officers	226
	Ethnic minorities employed in the Home Office	227
	Equal opportunities in criminal justice agencies	228
	Conclusion	231
10	**Conclusion**	233
	Ethnicity and criminal justice	233
	Ethnicity and crime	243
	New Labour, racism, crime and justice	253
	Guide to further reading	262
	Bibliography	270
	Subject Index	303
	Names Index	310

Series Editor's Preface

Our society appears to be increasingly preoccupied with crime and with criminal justice. Despite increasing affluence in the post-war period, crime has continued to rise – often at an alarming rate. Moreover, the pace of general social change at the beginning of a new century is extraordinary, leaving many feeling insecure. High rates of crime, high levels of fear of crime, and no simple solutions in sight, have helped to keep criminal justice high on the political agenda.

Partly reflecting this state of affairs, the study of crime and criminal justice is burgeoning. There are now a large number of well-established postgraduate courses, new ones starting all the time, and undergraduate criminology and criminal justice degrees are also now appearing regularly. Though increasing numbers of individual textbooks are being written and published, the breadth of criminology makes the subject difficult to encompass in a satisfactory manner within a single text.

The aim of this series is, as a whole, to provide a broad and thorough introduction to criminology. Each book covers a particular area of the subject, takes the reader through the key debates, considers both policy and politics and, where appropriate, also looks to likely future developments in the area. The aim is that each text should be theoretically-informed, accessibly written, attractively produced, competitively priced, with a full guide to further reading for students wishing to pursue the subject further. Whilst each book in the series is designed to be read as an introduction to one particular area, the Longman Criminology Series has also been designed with overall coherence in mind.

In this book, Ben Bowling and Coretta Phillips tackle one of the most important issues facing politicians, policy-makers, criminal justice professionals and criminologists today: that of racism. There is now a considerable body of empirical research in the UK and elsewhere that illustrates the extent to which people from minority ethnic communities are disproportionately subject to criminal justice intervention and penal sanction. Though we know a lot about the outcome we are still struggling in some senses to understand the processes involved. This is where Bowling and Phillips' book comes in. Taking the reader through criminological and social theory and through the vast quantity of research evidence they offer a series of insights into the nature and role of racism in contemporary criminal justice.

This is an important book. It manages to combine theoretical sophistication with an awareness of the importance of rigorous empirical evidence. This is especially crucial in an area such as this, fraught with difficult and controversial political questions. It is also, sad to say, still an unusual attribute in much contemporary criminology that too often sees theory and data as odd bedfellows. In addition, the authors of *Racism, Crime and Justice* bring their considerable experience of real world policy-making to bear discussing political options for tackling the problem of unequal justice. This book should be required reading for our politicians and policy makers. For criminologists – whether their interest be policing, sentencing, punishment or victimisation – this text will be invaluable.

Tim Newburn
London, September 2001

Acknowledgements

This book would not have been completed without the help of a great many people. We are grateful to Tim Newburn for suggesting this project and for nurturing us gently but firmly (and always with good humour) towards completion. Brian Willan signed us up at Pearson, and we were subsequently looked after by Pat Bond with the help of Pat Root and Tim Parker. Thanks also to Patricia Connell, Andy Zurawan, Debbie Barton, Jade Moran, Maria Docking and Steve Tong who collected and sorted material, chased references and helped to compile the bibliography. Jo Norton and Alex Campbell deserve special thanks for contributing ideas and information to chapter 2. We are grateful to the London and Cambridge University libraries, the Commission for Racial Equality and the Home Office for providing the books and to the Cambridge Institute of Criminology and King's College School of Law for providing financial assistance.

Lee Bridges and Eugene McLaughlin read the manuscript from front to back, talked us through our ideas and provided critical commentaries that greatly improved the text. Many people – among them Alison Liebling, Amanda Matravers, Bonny Mhlanga, Jennifer Douglas, Kirpal Sahota, Andrea Cork, Darnell Hawkins, Paul Wilson, Lee Jasper, Elaine Player, Jennifer Bostock, Robert Reiner, Loraine Gelsthorpe, Ann Haydock and Ken Pease – commented on work in progress and provided invaluable support, advice and constructive criticism. Colin Webster read the final draft and gave us much needed encouragement for the last lap. Colleagues and students at John Jay, Rutgers, Cambridge, Bramshill and King's heard us rehearse our arguments and shared their insights with us, some of which have doubtless found their way into the book.

We are grateful to Damaris Steele and Carolina Cordero who efficiently processed our words, to Johnny Boteler for casting a critical eye over the text and trimming it into shape, and to Anne Rix who worked long hours, painstakingly editing the text into its final form. Last, but not least, we want to thank our families and friends whose love and support made it all possible.

Ben Bowling, King's College London
Coretta Phillips, London School of Economics

Publisher's Acknowledgements

We are grateful to the following for permission to reproduce copyright material:

Ch2, Box 2.2 from National Statistics (2000) in *Census News*, National Statistics, London; Ch2, Box 2.3 from National Identity in *British Social Attitudes: the 15th Report by Jowell, R et al (eds)*, Dartmouth Publishing Company (Dowds, L. and Young, K. 1996); Ch4 Table 4.1 from Ethnic Minorities: Victimisation and Racial Harassment: Findings from the 1988 and 1992 British Crime Surveys in *Home Office Research Study 154*, HMSO, London, (FitzGerald, M. and Hale, C. 1996); Ch4 Table 4.2 from the 1992 British Crime Survey in *Home Office Research Study 132*, HMSO, London (Mayhew, P., Aye Maung, N. and Mirrlees – Black, C. 1993); Ch4 Table 4.3 from Young People and Crime in *Home Research Study 145*, HMSO London (Graham, J. and Bowling, B. 1995).

Whilst every effort has been made to trace the owners of copyright material, in a few case this has proved impossible and we take this opportunity to offer our apologies to any copyright holders whose rights we may have unwittingly infringed.

Introduction

Skimming through articles on crime and criminal justice in today's magazines and newspapers, the reader will find frequent references to 'race' and 'racism'. The same is true of books and journals in contemporary criminology. Whether the topic is crime, victimisation, disorder, drugs, the police or the prison, race and racism or the related ideas of ethnicity and discrimination seem continually to be at issue. Perhaps the most common observation is that people seem to have different experiences of crime and justice depending on whether they are 'white', or of Asian, African, Caribbean or some 'other' ethnic origin. Although there has been, for some time, a general agreement that race and racism *matter* (though perhaps they should not), there are many competing accounts (based on empirical evidence, theoretical position, personal experience and political perspective) of why they are relevant and how they impact on the experience of crime and justice. Three examples – victimisation, the prison population and employment in criminal justice occupations – illustrate what is meant.

- 'Ethnic minorities' – those of African, Caribbean and Asian origins – are at greater risk of criminal victimisation than their white counterparts and are the targets of specifically racist violence. The patterns of victimisation are agreed on by most people, but how are they to be explained? Some people say they are the result of socio-economic conditions; some point to white racism; others blame the victims themselves.
- Some ethnic groups – notably those of African and Caribbean origins – are much more likely than white people to be arrested by the police and imprisoned by the courts. Again, few disagree with the statistics; but how are they to be explained? Perhaps 'black' people are simply more likely to commit crime than 'whites'. Assuming this to be true, criminologists have debated the relative merits of biological, psychological, cultural and structural theories. Alternatively, perhaps

there are no 'ethnic' differences in offending. On this basis, critics have argued that discrimination within the criminal justice process results in black offenders being more frequently arrested and jailed than their white counterparts committing the same offences.
- People of African, Caribbean and Asian origins are strikingly under-represented (compared to their numbers in the workforce) as employees of the police and prison services and are more or less entirely absent among the senior ranks of the criminal justice professions. Yet again there are conflicting explanations. Some argue that ethnic minorities are simply reluctant to become employees of the 'system', or that there are socio-economic or educational barriers to their employment. Others point to racial discrimination in recruitment, selection and promotion procedures, and to the existence of an institutionalised 'racist culture' in the criminal justice occupations.

As these examples suggest, race and racism are often central to discussions of patterns of offending, victimisation and criminal justice. Indeed, the number of research studies describing the relationship between race and racism and patterns of crime and criminal justice processing has grown markedly, and there is now an extensive literature. Although there are several collections of essays addressing some of the topics in the field (for example, Gelsthorpe 1993, Cook and Hudson 1993, Marshall 1997, Tonry 1997), the only attempts to provide an overview are Paul Gordon's (1984) excellent text, Marian FitzGerald's (1993) contribution to the Royal Commission on Criminal Justice and David Smith's (1997) chapter in *The Oxford Handbook of Criminology*. There have been few attempts to interpret the research and statistics in the light of existing theories in criminology or the sociology of racism and ethnicity. This book is an attempt to pull together the literature on 'race' issues in English criminology[1] and to explore some key developments in the field.

---

[1] We think this is the best geographical and academic field to situate the present survey of the literature. Although 'British criminology' is often used in this context, in fact, the vast majority of empirical studies cited in the text were conducted in England though the government statistics do include Wales. Scotland has a different legal system and few research studies properly examine the situation there or indeed that in Wales or Northern Ireland. The theoretical work in British criminology has been heavily influenced by its counterpart in the USA so we have incorporated this work where appropriate and we refer to the original sources wherever possible, though sometimes we rely on US textbooks.

From pre-Scarman to post-Lawrence: racism, crime and justice 1979–2001

During the last two decades of the twentieth century, criminology and criminal justice policy gradually recognised the importance of racism in shaping the experiences of people from ethnic minorities in the criminal justice system. Until the early 1980s, Britain could, with some justification, be accused of being a 'White Man's Country' dispensing 'White Law', as encapsulated by two rather blunt book titles (Miles and Phizacklea 1984, Gordon 1984). At the end of the 1970s, the existence of racist violence was ignored by government and the police who said there was no reliable evidence that such a thing ever happened. The possibility that racism in policing and criminal justice practices impacted on the safety and liberty of ethnic minority communities was flatly denied. The government even rejected the idea that police and other statutory bodies should be covered by the 1976 Race Relations Act because it might slur their good name.

Twenty years later, this situation has changed significantly. Research and statistics compiled in the 1980s and 1990s demonstrated that people from ethnic minority communities face a disproportionate risk of both victimisation and criminalisation. This research evidence, together with hard-fought campaigns for justice, led a major public inquiry to conclude in 1999 that British society is 'institutionally racist'. When the findings of the Lawrence Inquiry were published it was admitted at the highest level that the institutions of government and criminal justice had 'collectively failed' to 'provide an appropriate and professional service to people because of their colour, culture or ethnic origin' (Macpherson 1999: 6.34). It was accepted by a government-appointed former High Court judge that discrimination, prejudice, ignorance, thoughtlessness and racist stereotyping explain ethnic minority communities' complaints that they are 'over policed ... and under protected' (ibid.: 45.7).

Between 1979 and 1999, the official view of racism shifted from denial to acknowledgement, to shame and a publicly stated commitment to change. Although there remain some who oppose the Lawrence Inquiry findings and recommendations, and there has been a backlash against the reform process, the overwhelming reaction has been to take the issues raised very seriously. But the Lawrence Inquiry has done more than that. According to the Home Secretary, the process of the inquiry 'opened all our eyes to what it is to be black or Asian in Britain today'. The Home Secretary should, of course, be better informed than most because of his responsibility for crime, policing, the administration of justice, prisons and race relations.

The overall goal of this book is to describe and explain how the experiences of offending, victimisation and encounters with the police and the criminal justice process vary among different ethnic groups. It also seeks to raise further questions emerging from the research that need to be answered if the criminal justice system is to meet a commitment to ensure the safety and liberty of ethnic minorities in Britain. The questions we aim to address include the following:

- To what extent does the experience of crime and victimisation differ among white and various ethnic minority groups and how are these differences to be explained?
- What is racist violence, how does it affect the safety of ethnic minority communities, how is it to be explained and what is to be done about it?
- What factors explain why there is a disproportionate number of people from some ethnic minority groups (and not others) stopped by the police, arrested, prosecuted and imprisoned? What part, if any, does racism play in this process?
- Can racism, where it occurs in the criminal justice system, be explained best by examining the prejudiced, stereotyping and discriminatory acts of individual criminal justice practitioners, the cultures of criminal justice organisations, or institutional racism? To what extent is racial discrimination systemic, cumulative or context dependent?
- What is the likely impact of current criminal justice policies on the safety and liberty of people from ethnic minority communities?

To answer these questions we draw extensively on the research and statistical evidence that has accumulated over the past 20 years to illuminate how white, black and Asian people fare in a range of different criminological contexts. However, we have found that the empirical research evidence does not tell the whole story.

There are big gaps in statistical and other research evidence, leaving major areas of crime and criminal justice decision making un(der)-researched. Among the most obvious gaps are empirical studies of offending *within* minority communities (for example, domestic violence), abuses of power by criminal justice practitioners (for example, deaths in custody), judicial decision making (to shed light on well-documented disparities in sentencing) and probation practice with offenders from ethnic minority communities. By identifying these gaps we aim to broaden the scope of debates within criminology and the sociologies of racism and ethnicity.

There are also limits to using a scientific or empiricist approach to explain complex social phenomena. The terms 'race', 'ethnicity', 'crime' and 'discrimination' are essentially 'contested concepts', the meaning of which varies from study to study depending on the researcher's perspective. Consequently, an apparently shared (but actually contested) vocabulary provides a weak conceptual basis with which to compare and contrast the evidence from several studies. In order to overcome the 'poverty of empiricism', on one hand, and theoretical confusion, on the other, we have found it necessary in the early chapters of this book to review theories of race and ethnicity, that have informed, and been informed by, debates within criminology.

We have found a tension between empiricism (which assumes the existence of an 'essence' of race and crime) and social constructionism (which conceptualises both as dynamic social processes). We approach the topic from the latter position, contending that race is not 'real' outside the racist ideologies and discriminatory practices which bring it into being. However, this sits uncomfortably with our empirical analyses of race and ethnic differences in rates of victimisation, offending and imprisonment. Our approach is to reject raciological and criminological essentialism while retaining race and ethnic categories in order to illuminate the racialised patterns of everyday human experience. We think it is important to subject the social construction of race and ethnicity to critical analysis because justice policy and practice are influenced by these categorisations, and they inform the media and public consciousness.

Finally, we have found that empiricist approaches have sidelined minority perspectives in criminology. Although there is extensive documentary evidence of ethnic minority communities' experience of victimisation, criminalisation and abuse within the criminal justice agencies, often this has been seen as distinct from research and statistical evidence and therefore omitted from reviews of the literature. This is a crucial weakness in earlier reviews of the evidence because empiricist research is often starkly contradicted by the case studies and other documentary sources compiled by monitoring groups, local law centres and organisations, such as the Institute for Race Relations and Runnymede Trust. During the process of researching and writing this text, the case for a specifically minority perspective has become increasingly pressing. Writing from this perspective we aim to reconcile the empirical evidence with accounts of lived experience and to ensure that these are properly represented in criminology (see Phillips and Bowling 1997).

We cannot claim to have resolved the tensions that have surfaced while writing this book. We find ourselves continually pulled back to our starting point which is that 'racialised' patterns emerge from the study of crime and justice and these require explanation. For example, if you walk into one of the Young Offenders' Institutions in the south-east of England today, you are likely to observe that the prison officers and governors will be almost exclusively white, while about half of the imprisoned young men will be from ethnic minorities, the majority of whom will be of African or Caribbean descent. We think that observable facts like this require explanation, and that such explanations are crucial to the struggle against racism and towards a safer and fairer society.

Organisation of the book

Chapter 1 provides an historical context for the study. It examines the origins of the 'race idea' and how this has influenced policy and practice towards ethnic minorities particularly in England during the latter part of the twentieth century. Chapter 2 aims to clarify such key terms as race, ethnicity, prejudice, discrimination, racism, equality and proportionality, and sets out the conceptual and legal basis for anti-discriminatory practice. Chapter 3 explores how criminological theory has used notions of race and ethnicity to explain the causes of crime and criminal justice practice. In chapter 4, we examine police and prison statistics on offending and victimisation. We describe the criminological preoccupation with the 'real' extent to which different ethnic groups are involved in crime, and identify the inherent conceptual and methodological problems involved. Chapter 5 examines racist victimisation directed specifically against ethnic minority communities and reviews the theoretical literature that attempts to explain these patterns. We then take three chapters to describe the divergent experiences of different ethnic groups in the criminal justice process, assessing the extent to which discrimination contributes to explaining the patterns that emerge. Chapter 6 examines policing and, in particular, the role of the police as 'gate-keepers' of the criminal justice process. Chapters 7 and 8 synthesise the empirical research on prosecution, sentencing, prison and probation and chapter 9 reviews the research on ethnic minority practitioners in criminal justice. In chapter 10 we evaluate the evidence taken as a whole and return to the questions raised in this introduction. Finally, we point tentatively towards an empirically grounded theory of racism, crime and justice and raise questions about future developments in this field.

Chapter 1

History

The origins of the 'race' idea

Although bodily differences – such as skin colour and facial features – and the *meaning* of those differences have been commented on for thousands of years, the idea of 'race' is a modern one, originating in the philosophies of the European Enlightenment. It is well established that ideas about race, nationality, ethnicity and cultural integrity were central to the work of late eighteenth- and early nineteenth-century writers such as Hume, Kant and Hegel. See for example, Gilroy 1993, 2000, Solomos and Back, 1996, Malik 1996 and Eze 1997. The 'race idea' is a key component of Enlightenment metaphysics, ethics, philosophy and science. Eze (1997) argues that the 'Age of Reason' was predicated upon the assumption that 'reason' could historically only come to maturity in modern Europe, while the inhabitants of areas outside Europe, who were considered to be of non-European racial and cultural origins, were consistently thought of as inferior with less rational, moral and evolutionary potential (ibid.: 4).

Enlightenment philosophers codified and institutionalised both scientific and popular concepts of race, articulating Europe's sense of cultural and racial superiority. From this perspective, 'reason' and 'civilisation' became almost synonymous with 'white' people and northern Europe, while 'unreason' and 'savagery' were located among the 'non-whites' outside Europe (Eze 1997: 5). David Hume, the great Scottish philosopher, for example, wrote in 1753, 'I am apt to suspect the Negroes and in general all other species of men (for there are four or five different kinds) to be naturally inferior to the whites' and 'there never was a civilised nation of any other complexion than white'. Such views were shared by Emmanuel Kant and many other philosophers of the era (Fryer 1984: 152–3, Eze 1997: 33).

The Swedish botanist Carl Linne (usually referred to as Linnaeus) laid the basis for the modern classification of plants and animals in the mid eighteenth century (Fryer 1984: 166). Linnaeus coined the term *Homo sapiens,* whom he further classified in a hierarchy largely based on skin colour with whites at the top (ibid.). In 1775 Johann Friedrich Blumenbach, a German physiologist and co-founder of 'physical anthropology', developed one of the most widely accepted racial taxonomies of the time. Blumenbach divided humanity into four, and later five, types – Caucasian, Mongolian, Ethiopian, Malay and American – based on detailed measurement of skulls. Joseph Arthur Gobineau has been called the father of racist ideology (Kleg 1993). In his 1853 essay on *The Inequality of Human Races,* the Comte de Gobineau set out his view that the decline of civilisation was due to the disease of 'degeneration' which occurred when racially superior nations allowed their populations to 'inbreed' with inferior stock. For Gobineau, 'the animal character, that appears in the shape of the pelvis is stamped on the negro from birth and foreshadows his destiny ... 'mental faculties are dull or even non-existent ... has an intensity of desire, and kills willingly, for the sake of killing'. The 'yellow' race by contrast, had 'little physical energy and inclined to apathy ... desires are feeble ... tends to mediocrity in everything ... has a love for utility and respect for order. His whole desire is to live in the easiest way possible.' By contrast, Gobineau described the Aryan race as beautiful, intelligent and strong. Moreover, only where Aryan blood existed could there be civilisation (ibid: 96–7). Gobineau's essay was influential in Germany and was quickly translated into English because of its appeal to white supremacists in the American South (Cashmore 1996: 152). Whether racial differences were to do with the process of 'civilisation' (Kant and Hegel) or 'degeneration' (Blumenbach, Gobineau), the belief that biologically separate races existed was axiomatic in the philosophy of the age.

It is in the period that these racial typologies and ideologies of racial superiority were being developed that racial slavery was in its ascendancy. Although African slaves were brought to England from the 1570s onwards, the transatlantic slave trade expanded dramatically in the seventeenth century. The process was accelerated by the increasing demand for sugar which had become essential to sweeten the fashionable new beverages – coffee, tea and chocolate. The consumption of sugar increased 20-fold between 1663 and 1775, the demand for which could not be met without the use of slave labour on West Indian plantations (Fryer 1984: 14). Ships left London, Bristol and Liverpool with commodities such as textiles, brass and copper made in Britain. In West Africa, these were bartered for slaves who were shipped in chains across the notorious middle passage to the West Indies. There, they were exchanged for sugar, spices, rum and tobacco which were carried back to British cities and sold. It was on this triangular trade that the shipping, manufacturing and other industries in Britain thrived and grew at the beginning of the factory age. The essential link was the slave trade (ibid.: 16–25, 33–58).[1]

---

[1] A crucial question is encapsulated by Fryer: 'Did race prejudice cause slavery? Or was it the other way round?' (Fryer 1984: 133). For Fryer, although there is evidence of race prejudice from the first European encounters with the people of

With the ending of the British slave trade in 1807 and slavery in 1833, the nature and form of race thinking transformed from a justification for the dehumanisation of slavery to a central ingredient in British imperial theory. At first, ideas about racial difference and hierarchy justified the extermination of the 'inferior' peoples that the Europeans encountered during the period of colonial expansion. For some, the extinction of 'natives' in the Americas, Australia, New Zealand, South Africa and Canada was 'nature's way of making room for a higher race' (ibid.: 172–5). Dr Robert Knox, the Scottish anatomist, wrote in his 1850 *The Races of Men*, 'Who cares particularly for the Negro, or the Hottentot, or the Kaffir? These latter have proved a very troublesome race, and the sooner they are put out of the way the better ... it matters little how their extinction is brought about' (cited ibid.: 175).

By the middle of the nineteenth century the supposed superiority of the European justified the acquisition and rule of the colonial territories and their inhabitants. A widely held idea among the British colonisers was that it was the divine destiny of the Teutonic or Anglo-Saxon race to rule and civilise the world. As Cecil Rhodes pondered as he wandered across the South African veld: 'As I walked, I looked up at the sky and down at the earth and I said to myself this should be British. And it came to me in that fine, exhilarating air that the British were the best race to rule the world' (cited ibid.: 183). The idea of superiority was linked to the notion of trusteeship in the colonial expansion in the second half of the nineteenth century. Statesman and philosopher, Edmund Burke saw the rights and privileges of colonial dominion as 'trust' that entailed a moral obligation towards the 'backward races'. Colonial subjects were seen as being akin to children or animals, needing care, nurture and improvement under a civilised and beneficent rule.

Drawing on theories of the inferiority of the 'lesser breeds' in foreign climes provided a new way of understanding and ruling the 'lower orders' of the domestic cities. Thus, the awful living conditions of the Irish and other poor whites of English cities was considered to be the result of racial degeneration (Pearson 1983: ix–xi, 69–73, Muncie 1999: 60). The 'fanciful Darwinian speculation' that informed these developments predicted that the growth of towns, overcrowded cities, the decline of individualism,

---

Africa and Asia, it was the 'drive for profit' that led English merchants to rise to the position of the foremost slave-trading nation of the world. As he puts it, 'There was big money in it. The theory came later' (ibid.: 134). Fryer makes a distinction between *race prejudice*, a contradictory, scrappy, cultural and psychological phenomenon, and *racism*, a 'relatively systematic and internally consistent' ideology that has acquired a 'pseudo-scientific veneer' that enables it to appear both rational and intellectually respectable. While prejudice serves cultural and psychological functions, racism serves economic and political functions (ibid.: 133–5).

family feeling and national pride would lead to 'perpetual lowering in the vitality of the "Imperial Race"' (Pearson 1983: 71).

From the early raciological theories briefly sketched here, there developed numerous strands of 'scientific racism' in the late nineteenth and early twentieth century, drawing on the evolving fields of ethnology, phrenology and palaeontology. In particular, the theories developed by Charles Darwin in his 1859 *Origin of Species* were adapted to explain the 'progress' of human societies. A newly emerging 'Social Darwinism' simplified ideas such as 'natural selection' and 'survival of the fittest' to posit that 'inferior' races would naturally disappear in favour of the 'stronger' European race (Solomos and Back 1996: 45). Such ideas led to the formation of the Eugenics movement, founded by Darwin's son-in-law, Francis Galton. The ideological basis for the Eugenics movement was set out in Galton's 1869 book *Hereditary Genius*. By the early twentieth century, mainstream anthropology was dominated by theories of 'racial hygiene', which aspired to the improvement of the stock of the white race and the extinction of the 'wretched, deformed and degenerate' (Nietzsche, cited by Burleigh and Wipperman 1991).

These beliefs informed racial supremacy in many countries, including Australia, South Africa, Sweden, England and the USA, including decisions about how to manage the perceived problem of 'racial degeneration' in both colonial and domestic contexts. Rooted in a common ideology, the early twentieth century saw the development of laws enforcing racial segregation and exclusion, such as 'whites only' immigration laws and the so-called 'separate but equal' Jim Crow laws in the USA, 'white Australia' immigration policies and South African apartheid. These laws operated by excluding and removing non-whites from areas of white settlement or prohibiting their rights to migrate, gain citizenship or own property; the prohibition of inter-racial marriages and other forms of miscegenation; pass laws restricting the rights of non-whites to travel; and segregated public facilities, such as buses, railways, hotels, restaurants and schools.

While race thinking was widespread across Europe in the early part of the twentieth century, it is of course in Germany during the period of Nazi rule between 1933 and 1945 that racism took its most virulent and horrific form. The notions of Aryan superiority and 'racial hygiene' was central to the machinery of the Nazi racial state. The *Law for the Protection of German Blood and Honour* (1935) forbade persons of German blood to marry or have sexual relations with Jews, gypsies or Negroes, or anyone who might have 'offspring likely to be prejudicial to the purity of German blood' (Burleigh and Wipperman 1991: 49–51). The racial anthropological and racial hygienic provisions in law and administration were supported by the work of academics and scientists from many disciplines. The German racial purification programme included research and experimentation on people designated 'racially impure' as well as policies of sterilisation and segregation intended to 'breed out' undesirable characteristics. The targets of these policies included people whose Germanness had been tainted by contact with other racial groups (such as the mixed race offspring of German women and French North African troops stationed in the Rhineland);[2] people with certain physical and mental conditions (such as schizophrenia and Down's syndrome); the 'hereditally asocial' (including people convicted of crimes or anti-social behaviour); and homosexuals. The notion of racial purification led ultimately to the persecution, internment and extermination of millions of Jewish people and others identified as racially inferior or impure (see also Goldhagen 1996).

Race and migration in Britain

After World War II, migration to Britain from former colonies became a practical possibility because of the ease and relatively low cost of global travel and labour shortages within the UK at a time of economic collapse elsewhere. Although a great deal of migration to and from Britain had occurred previously, it would, for the first time in its history, become an island that was not, exclusively, a 'white man's country' (Miles and Phizaklea 1984). The colonial enterprise had entailed inking the world atlas in pink (literally). In colonising not only the territory but also cultural resources and education, many people in various parts of the world were encouraged to consider themselves British subjects. There were, of course, anti-colonial struggles that would lead eventually to independence and new forms of national identity. Nonetheless, for many people in the West Indies, Africa, the Indian subcontinent and Hong Kong, England was the 'mother country' and London the metropolitan centre of the entire British Empire.

The inhabitants of the metropolis and its surrounding provinces held a quite different perspective, however, which is discernible in both political discourse and public opinion surveys of the period. In the late 1940s, the prospect of the arrival of significant numbers of people of different racial origins – despite the fact that they were, in common with their white counterparts, 'British subjects' – was discussed widely within government and the media (James and Harris 1993). The Royal Commission on Population reported in 1949 that immigration could be welcomed 'without reserve' only if the migrants were 'of good human stock and were not prevented by their religion or race from intermarrying with the host population and becoming merged into it' (cited in Holmes 1988: 210).

There had been immigration restrictions on people thought to be undesirable since the 1905 Aliens Act barred the entry into Britain of Jewish people fleeing the widespread pogroms in central and Eastern

---

[2] *Hitler's Forgotten Victims*, BBC.

Europe (Solomos 1993, Klier 1993). But the mass migration of the post-war period was of a different character in that the colonial migrants were legally indistinguishable from the mainland British and retained a right to settle in Britain even after the 1948 Nationality Act, which created a distinction between citizens of the Commonwealth and those of the United Kingdom and Colonies.

British race relations research in the 1950s and 1960s documented 'rejectionism' towards people migrating from the Caribbean, Africa and, somewhat later, from the Indian subcontinent, and official policies were concerned with 'managing' those who were now settling. Superficially, a *laissez faire* government policy existed that assumed that the New Commonwealth and Pakistan population would 'assimilate', a process which inferred that immigrants would be absorbed into mainstream (white) culture (Carter, Harris and Joshi 1993). However, as Clive Harris has shown, private correspondence between government departments reveals anxiety about 'coloured' migration from the mid 1940s, though this was not expressed publicly because it would appear discriminatory, jeopardising the 'Commonwealth ideal', damaging trade with the colonies and former colonies, and strengthening the hand of pro-communists arguing for a complete break from imperialist rule (ibid.).

The subsequent debate about race gained much of its potency from media and political debates about 'coloured' immigration and what were understood to be its consequences for the 'character and appearance' of the British people (Solomos 1993). After the 1958 Nottingham and Notting Hill race riots – in which black people were the targets of sustained violence – race became a key component of discussions on the economy, crime and nationhood in British politics. In the 1960s, the development of what amounted to a 'white Britain policy' was indicated by the introduction of the Commonwealth Immigration Act 1962 which severely limited the possibilities for 'coloured' would-be migrants from the New Commonwealth, while maintaining those from the mainly 'white' Old Commonwealth.

The key rationalisation for the 1962 Act was the perceived need to halt the arrival of 'coloured' immigrants because there existed only a limited ability to assimilate them into the host community. However, the Act failed to appease those who wished to see an end to immigration. In a 1964 by-election in the West Midlands town of Smethwick, the Conservative candidate, Peter Griffiths, campaigned largely on the basis of defending the interests of the local white majority against the influx of immigrants, beating the Labour Cabinet Minister Patrick Gordon Walker in what had been assumed to be a safe Labour seat. One of the campaign slogans heard during the election – 'if you want a nigger for a neighbour, vote Labour' – was defended by Griffiths as a 'manifestation of popular feeling' (Solomos 1993).

Although the Labour party had opposed the 1962 Commonwealth Immigrants Act, the Smethwick result had indicated the strength of popular feelings about race and the vulnerability of Labour on the issue of immigration. When Labour took office under Harold Wilson in 1965, it issued a white paper recommending further restrictions on immigration, a policy that had become an orthodoxy. As Roy Hattersley put it in 1965, 'without integration, limitation is inexcusable; without limitation, integration is impossible' (Smith 1989: 124, Fryer 1984: 381). The politics of immigration took a further restrictionist turn after a moral panic concerning the arrival of British citizens of Indian descent from the East African countries of Kenya and Uganda. Labour's new tough stance against immigration led to the second Commonwealth Immigrants Act in early 1968 introduced specifically to control the flow of East African Asians. The 1968 Act was condemned by *The Times* who described it as a shameful 'colour bar' (Solomos 1989).

Almost immediately, however, Labour was put on the defensive by Enoch Powell, the most powerful and eloquent speaker from the mainstream of British politics on the issue of race. In a notorious speech in Birmingham, April 1968, he warned of what he saw as the dangers of coloured immigration, emotively predicting the transformation of the nation and the inevitability of a war between the races. 'Like the Roman', he saw 'the river Tiber, foaming with much blood' (Hiro 1992: 247). Others spoke of their fears of Britain becoming a 'coffee-coloured' nation (Cyril Osborne cited in Hiro 1992, Solomos 1993). Powell urged further restrictions on coloured immigration, and later argued for 'a programme of large scale voluntary repatriation and re-emigration' of New Commonwealth settlers. He even proposed a Ministry of Repatriation to oversee the departure of 700,000 people at a cost of £300 million (Hiro 1992: 250).

Powell was forced out of the Conservative Shadow Cabinet as a result of this speech, but he remained an active back bencher and the extensive media coverage of the issues he raised continued until the period leading up to the 1970 general election. It was in this context and in what had become a cross-party consensus in favour of strict controls that the 1971 Immigration Act was passed. This was the last of three major pieces of legislation aimed largely at excluding Commonwealth migrants from Britain (Solomos 1989). A decade later, the first legislation of the post-1979 Conservative administration was the 1981 British Nationality Act, which not only consolidated and rationalised the discriminatory basis of previous immigration and nationality legislation (Solomos 1993) but also removed the automatic right of citizenship to a person born on British soil.

Changing perceptions of ethnic minority communities as disorderly

The experience among minority communities of being subjected to policing and criminal justice practices that singled them out for 'special attention' in Britain can be traced back to the 1960s when allegations of police going 'nigger hunting' were recorded (Hunte 1966). However, it is Stuart Hall *et al.*'s (1978) seminal work, *Policing the Crisis*, which shows most clearly how, on the basis of pre-existing beliefs about their supposed criminality, black people were, in practice, *criminalised*, subjected to extraordinary policing and punishment, and portrayed by the media, politicians and criminal justice agents as a 'social problem'. Black young men, in particular, became defined as an inherently criminal class. (See also Gilroy 1987, Solomos 1988, Keith 1993.) Hall *et al.* describe the demonisation of the British black population and the creation of a new and powerful 'folk devil'. This demonic status created a rationale for policing minority communities in a way which white populations (certainly those in the middle and 'respectable' working classes) had not experienced since the nineteenth century (Howe 1988: 13–16). That is, policing without consent and where oppressive 'swamp' tactics, brutality and racist violence were normal. For some commentators, policing black Britain was an extension of colonial policing which had existed for decades in the Caribbean, India and Africa, and which had now been turned inward to police the 'domestic colonies' (Sivanandan 1982, Fryer 1984, Howe 1988).

The politics of 'race and crime' became more explicit than ever in the 1970s. In the preceding years, Enoch Powell had given voice to, and made overt, or even respectable, fears about the results of coloured immigration on the race and culture of the British nation. This line of argument was built upon by the National Front, who campaigned on an openly racist platform of first exclusion, then repatriation of all coloured immigrants and for a clampdown on 'black crime'. In this milieu, Margaret Thatcher was elected to her first term as Conservative Prime Minister in 1979, publicly sympathising with white fears of being 'swamped by immigrants' and a tide of rising crime. Although the economic issues of unemployment and irresponsible trade unions were central to Thatcher's election campaign, for many commentators her success rested on the promise of 'more law and order' and 'an end to immigration' (Solomos 1993). The resulting empowerment of the police and immigration services, in the context of a deep recession and rising unemployment, increased the strains between black communities and the police. This relationship, which had become increasingly fractious by the end of the 1970s, collapsed vividly in the public disorder of Bristol in 1980 and then across the country in 1981.

There is no doubt that the inner-city disturbances in the London neighbourhood of Brixton in April 1981, then in Manchester, Liverpool, Birmingham and other towns and cities in July came as a shock to many members of the British public (Solomos 1993: 154). People familiar with the experience of black Britain had predicted disorder for some years (for example, Price 1979). But the images of rioting, burning, looting and the threat of a collapse of social order were brought home as scenes of pitched battles between police and people were beamed on to television screens across the country. In Brixton more than 300 people were injured, while many vehicles and 28 buildings were destroyed, some by fire.

For Lord Scarman, appointed to chair the public inquiry, the riots were 'essentially an outburst of anger and resentment by young black people against the police'. Although he noted that not all the people involved in the disturbances were black, Scarman placed race at the centre of his analysis of the two basic problems involved. First, he identified a problem of policing 'a multi-racial community in a deprived inner-city area where unemployment, especially among young black people, is high and hopes are low'. Secondly, he pointed to the social and economic conditions which 'beset the ethnically diverse communities who live and work in our inner cities' (Scarman 1981: 15).

Scarman's recommendations included identifying racial prejudice among recruits to the police service, recruiting more ethnic minority police officers, improving community relations and the handling of public disorder, supervising more closely front-line police constables, improving the management training of inspectors and sergeants (especially in conducting stop and search operations) and making the display of racially prejudiced behaviour a dismissal offence. To increase public confidence in the police a greater degree of consultation with the public was recommended, as well as introducing 'lay visitors' to make random checks on police stations and an independent element in the system for considering complaints against the police. Scarman's social policy recommendations included a 'co-ordinated response' to the 'problems of the inner city', involving the community in the planning, provision and management of local services. Social stability in the long term required strategies to promote: 'useful, gainful employment and suitable educational, recreational and leisure opportunities for young people, especially in the inner cities' (Scarman 1981: 205). Scarman concluded that, 'from the evidence of ethnic minority deprivation ... if the balance of racial disadvantage is to be redressed, positive action is required'. In his view, this needed no new legislation, but rather a 'clear determination' and 'positive effort by all in responsible positions' to 'enforce the existing law on racial discrimination'.

The Scarman Report was 'greeted with a wave of adulation' across the political spectrum (Kettle and Hodges 1982: 208). Conservative Home Secretary William Whitelaw and opposition Home Affairs spokesman Roy Hattersley welcomed it. David McNee, then Commissioner of the Metropolitan Police, called it 'fair and thorough'. The Association of Chief Police Officers (ACPO) described it as an 'objective study'. The press reaction was enthusiastic except the *Daily Mail*, which thought it was 'telling the police to turn a blind eye to black crime' and dismissed what it considered a 'call for positive discrimination' (Kettle and Hodges 1982).

The report received a mixed reaction from the black community. For critics on the left, the analysis was fundamentally flawed, simply echoing racist pathologies of black people (Gilroy 1987a). Scarman had failed to explain properly why black people were so angry with the police and how this was rooted in their experiences of oppressive policing. Most fundamentally, Scarman failed to 'grasp the nettle' in three areas of policing – the application of police powers (especially stop and search), the investigation of complaints against the police and police accountability (Bridges 1982, Howe 1988). For these commentators, unless the police could be brought under democratic control, continued frustration and anger were inevitable and further disorder a clear possibility.

As predicted, disorder flared again in 1985. The riots in September in the Lozells Road area of Handsworth in Birmingham resulted in the deaths of two Asian men and the injury of more than 100 people. The value of the damaged property was put at £7.5 million. A month later riots on the Broadwater Farm were triggered off by the death, during a police raid on her home, of Cynthia Jarret in Tottenham, North London. During the disorders, a community police officer, PC Keith Blakelock, was stabbed to death. More than 250 people were injured and there was widespread damage to property.

The media portrayal of the 1985 riots served to confirm the image of disorderly black communities trapped in a 'cultural pathology' of an 'alien character' (Gilroy 1987a). Gilroy describes how the view that blacks are a 'high crime group' whose criminality is an expression of their 'distinctive culture' became integral to British racism. This 'common sense' linked both public disorder and the street crimes of drug sale and robbery as an expression of black culture (ibid.: 109–11). Evoking Scarman, the media conjured up stereotypical images of pathologically disorganised black family life creating a predisposition for disorderly protest and street crime (ibid.: 103–6). After the Handsworth riot in 1985, the *Sun* front page headline read 'Hate of Black Bomber' next to a photograph of a black man holding a petrol bomb. For Solomos, these images 'established a linkage between race, crime and disorder much more firmly than the riots of 1980–1 had done'. Rather than interpreting the riots as a reaction against hostile policing and social and economic marginalisation, this time they were explained as a 'cry for loot', or simply an expression of *black criminality*, which, as such, required no further explanation (Solomos 1988).

In the wake of the 1985 riots, the Scarman Report was reprinted with a new preface that scolded the government for lacking urgency in implementing social and environmental improvements in the inner cities. Scarman bemoaned 'four years of lost opportunity – lost because so much more could have been done than was in fact done' (Scarman 1986: xiv). Indeed, many of the conditions which had commanded attention five years earlier had steadily worsened (such as unemployment, housing and welfare provision) (Solomos 1993: 160). In the inner cities in 1985, levels of unemployment were up to two or three times higher than in 1980–1 (Cross and Smith 1987). Moreover, nothing had been done to tackle racial discrimination and inequality (Solomos 1993: 160). As Scarman wrote in 1986, 'The government, over the last five years, has not tackled the core of the inner-city problem – the factor of racial disadvantage. You must tackle racial disadvantage, and that means adjusting all government policies to this end' (Scarman 1986: xvii).

After the mid 1980s, disorders involving black people as the principal protagonists were less frequently reported in the media and were either rarer or considered less newsworthy. Anxiety about race and crime was displaced to a large extent by a concern with youth in general (most of whom were, by default, white). The Poll Tax riot in Trafalgar Square – arguably the most serious peacetime disorder in London in the twentieth century – on 31 March 1991 symbolised both the end of the Thatcher era, and the myth that riot was a 'black thing'. It resulted in the injury of 500 police officers (60 of whom were hospitalised). Fifty vehicles were damaged or destroyed by fire; 394 shops and offices in prestigious Regent Street and Covent Garden were attacked (and some looted); 391 people were arrested, almost all of whom were white. In the summer of the same year, riots, burning, looting and wild driving displays in stolen cars were seen across Britain, famously in suburban areas of Cardiff, Oxford and Tyneside (Campbell 1993). In this period, nearly 500 'angry young men' were arrested and an estimated £12 million worth of property was damaged or destroyed. In the summer of 1992, more estates in England saw rioting and at the turn of the century disorders during the May Day anti-capitalist demonstrations became a regular feature of the spring calendar. In most of these *fin de siècle* riots, the protagonists have been almost exclusively white.

Among the few outbreaks of public disorder to merit official attention in the mid 1990s were the riots in the Manningham area of Bradford on 9–11 June 1995 (Bradford Commission 1996). These disorders erupted when two police officers passed 'a noisy group' of young Asian men playing football in the road. The officers intervened and, after a struggle, arrested three young men. During the course of the arrests a crowd gathered. Accusations and counter-accusations ensued, leading to the intervention of a large number of police officers. Although the official report of the inquiry argued that 'the direct cause of the disorder ... was the unacceptable behaviour of those relatively few people who behaved so anti-socially', Foundation 2000, a community organisation based in Manningham, concluded the riots occurred in the context of a 'severe loss of confidence in the police' because of police action that was 'highly questionable, extremely provocative and unreasonable' (Foundation 2000 1995).

Keith (1993: 252–5) argues that after the mid 1980s disorder in England had become 'naturalised'. When white youths rioted in the 1990s, there was relatively little surprise, compared with the shocked and outraged response a decade before. He also suggests that the changing demography of the rioters should not be taken as evidence of a resolution of the conflict between black youth and the police. Certainly, the media was still obsessed with questions of 'black criminality', robbery, drugs and disorderliness, but the debate about 'race' and riot was muted with few major events to focus upon. The material conditions which gave rise to the riots of the 1980s had not disappeared, and had in some ways worsened. As we describe in chapter 6, the (ab)use of policing powers, which provided both the context and immediate trigger for the riots, continued to be widespread and, indeed, increased during the 1990s. By the end of the decade, the police in England and Wales were conducting more than one million stop/searches annually, with young men from ethnic minority communities being targeted disproportionately. The questions of oppressive policing tactics, consent, legitimacy and accountability that were the focus of the Scarman reforms remained controversial. In chapter 10 we look at the linked, but broader questions of criminalisation, discrimination in the criminal justice process and the over-representation of black people in prison that had begun to be of concern within the ethnic minority communities from around the late 1970s. Whatever the changes in the way in which black communities were perceived during the late 1980s and 1990s, the extent of disproportionate criminalisation continued unabated and, indeed, if anything accelerated. While the number of white males in prison increased by 31 per cent between 1985 and 1999, the number of South Asian males in prison increased by 80 per cent and African/Caribbean males by 101 per cent (see chapter 8). Examining the various explanations for how this has come about is a major task of this book.

Changing perceptions of minority communities as vulnerable to attack

The history of racist violence in Britain is a long but discontinuous one (see Panayi 1996, Bowling 1999a). There is evidence of attempts at forced removal of people of colour since the time of Elizabeth I and examples of attacks against Jews in Britain stretching back to the twelfth century (Fryer 1984, Panayi 1996). The violent targeting of black and Asian sailors in British ports immediately after World War I (in 1919) and World War II (in 1948) is well documented (Jenkinson 1996, Panayi 1996). The late 1950s saw several anti-black riots in London, Nottingham and elsewhere (Panayi 1996). During the 1970s, the emergence of the 'skinhead' youth culture, and its link with the rise in popularity of extreme right political activism, was accompanied by an apparent increase in racist incidents. One of the earliest studies of the victimisation of ethnic minorities in Britain commented that

> While the East End is traditionally a 'high crime' area, there is clear evidence that the local Bengalee community has suffered physical attacks

and harassment over recent years on a totally different scale from that inflicted on the rest of the community... Behind the headlines is an almost continuous and unrelenting battery of Asian people and their property... The barrage of harassment, insult and intimidation, week in week out, fundamentally determines how the immigrant community here lives and works, and how the host community and the authorities are viewed.
(Bethnal Green and Stepney Trades Council 1978: 3–4)

The official recognition of the problem of racist violence targeted specifically against ethnic minority communities has also transformed over the past two decades. The period from World War II to the late 1970s was among the most viciously racist periods in British domestic history. Extreme racist attitudes were entrenched and widespread. Many British people strongly resisted the idea that black and Asian people should be allowed into the country and did their best to exclude them from 'their' neighbourhoods, workplaces and places of entertainment (Holmes 1988, Solomos 1993, Bowling 1999a).

During the 1970s, many people from ethnic minority communities were murdered by self-proclaimed racists. In Glasgow in 1975, for example, a National Front member shot dead a West Indian man. At the time he told the police, 'Niggers mean nothing to me. It was like killing a dog', and later claimed that his act was intended to 'boost emigration [and] start extermination' (*Searchlight*, undated). The following year, John Kingsley Read, leader of the British National Party, responded to the news of the murder of a Sikh youth in Southall, 'one down – a million to go' (Hiro 1992: 246). As well as violent racist attacks, there were 'mass outrages' directed against ethnic minority communities. This included a 'rampage' in 1978 by 50 neo-Nazi skinheads who ran down Brick Lane, East London, shouting racist abuse, smashing shop windows and causing many injuries. Marches by overtly racist organisations, such as the National Front, were common; participants dressed in skinhead 'uniform', adorned with racist insignia (such as swastikas and the emblems of the Waffen SS), carried Union Jack flags, co-opted as a symbol of British racism. Despite the extent of this explicitly *racist* violence, the government and the police bent over backwards to deny its racist content and to downplay its impact on ethnic minority communities.

The year 1981 is also a landmark in this history because it was when violence targeted specifically at ethnic minority communities was officially acknowledged and recognised for the first time in the publication of the Home Office Report, 'Racial Attacks'. Evidence of both extreme and 'everyday' racist violence and harassment was collected by campaigning groups in the late 1970s and early 1980s and this eventually led the government and the police to acknowledge the severity of the situation. Moreover, struggles to oppose racist violence had led to clashes between minority communities, their anti-fascist supporters and the extreme right and the police in a variety of locations, including Bradford and the London boroughs of Lewisham, Southall and Newham.

In January 1981, tragedy struck London's New Cross area when 13 young black people burned to death in a house fire. Suspicious circumstances – including the discovery of an unexploded incendiary device and a flood of racist hate mail – led many people then (and now) to believe that it was the work of right-wing racist extremists.[3] In the same week that the Scarman Report was published, then Home Secretary, William Whitelaw, admitted that racial attacks had a significant effect on minority communities and were 'more common' than previously supposed. Earlier denials were explained as the result of a 'lack of reliable information' (Home Office 1981; see also Bridges' 1982 critique of the Home Office Report).

An enormous amount of detailed evidence of the extent, nature and experience of racist harassment and violence has been assessed since the late 1970s. Government studies of police records have shown that racist incidents directed against black and Asian people are common (Home Office 1981, Seagrave 1989, Maynard and Read 1997). Successive sweeps of the British Crime Survey have shown that the real level of racist violence is more widespread still, with as many as 143,000 racist incidents occurring every year (Aye Maung and Mirrlees-Black 1994, Percy 1998). These surveys have shown that racist violence has a significant impact on minority communities, leaving them insecure and avoiding many public places for fear of attack. Surveys, police records, community organisations, law centres, local authorities and voluntary organisations have produced case studies and detailed descriptions of the effects of violent racism (see chapter 5). Successive government inquiries have confirmed this picture, one describing it as the 'most dispiriting and shameful aspect of race relations in Britain' (Home Office 1986). Local and central government reports have repeatedly called for more to be done (House of Commons 1994: xxxviii).

The Lawrence Inquiry: towards a new agenda

The questions of policing, racial prejudice and discrimination, inequality, accountability, fairness and justice raised in the Scarman Report leaped once again to centre stage in the mid 1990s. The focus this time, however, was not rioting and disorder, but the threat of violent racism to black and Asian communities. The *cause célèbre* which acted as 'lightning rod' to focus these issues was the murder, on 22 April 1993, of Stephen Lawrence, an 18-year-old black man stabbed to death in South London. Stephen Lawrence and his friend Duwayne Brooks were waiting for a bus

---

[3] The cause of the fire was never established beyond doubt and the first inquest arrived at an open verdict. (See Bowling 1999a: 61) The case remains controversial today.

in Eltham, South-East London, when a group of five or six white youths crossed the road towards them. One shouted 'what, what nigger?' and, with that, Stephen Lawrence was stabbed twice with a long knife; both stab wounds severed arteries and he was probably dead by the time an ambulance arrived. In 1997, an inquest jury returned a unanimous verdict that 'Stephen Lawrence was unlawfully killed in a completely unprovoked racist attack by five white youths' (Macpherson 1999). The police investigation failed to bring the killers to justice and was condemned as 'palpably flawed' and incompetent (ibid.).

Although very many people were the victims of murderous racism in 1990s Britain, the murder of Stephen Lawrence is the one which has come to symbolise the plight of all such victims, their families and communities. As Cathcart (1999) put it, the murder had a 'terrible purity' about it. The victim was a young man of unblemished character; the attack was entirely unprovoked; the racist motive was beyond question (or should have been); information came into the investigation very quickly; Stephen Lawrence's parents, Neville and Doreen, were respectable, hardworking, ordinary people who had high hopes for their son. They received broadly favourable media coverage from even the most unsympathetic quarters including the *Daily Mail* who published the names and photographs of the killers under the banner headline, MURDERERS, challenging the accused men to sue the newspaper if they were innocent. The events themselves and the campaign, which built up around the Lawrence family, appealed to people from all backgrounds. Despite the fact that they were of African/Caribbean origin, the plight of the Lawrences resonated with the sentiments of middle England. The message was clear: anyone could have lost a son in this way, anyone could be confronted by denial, ineptitude by the police and have no means of holding them to account for what had gone wrong.

Racism was rarely far from the headlines in 1993. Within the first few months of that year, Herman Ouseley became the first black chairman of the Commission for Racial Equality and called immediately for racist violence to be made a specific criminal offence. The newly appointed Commissioner of the Metropolitan Police, Paul Condon, made tackling racism his 'main priority'. John Major, then Conservative Prime Minister, condemned racism and xenophobia as morally repugnant in a speech to the Board of Deputies of British Jews. Yet the following years were characterised by a reluctance to take any practical action. The Commision for Racial Equality's recommendations for new legislation to strengthen the provisions of the 1976 Race Relations Act were rejected by the Conservative government, as were the calls to make racist violence a specific offence.

In the summer of 1993, Neville and Doreen Lawrence's request for a public inquiry into the murder of their son was turned down by Home Office Minister, Peter Lloyd. As Cathcart put it, Conservative Home Secretaries 'preoccupied with rising crime, had little interest in holding the police up to public scrutiny' (1999: 291). There is some evidence of back bench support for measures against racism from the Labour opposition, but the party leadership was silent on the issue of discrimination in policing until the run-up to the May 1997 general election when shadow Home Secretary Jack Straw expressed sympathy with the Lawrence family and raised hopes that, once elected, the Labour government would approve an inquiry.

On 31 July 1997, three months after their landslide election victory, Straw, now Home Secretary, announced the public inquiry into 'the matters arising from the death of Stephen Lawrence', chaired by a retired Scottish judge, Sir William Macpherson of Cluny. The inquiry took evidence from 88 witnesses and received 148 written submissions amounting to more than 100,000 pages of evidence. The report concluded that there was a series of fundamental flaws in the conduct of the investigation and that this was the result of 'professional incompetence, institutional racism and a failure of leadership by senior officers' (Macpherson 1999: 137). It documented a lack of direction, imagination and organisation of the murder investigation, and the insensitive and unsympathetic treatment of Duwayne Brooks and Mr and Mrs Lawrence. It documented the denial of the racist motive for the murder among at least five police officers, and the racist stereotyping of Duwayne Brooks at the scene when he was wrongly assumed to be one of the protagonists in a fight between youths rather than a victim of an unprovoked attack (Hall *et al.* 1998). It goes on to criticise the use of inappropiate and offensive language and the insensitive and patronising handling of Mr and Mrs Lawrence throughout the investigation. The report identified an absence of 'confidence and trust' in the police among ethnic minority communities. This was partly the result of a failure to respond properly to racist violence, but also stemmed from more widespread concern about the inequitable use of stop and search powers, deaths in police custody, racial discrimination and a lack of openness and accountability. In summary, the experience of the black community was described as being 'over policed ... and under protected'.[4]

The report made 70 recommendations, amounting to the most extensive programme of reform in the history of the relationship between the police and ethnic minority communities. It recommended that a 'Ministerial Priority' should be declared to 'increase trust and confidence in policing among ethnic minority communities' by eliminating racist prejudice and disadvantage and demonstrating fairness in all aspects of policing. The report recommended more vigorous inspections, and the application of freedom of information and anti-discrimination legislation to the police service. It recommended improvements in the handling of

---

[4] David Muir, representing black church leaders, cited in the Macpherson (1999) 'Stephen Lawrence Inquiry' paragraph 45.7, p. 312.

racist incidents, in first-aid training, in family liaison and in the handling of victims and witnesses. It also recommended improvements in training in racism awareness and cultural diversity and in employment, recruitment and retention policies, in handling discipline and complaints, and in the regulation of stop and search powers. Finally, it went beyond the police service to make recommendations for prevention of racist violence in the wider sense, including the role of education. In an action plan published by the Home Secretary in response to the Lawrence Inquiry, 56 of the 70 recommendations were fully accepted, five were accepted in part and seven were referred to the Law Commission to be subjected to further examination (Home Office 1999d).

The post-Lawrence era: from bad apples to root and branch reform

Scarman emphasised two principles of policing a free society which apply, by extension, to the criminal justice system as a whole – (1) consent and balance; and (2) independence and accountability (1981, para. 4.5–4.60). Scarman's proposals were intended to 'ensure that the police operate not only within the law but with the support of the community as a whole' (para. 4.60). Despite having identified these principles, Scarman's recommendations to resolve the problem of a system of policing and criminal justice, that was evidently out of balance, operated without the consent of the community and lacked proper accountability, now seem hopelessly weak. Whatever was done 'after Scarman', it became clear during the Lawrence Inquiry that the loss of 'confidence and trust' among ethnic minority communities had, if anything, worsened in the intervening 18 years. Rather than Scarman's 'mere tinkering' as Darcus Howe (1988) put it, re-establishing police legitimacy had to be addressed by a thorough examination of existing failings alongside appropriate remedies.

Scarman's analysis also failed to take proper account of the institutionalised racism that places an additional burden on ethnic minority communities. In simple terms Scarman rejected the suggestion that the police were institutionally racist. Rather than seeing racism as systemic, his diagnosis was that racial prejudice could be found only in the 'occasional ill judged remarks and behaviour of a few police officers' (Scarman 1981/6: para. 4.62). The problem was one of 'bad apples' within the service who could be identified on recruitment through 'scientific means' and whose prejudices could be removed through training in the awareness of cultural diversity. The Lawrence Inquiry, by contrast, condemned the practices of the Metropolitan and other police services and other organisations in British society as 'institutionally racist'. Although this allegation was denied until the last weeks of the inquiry, the Commissioner of the Metropolitan Police, the Association of Chief Police

Officers and the Home Office finally admitted it. As Jack Straw, the Home Secretary, commented:

> In my view, any long-established, white-dominated organisation is liable to have procedures, practices and a culture that tend to exclude or to disadvantage non-white people. The police service, in that respect, is little different from other parts of the criminal justice system – or from Government Departments, including the Home Office – and many other institutions.
>
> (*Hansard*, 24 February 1999, column 391)

Where Scarman was hesitant on the question of accountability, Macpherson was strident. Since the Lawrence Inquiry had concluded that the failings of the police were systemic and the result of insufficient accountability, it recommended the introduction of lay oversight into all areas of police work, and the creation of a fully independent complaints system. Crucially, the inquiry recommended bringing the police into the ambit of race relations law, a proposal that had been roundly rejected two decades earlier.

Conclusion

The perception of people from ethnic minorities as criminal and disorderly has a long history in Britain. People whose skins are not white have typically been seen as a problem for the social order, their very presence giving cause for concern. Often ethnicity has been taken as an indicator of proclivity to violence, deviousness and dishonesty. The social constructions of race and criminality have developed hand in hand. In its most extreme version, the presence of dark-skinned people has been defined as a problem because we are of an 'opposite race'. Such views have also sometimes acted as an explanation of justification for violence directed against ethnic minority communities.

In chapter 3 we examine the assumptions made by criminologists about the relationship between 'race', ethnicity, crime and punishment, and we explore the range of biological, psychological, cultural and socio-economic theories that have been proposed. These criminological 'theoreotypes', as Pitts (1993) describes them, reflect the beliefs of the broader public and, disturbingly, it is evident that these beliefs have formed the basis for the practice of criminal justice practitioners, such as police officers and judges.

This takes us to our next task which is to examine the relationship between racism, discrimination and criminal justice practices.

Chapter 2

Concepts

The aim of this chapter is to introduce and clarify the concepts that are commonly used to describe how crime and the administration of justice are experienced by groups of people identified by racial or ethnic difference. Our objective is to examine the notions of 'race' and 'ethnicity' to describe differences between people and the notions of 'racism', 'prejudice' and 'discrimination' used to describe the ways in which people think about, and act upon, these differences.

'Race' relations

Sociology expanded rapidly in the 1960s at the time of intense public discussion of immigration and anxiety about the arrival of settlers from the former colonies (Banton 1967). The central concern of race relations research was how social relations become defined as 'race' relations in specific contexts, such as 'frontier situations' of conflict over scarce resources, legal inter-group distinctions, indentured or slave labour, unusually harsh class exploitation, cultural diversity and limited group interaction, and migrant labour as an underclass fulfilling stigmatised roles in a metropolitan setting (Solomos and Back 1996: 7).

Applying theories gained from an analysis of race relations in a number of different places (such as the USA and South Africa), Rex and Moore (1967), Banton (1967) and others described the way in which race became a marker for the exclusion of migrants in such key areas as housing and employment. This exclusion led to the creation of a 'separate underprivileged class', whom they referred to as an 'underclass' (Rex and Tomlinson 1979). Several major research studies in Birmingham and elsewhere identified minorities who were systematically at a disadvantage compared with their white neighbours (being excluded from public housing, for example[1]) and, as a consequence, did not identify with white working-class culture, forming instead their own culture, community and politics. According to Rex and Tomlinson (1979) these took different forms within different immigrant communities. Within the Asian communities, for example, this took the form of capital accumulation and social mobility, while in the West Indian community it took the form of withdrawal from labour market competition and an emphasis on the construction of a black identity (Solomos and Back 1996, citing Rex and Tomlinson 1979).

The race relations problematic has been criticised on a number of grounds. With the notion of race as one of its central analytical categories, it reifies an essentialist notion of racial difference and contributes to the idea that 'races' are real, culturally or biologically meaningful entities. The race relations field also lent itself to the simplistic formulation that discrimination 'equals prejudice plus power', where whites have all the power and non-whites have none. While this 'macro' analysis might have some explanatory power at the global level, it fails to explain the experiences of racism and difference at the local level. The race relations problematic contributes to a superficial conceptualisation of racism as simply disordered attitudes and prejudices. This has been criticised as theorising racism as akin to a 'coat of paint', essentialising prejudice as an individual aberration. The approach over-simplifies a range of complexities that arise from everyday experience. By creating the dichotomous categories of blacks as victims and whites as perpetrators of racial discrimination, the experiences on each 'side' of the colour line become homogenised. Thus, differences of age, gender, class and wealth are submerged, as, more importantly, are the subtle differences within groups defined as black, white, Asian, Oriental, etc. Finally, 'race relations' research focused largely on ethnic minorities' *experiences* of racism, rather than attempting to examine the development and expression of racism among white communities.

Racism

Robert Miles rejects the possibility of a 'sociology of race', contending that the object of analysis should be racism understood from a Marxist perspective. For Miles (1989), racism is an ideology that is integral to the process of capital accumulation and class relations in capitalist societies

---

[1] They noted, for example, that 'residency clauses' prevented black and Asian immigrants from being offered local authority housing (Rex and Moore 1967), a policy supported by most white people in Sparkbrook, the area studied, where the slogan 'House Britons not Blacks' adorned several walls (Rex and Moore 1967: 202).

Box 2.1 Racism as an ideology

Many authors define racism as a 'doctrine, dogma, ideology, or set of beliefs' (Cashmore 1996). Common to most definitions of racism is:

> the belief that certain groups are innately, biologically, socially, morally superior to other groups, based upon what is attributed to be their racial composition (Kleg 1993: 95)

Ideas about 'race' can be found in many contexts, past and present. Over the past two hundred years, and still today, discourses with an explicitly racist content have been produced which primarily revolve around the following themes:

- 'race' is a natural, fixed biological and or cultural attribute, which explains differences in ability, resources and power;

- 'white' people (or Caucasians, Aryans, Europeans, etc.) are the most advanced 'race';

- inferior groups deserve to be subordinated by the superior group;

- people who are not 'white' are biologically and culturally inferior; imputed characteristics vary depending upon the group being referred to, but tend to revolve around a set of 'problems' with which they are associated;

- the 'mixing' of superior and inferior groups leads to degeneration of the superior;

- the presence of, and contact with, 'non-white' people is something to be avoided if at all possible and such people should be excluded or segregated, including the use of physical means such as forced repatriation or extermination;

- a Jewish conspiracy (or a Zionist occupational government, ZOG) is imposing a multi-cultural ideal on to white territory and should be resisted with force.

(see box 2.1). What has become known as the 'racism paradigm' has led to four areas of research. First, an analysis of the shift from biological to cultural racism. While the 'old' racism was based on an explicit belief in biological superiority, the 'new' racism (Barker 1981) is based on the notion of cultural superiority and the supposed ill-effects of other cultures on the (white) British national heritage or 'the English way of life'. Second, researchers examined the way in which employment, housing, policing and other spheres of social and economic life are structured, or patterned, by racism. The focus of analysis is then to uncover the role of racism in structuring the social, economic and political marginalisation of minority communities. Third, researchers examined the production and reproduction of racism within white, and especially working-class communities. Fourth, researchers explored the ways in which notions of race can be re-forged into a political colour of opposition and examined how 'political identities' spoken through race can be characterised as social movements, relatively autonomous from class relations.

The 'racism paradigm' has itself been criticised for over-simplification of the notion of racism which appears, in some accounts at least, as a 'single monolithic racism'. This, it has been argued, should be displaced by research which maps the multifarious historical formulations of *racisms* (Goldberg 1993). Others have argued that what is required is an understanding of *racialisation* – a process by which groups become socially constructed as 'races' in terms of the heredity of biological or cultural traits (Solomos and Back 1996, Back and Solomos 2000). The contemporary interest is on a plurality of *racisms,* exclusionary and practices based on 'racial' or ethnic criteria which are then used as the basis for access to resources. Central to this analysis is uncovering the process through which the qualities of social groups 'become fixed, made natural, confined with a pseudo biologically defined culturalism' (Back and Solomos 2000). This approach has also urged close attention to the complex linkages between colonialism and constructions of race, and the interplay between race, class and gender in specific situations. All of this points in the direction of DuBois's comment at the turn of the century that central to our understanding of the world is 'the capacity to live with difference'.

Racist ideas can be found in a range of contemporary contexts. They inform the philosophies of such organisations as Choice and the British National Party, as well as the Ku Klux Klan, Aryan Nations, the Posse Comitatus in the USA and numerous contemporary racist organisations in European countries. Many of these organisations have their own websites, linked by such networks as *Stormfront* for 'white pride worldwide'. Racist ideologies also permeate more popular sources of ideas, such as *Bulldog* magazine and white power music. The British National Party,[2] for example, makes its views on the topic of race central to its manifesto:

> Our nationalism is ethnic as well as political – in fact it is ethnic before being political. Britain's ethnic identity, based as it is on a mingling of English, Scottish, Welsh and Irish strains must be preserved. People of

---

[2] Since the collapse of the National Front after 1979, the British National Party has become the most electorally successful of the extreme right-wing parties. It gained notoriety in the mid 1990s when a local councillor, Derek Beackon, was elected in Tower Hamlets. The BNP leader gave a televised party election address in the 1997 general election campaign, where he spoke of the symbolism of the white cliffs of Dover. The results were weak, however. A total of 35,388 votes were cast for the BNP in 56 constituencies. The party polled no more than 7.5 per cent in their best seats.

other European strains can be absorbed into our population in limited numbers. Those of non-European origin cannot. [We are] racial patriots who value our own racial heritage and want to maintain it intact.

The British National Party point to a devotion to their 'own' race, with a right to self-preservation. They warn of high ethnic minority birth rates and bemoan the 'inevitable intermingling and intermarriage' that will result in the British nation becoming 'something wholly different, racially and culturally, to what it has been over the past centuries of magnificent British achievement'. As a solution to this 'problem', they suggest a programme of repatriation which would be, at first, voluntary and later compulsory for all non-whites, including those people whose parents or grandparents were born in Britain.

This kind of racism cannot be dismissed as 'natural' or 'neutral' dislike, as disapproval of or even as prejudice towards ethnic minorities. On the contrary, it is a well-developed ideology of race, which dominates the thinking of a sizeable number of extremists and affects a wider proportion of society.

'Race' without racism?

Kleg (1993) describes the problems that confronted researchers after World War II in attempting to establish a vocabulary with which to examine the social construction of 'race' as a cultural, historical and political phenomenon and to unearth the effects of racism on groups defined by reference to their 'race'. As Kleg points out, 'race' is fundamentally a biological concept and is often thought of as a signifier of genetic difference. He goes on to note that superficial biological features are taken as 'signifiers' of other characteristics, physiological, psychological and cultural. In 1950, the United Nations Education, Scientific and Cultural Organisation (UNESCO) attempted to disentangle the denotative biological aspects of race from its racist connotations, for example in its *Statement by Experts on Race Problems* (Kleg 1993: 78–81, Bonnett 2000: 68–9). The report concluded that: ' "race" is not so much a biological phenomenon as social myth. The myth of "race" has created an enormous amount of human and social damage. In recent years it has taken a heavy toll in human lives and caused untold suffering.' Kleg summarises the three salient features of this attempt to strip the discussion of 'race' differences from their biological origins:

1. Human variability constitutes a continuum. Regardless of the classification system used, whether typological or geographical, there is no agreement as to the taxonomy.
2. Racial designations are merely convenient labels for discussing and comparing physical similarities and differences among populations – race as something more tangible or concrete than an abstract construction is fiction.

3. These classifications do not imply any kind of biological or cultural hierarchy, and are frequently, if not always arbitrary. (1993: 79).

The UNESCO statement concludes that: 'neither in the field of hereditary potentialities concerning the overall intelligence and capacity for cultural development, nor in that of physical traits, is there any justification for the concept of "inferior" or "superior" race' (ibid.: 81). Nonetheless, the biological connotations of the very terms of debate reinforce the ideas of ethnic and racial essentialism, even while denying the validity of race as a valid and meaningful category. We return to the debate about racial classification later in this chapter.

Ethnicity

The problems that arise from using the biological concept of 'race' to describe a social phenomenon have led some to abandon the term 'race' in favour of *ethnicity* as a descriptive and analytical category. Like 'race' and 'racism', there is no universally agreed definition of the term 'ethnicity'. However, the term is intended to describe differences in groups (defined by such features as: a common geographic origin; migratory status; phenotypic features; language; religious faith; shared traditions, values and symbols; cultural features, such as literature, music and foods), without resort to the racist notions of superiority and inferiority (Kleg 1993).

The defining characteristic of an ethnic group is one that has either (or both) an internal sense of distinctiveness and an external perception of distinctiveness (ibid.: 32). For Kleg, an *ethnic group* or 'ethnos' may be defined as consisting of individuals who share a distinct culture and are 'bound together by ties of cultural homogeneity' that result in a 'common way of perceiving, thinking, feeling and interacting with reality' (ibid.: 38). Similarly for Floya Anthias the concept of ethnicity cross-cuts and transcends gender and class divisions, but posits similarity (on the inside) and a difference (from the outside). The language of ethnicity enables a discussion of the way in which 'ethnic resources' – language, culture, religion, gender relations – interplay with the class, gender and political resources and positionings of the group (Anthias 1992: 424). Ethnic groups that are in some way outside the mainstream of a particular society and who are the victims of prejudice, discrimination and scapegoating may be referred to as 'ethnic minorities' (Kleg 1993).

Despite the potential value of an analytical shift towards the study of ethnicity, there are a number of problems with its usage. There is a risk that the term will simply become a euphemism for race (Gilroy 1987a). Recall that, according to Kleg, ethnicity can be ascribed on the basis of 'phenotypic features'. As such, it sustains 'racial meanings' while rejecting the cruder terminology of race. As Susan Smith argues, ethnicity is either used to refer to culture or it is simply a way of 'signalling that black people are the object of concern' (Smith 1989: 13). Although conceding that cultural difference is important, Smith argues that the term ethnicity does not add to the analysis and is roundly rejected as a theoretically or politically valuable concept (ibid.: 13–14). As Sivanandan (1983) has argued, the notion of ethnicity obscures the problem of racism and weakens the political voice of black people by fragmenting it into diverse communities of interest.

New ethnicities

The criticisms of both the race relations problematic and the racism paradigm, and a reassessment of the role of culture in identity formation in the post-colonial era has led to a consideration of new ethnicities (Hall 1988). For Stuart Hall, the starting point is a need to re-theorise the concept of difference in a social context where analysis based on a black/white binary opposition will no longer suffice to express the newly emerging questions of culture, ideology and representation. He argues that ethnicity may be a way to examine the historical, cultural and political construction of subjectivity and identity. However, he cautions that a great deal of work is required to decouple the concept of ethnicity from its functions in the dominant discourse. Hall suggests a positive concept of ethnicity 'predicated on difference and diversity' that recognises that we are all 'ethnically located and our ethnic identities are crucial to our subjective sense of who we are'. As Hall indicates, 'we all speak from a particular place, out of a particular history, out of a particular experience, a particular culture, without being contained by that position' (ibid.: 258). The origins of the debate about new ethnicities can be traced by examining the way in which identities forged around the notions of 'black', 'white' and 'Asian' have been contested and re-worked. There is also the concern that an over-emphasis on, or celebration of, difference and diversity masks socio-economic inequalities and racist terror/victimisation (Sharma, Hutnyk and Sharma 1996).

Problematising blackness

Black was the political colour of opposition in 1960s England, following the American politics of representation during the civil rights era. The 'Black Power' movement gave a voice most obviously to African Americans and African/Caribbeans in Britain, but also established the principle of self-empowerment and offered a model for political action for other disempowered groups. For many post-colonial critics in the UK – including most importantly A. Sivanandan and Stuart Hall – the 'black experience' articulated the common experience of all post-colonial migrants, creating a coalition to unite the Asian, African and West Indian populations. For Hall (1988: 252–3), 'the term "black" was coined as a way of referencing the common experience of racism and marginalisation in Britain and came to provide the organising category of a new politics of resistance, amongst groups and communities with, in fact, very different histories, traditions and ethnic identities'. Black politics became a singular and unifying framework in which to build identity across ethnic and cultural differences, between different communities, in order to maintain a unified front against racist violence and state racism in immigration laws and policing.

Although a 'black identity' became 'hegemonic' over other ethnic/racial identities, homogenising cultural, class and sexual difference, obviously these other sources of identity did not disappear (ibid.: 252). As the extraordinary diversity of social experiences and cultural identities re-emerged, the politically and culturally constructed category of 'black' was increasingly challenged as a 'fiction', however necessary it had been.

The focus on a black–white dualism emphasised the various minorities' shared experiences of racial exclusion, but as Modood argues, the *differences* are as significant as the similarities between the various minority groups' 'life chances' (Modood and Berthoud 1997: 8). Earlier Modood (1988) argued that the use of the term 'black' 'sold short' the majority of people it was intended to circumscribe, in particular those from the Indian subcontinent. Anthias and Yuval-Davis (1992: 144), point out the term 'black' also had the effect of excluding people from other developing regions, such as North Africa, the Middle East and Latin America, as well as those excluding 'white' minorities, such as the Irish, who suffer social, economic and political exclusion.

A further aspect of the 'end of innocence' brought about by a reconsideration of the analytical and political value of an inclusive 'black identity' emerges from the study of black nationalism. Although black communities are very diverse politically and culturally, African nationhood has sometimes been forged on racial essentialism. Although Afrocentric movements have made enormous contributions to black community development, it must also be ackknoweldged that the nationalism of Marcus Garvey and Louis Farrakhan also shares the idea of a mythologised past, concern for racial purity, separatism and anti-miscegenation, the idea of a chosen people and a 'racially exclusive' homeland (Gilroy 2000, esp. pp. 205–37).

Problematising Asianness

The events surrounding the publication of Salman Rushdie's 1989 book *The Satanic Verses* jolted the debate about 'race' and ethnicity out of the narrow groove where it had stuck in the 1980s (Modood 1992). The analytical vocabulary of neither the 'race relations problematic' nor the 'racism paradigm' could cope with the debate about 'religious absolutism' and Islamaphobia that centred on *The Satanic Verses* itself and reactions to it, such as public book burning and the Ayatollah's *fatwa* (which resulted in Rushdie going into hiding). Neither was the existing vocabulary able to articulate the experiences of working-class Muslims living in English towns (ibid.). What became known as the 'Rushdie affair', more than any other set of events, challenged the utility of the political category 'black' in the changed social and political environment of the 1990s. In particular, the emergence of religious and communal movements within minority communities became as much a focus of interest as the relationships between white and minority communities.

Tariq Modood's empirical test of the views of British South Asians, found that about one-fifth thought of themselves as being 'black' while about two-thirds rejected the label (Modood and Berthoud 1997 294–5). This black identity appears very important to many of those interviewed, while, for others, it was linked to situations where they were made to feel self-consciously 'black' or 'Asian'. Unfortunately, however, Modood and Berthoud did not explore the extent to which their interviewees would classify themselves as 'South Asian', his own preferred collective noun. A contrasting view is held by Anthias (1992), who argues that in Britain the principal countries represented by the category Asian – signified by skin colour and region – are more likely to use the categories of Indian, Sikh, Gujerati or Pakistani as the principal source of their identity. Just as Modood and Berthoud argue that 'black' conceals as much as it reveals, the term 'Asian' also glosses over important historical, cultural, religious, political and socio-economic differences between groups, despite their shared origin in the Indian subcontinent.

Problematising whiteness

One of the central assumptions of modern racism is that there exists an *essence* of the 'white race'. As we have seen, in chapter 1, the 'race idea' originated in the seventeenth century, as Europeans colonised the Americas and homogenised all classes into a new status: members of a 'white race'; Caucasian, Aryan, Germanic and Anglo-Saxon all being synonyms for 'white'. Writers of the day gave these ideas scientific credibility and these underpinned claims of the naturalness of European colonial domination and the 'common-sense' claims of superiority. In the colonial context, whiteness provided privilege even within systems of slavery and indenture that were, in fact, experienced by people of all colours. Even today, whiteness remains tied up with the notion of superiority (Hall 1988, Runnymede Trust 2000).

Whiteness defies definition because it has an 'everything and nothing quality', as Dyer (1988) put it, and thus the idea of 'being normal' has been colonised by the idea of 'being white' (cited by Back and Solomos 2000). It is easier, therefore, to define what 'whiteness' *is not* rather than what it *is*. It is not a 'biologically defined group, a static taxonomy, a neutral designation of difference, an objective description of immutable traits, a scientifically defendable division of mankind, or an accident of nature unmoulded by the hearts of people' (Haney Lopez 1996: 107). It could be defined as 'a social construct, a legal artifact, a function of what people believe, an unstable category tied to particular historical moments' (ibid.: 546).

The boundaries of the category of whiteness are constructed by deciding who does not fit within it and may, therefore, only be defined by a double negative: 'they are those who are not non-white'(ibid.:28). The notion of whiteness becomes problematic when its boundaries are tested. There have been numerous historical contexts in which the question has been raised: what counts as white? In the USA, the 'one drop rule' meant that an individual who had any known African ancestry would be classified as 'Negro', and this circumscribed the political franchise, rights to own property, and freedom of movement and association until the Civil Rights Acts of the 1960s. A fundamental problem with this kind of classification is that, despite the historical attempts to maintain racial boundaries, all people are 'mixed' both in terms of their genetic make-up, history and physical appearance. Those people whose appearance lies at the boundary of whiteness are able to 'pass for white' under some circumstances but not others.

Problematising whiteness has also led to an analysis of the social construction of 'white ethnicities'. Although the notion of 'white' has served the purpose of uniting all Europeans at various historical junctures, other racial taxonomies subdivided whiteness into finer gradations, such as between those of Anglo-Saxon, Celtic and Mediterranean origin (see Kleg 1993: 72–5). It becomes clear that the notion can include and exclude a wide range of different ethnic groups, and that categorisation as white is socially, historically and geographically contingent. Nazi German categories used to document racial identity distinguished between Aryans and Southern Europeans in the same way that the Metropolitan police distinguish between 'Caucasian' and 'Mediterranean' or 'dark-skinned Europeans'. These 'whites of a different colour'– including Italians, Spanish, Greeks, Turkish, Cypriots and Maltese – have historically faced racism in, for example, occupational colour-bar and in restrictions on migration, and have, at various times, been thought of as a 'problem' in Britain. Another significant example is that of people who have one African/Caribbean and one 'white' parent. Logically one might argue that such people could easily be categorised either as 'white', 'black' or 'mixed', but because the original police definition of 'black' included anyone who 'looks black', people with one black parent, or even one black grandparent, are likely to be categorised as 'black'.

There is evidence of physical violence and intimidation directed against 'white ethnic groups', such as the anti-Italian riots in 1940 (Panayi 1996). An echo of the 'othering' of Italians can be heard in the 1966 film, *The Italian Job*. Michael Caine, playing a plucky English villain, is blocked by the Mafia from getting to Milan, his target for an audacious gold bullion robbery. His two E-type Jaguars and an Aston Martin convertible have been rolled over a cliff by the Mafiosi. The camera gives us a close-up on the Mafia boss flanked by a mountainside of armed men in black suits and dark glasses. A defiant Caine says, 'You'd be making a grave error if you kill us. There are a quarter of a million Italians in England and they would be made to suffer. Every restaurant, café, bar, drinking den and nightclub in London, Liverpool and Glasgow will be smashed. Mr Bridger [the gangland boss] will drive them into the sea.' For a tense moment, the Mafia boss reflects, then orders the mob into their fleet of black Alpha Romeos and disappears.

The question of the relationship between Jewishness and whiteness is also problematic. Anti-Semitism is among the most obvious manifestations of racism against white people. This ideology conceives of Jews as an alien, hostile and undesirable group, and has been present in all major European countries, resulting in both 'popular' and politically driven anti-Semitism throughout Europe. In England, the arrival of Jewish migrants from Eastern Europe in the late nineteenth and early twentieth centuries was greeted with hostility, pseudo-scientific tracts identifying the Jews with disease and degeneration.

Reflection on whiteness has drawn attention to the ethnicities of the British Isles. The establishment of the Scottish Parliament and National Assemblies in Wales and Northern Ireland have been accompanied by an increasingly vocal English nationalism, calling for an English Parliament and regional assemblies. For Jeremy Paxman (1999), the attempt to define Englishness begins by defining its difference from, and opposition to, other British nationalities. The Welsh are caricatured by the English as 'wheedling duplicitous windbags, full of bogus sentimentality' (ibid.: 46). One critic asserted in 1997 that 'Wales enjoys a panoramic range of prejudice. We all know that the Welsh are loquacious dissemblers, immoral liars, stunted, bigoted, dark, ugly pugnacious little trolls' (ibid.), while the 'less abusive' English prejudice against the Scots sees them as tough, cantankerous, bloodthirsty traitors and drunks (ibid.).

People of Irish origin have also experienced discrimination and social and political exclusion. For example, Rex and Moore (1967) found that the Irish were seen more than any other group as being responsible for the declining conditions in an inner-city area. The Irish have also been constructed by the English as being inferior to them and as being of low intelligence and drunkards (Mac an Ghaill 1999: 78–80, Paxman 1999). Such stereotypes are implicated in discrimination against the Irish community in Britain in a range of settings, including migration, health, education, policing and welfare rights. Pearson (1983) notes that Irishness was a key component in the social construction of criminality in the eighteenth and nineteenth centuries in England, illustrated by the corruption of an Irish name providing the contemporary term Hooligan to describe a person with disorderly, drunken and violent tendencies. Such evidently racist ideologies and discriminatory practices provide part of the context for the construction of complex Irish identities, further problematising the alternatives of white and British identity.

What remains of Englishness? Attempts to define it flounder on its contradictions (for example, Paxman 1999) and these are sometimes resolved by elevating unique aspects of the culture – 'queuing perhaps, or the sound of leather on willow' – to stand for a pure and homogenous nationality (Gilroy 1997a:69). However, the idealised notions of 'fair play' and tolerance are frequently undermined by a quiet and unspoken sense of superiority (Hall 1988). Despite the appeal to culture, Englishness is often implicitly defined by a 'racial' characteristic, that is, whiteness (Runnymede Trust 2000). In the process of creating a culturally constructed sense of national identity, a 'closed, exclusive and regressive form' of Englishness was created by marginalising, dispossessing, displacing and forgetting other ethnicities (Hall 1988: 258). This raises the questions posed by Paul Gilroy (1983: 49–63), to what extent are blackness and Englishness mutually exclusive categories, and what are the prospects for the development of a black English identity?

Whiteness has an 'everything and nothing' quality and is the norm against which other ethnic groups are compared. In our analyses throughout this book, on the questions of disproportionality and 'over-representation' of ethnic minority groups in relation to offending, victimisation, criminal justice processing and imprisonment, we have assumed the appropriateness of comparison against an undifferentiated, homogenous 'white' norm. This position is clearly problematic on a number of grounds. What, for example, is the logic of making comparisons with a group who differ so markedly from minority communities in their demographic profile, geographical spread and social and economic circumstances? Does this formulation imply that a particular rate of victimisation or imprisonment is 'normal' for an English citizen, and is this the benchmark against which all 'other' ethnic groups should be compared? This formulation ignores the fact that there are stark differences between groups *within* white communities, depending on where exactly they live, their social class, age, etc., and that these are frequently just as great as those between the white majority and ethnic minority communities.

It must also be remembered that these differences in the way in which whiteness is constructed also have relevance for thinking about different 'white experiences' of crime and justice. Thus, the undifferentiated white prison population is comprised of people with very different experiences. We know, for example, that Irish people are disproportionately stopped and searched by the police (Young 1992) and make up a significant proportion of the prison population (Walmsley, Howard and White 1992). This raises all kinds of questions about the reasons for this over-representation and places the discussion of the social construction of 'Irish criminality' squarely within the same field as the social construction of 'black criminality' (see chapter 4).

Hybridity

Except for those who cling to discredited raciological thinking, it is accepted by most people that 'race' is not real, in the sense of discrete, biological or cultural categories, and that attempts to categorise are contradictory and flawed. This recognition has focused discussion on the notion of hybridity, which can be seen as the essence of the post-modern condition. The rejection of the notion of 'pure' races suggests that all human beings are phenotypically hybrid, comprised of a genetic mixture that defies the claims to a single origin, or even a finite number of different origins. At the boundaries of colour – especially those protecting the notion of 'whiteness' – there have always existed people who disrupt the process of racial categorisation. As Maria Root puts it 'the presence of racially mixed persons defies the social order predicated upon race, blurs racial and ethnic group boundaries, and challenges generally accepted proscriptions and prescriptions regarding inter-group relations' (Root 1992: 3).

The notion of hybridity has been used to explore cultural syncretism and an analysis of human identities that do not possess fixed, permanent, essential qualities (Solomos and Back 1996: 132–45). Recent studies of 'mixed-race' people in numerous contexts have allowed the possibility that an individual can have simultaneous membership and multiple, fluid identities with different groups (Root 1992: 6). For example, Les Back interviewed young Londoners whose parents were various combinations of black, white and Asian and found that young people could both identify themselves as having a 'mixed race' identity and locate themselves within a notion of blackness (Back 1996: 242). The experience of 'ethnically mixed' children will become increasingly important as this population grows. In the fourth Policy Studies Institute survey of ethnic minorities in Britian, Modood and Berthoud (1997) found that 39 per cent of children classified as being of 'Caribbean' origin had one white parent, though this was far less common among other ethnic groups (15 per cent of people classified as 'Chinese', 3 per cent of Indian/African Asian and 1 per cent of Pakistani and Bangladeshi had one white parent).

There are four qualifications that need to be raised about the interest in hybrid identities. First, the notion of 'mixed race' can contribute to reifying racial categories and essentialising 'race'. By declaring some individuals to be 'mixed', this can imply that there are other, pure, races from which this hybrid admixture has been formed. Second, while the celebration of hybridity contributes to the construction of positive identities for the extraordinarily diverse individuals and communities whose experiences are now being documented, an equal concern must also be paid to the presence of anti-miscegenationist sentiments and politics both historically and in the present day (Small 1991, Root 1992). Local ordinances prohibiting 'racial mixing' can still be found in US state legislatures, despite a Supreme Court ruling them unlawful in 1967 (Spickard 1989, cited in Root 1992: 7). Third, 'mixed race groups' have sometimes been manipulated in struggles between groups structured around black/white social divisions, often being encouraged to provide a barrier against the 'dangers' of black emancipation imagined by whites (James 1938). In South Africa, the 'Cape coloured' population (together with the Indians) were given a privileged status, such as limited political representation denied to the 'blacks'. Fourth, 'pure' religious and cultural identities can be the *end result* of hybridity rather than a return to some earlier forms of belonging (Bhatt, cited by Solomos and Back 1996: 145). For example, although Hitler detested the idea of 'racial' or cultural mixture, Nazi ideology did not represent *simply* a return to a mythic past of racial and cultural purity. Rather, fascism has a 'syncretic' quality as illustrated by the swastika, a symbol that has been present in a variety of different cultures and whose meaning has been the site of cultural and political struggle before, during and after the Nazi regime (Solomos and Back 1996: 145–53).

Connecting 'race', ethnicity, gender and class

Human *experience* is mediated by one's 'ethnic origin' and this is shaped by beliefs about racial difference and the ways people act upon them. In a similar way, being male or female, gay or straight, rich or poor, an urban or rural dweller shapes our experiences. The subject of this book dictates that racism and ethnicity are at the centre of our analysis, but we are also concerned to uncover the *intersections* with other social divisions and in particular gender and class (Mama 1984, Wilson 1978, Mirza 1997, Patel 1997). For example, ethnic minority women's relation to the British economy cannot be equated with, or reduced to, that of their male or female counterparts; rather black and Asian women have played a specific and unique role in the workforce and union activism (Mama 1984: 36).

The location of black women in the workforce reflects and compounds inequality. Black women workers are to be found '[i]n the lower echelons of all the institutions where we are employed (this in itself reflects the patterns of a segmented labour market) where the work is often physically heavy (in the factories and the mills no less than in the caring professions), the pay is lowest, and the hours are longest and most anti-social (night shifts for example)' (Mama, 1984, 1997: 37). The effects of gender inequality extend beyond the workplace and income inequalities to the experiences of community and social life in general and to the experiences of crime and justice in particular. As Chigwada-Bailey puts it, the forces of 'race', class and gender, work *in combination* to the detriment of minority women. Living in a society where the dominant culture, values and institutions are 'white', and where society is devised and run by men, the privations of life at the bottom of the economic scale are often combined and compounded for black women (Chigwada-Bailey 1997: 11). While it is helpful to examine one aspect of disadvantage alone, the full situation is only discernible through an analysis of the 'combination of oppressions' (Rice 1990, Chigwada-Bailey 1997).

'Race' and 'ethnic' categorisation

The collection of statistics coded by race, ethnicity and nationality has been controversial in numerous contexts. In Germany, for example, the fact that the Nazi state used racial and ethnic categories in its bureaucratic systems to facilitate the 'final solution to the Jewish question' led, after World War II, to the elimination of all such variables from official information systems. A lesson on the unintended consequences of recording and documenting citizens based on 'race' or ethnicity (for apparently benign purposes) can also be drawn from the Dutch experience. In the Netherlands, town hall records contained population registers that included religious affiliation. These records were of value, even indispensable, to the occupying Nazis in identifying and deporting Jews to concentration camps where many died.

The compilation of 'race-coded' statistics by police agencies in Britain can be traced back to the late 1960s, but was not revealed publicly until 1975 when the following categorisation, used by the police, was made public: IC1 – White-skinned European type; IC2 – Dark-skinned European type; IC3 – Negroid type; IC4 – Asian type; IC5 – Oriental type; and IC6 – Arabian type. Gutzmore noted that the police decide what 'race' people are coded as, and also that neither all suspects nor all offences were 'racially coded' because in most cases the victims had no idea whom to suspect. Gutzmore (1983) raised the question of why only statistics on crime in which blacks are 'purported to be over-represented' were published by the police.

Because human variability is a continuum, any taxonomical scheme is bound to be arbitrary and problematic. The arbitrariness of the British police system of categorisation is self-evident. The problem remains that in many analyses of ethnicity and crime and justice issues, especially those that draw on government statistical sources, undifferentiated 'white', 'black' and 'Asian' categories are used, thereby concealing ethnicities based on national, regional, class or other identities. As Montagu puts it in his book *Man's Most Dangerous Myth*, first published in 1942, 'we must guard against subscribing to a lexicon of unsound terms of which we elect ourselves guardians and make ourselves the prisoners of our own vocabularies' (Montagu 1997: 46)

British Census definitions

In the 1981 Census, estimates of the ethnic origins of the UK population were calculated on the basis of the place of birth of the head of the household polled. The Census included an estimate of the 'New

34 Concepts

Commonwealth and Pakistan' (NCWP) population, countries of the Caribbean, Africa and the Indian subcontinent and excluded the countries of the 'Old Commonwealth', including Australia, Canada and New Zealand. Interestingly, the 'white' countries of the New Commonwealth – such as Cyprus and Malta – were excluded from this NCWP category.

Box 2.2 A question of ethnicity

1991 Census ethnic question	2001 Census ethnic question
Ethnic group – please tick the appropriate box	**What is your ethnic group?** Choose ONE section from A to E, then tick the appropriate box to indicate your cultural background.
White	**A White** ☐ British ☐ Irish ☐ Any other white background, *please write in*
	B Mixed ☐ White and black Caribbean ☐ White and black African ☐ White and Asian ☐ Any other mixed background *please write in*
Indian **Pakistani** **Bangladeshi**	**C Asian or Asian British** ☐ Indian ☐ Pakistani ☐ Bangladeshi ☐ Any other Asian background *please write in*
Black Caribbean **Black–African** **Black** – Other please describe	**D Black or Black British** ☐ Caribbean ☐ African ☐ Any other Black background *please write in*
Chinese **Any other ethnic group** (please describe)	**E Chinese or other ethnic group** ☐ Chinese ☐ Any other, *please write in*

Source: OPCS (1993)
National Statistics (2000).
Note: The order of the 1991 Census has been re-arranged to enable a comparison with the 2001 Census.

After much debate, the 1991 British Census included, for the first time, a question on 'ethnic group', and this was modified slightly for the 2001 Census.

As can be seen, this categorisation of 'ethnicity' is a curious combination of adjectives describing 'colour' (white and black) and geographical location (Caribbean, African, Asian Indian, Pakistani, Bangladeshi and Chinese). Interestingly, the form also refers to 'your cultural background'. This list and that used for the 2001 Census, can only be understood in the specific historical, geographical and political context of post-colonial England and Wales (see box 2.2)

The absurdity of official ethnic categorisation is revealed by comparing American and British definitions of the term 'Asian'. In the USA, the Census category 'Caucasian/white' historically included not only the 'original peoples of Europe', but also 'North Africa, the Middle East, or the Indian subcontinent' (Root 1992). Therefore, most people defined as Asians in Britain would, in the past at least, have been classified as 'white' in the USA. To confuse matters 'Asian' in the USA is used to describe people from 'the Far East', South-East Asia and the Pacific Islands. These 'Asian Americans' would, in Britain, be categorised as 'Chinese' (Banton, 1988).

No set of ethnic or racial categories can resolve the question of identity and representation. The statistics collected by criminal justice agencies – based on stops, searches, arrests, cautions, convictions and prison sentences – are not how communities see themselves, but how individuals are seen by others, in this case, as they are seen by the agencies of the state, the primary definers of who is, or is not 'black', 'white' or 'Asian'. The primary definers of ethnicity also decide what counts as a crime and which crime deserves to be punished, a point that we return to in chapter 4.

Table 2.1 The population of Great Britain by ethnic origin, Census 1991

Ethnic origin	%	N
Total population	100.0	54,888,844
White	94.5	51,873,794
Total ethnic minority	5.5	3,015,050
Black–Caribbean	0.9	499,964
Black–African	0.4	212,363
Black–Other	0.3	178,401
Indian	1.5	840,255
Pakistani	0.9	476,555
Bangladeshi	0.3	162,835
Chinese	0.4	156,938
Other Asian	0.4	197,534
Other	0.5	290,206

Prejudice, attitudes and stereotyping

Much early 'race relations' research was concerned with the social psychology of attitudes, prejudice and stereotyping and these ideas are still central to many contemporary discussions. In the USA in the late 1940s, MacIver (1948) made an analytical distinction between discrimination as a form of behaviour and prejudice as an attitude. In this formulation, a prejudiced person did not necessarily or always discriminate and discrimination was not necessarily the result of prejudice (Banton 1994: 7). The classic social psychological definition of an attitude is 'a mental and neural state of readiness to respond, organised through experience, exerting a directive or dynamic influence upon the individual's response to all objects and situations with which it is related' (Allport 1935, cited by Kleg 1993: 118). This definition sets out both the *cognitive* (relating to thought) and *affective* (relating to feeling) natures of attitude, based on past experiences, which provide a framework for interpretation. Central to Allport's definition is the idea that attitudes indicate a 'readiness to respond' and 'set the stage for action'. They are not *in themselves* a form of behaviour but they do have a 'directive' or 'dynamic' influence on behaviour.

The term *prejudice* in common usage is often taken to mean simply prejudging a person or thing. However, social psychologists include a more complex set of attributes. A social psychological definition of racial prejudice is 'a readiness to act, stemming from a negative feeling, often predicated upon a fixed over-generalisation or totally false belief and directed toward a group or individual members of that group' (Kleg 1993: 114). Although prejudices can be positive as well as negative, the term usually has negative connotations in the area of race and ethnicity. Among different types of prejudice are *ethnocentric beliefs* (a set of beliefs that judges other groups as inferior to one's own), *over-generalisation* (a belief about members of a group that is not actually true of all or even most members) and *falsehood* (an extreme form of what is sometimes thought of as over-generalization in which an entirely false attribution to an individual or group is taken as characteristic of the entire group). The constellation of prejudices towards outgroups is known as *xenophobia*, and surveys indicate that such attitudes are widespread in Britain and elsewhere (see box 2.3).

In his 1922 book *Public Opinion* Walter Lippmann coined the term *stereotype* to mean the 'pictures inside the head' stimulated by a person thinking about themselves or other people. In Lippmann's terms, stereotypes are an individual's 'perceived reality', based on a combination of information from the world of immediate experience together with personal ideas constructed from cultural values, desires and past experiences. As Kleg (1993: 137) suggests, stereotypes are important because they stamp themselves upon reality and transform reality to fit the stereotype.

Box 2.3 English xenophobia

That xenophobic stereotypes and prejudices are widely dispersed throughout society can be illustrated in surveys of public opinion about prejudice.

Endorsements of xenophobic sentiments among a random sample of English people

% who	
disagree that immigrants are good for the economy	37
agree that immigrants increase crime rates	25
disagree that political refugees should be allowed to stay in Britain	25
disagree that immigrants make Britain open to new ideas and cultures	17
say that immigrants take jobs away from those born in Britain	48
agree that the number of immigrants should be reduced	64
Base	856

This survey suggests that xenophobic opinions are widespread. For example, about two-thirds of the predominantly white English population think that the number of immigrants should be reduced. These patterns are not uniformly spread across the population but cluster within certain groupings. *Supra-nationalists* tend to be 'unmoved by the symbols of nation', are younger, female, better educated and rather more likely to read the *Guardian* or the *Independent* than the *Daily Express*. At the other extreme are the John Bulls who hold the strong national sentiments and exclusionary views. This group has few educational qualifications, hold authoritarian values and reads the *Daily Mail*.

Source: Dowds and Young (1996: 147).

Psychologists do not see stereotyping as the exclusive preserve of bigots, but, rather, as a central feature of human cognitive and affective functioning. Stereotypes are part of the mental process that 'fills in the gaps' between the stream of information about the world perceived by the observer and his or her *interpretation* of it. This 'filling in' process may form highly distorted images of what is real and these, in turn, may lead to further distortions when stereotypes are used to fill in bits of information in the future (ibid.: 140). Racial stereotyping is the application of a generalised mental picture to all members of a particular group (Tajfel

1969). Stereotypes are an important aspect of prejudice because the process of categorising people into 'racial' or 'ethnic' groups creates a *mind set* on the part of the perceiver. This 'mind set' leads the perceiver to select and interpret traits that members of the group *seem* to have in common. In some cases, this may include the creation of traits that 'reside only in the mind of the perceiver' (Kleg 1993: 147).

Recently, Stuart Hall *et al.* (1998) have contributed a structural account of the content and formation of racial stereotypes. They argue that racial stereotypes in Britain are part and parcel of a way of thinking about contact with people from other parts of the world, and are diffused through every level of British society. No society is wholly or inevitably 'racist', nor are racial stereotypes universally held; rather, they vary from period to period, group to group, situation to situation (ibid.: 5). Hall *et al.* propose that the use of racial stereotypes is related to marking and sustaining the differences between 'us' and 'them'. They argue that stereotyping is *structural*, persisting over time in the 'unconscious thought processes and long-term collective memory of groups'. These processes, they argue, are embedded in the routine daily conduct of individuals as well as the culture of social institutions. Such prejudices and stereotypes affect the way organisations work and remain stable over time. However, the use of stereotyping is 'contingent', depending on individuals and the circumstances in which they find themselves in.

Discrimination

Attitudes, prejudice and stereotypes are 'all in the mind'. What is more important is not what people think, but how they behave and how their thinking affects their behaviour. This link between attitudes of mind and forms of behaviour is explored by the social psychology of discrimination, scapegoating and aggression. Allport (1954) described the levels of aggression in 'acting out' prejudice to be on a five-point scale, ranging from the most mild forms of *antilocution* (or defamation), *avoidance* and *discrimination* to *physical attack* and *extermination* at the most extreme. A modified version of Allport's continuum is shown in Figure 2.1. For present purposes, discrimination is the most important form of behaviour, though we return to the questions of physical violence in chapter 4.

Discrimination consists of unequal, unfavourable and unjustifiable treatment based on a person's sex, gender, 'race', ethnicity, culture, religion, language, class, sexual preference, age, physical disability or any other improper ground. It includes refusal to offer employment, pay fair wages, to provide housing or medical treatment or to provide a commercial or social service. Discrimination directly restricts civil liberties, such as voting rights, the right to be tried by a jury of one's peers and freedom of movement and association. It can also take the form of harassment, attack, exclusion and expulsion. Some theorists emphasise an investi-

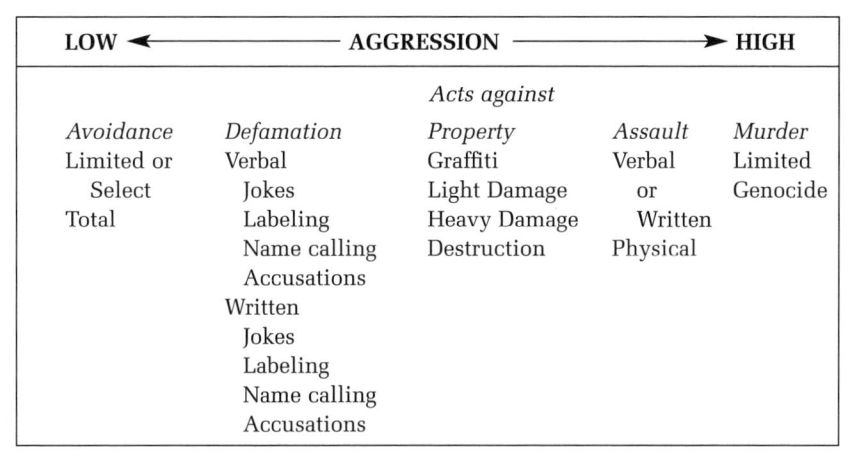

LOW ←		AGGRESSION		→ HIGH
		Acts against		
Avoidance	*Defamation*	*Property*	*Assault*	*Murder*
Limited or	Verbal	Graffiti	Verbal	Limited
Select	Jokes	Light Damage	or	Genocide
Total	Labeling	Heavy Damage	Written	
	Name calling	Destruction	Physical	
	Accusations			
	Written			
	Jokes			
	Labeling			
	Name calling			
	Accusations			

Figure 2.1 Kleg's continuum of aggression, drawing on Allport (1954)
Source: Milton Kleg (1993) *Hate Prejudice and Racism*

gation of the 'life form' of discrimination and its roots in local histories, as well as the development of racist and ethnocentric beliefs. Others emphasise the *effects* of discrimination in creating disadvantage and limiting the life chances of those discriminated against.

A distinction can be made between direct and indirect discrimination. Among the best examples of *direct discrimination* are those which have been enshrined in law. The South African apartheid legal system, for example, prohibited black people from voting or participating in the political process, created separate 'white' residential areas and schools, and also prohibited 'mixed marriages'. Similarly, restrictions on women's ability to own property or to vote etc. have been in place in many countries and still exist in some places, including some cantons of Switzerland. An explicit ban on the employment of openly homosexual people in the police or military is another example of direct discrimination. Such legal restrictions have obvious and wide-ranging consequences for fairness and social justice.

These *de jure* forms of discrimination are easy to identify and criticise as unjust. Even when there are no laws promoting or requiring discrimination, however, people are often still directly excluded or singled out for unfavourable treatment. In many criminal justice agencies (including police, prisons and the courts) explicit, overt and direct discrimination has led to informal restrictions – known as the 'colour bar' – on the employment of people from ethnic minorities and of women. Discrimination also contributes to explaining why there are often marked inequalities in service provision (Brown 1997). Sometimes discriminatory practices persist even in the face of laws or policies designed to eliminate discrimination. This *de facto* discrimination can be the result of covert activity – that which is intentional, but hidden – but can also be the result of indirect discrimination.

Indirect discrimination refers to treatment which might be described as 'equal' in a formal sense between different groups, but is discriminatory in its *actual effect* on a particular group. The 'minimum height' requirement for appointment as a police officer in some jurisdictions is an example of indirect discrimination. Clearly, women and people from some ethnic minority groups are less likely than white males to be able to meet the minimum requirement. This regulation would clearly have the effect of restricting job opportunities for some groups, and is therefore discriminatory, particularly since height is irrelevant to the job of being a police officer. Sometimes indirect discrimination occurs knowingly but covertly excluding women, homosexuals or people from ethnic minority communities – but there are many other instances where such exclusion appears to be neither conscious nor deliberate. For example, few criminal justice agencies provide services for non-English speakers. Although it is probably not the intent of these organisations specifically to exclude non-English speakers, this is, in fact, what happens and can be seen as having an indirect discriminatory effect.

Institutional racism

The term 'institutionalised racism' was introduced by Carmichael and Hamilton (1968) who wrote that racism in America is 'pervasive' and 'permeates society on both the individual and institutional level, covertly and overtly' (see Miles 1989: 50, Cashmore 1996: 169–70). Cashmore sees institutional racism as an analytical tool to examine how: 'institutions can operate along racist lines without acknowledging or even recognising this and how such operations can persist in the face of official policies geared to the removal of discrimination' (Cashmore 1996: 172). Lea defines institutional racism as occurring when racist actions are 'built into the policy or mode of operation of institutions irrespective of the attitudes of the individuals who carry out the activities of the institution' (Lea 1987: 148). By way of illustration he points to the possibility that 'racist immigration laws may be administered by officials and police officers irrespective of their individual attitudes to immigrants'. He adds that, '[c]onversely racist practices may originate at the level of individual behaviour irrespective of the formal policies and the general operations of the institutional framework within which the individual is operating' (ibid.: 149).

Susan Smith argues that 'although a hallmark of institutionalised racism is detachment from the intentionality of individual managers and administrators ... some racist practices must be regarded as the product of *uncritical* rather than unconscious racism' (1989: 101, emphasis added). That is, practices with a racist outcome are not engaged in without the actor's knowledge, even if they have failed to consider the consequences of his or her actions for black or Asian people. Smith also points out that:

institutionalised racism is not a process confined to housing or any other single system of resource distribution. It is rather, a pervasive process sustained across a range of institutions – housing, education, employment, health and social services – that have procedures which combine to produce a mutually reinforcing pattern of racial inequality. This acknowledges that virtually all large organisations concerned with the allocation of power and resources develop conventions which distinguish the deserving from the undeserving and the reputable from the debased, in order to help prioritise applicants queuing for goods and services. Virtually all these conventions invoke 'racial' attributes, tacitly or explicitly, as a criterion for exclusion or inclusion in the dispensation of scarce resources.

(ibid.: 102)

Without losing sight of the importance of the overt expression of racism, individual prejudices and direct discrimination, indirect 'institutional' racism has become the focus for many critics because it is both more subtle and potentially more pervasive. All definitions of institutionalised racism have a set of common themes, encapsulated by the Lawrence Inquiry as:

The collective failure of an organization to provide an appropriate and professional service to people because of their colour, culture, or ethnic origin. It can be seen or detected in processes, attitudes and behaviour which amount to discrimination through unwitting prejudice, ignorance, thoughtlessness and racist stereotyping which disadvantage minority ethnic people.

(Macpherson 1999, para. 0.34)

Contextual discrimination

No one theory of discrimination, whether it is based on notions of individual attitudes, organisational or national cultures, or iniquitous social structures, fully explains why racism and racial discrimination appear to be concentrated into 'pockets' of the criminal justice system – within specific police stations or certain parts of the prison service or judiciary. The concept of contextual discrimination is defined by Walker, Spohn and DeLone (1996) as that which occurs in certain places, situations or contexts. Thus, for example, the extent and nature of cultural racism can differ from one police station to another (Foster 1989), or between one Crown Court and another (Hood 1992). The extent of discrimination can also differ for the processing of different kinds of offences or different victim–offender relationships. It might also be that at certain times discrimination occurs but not at others. Contextual discrimination also provides a way of thinking about how discrimination changes over time – between the middle of the twentieth century (prior to any anti-discrimination legislation) and the beginning of the twenty-first century (as a third Race Relations Act is implemented), and between places (comparing Britain to the USA or South Africa).

A theory of 'contextual discrimination' suggests that discrimination is likely under certain specific conditions but not under others. This raises the question of what kinds of conditions enable discrimination to occur. There are some obvious factors such as the extent to which discrimination is enshrined in law or where anti-discriminatory legislation is in place and the extent to which such behaviour is actually sanctioned. The ethnic composition of a particular organisational context and the extent to which ethnic minorities within those organisations are empowered must also make a difference. For example, when African, Caribbean and Asian people made up only a tiny minority of the British police service (in the late 1970s) many white police officers felt able to use extreme racist language with impunity. In early 1980s London racial prejudice was 'pervasive' in the Met and racialist talk was 'expected, accepted and even fashionable', even among senior officers (Smith and Gray 1983: 355). In organisations where people from African, Caribbean and Asian communities hold senior positions, this situation seems less likely to occur.

A further set of considerations in identifying the contexts where discrimination is likely are aspects of the organisational structure, particularly the extent of oversight and accountability. FitzGerald (1993b), in her contribution to the Royal Commission on Criminal Justice, noted that where the following conditions (either singly or in combination) apply 'discrimination is likely':

- where there are no clear guidelines about the criteria on which decisions should be taken;
- where decisions depend on subjective judgements rather than (or in addition to) objective criteria;
- when there is considerable scope for the exercise of individual discretion;
- where there is no requirement to record or monitor the reasons for decisions;
- where local and organisational cultural norms (rather than the requirements of service delivery) strongly influence decision making.

As FitzGerald notes, many criminal justice decisions are taken in such circumstances. The key point is that discretion exists where officers are free to make a choice among possible courses of action or inaction (Lustgarten 1986). Clearly, where there are detailed rules about how an individual criminal justice agency may – and in particular must – act, discretion is low. However, discretion will remain high even in the presence of these rules if no record is made of the decision and where there is little or no supervision. Accountability and discretion are linked; where accountability and visibility of decisions are low, there exists a greater degree of discretion and discrimination is more likely.

This analysis is helpful for understanding the impact of discrimination in criminal justice, but what has not been explored, to our knowledge, is any analysis of where wide discretion, lack of control and accountability are evident in the criminal justice system. Hypothetically, those parts of the criminal justice system where discretion is wide and accountability low will be those where disproportionate outcomes are most prevalent. Conversely, where an evidence-based, recorded, monitored decision-making regime exists, discrimination will be less common.

Equal treatment, equal opportunity or equal outcome?

The discussion of discrimination leads to the question of what counts as 'equality'. Arguably, a full consideration of what counts as discriminatory is not possible unless we can conceptualise a system that is without discrimination. Three approaches to understanding equality can be discerned.

The *equal treatment approach*, aims to establish 'formal equality' (Smith 1997a) and assumes that because all people are equal, they should be treated identically. However, this approach can deal only with direct discrimination. It does not address indirect discrimination because it fails to recognise differences in experiences and needs. This may be regarded as synonymous with the 'individual justice' model proposed by McCrudden, Smith and Brown (1991). It has also been described as the 'colour-blind approach' because it does not recognise that cultural differences make the application of a mono-cultural 'one-size-fits-all' approach to service provision unfair. The experience of elderly people from ethnic minority communities shows that although service providers thought their services were 'open to all' in the 1980s, they were *de facto* designed for white English elderly people and did not recognise differences in diet, health needs, etc. found within different communities (Bowling 1990). Moreover, the colour-blind approach does not accept that racism exists in any sphere, so cannot respond to people's actual experiences of discrimination.

The *level playing field* or *equal opportunities approach* recognises the fact of cultural difference and accepts that discrimination has created, over time, patterns of inequality that the 'equal treatment approach' cannot address. This approach therefore seeks to tackle the conditions which prevent minorities from competing fairly. This approach is concerned with outcomes, but is wary of the application of quotas (preferring instead to identify *targets*) and takes a long-term view of when proportionality will be achieved.

The *equal outcome approach* focuses attention on the outcomes or end results of policies and programmes, imposing an expectation that an absence of racial disproportionality would be a hallmark of a non-discriminatory system. Thus, there would be demographic parity within a particular organisational setting (in employment and promotion, for example) and in service delivery (evident in patterns of satisfaction, complaints, etc.). This model is consistent with McCrudden, Smith and Brown (1991) 'group justice model'.

The term 'proportionality' refers to the extent or degree to which something appears to be appropriate or in 'proportion' with something else. The term disproportionality has been used in criminology to describe a disparity, or imbalance, in patterns of crime or the administration of criminal justice. For example:

- the extent to which a punishment is unduly harsh, proportionate to the gravity of the offence being punished;
- the extent to which police powers are used in proportion to the extent and seriousness of the offence;
- rates of imprisonment in proportion to the demographic characteristics of the general population;
- rates of offending or victimisation in proportion to the demographic characteristics of the general population;
- rates of employment in the criminal justice professions in proportion to the demographic characteristics of the workforce.

The notion of proportionality is central to desert theories. A sentence of the court could be described as disproportionate if a person convicted of a minor offence were sentenced to a long period of custody or if a judge or magistrate fails to take into account mitigating circumstances. If people of African/Caribbean origin are more frequently given custodial sentences in comparison with their white counterparts, even once all legally relevant variables are taken into account, this constitutes disproportionality.

Identifying disproportionate outcomes of the criminal justice process is a necessary but not sufficient step towards establishing discrimination. In human rights jurisprudence, disparities in the treatment of women and people from ethnic and other minorities can be taken as *prima facie* evidence of discrimination which can be tested by assessing the extent to which differences can be explained by legitimate factors. Where disparities are shown to be unjustified, discriminatory practices may be ruled unlawful and complainants are entitled to redress.

Disadvantage

There is no shortage of examples of where ethnic minority communities appear to lose out, and these are by no means restricted to criminal injustice. The social and economic *disadvantages* experienced by people of African, Caribbean and Asian origin have been documented in a range of spheres including employment, housing, education, health and social services.

Exploring the extent and nature of these disadvantages is important to understanding ethnic minorities' experience of crime, victimisation and the criminal justice process because these broader economic and social factors provide the context within which these experiences unfold (see box 2.4).

Box 2.4 Policy Studies Institute surveys of disadvantage

Since the 1960s there have been numerous studies of racial discrimination and disadvantage. Among the most important of these is a series of surveys conducted by the Policy Studies Institute (PSI). The key studies and their findings are summarised below:

1966   Ethnic minorities are consistently in jobs below the level to which they are qualified. Overwhelmingly in manual work, they are confined to a limited number of industries. Some employers flatly refuse to employ 'coloureds', others do so only when insufficient white workers are available. Overt exclusion from public and private sector housing is widespread with properties only available in areas white people are leaving. Segregation in residential settlement results. Objective tests in housing and employment reveal that 'colour' is the focus for discrimination (Daniel 1968).

1974   Little progress since 1966 with patterns of discrimination and disadvantage enduring (Smith 1977).

1982   Some progress, but minorities are still concentrated in a limited number of occupations, earn lower wages and are more likely to be unemployed than their white counterparts. Residential segregation still evident with ethnic minorities concentrated in urban areas, especially in the poorest parts (Brown 1984).

1994   Still a great deal of disadvantage among ethnic minority groups, but patterns of differentiation are now apparent. People of African, Caribbean and Indian origin (with the exception of African Asians) experience disadvantage, but less acutely than those of Pakistani and Bangladeshi origin. In socio-economic terms, people of Chinese and African Asian origin have reached a position of broad parity with the white population. (Modood, Smith and Brown 1997).

Geography, urbanisation and housing

Compared with countries such as South Africa or the USA, the UK is relatively 'integrated' rather than segregated. There are no *de jure*, or even *de facto* areas where only whites can live, though there are areas where the non-white population is extremely small. Conversely, there are no areas where *only* ethnic minorities live. Indeed, there are very few local authority areas where whites are in the minority and none where whites are other than the numerically dominant group. However, Susan Smith's (1989) analysis of patterns of residential settlement at the finest level of detail shows that Britain is actually highly segregated. Based on 1981 Census data, Smith showed that about half the white population lived in neighbourhoods containing *no* black residents while only about one in 16 white people lived in a neighbourhood with an ethnic minority population greater than 5 per cent. As Smith puts it, 'black people are disproportionately likely to live in the country's most deprived and disadvantaged neighbourhoods'. Ethnic minorities tend to live in urban areas; to occupy the older, poorer housing stock; and to live in the parts of cities where urban decay is most pronounced. Minority communities cluster where a range of services including education, health care, crime prevention and victim support are 'in greatest need but shortest supply' (ibid.: 39).

Part of this geographical concentration of ethnic minorities can be explained in terms of patterns of settlement based on preference. It is probably true, for example, that people tend to settle near where friends and family have settled. However, Smith shows there are clear individual, community and institutional factors which shape patterns of residential settlement. For example, until local authorities were forced to comply with the 1976 Race Relations Act, local authorities had policies which disadvantaged black and Asian people seeking accommodation, such as the requirement for a certain period of residency or 'sons and daughters' policies which favoured relatives of existing tenants. In the private sector, estate agents have avoided showing houses in white areas to prospective ethnic minority buyers while private landlords have refused to let flats to ethnic minority tenants. In sum, their disadvantaged position reflects 'systematic inequalities dispensed by the interaction of the labour market with the housing system' (ibid.: 39).

A Commission of Racial Equality study of the role of local authorities in housing provision found systematic differences between members of different ethnic groups in housing allocation. Black and Asian families were more likely to be allocated flats rather than houses, and were residents of less popular estates with fewer amenities (Mason 1995: 84). Peach and Byron (1993) found that these differences were most pronounced for African/Caribbean female heads of households, who were most likely to be located in the poorest housing (cited in Mason 1995: 85).

A 1990 Commission of Racial Equality report entitled 'Sorry, It's Gone' found racism to be pervasive in the private rented sector, and that minorities were more likely to be rented only the poorest quality of private accommodation, or not rented to at all. This partly explains the overrepresentation of minority group members in the homelessness statistics. Research in London, for instance, found that ethnic minorities are up to four times as likely to become homeless as white households (Skellington 1996: 141). There is a high representation of certain minority groups, particularly Indian, African Asians and Pakistanis, who own their own homes. However, a 1992 government report indicated that over 1.3 million dwellings in England were unfit to live in (90 per cent of which were owner occupied), and four-fifths of Indian households were found to live in such dwellings (ibid.: 143–4).

Education

Mason's (1995) overview of racism in the education system concluded that 'many schools and teachers have been at best ill-informed and insensitive, frequently ethnocentric ... and at worst, explicitly racist in their treatment of pupils of minority ethnic origin'. Research has revealed a range of widespread negative experiences, from being excluded as a result of religious or cultural non-conformity, the misdiagnosis of medical or educational problems and an unwillingness by teachers to accept the nature of racist attacks, to disproportionately harsh reactions to the behaviour of ethnic minority students (for example, Bourne, Searle and Bridges 1994, Wright 1994). Recent initiatives to enlarge 'parental choice' have had a particularly negative impact on ethnic minority students and their families. As Bourne *et al.* (1994) put it, 'children whose parents are unable ... to play the new "market" of social choice ... find themselves cut adrift with no effective means, formal or informal, of exercising their basic right to education'. It is neither surprising, perhaps, that disaffection is expressed by students, nor that many ethnic minority groups are demanding the establishment of schools that serve their needs and meet their expectations (Mason 1995).

The Office for Standards in Education (OFSTED) (1999) reported that while achieving equal levels with white students at primary level, black Caribbean students' performance declined significantly at secondary level. Modood and Berthoud (1997) found that Bangladeshi students had the lowest level of post-16 qualifications, followed by black Caribbean and white students, while the best-qualified groups were the Chinese, African Asians and Indians. Young ethnic minorities on training programmes are much less likely to benefit from being in employment than their white counterparts, and this is particularly marked for black and Asian young people (Pathak 2000). Much of our interpretation depends on which particular ethnic group and which age group is being studied, and also needs to bear class and gender in mind, since some studies indicate that black Caribbean girls are high achievers. These findings reveal the problematic nature of the notion of 'underachievement'. It is also important to consider how 'achievement' is being measured, as studies generally use crude examination results as the yardstick. What does seem clear is that black Caribbean students in secondary schools under-perform in comparison with their white peers. Interestingly, there is later a marked upturn in this group's achievement – particularly black women – in post-compulsory education (Modood and Berthoud 1997).

A recent Commission for Racial Equality study described the extent of school exclusions as 'alarming'. With an estimated 10,000–14,000 permanent exclusions during 1995/6: 'schools are at present effectively dumping the population of a small town each year' (Commission for Racial Equality 1997). A MORI survey estimated that there may be as many as 20 times the number of students excluded as official figures would suggest. The DfEE's figures for 1998/9 show that black Caribbean students form only 1.5 per cent of the school population but 5.7 per cent of excluded pupils, making them almost four times more likely to be excluded than their white counterparts (DfEE 2000).

Several studies have examined the various factors resulting in the disproportionate exclusions. These include: racist or stereotypical perceptions of black students as having particular 'behavioural' and 'cultural problems'; socio-economic deprivation; racial harassment and provocation; teachers, under increased time constraints, are often unable to deal effectively with individual students; cuts in spending on special education needs provision and alternatives to mainstream schools; and a curriculum which can seem irrelevant to some students. There is also some evidence that black Caribbean boys are excluded for behaviour that would not usually result in an exclusion for their white counterparts. Most worrying is that many excluded students disappear from the education system altogether. An Audit Commission survey revealed that only 15 per cent of those students who are permanently excluded return to school. Thus, discrimination and exclusions can lead to cumulative disadvantage for ethnic minority students in terms of their future competitiveness in the labour market.

Employment and unemployment

As David Mason (1995: 43) points out, economic resources are often key to people's ability to control other aspects of their lives. Trevor Jones (1993: 112) describes unemployment among minority groups as 'hypercritical'. That is, in times of recession, ethnic minority unemployment increases faster than that of white people, whilst in times of recovery these rates fall more rapidly (see Skellington 1996: 220, figure 10.3). The Labour Force Survey's (Home Office 2000b) employment rates for spring 1999 reveal that while 75 per cent of working-age whites were in employment, the percentage was only 40 per cent for Pakistanis/Bangladeshis, 50 per cent for those of Chinese origin, 61 per cent for blacks and 65 per cent for those of Indian origin (Home Office 2000b). A study by the Department of Employment found that ethnic minority unemployment rates are consistently higher than whites within the same broad levels of qualifications (Skellington 1996: 222). Unemployment particularly affects young people (16–24), which is significant because of the relatively young structure of minority groups within Britain. In the autumn of 1994 in the 16–24 age group, 51 per cent of African/Caribbeans, 33 per cent of Bangladeshis, and 30 per cent of Indian men were unemployed compared with 18 per cent of white men in the same age group.

Certain groups, most notably African Asians and Indians (Skellington 1996: 222), have penetrated to a remarkable extent into certain professions. However, as Trevor Jones (1993) shows, there is also strong evidence that other minority groups remain at substantially lower job levels than whites, most notably Bangladeshis and Pakistanis (Skellington 1996: 222). In general, minority workers are more likely to be unemployed and in lower-level employment than their white counterparts (Mason 1995: 58) and so are under-represented in the highest occupational categories, and over-represented in manual work (Modood and Berthoud 1997: 100). The Equal Opportunities Commission (EOC) showed that skilled minority women are twice as likely as white women to be unemployed, or over-qualified in inferior employment (Skellington 1996: 221).

Income

The 1995 Policy Studies Institute survey showed that the mean weekly earnings of all ethnic minorities was £296 compared to £336 for whites. Bangladeshis had the lowest weekly income of of £191 (Modood and Berthoud 1997: 113). Jones (1993) argues that local analysis is more meaningful than national averages, on the basis of which he identified earning differentials between white employees and those from minority ethnic groups ranging between 10 and 30 per cent.

These patterns might be perpetuated and compounded by the ways in which people find employment, that is, often through informal networking. However, this does not account for all disadvantage. A report by the Commission for Racial Equality (1995) showed that out of 300 leading companies only one half were beginning to put racial equality policies into practice, with very few moving from a stated commitment to practical action (Skellington 1996: 228). A method to investigate this has been to submit job applications from candidates matched in every way except ethnic origin (Mason 1995: 59, table 5.7). This research revealed some alarming differences in the way in which applicants are treated, with white applicants 30 per cent more likely to be treated more favourably overall than those of minority ethnic origin (Mason 1995: 59).

Poverty

Long-term unemployment, educational under-achievement, low pay, lone parenting, overcrowding and poor housing, can all be defined as indicators of poverty and are more likely to afflict people from ethnic minorities. For example, 18 per cent of the white population are in the poorest 20 per cent of the population, compared with 33 per cent of the non-white population (Skellington 1996: 108). The London Research Centre reported disturbing incidences of multiple deprivation affecting minority ethnic groups in particular in the capital (ibid.: 108, figure 4.9, 145). Berthoud (1997) indicates that this is even more pronounced for some groups, and suggests, for instance, that 80 per cent of Pakistani and Bangladeshi households fell below a poverty benchmark, which affected only 20 per cent of the white population. While extended families seem to be more vulnerable to poverty, this is also a problem faced by lone parent households, who are particularly vulnerable to low pay and expensive childcare. This is a critical point, given that African/Caribbean families are more than three times as likely to be lone parents (Skellington 1996: 99). Berthoud (1997) showed that people of Caribbean descent have exceptionally high levels of rent arrears and are more likely to experience money worries (ibid.: 99, figure 4.5).

Family

One significant trend among the community of African/Caribbean origin is a low emphasis on formal marriage across every age group, compared with the white population. A recent study suggested that about one-third of Caribbean families with children had a 'never married' mother, more than five times the proportion among whites (Berthoud and Beishan 1997: 56; Skellington 1996: 60). Thus, large proportions of children of Caribbean origin do not live with their fathers and may not know him (Berthoud and Beishan 1997: 57). The extent of single-parent families is important, because three in five one-parent families are living on or below the margin of poverty, compared with one in five two-parent families (Skellington 1996: 51). Nonetheless, Caribbean lone parents were significantly more likely to be in work than white lone parents (Berthoud and Beishan 1997: 57).

In contrast, Asians were much more likely to marry than whites, with an accompanying low rate of divorce and separation. Although South Asian women are similar to white women in the age that they have children and the number they have, they are more likely to live in the same house as their partner's family, whereas white people tend to live separately from their parents once they have their own families. People of Pakistani and Bangladeshi origin differ in that they tend to start their families earlier and finish later with more children. The result is that both South Asians and the latter groups are characterised by larger, extended families (ibid.: 58–9). Pakistanis and Bangladeshis, who are most likely to have lower incomes than whites, live in the poorest of housing in overcrowded conditions. These groups, which tend to be characterised by complex and large family households, approximate to family structures and parenting practices in Pakistan and Bangladesh (Modood and Berthoud 1997: 354). In a similar way, Modood argues that Caribbeans, with a low emphasis on marriage and who have a high proportion of one-parent families, also approximate structures of living in the Caribbean. Maintaining this position against assimilation (whether intentionally or unintentionally), these groups are frequently penalised – not just economically but also morally.

There is an increasing trend among ethnic minority group members to choose white partners in cohabitation, marriage and child rearing. This is more prevalent among Caribbeans than among Asians. With one-half of Caribbean men, a third of Caribbean women, and one-fifth of Indian and South Asian men having a white partner (ibid.: 316). However, because the ethnic minority population is so small only about 1 per cent of all partnerships in the population as a whole are 'mixed'. The British Social Attitude (BSA) surveys reported on different occasions over the period of 1983–91 that about three-quarters of white people have said that they think that other whites would mind if a close relative were to marry a black or Asian person (ibid:. 316).

Discrimination, disadvantage and diversity

This overview of the extent of the experiences of discrimination and disadvantage shows that there are some striking differences as well as similarities between groups. In particular, the African/Caribbean groups and Bangaldeshis, and to a lesser extent Pakistanis, have found that the particular nexus of disadvantages have afflicted them to a much greater extent than those facing groups of Indian and African Asian origin. These differences emerge from historically structured differences in their economic position immediately after migration, success in the education system and subsequent success or failure in the labour market.

Anti-discrimination law

The right to equality before the law and protection against discrimination are central to conceptions of human rights. Protection against discrimination is recognised in Article 1 of the 1945 United Nations Charter, Article 7 of the 1949 Universal Declaration of Human Rights and Article 14 of the European Convention on Human Rights. The European Convention on Human Rights, now incorporated into British domestic law in the 1998 Human Rights Act, calls for human rights to be secured 'without discrimination on any grounds such as sex, race, colour, language, religion, political or other opinion, national or social origin, association with a national minority, property, birth or other status'. The International Convention on the Elimination of All Forms of Racial Discrimination (1965) is more stringent. This requires governments to review national and local policies, and to 'amend, rescind or nullify' any laws or regulations which have the effect of creating or perpetuating discrimination (Banton 1996) and also makes it a duty to promote tolerance and equality of opportunity.

In Britain, Race Relations Acts of 1965 and 1968 prohibited direct discrimination on the grounds of 'race', established a network of race relations councils, co-ordinated by the Race Relations Commission, and funded welfare agencies. The race relations legislation of the 1960s was criticised for being limited in both intention and impact, partly because of its focus only on *individual* and *direct* acts of discrimination and partly because the resources allocated to enforce the law were inadequate to the task (Solomos 1993: 83–6). The 1976 Race Relations Act extended the law to prohibit indirect discrimination and created the Commission for Racial Equality. This allocated funding for local community relations councils who employed advisers to take up discrimination cases.

Indirect discrimination has most successfully been challenged in the US courts. The plaintiff establishes a *prima facie* case of discrimination by producing detailed statistics of a generic practice, usually in employment, which has had an adverse effect on a particular group. The burden of proof then shifts to the employer to show that the allegedly discriminatory condition or requirement which produces a disproportionate outcome is justified by 'business necessity' (Fitzpatrick, Hegarty and Maxwell 1995: 153). Moreover, plaintiffs can rebut the defence of business necessity by showing that other, non-discriminatory requirements would be equally effective. Applying anti-discrimination law to the criminal justice context would involve examining a range of criminal justice processes – such as employment, service delivery to the public (and perhaps arrrest and imprisonment) and assessing the extent to which the outcomes of these processes are disproportionate. Having established a *prima facie* case of discrimination, the burden of proof would then fall to the state to demonstrate that the practice in question was justified by reference to some other criterion, broadly compatible with 'business necessity'. Even if such a justification was demonstrated, it would still be necessary to show that no equally effective practice could be used which would not impact disproportionately on ethnic minority groups.

Section 95 of the 1991 Criminal Justice Act was introduced amid concerns about racial discrimination within the criminal justice system. The Act makes neither direct nor indirect discrimination unlawful, but requires the Home Secretary to publish information 'facilitating the performance by such persons of their duty to avoid discrimination against any persons on the ground of race or sex or any other improper ground'. The obvious limitation to Section 95 is that once information is collected which produces a *prima facie* case of discrimination, there is no specific *requirement* on the criminal justice agency or the Home Office to do anything about it and no enforcement mechanism. For example, if statistics collected under the Act show – in customer satisfaction surveys – that ethnic minorities who suffer victimisation receive a poorer service than their white counterparts, Section 95 imposes no legal requirement to ameliorate the effects of discriminatory practice once they have been discovered. It is also a weak provision in that it encourages officials to *avoid* discrimination but not actively to *eliminate* discrimination.

Race Relations (Amendment) Act 2000

The Race Relations (Amendment) Act 2000 applies anti-discrimination principles for the first time to public services, including the police. The Act is an amendment to the 1976 Race Relations Act, removing from the Act the exemption for the police and other public authorities and for 'acts done for the purpose of safeguarding national security'. In theory, this means that individuals can take racial discrimination cases against criminal justice agencies through the civil courts for redress. The Act extends the liability of chief officers of police and police authorities for acts of police officers by defining them as employees for the purposes of the Act. Thus the chief officer is liable for all police actions done in the performance of duty and all compensation costs or expenses are to be paid out of the police fund.

It is too early to tell what the effectiveness of the legislation will be. However, it was unfortunate that the government attracted controversy during the drafting of the bill by including a clause restricting the scope of the Act to direct discrimination. Since the Lawrence Inquiry (Macpherson 1999) had identified institutional racism, definable in legal terms as indirect discrimination, as a key factor in explaining the failure to respond appropriately to people from ethnic minority communities, many people were astounded that the bill had been circumscribed in this way. It was only after the threat of a Lords revolt reminding the Home Secretary that the Lawrence Inquiry had recommended that 'the full force of Race Relations legislation should apply to all police officers', that the bill was amended to include indirect discrimination.

Two broader changes may have an impact on the implementation of this Act. First, the 1998 Human Rights Act came into effect on 1 October 2000 with the effect that cases where people believe their human rights have been violated can pursue legal action through the UK courts rather than having to travel to Strasbourg. Cases brought under Article 14 prohibiting discrimination in securing convention rights – including the rights to life and security of the person, to family life and against detention – will provide test cases for the new Act. At the same time, there are significant international developments. At the European level, the Amsterdam meeting of Heads of State agreed to strengthen the European capacity to act against discrimination by introducing Article 13 of the treaty establishing the European Community (Bowling, Malik and Wintermute 2000). This Article goes beyond Article 14 of the ECHR because it creates a general principle of non-discrimination and lays down a legislative framework to be implemented by member states to provide for directly enforceable judicial remedies before national courts (Commission of the European Communities (1999), para. 2.3.2).

Conclusion

In this chapter we have attempted to clarify the terms used in contemporary debates about racism and ethnicity in Britain. As we have seen, the key terms in this discussion are *essentially contested*: they mean different things to different people. These variations in meaning depend on various factors, including whether the concepts have their origins in biological, psychological, sociological or political economic theories. As a result, there is frequently *conceptual conflation*, where researchers share a vocabulary for discussing phenomena, but the meanings ascribed to the terms vary from one researcher to the next. There is also *conceptual inflation*, where terms used have multiple meanings, even when used by the same author. The widely used, but essentially contested, vocabulary of 'ethnic' and 'racial' difference often leads to confusion and must be used with care. With these pitfalls in mind, we set out in chapter 3 to examine the ways in which criminology has incorporated these concepts into its theoretical and empirical endeavours. Understanding the origins of these terminologies also provides an important context for the subsequent chapters that examine the research and statistics employing 'race', ethnicity, racism and discrimination as central analytical categories.

Chapter 3

Criminological theory

The aim of this book is to develop a theoretically informed account of the way in which racism and ethnicity shape experiences of crime and criminal justice in England. However, there are a number of difficulties that present themselves in attempting this task. The first question is: *what needs to be explained?* The topics approached in this text include victimisation, involvement in criminal behaviour, arrest, criminal justice processing and imprisonment. Although these issues are clearly linked, they must not be conflated in the way of some authors who use 'arrest', 'criminal involvement' and 'criminality' as though they were interchangeable. In our view, it is important to explain the evidence that specific ethnic groups appear to be involved in (or *avoid* involvement in) specific forms of deviant behaviour, while at the same time examining ethnic differences in the way suspected individuals are drawn progressively further into the criminal justice process. However, these phenomena should not be treated as though they were one and the same thing.

Many criminological theories start, explicitly or implicitly, from the assumption – examined in detail in chapter 4 – that there are *real* ethnic differences in involvement in crime. Theories of behaviour based upon *a priori* assumptions about ethnic minority 'criminality' are bound to be questionable. Most theoretical approaches are highly speculative (which is, of course, in the nature of theory). Many have little or no supporting data and are refuted when tested empirically.

Criminological literature in this field is extraordinarily extensive and diverse. Theorists from almost every 'parent' discipline – from genetics and physiology to history and political economy – have commented on 'ethnic' and 'racial' differences in crime and differences in the treatment of different groups in the criminal justice process. Moreover, within each discipline the matter has been examined from every conceivable philosophical, ideological and political perspective. Many theories, in common with those of their parent disciplines, are based on experience in other countries, particularly in the rest of Europe and North America. While these theories have found adherents in the mainstream of British criminology, they tend often not to have been applied specifically to empirical problems in the British context. This should be borne in mind and is designed to provoke thought rather than to promulgate a particular version of the 'truth'.

The aim of this chapter is to introduce the reader to the theoretical literature on 'race' and crime. In organising this material we have drawn on and elaborated on Reiner's (1993) three contrasting frameworks of explanation; namely, 'individualist', 'cultural' and 'structural' accounts. Although an attempt has been made to provide an assessment of each line of enquiry in this chapter, a full assessment of each theoretical approach must be returned to in the conclusion once the empirical data have been explored in subsequent chapters.

Classical and control theories

One origin of the criminological enterprise is the classical theories of Jeremy Bentham and Cesar Beccaria. Emerging in the 'age of Enlightenment' and at the end of the 'barbaric' 'bloody codes' of the eighteenth century, classical thinking provided the framework that underpinned modern penology and the birth of the prison (Foucault 1977). The classical school developed theories based on the notion that crime was a voluntary action made by a free-willed individual. The motivation for crime could be understood as the calculation made by the 'reasoning criminal' weighing up the benefits of crime against the potential costs of detection and punishment. Punishment, from the classical perspective, should be swift, certain, proportionate to the crime and restricted to the individual offender. Classical theories formed the basis for a range of theories throughout the twentieth century and underpin contemporary thinking about crime. 'Neo-classical' theories include 'control theories' that emphasise the individual's bonds to society (Gottfredson and Hirschi 1990), 'rational choice theories' that emphasise offender decision making (Cornish and Clarke 1986), 'deterrence theory' that emphasises the impact of sanctions on offending rates at the population level (von Hirsch *et al.*, 1999) and 'incapacitation theory' that emphasises the effect of the prison in keeping offenders out of circulation.

Classical theories have not been greatly concerned with the questions of 'race' or ethnicity, except with the penological question of proportionality in sentencing (von Hirsch 1993, von Hirsch and Roberts 1997, Tonry 1994, 1995). This omission is perhaps because the 'reasoning criminal' as an individual human agent is not a focus for study from this perspective, and some classical theorists specifically reject the need to examine the social and economic 'causes' of crime. The focus is, instead, on thinking about the relationship between opportunities to commit crime, the risks of detection and the severity of punishment. A problem for classical theory is that where controls are targeted against particular ethnic groups – subjecting them to a disproportionate degree of police enforcement or punishment, for example – this does not appear to result in greater conformity or lower levels of crime. On the contrary, the opposite is more often claimed to be the case. Disproportionate involvement in crime is used to justify more extensive levels of enforcement and punishment. Classical theory has also been characterised as deterministic, metaphysical and paying too little attention to the cultural and structural contexts within which individual decisions are taken.

Tyler is critical of compliance-deterrence theories because, although social control is 'attractively simple', the legal system cannot function if it can only influence people by manipulating rewards and costs; such strategies consume huge amounts of public resources and are in constant peril of disequilibrium and instability (1990: 22). Moreover, all authorities rely, at least in part, on voluntary acceptance to ensure compliance. Even in rigid hierarchies (such as the army) or closed institutions (such as the prison) order depends not on coercion, but on voluntary compliance based on legitimate authority. Tyler argues that it is normative influences that lead to compliance through 'internalised obligations' (ibid.: 24). The normative perspective focuses on the values that lead people to comply voluntarily with legal rules and the decisions of legal authorities (ibid.: 161). Tyler's empirical work shows a direct link between experiencing fair procedures in dealings with police officers and judges, and subsequent behaviour in relation to the law. When people are unfairly treated, they then view the authorities as less legitimate and, as a consequence, are less likely to obey the law in their everyday lives (ibid.: 107–8).

Biological and psychological theories

A second major theoretical movement in modern criminology is *positivism*, an approach based on methods in the natural sciences. Cesare Lombroso's *Criminal Man* (1876) is usually cited as the most influential of the 'new' scientific criminologies and its focus on the idea of the 'natural born criminal' (see also Ferri 1895, reviews by Mannheim 1965, Taylor, Walton and Young 1973). Lombroso believed there was a direct link between criminality and 'race'. Based on post-mortem examinations of soldiers, convicts and 'lunatics', he concluded that 'many of the characteristics found in savages, and among the coloured races, are also to be found in habitual delinquents'. Among the things 'in common', he found, were 'thinning hair, lack of strength and weight, low cranial capacity, receding foreheads, highly developed frontal sinuses ... darker skin, thicker, curly hair, [and] large or handle-shaped ears' (Lombroso 1876). On the other hand, '[T]he white races ... represent the triumph of the human species, its hitherto most perfect advancement' (Lombroso, cited in Miller 1997: 185).

Similar ideas were developed in Britain by, among others, Galton (1869) and Goring (1913) who drew on Darwin's (1859) *The Origin of Species*, to develop the notion of the *heritability* of social characteristics, such as physical fitness, social undesirability, alcoholism, poverty and criminality. This line of reasoning led Galton to found the Eugenics movement (often referred to as a 'pseudo science') that linked the study of human heredity to the development of selective policies to improve the 'human stock'. The political goal of Eugenics – which was widespread in Europe, North America and elsewhere from the late nineteenth century – was to encourage the elite to have children while discouraging reproduction among 'mental defectives' and others 'intellectually least endowed'. In the US, for example, biologists and physicians assisted state legislators in Kansas, Indiana and elsewhere, with gathering up those people seen as 'socially undesirable' and embarking on an extensive programme of involuntary sterilisation. Those seen as undesirable by eugenicists included a wide range of individuals and classes – including criminals, 'negroes', idiots, tramps, poor farmers, slum dwellers, unskilled labourers and immigrants (Miller 1997: 188).

The 'Lombrosian project' to identify the biological causes of crime has continued sporadically throughout the twentieth century and is still in progress today. Herrenstein (1995: 56), for example, concludes that 'chunky' or mesomorphic people (that is muscular and large boned) are more likely to become criminals, as are those with neurological, biochemical and metabolic abnormalities (ibid.: 57). Mednick and others contend that 'criminogenic characteristics' are genetically transmitted, especially among 'recidivistic' criminals. They suggest that a range of biomedical factors are criminogenic, which are 'especially likely to predict criminal outcome when combined with adverse social environments' (Brennan *et al.* 1995: 88). Moreover, these authors conclude that '[a]ntisocial individuals have been found to be less responsive to punishments than are controls' with the consequence that '[r]ehabilitation through criminal justice system punishment may be an unrealistic goal for some criminals' cited by Vold, Bernard and Snipes 1998). This biomedical and genetic research has been controversial to such an extent that a conference to explore the relationship between crime and genetics was cancelled in 1992 after protesters charged the conference organisers with racism. Some scholars working in this area deny a direct link to 'race'. However, the research on the 'genetics of crime' is conducted by the same researchers using the same theoretical frameworks and methodological tools as those examining the genetics of race.

An offshoot of the Lombrosian project is psychological positivism. Among the underlying assumptions of this approach is that behaviour, including crime, has a biological basis and also that 'race' is a biologically meaningful concept. Probably the most commonly researched psychological 'determinant' of crime is intelligence and, specifically, IQ (see Wilson and Herrenstein 1985, Herrenstein 1995, Farrington 1997: 385–7). Citing Hirschi and Hindelang (1977), Herrenstein describes the conclusion that criminals have lower than average IQ as being 'among the prime discoveries in criminology' (1995: 51). The study of links between IQ, 'race' and crime has also been controversial. For example, Nobel Prize winner William Shockley speculated in a 1976 speech before the American National Academy of Science that differences in IQ between African/Americans and European/Americans might be solely due to genetic differences, and that these might also explain differences in poverty and crime rates (cited in Vold, Bernard and Snipes 1998: 59). This line of enquiry was subsequently pursued by such authors as Arthur Jensen (1969), and, most recently, by Richard Herrenstein and Charles Murray (1994) in their best-selling book, *The Bell Curve*. A review of *The Bell Curve* conducted by the American Psychological Association concluded that its major conclusions were wrong (cited by Vold *et al.*, 1998: 66). The problem, explained in detail in chapter 2, is that the biological notion of 'race' used by this research is conceptually and empirically unsustainable. A study published by population geneticists at the same time as *The Bell Curve* (Cavalli-Sforza, Menozzi and Piazza 1994) found that once the genes for coloration and stature are dealt with, differences between and among individuals are so great as make the concept of 'race' virtually meaningless. Cavalli-Sforza, Menozzi and Piazza conclude that 'there is no documented biological superiority of any race however defined. There are some superficial traits like skin color and body build. They are striking and we notice them. That is what misleads us. It makes us think races are very different. They are not, when we look under the skin' (cited in Miller 1996: 179).

The political and policy implications of these lines of research must also be borne in mind. The basic thrust of this research is that the 'causes of crime' lie fixed in the mind or body of the criminal and, consequently, are not amenable to change through social intervention. This has led some researchers to argue for the abandonment of attempts to rehabilitate offenders (Vold, Bernard and Snipes 1998) and others to recommend the incarceration of people with an 'anti-social personality disorder' until they are middle-aged (ibid.). Others have gone further to argue that people with this 'disorder' should be executed (Guze 1976, Ewing 1991 cited in Vold, Bernard and Snipes 1998: 100). Although 'race' is not always mentioned by positivists the issue is rarely far from the surface. Either 'race' appears implicitly linked with crime through its associations with other factors such as IQ scores or 'impulsivity', or the fact that black people are over-represented in prison is taken as a self-evident indication of the relationship between crime and psychobiological dysfunction among people of 'non-European' origin. Most troubling are the continuities between the theories of the nineteenth-century eugenicists, the 1930s criminal-biologists and contemporary researchers studying biology and crime.

The more general problem with individualistic accounts is that they become detached from the social contexts within which human action occurs. Criminological research and popular debate is suffused with individualistic explanations for poverty, deviance, drug abuse and disorderly behaviour. To paraphrase Laurie Taylor (2000), a considerable imaginative effort is required to abandon these individual accounts for the less immediate and more abstract stories that sociologists have to tell about the influence of culture and social structure on everyday lives[1]. It is to these theories that we now turn.

Cultural theories

Cultural theories focus attention on the norms, values and patterns of daily life to be found in a society as a whole or within specific 'subcultural' groups. While cultural theorists may share a common concern with describing the 'way of life' among particular groups in a society, different frameworks are used to explain the development of particular cultural forms and how these shed light on patterns of crime and deviance. There are major differences, for example, between conservative, liberal and radical analyses of culture.

Conservative cultural theory: the underclass and 'undeserving poor'

Conservative conceptions of culture draw on a tradition that is linked to social Darwinism discussed above. From this perspective, the 'dishonest' or 'undeserving' poor are thought to be afflicted by a 'culture of poverty' characterised by 'illegitimacy', 'fecklessness', drop-out from the labour force, drug abuse, alcoholism and violent crime. The resulting 'underclass' is explained largely to be the result of cultural weakness resulting from 'welfare-dependency', an absence of working parent role models and an absence of male responsibility for partner and children. Charles Murray (1990), one of the most prominent of these theorists, argues that without the 'civilising forces' of adult authority and the routines of work, 'young men remain barbarians'. Although the 'underclass' theorists in Britain have not focused on 'race' and ethnicity to the same extent as in the US (where the underclass is seen largely as black and Hispanic), commentators have noted that some ethnic minority communities – especially poor black communities – can be characterised as part of the 'underclass' in Britain.

---

[1] Laurie Taylor, *Guardian*, 21 June 2000

This perspective has been criticised because it tends, implicitly or explicitly, to generate false 'pathologies' of the lives of poor people who are seen as the cause of their own problems through feckless or irresponsible behaviour. More careful examination of daily life for unemployed or casually employed people reveals that supposedly 'pathological' forms of behaviour are functional adaptations to the reality of joblessness. For underclass theorists, deviance is seen either entirely as a matter of choice (invoking classical theory) or unalterable because of biological destiny (invoking positivism). Consequently, no account is taken of the way in which life chances are structured by political economic forces (such as employment and housing markets) that are largely beyond the control of individuals.

Liberal cultural theory: social disorganisation and criminal areas

The researchers at the University of Chicago such as Clifford Shaw and Henry McKay had an enormous influence of Anglo-American criminology. The 'social' or 'human ecology' conducted between the 1920s and 1940s examined different communities, neighbourhoods or areas of cities to identify and explain patterns of employment, health and delinquency. Shaw and McKay (1942) observed that patterns of immigration into Chicago were part of related processes of economic and occupational segregation. Newly arrived immigrant groups tended to become concentrated into particular sections of the city, though African/Americans were dispersed throughout deteriorated neighbourhoods. Upon arrival each group tended to be pushed into the areas of lowest economic status. All ethnic groups except for African/Americans, Latinos and native Americans worked their way out of these 'zones of transition' towards more affluent suburbs, their places being filled by the next migrant group. These ideas were applied to the UK by, among others, Rex and Moore 1967.

Although social disorganisation theory is based on neighbourhood contexts, it also provides a basis for liberal theories of deviant subcultures (Cohen 1955). This perspective sees some neighbourhoods as 'socially disorganised', meaning that conventional traditions have disintegrated along with neighbourhood institutions that effect control over the behaviour of children. In these 'criminal areas' – often found in the 'zone of transition' or 'inner cities' located between the commercial centre of cities and the suburbs – there are not only insufficient means to educate conventional norms, but there are also 'criminal networks' that provide an alternative (Morris 1958). In such a context, criminal behaviour may sometimes be accepted, even approved of by communities.

Growing out of the Chicago School (Vold *et al.* 1998: 91) were studies of specific 'criminal subcultures' that described the unique knowledge, beliefs, values, codes and tastes that differ in some way from the main or dominant culture (Cohen 1955). Such theories also tend to draw on more structural analysis by introducing the Mertonian notion of 'strain' caused by the inability to achieve middle-class goals through conventional means and the 'delinquent solutions' that result (Downes 1966).

Liberal theories II: the subculture of violence

Wolfgang and Ferracuti (1981) drew on the theories of Cloward and Ohlin (1961) to propose a theory of the 'subculture of violence'. They argue that the significance of a jostle, a slightly derogatory remark, or the appearance of a weapon in the hands of an adversary are stimuli 'differentially perceived' and interpreted by blacks and whites, males and females. They suggest that a quick resort to violence 'as a measure of daring, courage or defense of status' is a 'cultural expression', especially for lower socio-economic class males of both 'races'. With peer groups comprised of people sharing these cultural traits, 'physical assaults, altercations, and violent domestic quarrels that result in homicide are likely to be common' (Wolfgang and Ferracuti 1981: 141).

Wolfgang and Ferracuti (1981) refused to speculate about the origins of these cultures, though they suggested that they might lie in social conditions suggested by Cohen (1995) and others from the Chicago School. The underlying conditions were not of interest because the subculture itself explained the violence, and this subculture had arisen for historical reasons and was transmitted from generation to generation. However, as one review put it, 'the subculture of violence thesis is perhaps one of the most cited, but one of the least tested propositions in the sociological and criminological literature', the original thesis being based on speculation rather than evidence (Cao, Adams and Jensin 1997: 367). These authors tested the Wolfgang and Ferracuti thesis using the US General Social Survey (which measures attitudes to a wide variety of issues). Cao, Adams and Jensin found, contrary to what would have been expected from the subculture of violence thesis, that 'white males express significantly more violent beliefs in defensive or retaliatory situations than blacks and that there is no significant difference between white and black males in beliefs in violence in offensive situations' (ibid.: 374), a finding confirmed by many earlier studies. The authors conclude that this evidence contradicts Wolfgang and Ferracuti's implication that African/American culture has a value system which embraces violence (ibid.: 376).

This theorising has been influential in shaping thinking about crime among ethnic minority communities in Britain. The idea that black and Asian people, especially young men, would form criminal subcultures has been central to various interpretations of 'disproportionate black crime', based largely on analyses of official statistics, such as arrest rates. Lea and Young (1984), for example, argue that 'the economic alienation of young black people gives rise to a culture with a propensity for crime'. This culture is seen as 'improvised' from aspects of 'imported' elements of

Caribbean cultures forged in the context of the UK. Deviance within black British culture, Lea and Young speculate:

> [i]s not a hand-down from the previous generation of immigrant parents as the conservative thesis of 'alien cultures' would suggest. Rather, it is an improvised culture based on the import of elements from the West Indies by kids most of whom either have never been there or left when they were very young ... [s]uch culture is widely disapproved of by the older generation of West Indian immigrants and is, furthermore, a minority and deviant subculture within the West Indies itself.
>
> (1984: 127)

Liberal cultural theories have been criticised for developing a reified notion of culture that becomes simply another form of 'cultural pathology', similar to the conservative 'underclass' theories and individual positivism. As Gilroy argues, 'the emphasis on black culture legitimates the idea that any black, all blacks, are somehow contaminated by the alien predisposition to crime which is reproduced in their distinctive cultures, specifically their family relations' (1987b: 112). This, for Gilroy, represents a 'capitulation to racist logic'.

Radical theories of culture: the Birmingham School and beyond

Radical theories of culture aiming to offer a corrective to the ethnocentricity of the field grew out of the work of the Centre for Contemporary Cultural Studies at the University of Birmingham in the 1970s (for example, CCCS (1982)). From this perspective, culture is a field articulating the 'life-world of subjects' and the 'structures created by human activity' (Gilroy 1987a). Thus, the active, dynamic aspects of cultural life are emphasised as a means of challenging both absolutist notions of 'race' and ethnicity, and static, reified notions of culture. For Gilroy, crime within black communities cannot be explained through liberal versions of 'criminal subculture' theory that sees black law-breaking as an integral element in black culture (ibid.: 72–9). Rather, offending itself is explicable primarily through a broader analysis of political and economic forces: '[i]t is no betrayal of black interests to say that blacks commit crime, or that black law-breaking may be related to black poverty as law-breaking is always related to poverty' (ibid.: 75).

It is not that culture is unimportant for Gilroy; on the contrary, he argues that black cultures are central to understanding the black experience in Britain. Unique cultural forms including, but not restricted to, literature, scholarship, the visual arts, music, poetry, dance, fashion and politics are not only the media through which black life in Britain is experienced, but have also become a determining force of urban Britain as a whole (Gilroy 1987a). Among the elements examined by Gilroy are the 'diaspora' relationship between British black cultures and those in other places (especially the USA and the Caribbean), the dynamic relationships between black and white youth in Britain, and the articulation of discourses of black liberation and a critique of capitalism in music and political action (ibid.).

Critical cultural studies of 'race and crime' have been criticised as being 'idealist' or 'romantic' by 'left realists', such as Lea and Young (1984), who emphasise the 'reality' of crime victimisation and its damaging effects on individual victims and working-class people more generally. They point out that most crime is both intra-class and intra-ethnic, so to see offences committed by black people as 'revolutionary' is to idealise damaging forms of behaviour. Such romanticism is rejected by Hall *et al.* (1978) and by Gilroy (1987a) who maintain simply that under-theorised notions of black culture are unhelpful. As Gilroy suggests, 'the possibility of a direct relationship between ethnicity, black culture and crime is an altogether different and more complex issue which requires detailed historical investigation and which is likely to end, as previous attempts to quantify crime itself, only in raising further yet more speculative questions' (Gilroy 1987a: 118).

Structural theories

Structural theories depart radically from individual and cultural theories in that they see political, economic and social forces as the dominant, if not determinant, means of explaining the functioning of society. The Marxist approach, rooted in an historical analysis of political economy, sees the processes of criminalisation as one means that the state has of managing the central contradictions of capitalism, such as periods of 'surplus labour', and the problems, such as poverty and frustration, that arise from joblessness (Bierne and Messerschmidt 1995). State power, exercised through the medium of law, sustains dominant economic class interests and seeks fundamentally to protect private property. In a society divided by class, gender and ethnicity, law perpetuates inequalities. When the struggle between economic classes becomes acute, the law acts as a repressive force.

Marx and Engels considered crime to be functional in capitalist societies. It 'render[s] a service by arousing the moral aesthetic sentiments of the public, interrupting the monotony of bourgeois life, diminishing competition among workers, removing excess labour from the market place and contributing to the development of productive forces' (Marx 1961: 385–7). However, Marx and Engels also referred to the impact of the *demoralisation* that resulted from the terrible living and working conditions among the mass of the population during the industrial revolution. This psychological condition led either to rebellion or to crime. Engels's comment that theft is 'the most primitive form of protest' (1845: 502–3) has led to the caricature of Marxism defining crime as a political act. The point, however, is that the inequalities of class exploitation led to working-class crime as 'the earliest, crudest, least fruitful form' of rebellion.

A critical theory of ethnicity, social structure and criminal justice in Britain

The starting point for a critical theory of racism and crime is immigration law which 'defines the presence of black people – not white racism – as the problem' (Gordon 1984). From this perspective, external immigration controls and internal controls of both 'illegal immigration' and 'ethnic crime' were a direct response to the appeals of an explicitly racist constituency which felt that there were 'too many blacks' and that those who were here required extra measures of control (Sivanandan 1982, Gordon 1984, Miles and Phizacklea 1984, Miles 1989, Solomos 1988, 1993, Smith 1989). For the police, courts and prisons, black people were defined as a 'law and order' problem – 'disorderly', 'unruly', inherently 'criminal', even part of the 'enemy within' (Scraton 1987). Consequently, black and Asian people were targeted by the police for 'exceptional' responses because they were dealing with an 'exceptional problem' (see also Keith 1993, Solomos 1988, Gilroy 1987a and b). At the same time that the practices of the criminal justice system criminalised – literally 'turned into criminals' – part of the black community, the 'white public was shown a black population extensively involved in criminal activity of one kind or another, facing serious charges and special procedures in the courts, represented disproportionately in the prison population, creating a serious problem for prison management' (Gordon 1984: 137–8).

For critical theorists, racism and criminalisation are not ends in themselves, but the result of a specific crisis of the capitalist economy in Britain (see Gordon 1984, Hall *et al.* 1978, CCCS 1982, Sivanandan 1982, Scraton 1987). Economic restructuring creates structural crises – including unemployment alongside skill shortages; the collapse of infrastructure and resources in education, health and housing; and crises of authority and legitimacy for the state. In this context, the most economically marginalised – among whom are working-class black and Asian people – are forced to accept the worst housing in the worst areas, in which schools are under-resourced and cannot attract good teachers, where public housing is in shortest supply and greatest demand and where employment prospects are bleak. From this perspective, confrontation between police and ethnic minorities was higher in the black community for three reasons. First, immigration controls defining black people as a 'problem' led to antagonistic contacts. Second, cultures of resistance against state and racist repression were 'forged in the context of direct imperialist repression'. Third, the second generation increasingly refused to accept the discrimination and abuse that their parents had been forced to put up with.

Connecting the discourses of racism and racial discrimination with the history of the British economy, Gordon (1984) notes that black people came to Britain to meet a labour shortage and inevitably ended up doing the jobs that white people did not want. They were paid less, enjoyed fewer benefits and the British state did not have to bear the costs of their upbringing. Once the *labour shortage* in the post-war boom years became an *employment shortage* in the 1970s and beyond, black people were no longer required by the state and increasingly became seen as a problem that should be responded to first by 'stemming the tide' and second by 'repatriating' those who had already settled. The problem for the state was that ethnic minorities were neither prepared to 'go back to your own country' as both policy, political rhetoric and the slogans of racist thugs urged them to do. Nor were they prepared to accept acquiescently their status as second-class citizens. The inevitable result of a contradiction between the requirements of a racist state and the rights of minority communities is struggle by the black community against racist immigration policies and deportation, against racist conduct by the police and defence campaigns for those wrongly convicted or abused by the police (Gordon 1984, 1987)

Contributions to the 'race and crime' debate from a radical structural perspective situate deviant behaviour in its social, political and economic context. Such accounts also focus attention on both the context for and mechanisms of law enforcement and criminalisation. However, the reluctance to engage with the question of the actual forms of offending, or to uncover the experience of involvement in crime within different ethnic groups (focusing instead on documenting struggles with the system), has left a theoretical void in critical analysis in Britain.

Strain theories

Robert Merton's (1938 [1963]) writings on deviance drew on Durkheim's notion of anomie, arguing that social structures exert a pressure on people in society to engage in 'non-conformist' rather than 'conformist' conduct. Merton's central thesis was that crime is a result of a lack of fit or 'strain' between culturally prescribed goals and the socially structured means of obtaining them. The reaction to this 'lack of fit' includes conformity, innovation, ritualism, retreatism or rebellion. The evidence set out in chapter 2 showed that some, but not all, ethnic minority populations are systemically discriminated against in a range of social and economic contexts which, taken together, can be defined as social exclusion that might have the effects predicted by Merton.

Much criminological theory has been concerned with the relationship between economic patterns and crime in general, and the links between unemployment, poverty and crime in particular. Stephen Box reviewed all the available evidence from time-series studies of unemployment and crime concluding that the two are causally linked, particularly for young males (1987:78). Cross-sectional studies allow an investigation of the relationship between unemployment and crime at both the population and the individual levels. Again, Box found that the weight of research evidence supports the contention that there is a weak but significant causal relationship between overall unemployment and crime, though accounts had to be taken of the *meaning* and *duration* of unemployment (Box 1987: 97).

The *Gini coefficient* has been identified as one of the key standard measures of 'income inequality'. This statistic is derived by calculating the relationship of the income of the top earners in society (the wealthiest 5 per cent, for example) as a proportion of society's total income (ibid.: 86–7). In Britain (as in many societies) high incomes are concentrated in small groups of the population, with the wealthiest in society earning a significant proportion of the total resources. This gap between rich and poor is expressed in the Gini coefficient. As Box suggests, this 'objective' measure of income inequality has a 'subjective' counterpart, commonly referred to as 'relative deprivation', that is the experience of poverty in a society which emphasises equality and where individuals are socialised to aspire to material success. Box's review of the evidence up to the mid 1980s found that every study found a statistical and 'maybe even a causal relationship' between income inequality and property offences and violence except for homicide. In a similar vein, Lea and Young place a strong emphasis on discontent as a product of *relative* rather than *absolute* deprivation (1984: 81).

Applying structural theories to the contemporary experiences of ethnic minorities in Britain, one would predict that all groups – and in particular those of African, Caribbean, Pakistani and Bangladeshi origin – would be at greater risk of being involved in crime because the evidence has consistently shown higher rates of unemployment, relative and absolute poverty, exclusion from labour and housing markets among the same communities. The implications of this are, as Jefferson puts it:

> If black over-offending constitutes at last part of the explanation for their high arrest rates, then it puts back squarely on the agenda the question of disadvantage and crime. For if blacks are disproportionately involved in known offending behaviour, they also have much higher rates of social disadvantage ... Since known offenders are disproportionately drawn from the ranks of manual workers, the unemployed and the socially deprived, the higher black arrest and offender rates should not particularly surprise.
> (Jefferson 1991: 181)

There are a number of limitations of the structural accounts, however. First, they all risk the accusation of economic determinism, seeing unemployed, poor or otherwise marginalised people as being propelled into offending, like automatons, lacking human agency, the capacity to think for themselves and act on the social world. Where structural accounts have failed to take account of human agency, they also fail to explain differences *within* similarly marginalised groups. For example, purely structural accounts cannot explain why one unemployed young person, truanting from school, will take a chance and attempt to snatch a purse while his neighbour, from the same ethnic group, spends his afternoon at home watching the TV. A specific problem for structural theories is the relative *under-representation* of Asians in prison in stark contrast to the striking over-representation of black people, even though some Asian groups – most notably Bangladeshis – have similar rates of unemployment, poor housing and concentration into the 'inner cities'. This certainly contradicts the view that crime rates can be predicted through multi-variate analysis of economic variables and leaves structural theorists to undertake a more controversial analysis of cultural difference.

Labelling theory

A major departure from orthodox criminology can be found in the work of Howard Becker for whom deviance does not exist in an 'abstract or absolute sense', but is an act in which *a rule is enforced* against a form of behaviour. Not all people who are labelled deviant have actually broken a rule (because the process of labelling is not infallible) while not all those who break rules are labelled deviant. The process of labelling depends on who commits the act and who feels harmed by it; as a consequence, rules are applied more frequently on some people than others. Sometimes, people feel as though they are being judged according to rules they had no hand in making and do not accept the rules forced upon them by outsiders (Becker 1963: 221). By and large, conflicts over what is and is not appropriate behaviour in any given situation – and the extent to which it becomes defined as 'crime' – are resolved by economic power which enables the dominant group to force their will on others without their consent.

Lemert (1951) proposed the distinction between 'primary' and 'secondary' deviance. For Lemert, primary deviance does not result in any changes in the deviant's reputation and future conduct that are the consequences of social reaction to censure. Secondary deviance is then 'caused' by the social reaction to initial deviance. Labels have important consequences for self-image as well as relationships with family and friends. Sometimes such labelling can have a powerful 'self-fulfilling prophesy', where a series of negative effects – such as loss of earnings, employment or housing – result directly from the acquisition of the label. An extension of Lemert's thesis is the notion of 'deviancy amplification' (Wilkins 1964, Young 1971, Lea and Young 1984). In this account, 'real deviancy' – itself the result of relative deprivation, youth unemployment, racial discrimination and the denial of legitimate opportunities – is *amplified* as a result of police action targeted against ethnic minority youths.

Feminist perspectives in criminology

The starting point for feminism is the observation that society treats women unequally and unfavourably. It sets out to explain the mechanisms of women's oppression and to achieve women's liberation (Tuttle 1997: 107). Feminism takes many forms, but there are core elements distinguishing it from other forms of social theory. Most feminists would agree that gender is a complex social and cultural product related to, but not simply derived from, biological sex differences and that *gender relations* order social life and institutions. The often taken for granted constructs of 'masculinity' and 'femininity' are asymmetric and contribute to ideologies and practices of male superiority in the social, economic, political and domestic spheres. Corresponding systems of knowledge are *gendered* so as to reflect a male view of the social world. In order to develop a more complete understanding of society, feminist thinkers argue that women should be at the centre of intellectual enquiry rather than being peripheral or invisible which is often the case (Daley and Chesney-Lind, 1988 cited by Bierne and Messerschmidt 1995).

Feminist scholarship has had a profound impact on English criminology, identifying new subjects of study and developing radically new theoretical perspectives and insights into effective ways of practical engagement. Feminist scholars exposed the now obvious but hitherto unacknowledged fact that Anglo-American criminology had been 'the criminology of men' (Gelsthorpe and Morris 1990: 3). Most of the theories of criminality described above were developed from, and validated on, male subjects and it is striking that the vast majority of empirical and theoretical literature in criminology completely ignores the role of women and gender relations. The problem with 'man made' theories is not inherent in the focus on men to explain crime and conformity, but in over-generalising these theories to include *all* criminals, defendants and prisoners. Conventional criminological theories based on study of only half the population were thought to have a 'general' application. While it was assumed that the theories would apply to women, 'most do not' (ibid.: 3).

Early theories of 'female criminality' have been criticised as based on stereotypical views about women, sexuality, conformity and social weaknesses. They are more likely to feature biological or psychological pathologies than theories of crime among men (see Brown 1990). Critiques of conventional approaches were followed by the work of Freda Adler who argued that women took on what have been seen as masculine qualities as they moved into the previously male world of the competitive marketplace. Such characteristics as competitiveness and aggression in the marketplace are echoed in a change in patterns of crime. Thus, there are 'increasing numbers of women who are using guns, knives and wits to establish themselves as full human beings, as capable of violence and aggression as any man' (Adler 1975, cited by Vold *et al.* 1998: 276). Rita

James Simon (1978) supported Adler's view of a gradual increase in the types and volume of crime committed by women but argued that as they moved out of traditional gender roles women encountered many more *opportunities* to commit crime. Both Adler and Simon's theories 'argued that liberation from traditional women's roles would result in increasing crime committed by women', a contention that has been debated ever since (Vold *et al.* 1998). This 'liberation thesis' has implications for thinking about the rising prison population in the 1990s and also for exploring differences in rates and patterns of offending among women of different ethnic groups who differ in the extent to which they are free from male control.

Feminist research uncovered aspects of victimisation that had hitherto gone unexplored and ensured that violence against women – such as rape, sexual assault and domestic violence – was placed firmly on the research and policy agendas. Ethnic minority women's experiences of poverty, social exclusion and gender inequality have consequences for the general quality of their lives. They face a greater risk of assault and an economic situation that exacerbates their vulnerability, such as unsocial hours and reliance on public transport (Rice 1990: 61). Racism also has implications for sexual violence. Beliefs about black female sexuality create greater risks of sexual violence which in turn leads to a 'particular fear' of white men among black women (ibid.). Economic, social and political marginalisation impact on the quality of liberty and justice. Poor people have fewer freedoms than the rich, and can ill afford to pay the high financial price of achieving justice.

Feminist research has also been concerned with women's experiences in the criminal justice process. Chigwada-Bailey (1997: 11) argues that 'race', gender and class are three compounding forces that create a greater potential for unequal treatment in the criminal justice process. Rice refers to this as the 'triple oppression of race, class and gender' and argues for a black feminist perspective which underlines the theoretical consideration of the experiences of black women (Rice 1990: 57). She comments that because 'black criminology' focused on men while 'feminist criminology' focused on white women, the unique social, cultural and economic experiences of black women were overlooked. For example, the extent of low-wage work and return to work soon after childbirth provide a very different context for social life. Rice also argues that black girls develop early on a particular set of subcultural values which stress strength, independence, resilience and perseverance and which are necessary in the face of a racist and sex-segregated labour market. However, these qualities, when judged by ethnocentric standards, are viewed as 'unfeminine' (ibid., Chigwada-Bailey 1997). Existing criminological theories simply sustained stereotypical thinking (Rice 1990).

Masculinity theories

Problematising gender turns attention to the social construction of femininity and masculinity, raising new questions about one of the most consistent findings in criminology – that men have higher rates of offending than women. There are a number of strands of criminological theory that draw upon some notion of masculinity as a central explanatory theme. These originate from observation by feminist researchers that, while the vast majority of criminal offences are committed by males, the reasons for this are rarely explained, or even commented upon. Recent research on masculinity and crime has sought to go beyond a simple association of masculinity with 'machismo' so as to examine diverse *masculinities*, mediated by class, ethnicity, geography and other aspects of social context (Newburn and Stanko 1994: 1). Rather than masculinity being an ideal that all men aspire to and simply internalised by successive generations of male children through institutional socialisation, what is required is an analysis of 'masculine subjectivity' (Jefferson 1997).

Jefferson's analysis of 'youth crime, underclass males and black masculinity' is an attempt to theorise the impact of global transformations on' subordinate and marginal masculinities across the developed world' (Jefferson 1997: 549). Jefferson notes some of the early research on growing up male, including Cohen's (1955) subcultural analysis, covering the experience of 'status frustration', of growing up working class in a world dominated by middle-class values, and the reworking of those themes by Willis (1977), among others. More recently, Collinson (1996) analysed the ways in which 'structurally excluded males accomplish masculinity in creating a street style of spectacular consumption, excessive drug use, and living life on the "edge" in pursuit of a reputation for being "mad" (see also Bourgois 1995). All of these accounts, according to Jefferson, are about the effects of the restructuring of the global economy on 'subordinated' or 'marginalised' masculinities. For Jefferson, there is a requirement to look more closely at the 'psychic' as well as the social dimensions of exclusion.

Colonialism, ethnicity and crime

The work of Franz Fanon, an influential psychiatrist from Martinique, is a starting point for 'colonial theory', developed from elements of Marxism and psychoanalysis. Fanon observes that the 'black' is demonised, subjected, denoted as inferior and juxtaposed against the idealised 'white' portrayed as superior and placed in a position of power over the other. This, according to Fanon, has created a massive psycho-existential complex located squarely in the history of slavery and western colonialism (Fanon 1967: 14). This political economic experience has impacted not only on the material social and economic lives of the colonised people, but also on the language, culture and ultimately the psyche. The historical experience of colonisation and subjugation and the contemporary experience of social, economic and political marginalisation led to a 'feeling of insignificance' and to an insularity that becomes 'unbearable' because the goals and standards of success in the white world are defined in ways which make this impossible to achieve (ibid. 51).

Drawing on Fanon (1967) and Staples (1975) 'colonial' thesis, Mama confronts the controversial question of whether 'socially oppressive circumstances produce more intra-communal violence, including wife beating and other abusive behaviour' (1996: 20). She argues that poverty, overcrowding and fear of police harassment, that characterise many black communities, are all likely to exacerbate problems within relationships, increasing the likelihood of physical violence. Mama notes the 'devaluation of black womanhood' that occurred under imperialism and colonialism in Africa, Asia and the Caribbean may also contribute to the historically based demonstration of contempt. Mama concludes that although the physical abuse of women occurs across all cultural groups and socio-economic classes and in a range of social and political conditions, the forms and dynamics of this abuse have culturally specific content.

Mama describes the experiences of women of African, Asian and Caribbean origin who survived violence both at the hands of the state and at the hands of their menfolk. As Mama puts it 'black women, like black men, have their lives circumscribed and limited by widespread racism in British society, but inestimable numbers are also subjected to extremely oppressive and often violent behaviour from the men they live with'. While both men and women share experiences of immigration control, racist attacks and coercive policing, 'black women are also expected to continue to show sympathy and understanding when the men that live with them also turn violent' (1996: xiii). Many women have to abandon their home to escape violent men; many women and children are seriously injured physically by the violence and emotionally by the breakdown of relationships. As a consequence many women experience homelessness in a context where limited resources, racism and sexism within the statutory agencies affect their struggle to find temporary accommodation, rehousing, financial support and legal assistance.

Colonial theory shifts the focus of the study of crime from the victims of oppression to exploitative social systems and facilitates an examination of the historical process of structural oppression (Tatum 1996). In short, it 'illuminates the relationship between structural oppression, alienation, crime and delinquency'. The application to criminology of post-colonial theory needs development to explore the effects of oppression and alienation on real lives. A theoretical tension between race and class remains, consequently the theory says little about the structural oppression experienced by working-class and economically residualised whites.

The criticisms are answered to some extent by Cornel West (1991) who argues that 'liberal structuralists' (who highlight the structural constraints on the life chances of black people) and 'conservative behaviourists' (who stress the 'behavioural impediments' to black upward mobility) have stifled productive debate. Neither fully acknowledges that the 'structures and behaviour are inseparable, that institutions and values go hand in hand' and that 'how people act and live is shaped – though in no way dictated or determined – by the larger circumstances in which they find themselves' (ibid.: 37). West argues that the notion of structure cannot be seen simply in terms of economics and politics, but that 'culture is quite as structural as the economy or politics; it is rooted in institutions like families, schools, churches, synagogues, mosques, and communication industries (television, radio, video, music)'.

For West, black America faces 'a nihilistic threat to its very existence'. This is not only a matter of 'relative deprivation and political powerlessness', but a sort of 'collective depression', 'sense of personal worthlessness', social despair and self-destructiveness which is widespread in African/American communities. This nihilism, is to be understood not in the sense of an articulated philosophical doctrine, but as the 'lived experience of coping with a life of horrifying meaninglessness, hopelessness and (most important) lovelessness' (ibid.: 42). This, according to West, results in a numbing detachment from others and a self-destructive disposition towards the world. Life without meaning, hope, or love 'breeds a cold-hearted, mean-spirited outlook that destroys both the individual and others' (ibid.: 40).

This crisis in West's view has not been acknowledged by liberals because they focus exclusively on economic and political structures and fail to understand the *structural character of culture.* There has also been a 'sheer failure of nerve' stemming from a fear that if values are discussed this will take the focus away from structures. This, warns West, 'leaves the existential and psychological realities of black people in the lurch' (ibid.: 39). The failure of the conservative behaviourists is even more profound, and has contributed to nihilism. Conservatives talk about values and attitudes as though political and economic structures do not exist. Although they tell black people to be agents not victims, they fail to take account of the 'lingering effect of black history' and, this ahistorical perspective contributes to nihilism within black America by justifying cutbacks for poor people who are 'struggling for decent housing, child care, health care and education' (ibid.: 39).

West argues that corporate market institutions have contributed to the 'commodification of pleasure', creating seductive ways of life, a culture of consumption that 'capitalises on every opportunity to make money' (ibid.: 41). This, in turn, contributes to 'undermining traditional morality in order to stay in business', in the culture industries in particular. In common with their white neighbours, black Americans are influenced by 'images of comfort, convenience, machismo, femininity, violence and sexual stimulation that bombard consumers' (ibid.: 42). These 'seductive images' contribute to a market-inspired way of life which edges out the non-market values, such as 'love, care, service to others', characteristic of earlier generations (ibid.: 43). The predominance of this way of life among those living in poverty-ridden conditions, with a limited capacity to ward off self-contempt and hatred, results in the nihilistic threat in black America. A combination of the market way of life and poverty-ridden conditions, black existential angst has directed most of the anger, rage and despair towards fellow black citizens, especially black women. Nihilism, argues West, is not overcome by arguments or analyses; it is tamed by the ethics of care and love (ibid.: 43).

Conclusion

The notions of 'race' and ethnicity have been infused into criminological thought throughout its history. The search for the biological causes of crime has been a criminological obsession since Cesare Lombroso 'discovered' the atavistic man: a dark-skinned, curly haired criminal type. The history of biological determinism and the search for 'pure' race differences in crime is a disturbing one. The endeavour is based on the idea that there is an essence of both 'race' and 'crime', and that the two are 'linked'. The twentieth-century 'criminal biologists', 'racial hygienists' and eugenicists contributed to state practices, such as sterilisation, segregation, mass incapacitation and even extermination (Burleigh and Wipperman 1991: 167, Miller 1997). Cultural and structural theorists have also applied their thinking to the 'race' and crime debate. Even those theories that eschew the categories of 'race' tend to fall back on notions of ethnicity that remain suffused with racial meanings. Understandably, many criminologists avoid this controversial field altogether and reject the study of ethnicity and crime as 'dangerous'.

We lack any convincing theoretical account of offending within ethnic minority communities in Britain. Crime must be placed in its historical, political, social and economic context. It is also important to examine the social construction of crime and the way in which 'race' and ethnic categorisation contribute to the process of criminalisation. No theory of crime is complete without an account of the relationship between deviance and censure. For this reason, we will not be in a position to develop an empirically grounded theory of crime within ethnic minority communities until we have had an opportunity to examine their experience in the criminal justice process in the later chapters of this book.

Many theories start from an implicit or explicit assumption that ethnic minority groups will be 'predisposed' or in some other way 'at risk' of becoming involved in crime. However, in the English context, there have been few attempts to explore the contexts in which offending occurs and fewer still attempts to explain involvement in crime from the offender's perspective. The evidence about ethnicity and involvement in crime is largely restricted to statistics based on arrest and imprisonment and, more recently, surveys of victimisation and self-reported offending. It is to these studies that we now turn.

Chapter 4

Offending and victimisation

Until recently, the 'race and crime' debate has been preoccupied, to the exclusion of many other issues, by the question of whether people from ethnic minorities are more (or less) likely to commit criminal offences than those from the white majority population. The debate has turned largely on an analysis of 'official' crime statistics – especially arrest and prison data – that show marked variation for different ethnic groups. Where elevated rates of official offending are identified, the debate is often polarised into the formulation: 'is this because the criminal justice system treats black people unfairly, or because black people are more likely than others to offend?' (Smith 1997b). This question is one of the most controversial in the field of criminology.

Criminal statistics have assumed a position of great importance in the debate about discrimination. If the extent of 'actual' offending is no greater among black or Asian people than among whites, then disproportionate arrest and imprisonment rates are more likely to be the result of discrimination in the criminal justice process. Conversely an elevated '*actual*' rate of offending undermines the statistical basis for the 'discrimination thesis' considerably. Criminal justice statistics have many flaws as indices of behaviour. Nonetheless, they are commonly taken as facts about 'black criminality' and, therefore, a critical examination of these statistics (and also survey data) is warranted.

The 'race and crime' debate has largely been detached from discussion of ethnic differences in the extent and nature of victimisation and how patterns of offending and victimisation interrelate. Here, our concerns are with what might be termed 'ordinary victimisation', focusing specifically on household offences such as burglary and theft, and violent offences such as assault, robbery and murder. We consider the question of racist victimisation in the following chapter.

The social construction of ethnicity and criminality

The public, in general, has little direct experience of crime, especially its most serious forms. Consequently, the role of the media must be considered in relaying the dominant definitions and understandings of crime to the public at large (Hall *et al.* 1978: 30). Numerous authors, among them Cohen (1972) and Pearson (1983), have noted that the social construction of crime and criminality bears sometimes only a tenuous relationship with the extent of actual deviance. This has led some authors to the view that the relationships between criminality and ethnicity are *mythical*, and, therefore, attempting to estimate the extent of 'black' (or indeed 'Asian') crime is a flawed enterprise.

The histories of 'race' and of 'crime' show that the idea of 'the racial other' has been central to European thinking in the modern period. Long before extensive contact between Europeans and people from other parts of the world, certain groups were portrayed as having a specific set of physiological and characterological attributes which attach to their skin. Those designated as 'black', African, or African/Caribbean have consistently been attributed characteristics such as stupidity, laziness and violence; those designated 'Asian' have been attributed characteristics such as deviousness, dishonesty and insularity; while those designated 'white' have been ascribed the attributes of honesty, integrity and superiority of mind and character.

Not everyone who is referred to as 'white' escapes the portrayal as a criminal type, however. As Geoffrey Pearson (1983) has pointed out, the notion of the 'dangerous classes' is one that transcends race and serves to identify specific white groups as inherently criminal. Thus, 'white' groups such as the Irish, Maltese, Russians, Jews and others have, at specific times, been thought of as a problem for the social order in England. Indeed English people are themselves sometimes considered a problem, for example in the context of football violence in continental Europe. It is interesting to note that in Germany the arrest rate for British nationals is disproportionately high in comparison to that for German nationals. The arrest rate for British nationals is rather higher than the rate for people of Turkish origin, and rather lower than those originating in Morocco, Yugoslavia and Poland (Albrecht 1997).

Paul Gilroy points to ancient images of black lawlessness – such as 'stowaways, drifters, pimps, and drug dealers' – recurring in modern forms – such as 'muggers, illegal immigrants, black extremists and criminal Rastafarians'. The 'black folk devil', he argues, 'has acquired greater power with each subsequent permutation' (Gilroy 1987b: 145). Images of black criminality not only echo, but draw upon, the biological and cultural racism of earlier eras (see chapters 1–3). However, there was a period in British history when the question of whether ethnic minority communities had more or less involvement in crime was far from settled.

Indeed there was a strong official line that maintained that ethnic minority crime rates were rather lower than the communities among whom they settled. Rather than crime, *per se*, the earliest pronouncements about the problem of 'race' in Britain in the 1940s and 1950s clustered around anxieties and images of sexuality and miscegenation (Gilroy 1987a, b: 79). As time passed attention was drawn to the 'problems' of crime and disorder which had become identified with minority populations, ironically, as a result of the racist riots directed against them (see chapter 5). Until 1972, the official view was that:

> The conclusions remain beyond doubt: coloured immigrants are no more involved in crime than others; nor are they generally more concerned in violence, prostitution and drugs. The West Indian crime rate is much the same as that of the indigenous population. The Asian crime rate is very much lower.
>
> (House of Commons 1972: 71)

The government's response to the Select Committee Report in 1973 shared the view that black criminals formed a minority within an overwhelming majority of law-abiding citizens (Gilroy 1987a, b). However, the police position turned 180 degrees between 1972 and 1976 (Gilroy 1987b: 92). The Metropolitan Police date their change of opinion from 1974 when their 'concern began to grow' about the involvement in crime among 'black youth'. This shift can be explained in a number of ways.

First, there is the evidence of growing conflict between the police and black communities that was described in chapter 1. Thus, the visible conflicts that occurred in numerous places across the country from the mid 1970s onwards, in places as far apart as Chapeltown in Leeds and Notting Hill in London, increased in frequency and intensity (Institute of Race Relations 1979, 1987). The Metropolitan Police 'memorandum' to the 1976 Home Affairs Committee stated that 'the potential for conflict' existed in 'every law enforcement encounter' between the police and West Indians. The police also identified 40 incidents with the potential for large-scale disorder between police and black youths that had occurred in the previous year (House of Commons 1976).

A second reason for this change of official view was that the police started to collate and develop statistical material that set out specifically to demonstrate the involvement of black people in certain forms of crime, particularly 'the degree of involvement by black youth in robbery and theft [from the] person offences in some areas'. For example, a report that 'muggings' increased 129 per cent in the five years 1968–72 received much publicised headlines when it was published in 1973 (Hall *et al.* 1978: 13–17). On the basis of these statistics, the Metropolitan Police concluded that 'our experience has taught us the fallibility of the assertion that crime rates amongst those of West Indian origin are no higher than those of the population at large' (cited in Gilroy 1987a: 94). On numerous subsequent occasions, the police have published statistics linking crime with black people. For example, the release of figures in January 1975 by the Metropolitan Police from a study of victims' descriptions of assailants in the Brixton area of London showed that 79 per cent of robberies and 83 per cent of offences of theft from the person were carried out by black people (Solomos 1988: 107). This study was widely reported in the media and helped to attract attention to the 'growing problem' of black involvement in crime (ibid.) In a critical account of this development, Gutzmore (1983) argues that the police handling of the issue of 'black crime' and 'mugging' appears to be conscious political manipulation. The racially coded statistics were based on a conflation of a number of offence categories and resulted in sensationalising a very small percentage of all recorded crime. This was used to dismiss claims of discrimination as unjustifiably putting police officers on the defensive. The publication of the statistics, for Gutzmore, did little more than provide a basis for the state's campaign of criminalisation echoing the police perception of a 'rising tide of black crime' referred to by Scarman (1981). This point is related to the third reason for the change in official view which is the way in which images of 'black criminality' were constructed over this period. As Gilroy (1987a: 76–9) puts it, criminality became entrenched, or 'fixed', in the definition of blackness (see also Solomos, 1988, 1993: 99–107). The media and political reactions to the public disorders of the late 1970s and 1980s also contributed significantly to popular understandings of black people as disorderly and criminal.

In suggesting that 'black criminality' is myth, Gilroy and others are not arguing that black people do not or cannot commit crime, nor are they intending to 'invoke a pastoral definition of the black communities or the inner cities as places where crime did not occur', but pointing rather to the need to examine the 'images and representations of black criminality which ... have achieved a mythic status in the lexicon of contemporary race politics' (Gilroy 1987b: 118). The problem, then, is that 'myth' and 'reality' are inseparably bound together. The myth inspires the practices of the criminal justice system – as evident in proactive policing and responses to gatherings of black people in public space – which leads to the production of statistics, and this, in turn, feeds the myth. Since the two cannot be disentangled, the exercise of attempting to uncover the 'real' crime rates is futile and perhaps even dangerous. Gilroy is adamant on this issue:

> We challenge the categorisation of crimes according to the skin colour of their perpetrators, but we must go deeper still and face the question of whether black crimes and criminality are distinct and separable in any other sense. This will not be resolved by empiricist haggling over official crime statistics even if they are the product of class struggle.
>
> (Gilroy 1982: 146)

The construction of 'Asian criminality' has assumed a very different character from that of black or white criminalities. In general, images of Asian communities portray a community that is 'inward looking', 'tightly knit', self-regulating, passive and ordered by tradition and with strong family ties. Asian youth were largely absent from the debates about urban unrest of the 1980s, but more recently several studies of deviance within British communities of Pakistani and Bangladeshi origin have begun to shift debates within criminology (Webster 1997, Desai 1999, Wardak 2000, Alexander 2000a, b).

Mawby and Batta's study (1980, cited by Webster 1997) of *Asians and Crime: The Bradford Experience* found that, despite being over-represented in 'high risk' categories (working class, poor, inner city, etc.), 'crimes by Asians are either intra-racial or minor' (see also Stevens and Willis 1979). Mawby and Batta (1980) suggest a cultural theory based on an analysis of the strengths of South Asian family. They argue that, despite the experience of economic and social deprivation, community informal controls are greater and that young people were committed to the norms of the extended family system and the protection of *izzat*, or family prestige. Studies two decades later found that many Pakistani and Bangladeshi young people remained 'conformists' and emphasised the desire to avoid bringing shame on the family name (Webster 1997) and accepted the traditional strategy of avoiding conflict in the face of racist assault by staying away from 'white areas' or taking the elders' advice to 'turn the other cheek' when they were attacked (Desai 1999, Webster 1997).

However, these recent studies have also found other groups of Asian males who were willing to take the risks involved in moving about town and were rebelling against their parent culture (Webster 1997, Desai 1999). Others – the 'local heroes' – were older combatants who had their roots in the self-defence movements that evolved within Asian communities as a response to the racist violence of the 1970s and 1980s and were known locally 'for defending Asian territory and attacking whites'. While these instances challenged the conventional image of Asian youth as passive victims, the 1988 'Rushdie Affair' marked a more decisive shift. Young men were seen on the street burning copies of *The Satanic Verses* and the episode was constructed as linked with Islamic militancy elsewhere, itself seen as an 'aggressive religion' (Desai 1999: 8). There were numerous television and radio documentaries focusing on the 'Asian gang' throughout the 1990s (ibid.: 8–9). This new 'discourse of Asian criminality' was replicated in national and local newspapers, drawing on images such as 'Tigers in a Cage', illustrated with a photograph of angry and defiant Bengalis seen through the mesh fence of a children's playground. Alexander (2000b: 234 and 243), considers this a process of 'racialization of Muslim communities, and particularly their reinvention as "the Underclass", the embodiment of social and cultural dysfunction and danger' and as 'the latest incarnation of the black youth folk devil'. Her account of the experiences of young Bengali men in South London provided many examples where the gang label was wrongly ascribed, particularly in episodic instances of violence between groups of young people. Essentially, this labelling ignored the more fluid nature of gender, age, ethnic and community identities and friendship patterns.

Desai argues that while the media construction of the 'Asian gang' is important, other factors, such as the growth in the Bengali population in the late 1980s and 1990s, an increasing number of adolescents in the population and the experience of a generation growing up, shifted the perception within the community that now saw that it had as much right to live in England as its white counterparts, and with this new sense of entitlement developed, a confidence and assertiveness. The need to invert a deeply ingrained stereotype of passivity attracted some to images of black youth culture, elements of which were borrowed to create the 'Bengali Bad Boy' image. This was opposed to the local image of weak passive Asian people, but also the 'Abdul Hashim', the stereotypical subservient Bengladeshi (Desai 1999). Desai argues that incivility, the recourse to violence to resolve problems and an aggressive sense of localism and territorial aggression expressed between groups has existed for generations in Camden when the neighbourhoods were all white. Desai concludes that: 'The so-called "Asian Gang" is a product of a particularly British form of working class masculinity' (ibid.: 298).

The work of both Desai and Webster indicates that the new found strength of Asian young men, which was forged in a struggle of resistance against white racist attacks, also gave rise to retaliatory attacks. In particular, the murder of Richard Everitt in King's Cross in 1994 by a group of Bangladeshi youth contributed to growing white fears of racist attack and to consider local Muslim youths as a violent, criminal, knife-carrying group hostile to the white community, and this image has become increasingly prevalent. Recently, under the *Guardian* headline, '"No go for whites" in race hotspot', a report claimed that a rash of attacks – including an assault on a white schoolboy by a group of 12 Asians – had given rise to claims that streets in Oldham had become no-go zones for whites. (*Guardian*, Friday 20 April 2001).

Domestic violence within Asian communities has been relatively neglected until recently (Southall Black Sisters 1989, Sarwar 1989, The Gurdip Kaur Campaign 1989, Patel 1997). Macey argues that Bangladeshi young men use violence to control women's behaviour in the name of protecting the family honour. As Patel puts it, 'the choice for women who dare break out of the very narrow confines of the roles prescribed by religion and culture is stark; either they remain within the parameters of permissible behaviour, or they transgress and risk becoming pariahs within their own community' (Patel 1997: 263). Measures to keep women in their place include slander and rumour, threats and violence in the home and the 'phone mob' who use aggressive phone calling to pressurise liberal parents to force women to stay at home. Patel describes the 'bounty hunters' who will, for a fee, locate and return to their families young women and girls who have run away from home, some to escape violence, abuse, restrictions on movement and forced arranged marriages (ibid.: 265).

The issue of violence against women in the home places the issue of male violence squarely at the centre of understandings of crime and victimisation and thus connects back to violence committed in the public sphere. Macey (1999), for example, concludes that 'the involvement of young men of Pakistani origin and Muslim faith in violence', including drug use, violence against women, street harassment and involvement in public disorder 'has grown in recent years'. This increase in anxiety about 'Asian youth' has accompanied the growth of the male prison population of Pakistani and Bangladeshi origin. The first Muslim adviser to the prison service was appointed in 1999 on publication of statistics which showed that the number of prisoners of Islamic faith more than doubled from 1,840 to 4,355 between 1990 and 1999 (Desai 1998:8, Home Office 2000a).

The power of myths makes all discussions of ethnicity and offending deeply problematic and we share Gilroy's concerns about how the empirical data summarised in this chapter may be used. However, we are also troubled by the sense that if the 'empiricist haggling' ceases, there will be some people who will consider the matter settled and simply accept criminal justice statistics as a reflection of 'real' rates of offending. Moreover, there remain the questions of community safety and protection from victimisation which concerns all parts of the community.

Defining crime

Defining crime is notoriously difficult. A preliminary definition might be any act that breaks a criminal law. However, what is lawful in England in the year 2000 might be criminal in another country or made illegal here in ten or twenty years' time. It is also evident that not all dishonest or violent acts become defined as crimes, nor are they responded to in the same way by victims, the police and the legal system. Differences in the extent to which deviant acts are responded to as crime depends on local traditions and practices. The dispensation of 'justice' is known to differ 'by geography', and by class, gender and ethnicity. Police and judicial discretion exerts a powerful impact on who becomes defined as criminal and who does not. Consequently legal definitions provide only a partial answer to the problem of defining crime.

Definitions of crime based on morality are subject to the same kind of difficulty. What are seen as good, bad and criminal are not absolute, but also change with time and place. Using 'social harm' as a defining criterion for crime falls down in rather the same way as using legality: acts that result in the most serious harm are not always unlawful, while relatively harmless forms of behaviour are often subject to serious punishment. The process by which crimes are defined and prioritised is not a neutral one. Rather, the focus of both criminology and the criminal justice process is on crimes of the powerless – typified as 'street crime' – rather than crimes of the powerful, such as fraud, environmental pollution, health and safety violations, corruption and the abuse of power. The crimes of the powerful often escape punishment, despite the evidence which suggests that these are more harmful – resulting in much more extensive death and injury – than the crimes that are typically the focus of public anxieties. Possessing cannabis, for example, is much more likely than corporate manslaughter to be punished by imprisonment.

Official statistics on ethnicity and offending

Attrition in the criminal justice process

The most common basis for discussing 'race' or ethnic differences in offending are the official statistics, specifically arrest and imprisonment rates. Indeed, many studies have relied more or less exclusively on criminal justice records. Analysis of the characteristics of offenders based on criminal records is limited, however, by the fact that in only a very small minority of offences that occur is an offender identified and in a smaller percentage still does that person end up convicted and sentenced to imprisonment (see figure 4.1). Home Office (1999d) figures indicate that 24 per cent of offences reported to the British Crime Survey are recorded by the police; in 26 per cent of these recorded offences an offender is identified (referred to as a 'clear-up'); and half of these detected offences result in a conviction. The end result of this attrition is that only about 2 per cent of offences result in the conviction of an offender (Home Office 1999d).

There is clearly a great deal of scope for individual discretion to affect who is, and who is not, filtered out of the process between the 'criminal act' and conviction. In this process, decisions are taken by victims, police officers, court officials, juries and judges, all of whom have varying degrees of discretion in their decision making about who should be 'filtered in' and 'filtered out' of the process. Furthermore, only about one-sixth of offenders who are convicted and sentenced by the courts receive a custodial sentence. Overall, fewer than one-third of 1 per cent of all offences that actually occur will result in a custodial sentence, suggesting that prison statistics tell us about an *atypical* group who are in prison. It would obviously be a mistake, therefore, to extrapolate from the characteristics of the prison population to make generalisations about the population of offenders (Coleman and Moynihan 1996: 98). Chambliss and Nagasawa (1969) say bluntly: 'the notion that official statistics provide a reliable index of either actual or relative involvement in crime is quite wrong'.

Although we concur with Keith Bottomley and Ken Pease (1986: 86)

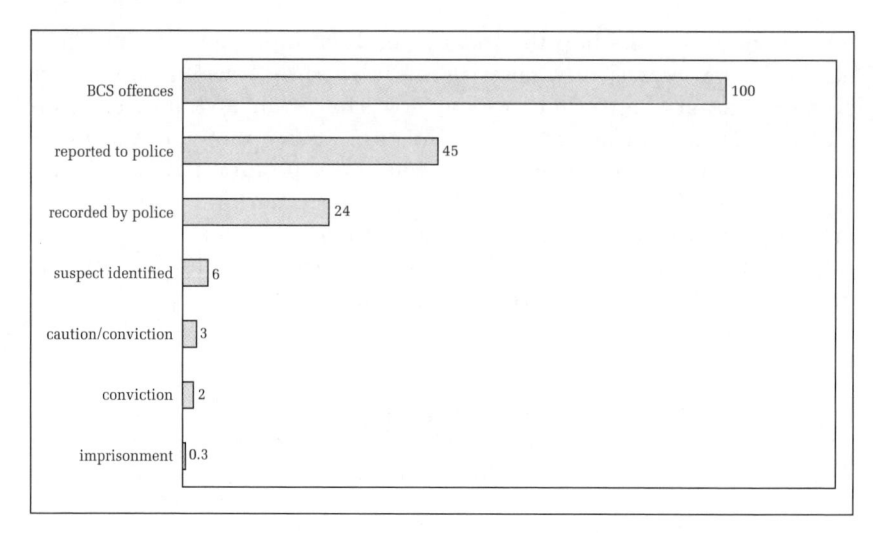

Figure 4.1 Attrition in the criminal process
Source: Home Office, 1999d

Stage	Value
BCS offences	100
reported to police	45
recorded by police	24
suspect identified	6
caution/conviction	3
conviction	2
imprisonment	0.3

that it is 'especially dangerous' to reach conclusions about ethnic differences in offending based on recorded crime statistics, examining these figures remains an important task. Recorded crime statistics are commonly the basis for public discussion about crime. Despite what we know about the weaknesses of official crime data, the extent of crime, its rise and fall and its seriousness as a social problem is routinely assessed and discussed in the media using these figures. It seems likely that public discussion about 'race' and crime will continue to draw on media interpretations of official statistics for the foreseeable future. Despite attrition in the process and the potential for bias that this introduces, criminal justice statistics are not completely meaningless. These statistics tell us who is detected for particular types of offences, who is processed by the system and who ends up in the custody of the prison service. They tell us who has become officially labelled as offenders. As long as it is understood that these figures comprise a *record of decisions taken by the criminal justice agencies* (which we critically examine in chapters 5–7) they can contribute to understanding crime and justice. We feel a responsibility to interpret these data because they have such power and prominence in criminal justice policy and practice. They are necessary to explore any evidence of both elevated offending rates and discriminatory practices by decision makers in the criminal justice process.

Arrest rates

Of approximately 1.3 million arrests for notifiable offences made in England and Wales in 1998/9, 93,000 arrestees (7 per cent) were

Offending and victimisation 85

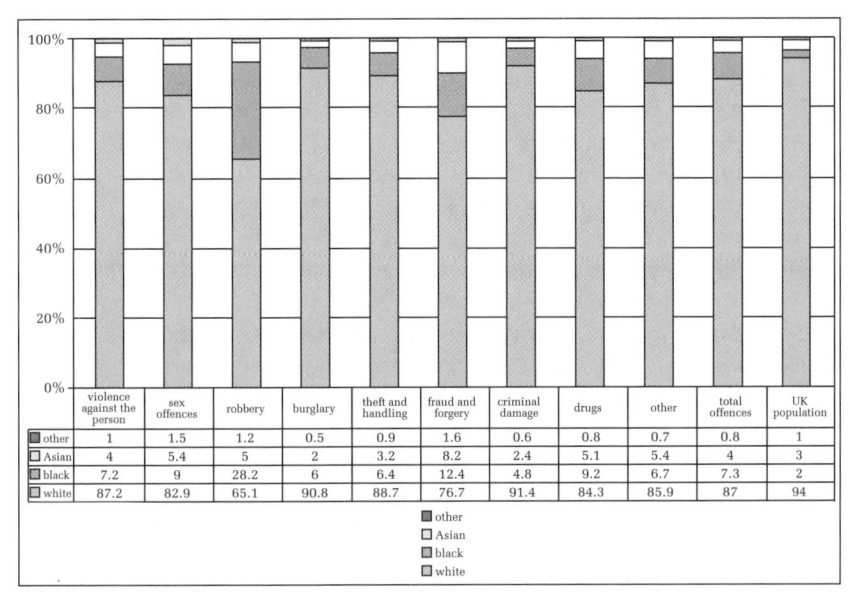

	violence against the person	sex offences	robbery	burglary	theft and handling	fraud and forgery	criminal damage	drugs	other	total offences	UK population
other	1	1.5	1.2	0.5	0.9	1.6	0.6	0.8	0.7	0.8	1
Asian	4	5.4	5	2	3.2	8.2	2.4	5.1	5.4	4	3
black	7.2	9	28.2	6	6.4	12.4	4.8	9.2	6.7	7.3	2
white	87.2	82.9	65.1	90.8	88.7	76.7	91.4	84.3	85.9	87	94

Figure 4.2 Arrests for indictable offences by ethnic origin, England and Wales 1999/2000
Source: Home Office, s. 95 report.

recorded as black, 51,300 (4 per cent) Asian and 12,600 (1 per cent) 'other' non-white groups (Home Office 2000c) (see figure 4.2). The black/white arrest ratio varied from 3.8:1 in London to over 7:1 in Hertfordshire. Arrest rates for Asians were greater than those for white people in ten police force areas, rising to a ratio as high as 3:1 in Thames Valley. Police recorded arrest data indicate that ethnic differences in patterns of arrest rates vary widely between offences and between police force areas. Examining arrest rates per head of population, whites were arrested in 1999/2000 at an average rate 26 per 1,000 population, with corresponding figures of 113 for blacks, and 37 for Asians (Home Office 2000c: 22).

On the face of it, these data suggest that ethnic minority communities – especially those of African and Caribbean origin – are more likely to be arrested *per capita*. It must be remembered, however, that arrest rates for the general population take no account of the fact that younger people and males are more likely to be arrested by the police. It is also evident that arrests are generally higher in urban areas and, in particular, in those 'inner-city' areas where ethnic minority communities are concentrated. This begs the question: to what extent is the disproportionate ethnic minority arrest rates simply the result of residence in an area with a higher than average likelihood of arrest (Stevens and Willis 1979)? We return later in this chapter to address the question of whether disproportionalities still remain when relevant social and demographic variables are taken account of.

Imprisonment rates

Prison data represent the 'end point' of the criminal justice process. That is, people who have been arrested, charged, convicted, sentenced and held in prison service custody. On 30 June 1999, there were 12,120 people from ethnic minority communities in English and Welsh prisons out of a total prison population of 64,529, accounting for 18 per cent of the male prison population and 25 per cent of the female prison population (Home Office 2000). Including British nationals only 10 per cent of the male prison population are black, 2 per cent Asian and 2 per cent are of 'other' ethnic origins. Of the female prison population, 22 per cent are black, 1 per cent Asian and 2 per cent are of 'other' origins. These figures compare with an ethnic minority population that makes up 5.5 per cent of the general population of England and Wales, comprising 1.7 per cent black, 2.7 per cent Asian and 1.1 per cent of 'other' ethnic origins. Nonetheless, compared with whites, many, *but not all*, ethnic groups have higher rates of incarceration. As can be seen from figure 4.3 – based on British nationals in prison in 1999 – the incarceration rate per 100,000 population of England and Wales was 184 whites compared with 1,265 blacks, 260 Pakistanis, 74 Bangladeshis, 93 Indians, 44 Chinese and 914 'other Asians'.

The fact that official statistics such as arrest and imprisonment rates 'over-represent' people of African and Caribbean origin and some people of Asian origin has been taken by some as an indication of greater criminality among ethnic minority populations (Smith 1997a). This conclusion, in itself, is quite wrong because official statistics are the *product of*

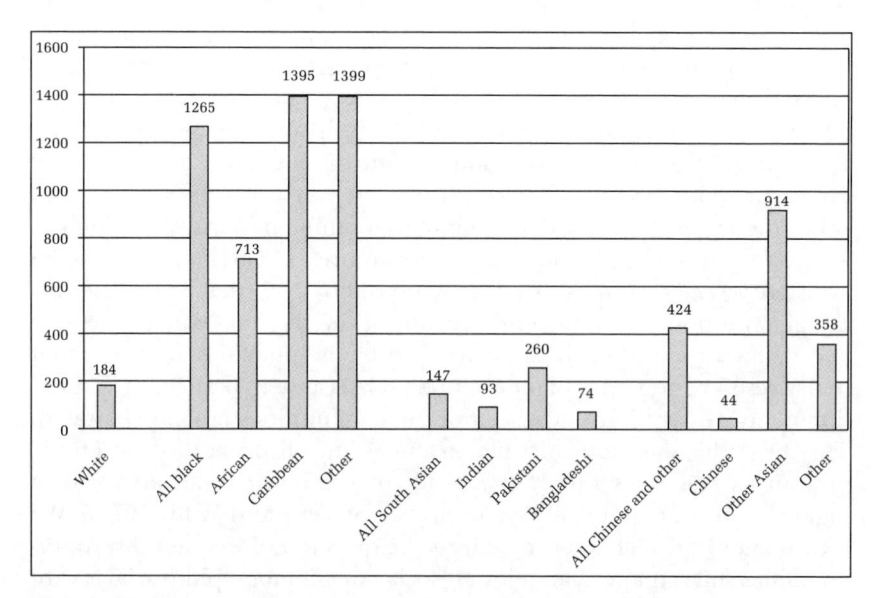

Figure 4.3 Incarceration rates, ethnic group, 30 June 1999

criminal justice practices. While data collected by the criminal justice system are 'real', they should be seen as records of organisational decisions, categorisations and actions. We examine decisions taken by police officers, court officials, magistrates and judges in chapters 6–8. As we argued in chapter 2, most criminal justice agents have wide discretion in their decisions to take formal action – to arrest, charge, prosecute or imprison – and where discretion is widest and decision making least visible there is the greatest scope for discrimination. Consequently, criminal justice statistics cannot be seen, as a measure of offending as a phenomenon, in any sense separable from the organisations that produce them.

Risk of victimisation

Since the late 1980s, government funded victimisation surveys have gathered 'booster samples' of respondents from minority communities to allow analyses of how patterns of victimisation vary by ethnic origin. The first firm evidence that ethnic minorities were more 'at risk' of victimisation relative to their white counterparts came from the 1988 British Crime Survey which included a large enough sample of black and Asian people to compare their experiences with white people (Mayhew, Elliot

Table 4.1 Differential risk of victimisation by ethnicity (percentage victimised once or more, 1988 and 1992 British Crime Survey), selected offences

	White	Black	Asian	Indian	Pakistani
Burglary	5.8	**11.1	**7.8	**8.1	7.5
Vehicle theft	19.1	**27.3	21.0	20.8	22.6
All household offences	30.8	**34.8	**36.2	**35.9	**39.5
Assault	3.4	**5.9	4.0	3.3	5.1
Threats	2.5	3.3	**4.5	3.7	**6.2
Robbery/theft from person	1.3	**3.2	**3.1	**2.9	2.1
All personal offences	9.7	**13.9	**13.0	*11.8	**14.7
Number interviewed	19,294	1,776	1,976	1,236	596

Sources: FitzGerald and Hale 1996:11.
Percy (1998: 35, table A2.1) provides same data for 1995 and Kershaw *et al.* (2000: 70, table A2.11) for 2000.
Notes:
* Significantly different from whites at the 10 per cent level.
** Significantly different from whites at the 5 per cent level.

---

[1] This involved interviewing, in parallel with the main sample, a 'booster sample' using a technique known as 'focused enumeration'. This entailed asking each person in the main sample whether any of their immediate neighbours were of African, Caribbean or Asian origin and, if so, the interviewer called on them to be interviewed.

and Dowds 1989)[1]. The 'headline' results were striking. In the 14 months prior to the survey, one white person in every ten (9.6 per cent) had experienced some form of violent crime compared with nearly one in six Afro-Caribbean people (16.1 per cent) and one in seven Asian people (14.8 per cent) (ibid.). More recently, the data from the 1988 and 1992 British Crime Surveys have been combined to enable a close examination of the comparative extent of victimisation for both violent and property crime experienced by different ethnic groups (FitzGerald and Hale 1996). The findings are set out in table 4.1. The patterns are also confirmed in the 2000 British Crime Survey (see Kershaw *et al.* 2000).

The British Crime Survey indicates that all ethnic minority groups are at greater risk of victimisation than whites for both property and violent offences (FitzGerald and Hale 1996, Percy 1998, Kershaw *et al.* 2000). Taking only the more serious offences, it is evident that all minority groups are at greater risk than whites of household burglary (strikingly so when only burglaries with loss are examined) and all are at greater risk of robbery and thefts from the person. FitzGerald and Hale (1996) found that about 6 per cent of white respondents said that they were burgled in the previous year, this was the experience of 11 per cent of black and about 8 per cent of Asian respondents. The same study reported that just over 1 per cent of whites said that they had been robbed, this was the case for about 3 per cent of blacks, 4 per cent of Indians and 6 per cent of Pakistanis. The British Crime Survey has shown consistently that the weight of victimisation falls disproportionately on ethnic minority communities relative to their numbers in the general population (see Percy 1998; Kershaw *et al.* 2000).

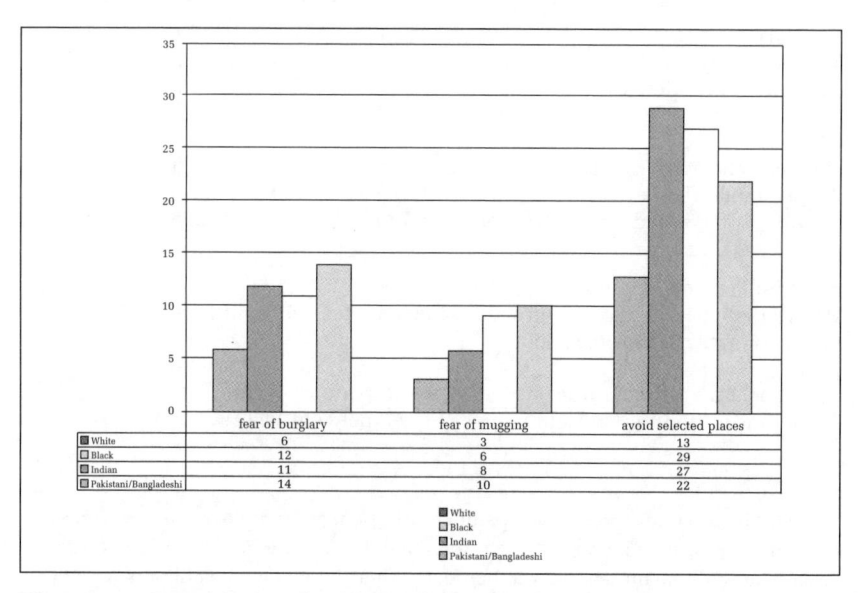

	fear of burglary	fear of mugging	avoid selected places
White	6	3	13
Black	12	6	29
Indian	11	8	27
Pakistani/Bangladeshi	14	10	22

Figure 4.4 Fear of crime by ethnicity (1995 British Crime Survey)
Source: Percy (1998: 33)

Fear of crime

Given that respondents from ethnic minority communities are generally at greater risk of criminal victimisation, it is not surprising to find that these same people perceive themselves to be at greater risk of crime. For example, while 20 per cent of whites thought it either 'very or fairly likely' that they would be burgled in the coming year, this was the perception of 30 per cent of black respondents and 38 per cent of Asian respondents (see Kershaw *et al.* 2000). A similar picture emerged for 'mugging'; twice as many people from ethnic minority communities thought they were certain or very likely to be 'mugged' (ibid.). The BCS also asks people whether they are 'worried about' specific types of crime. Figure 4.4 shows that worry about crime was much higher among ethnic minorities, especially Asians, compared with white people.

Percy (1998) found that on the street, and especially at home alone at night, people from ethnic minorities felt less safe than white people and that feeling of lack of safety affects individual freedom of movement. For example, people from ethnic minorities (Pakistanis and Bangladeshis in particular) avoid going out at night for fear of crime, avoid walking near certain types of people and are *always* accompanied when walking out after dark (ibid.). More detailed analysis showed that while 13 per cent of white respondents said they avoided certain places or events (such as football matches, night clubs, theatres or pubs) because they fear crime or violence, this was true of 29 per cent of blacks, 27 per cent of Indians and 22 per cent of Pakistanis and Bangladeshis (see figure 4.4). Although the relationship between the experience of crime and fear of crime is a complex one, ethnic differences in perceptions of risk appear, to a large extent, to be influenced by their actual risk of crime. The nature and extent of fear of crime are also affected by the experiences of friends and neighbours, crime reported in the media as well as the individual's capacity to protect or defend themselves against crime.

Victims' description of suspected offenders

Victimisation surveys have also been used to discover who victims believe offenders to be (Mayhew, Aye Maung and Mirrlees-Black 1993: 91–2; FitzGerald and Hale 1996; Smith 1997b: 713; 730–1), but give only a limited, and potentially distorted, picture of offender behaviour. Survey data indicate that in only about 35–40 per cent of cases can the victim attempt a description of the offender. However, this does not equate to 35–40 per cent of *all* offences, because less than 20 per cent of survey recorded crime and only 2 per cent of officially recorded crimes are 'personal crimes' (such as theft from person and assault) where the offender is identifiable. The vast bulk of crimes are vehicle crime (36 per cent), theft (28 per cent), burglary (9 per cent) and vandalism (7 per cent) where the victim will usually only rarely have any idea of who the offender was (Mayhew, Aye Maung and Mirrlees-Black 1993: 58).

Although some victims of crime actually see who the offender was (or come to know by some other means), others only *suspect*, or make assumptions about the perpetrators involved. It is possible that estimates of the relative involvement of different ethnic groups in crimes, as reported by victims, are affected by stereotypes and culturally determined expectations. Stevens and Willis (1979), in their early study of arrests in London, found that the likelihood of criminal incidents coming to police attention is affected by the ethnic origin of the offender. Their data suggested that white victims of violence committed by ethnic minority perpetrators reported their victimisation to the police in situations where they would not have done if the perpetrator had been white, and this was particularly true where the incident did not cause any injury to the victim. Shah and Pease (1992) note that the police may mis-record either the ethnic origin of the offender or the nature of the 'assault'. They also suggest that there may be other distinguishing features of offences committed by ethnic minorities that lead white victims to report them to the police even when no injury has been sustained. In line with the findings of Stevens and Willis (1979), Shah and Pease (1992) found that where no injury was inflicted, victims were more likely to report crimes where the offender was from an ethnic minority group (36 per cent) than where the offender was white (25 per cent).[2] Conversely, where injuries were inflicted, and particularly where they required medical attention, victims were more likely to report crimes where the offender was white than where they were of ethnic minority origin. FitzGerald and Hale (1996) using the 1988 and 1992 British Crime Surveys have shown that this pattern holds for whites and Pakistanis (where the offender was black), while black people were more balanced in their reporting and Indians were less likely to report offences involving black offenders. This, of course, only relates to the proportion of offences for which victims see the offender.

A more controversial objection to victim accounts is the evidence of 'racial hoaxes' where victims of crime have deliberately misled law enforcement agencies and the media, claiming that the perpetrators were of a particular ethnic origin. In the USA, there have been numerous instances where white victims have falsely claimed to have been victimised by African/Americans. Among the best known of these is the case of Susan Smith, a white South Carolina mother, who told the police that she had been the victim of a carjacking. According to Smith, an armed black male, 20–30 years old, drove off with her two sons aged three and 14 months. Nine days after an extensive federal and state manhunt, Smith confessed to driving her car into a lake with her children strapped into their car seats

---

[2] Shah and Pease (1992) analysed victimisation reports where the ethnic origin of the offender is described using the 1982, 1984 and 1988 British Crime Surveys (BCS) to examine these possibilities in relation to personal crimes (including assault, wounding, rape, indecent assault, robbery and attempted personal crimes).

Table 4.2 Ethnic origin of offender[1] by ethnic origin of victim, combined 1988 and 1992 British Crime Survey[2] (per cent)

	White victims	Black victims	Asian victims
Violence[3]			
White offender	88	51	62
Black offender	3	42	11
Asian offender	1	1	19
Other/mixed group	5	3	7
Unknown	3	3	1
N	628	108	59
Mugging[4]			
White offender	49	16	20
Black offender	32	58	55
Asian offender	1	–	10
Other/mixed group	8	13	8
Unknown	10	13	9
N	103	30	41

Notes:
1 Based on all cases where the victim could say something about the offender.
2 Source 1988 and 1992 British Crime Survey core and ethnic minority booster samples (weighted data). See Mayhew, Aye Maung and Mirrlees-Black (1993: 92, table 6.8).
3 Violent offences include wounding and common assault
4 Mayhew, Aye Maung and Mirrlees-Black describe the term 'mugging' as a 'popular rather than legal term. Used in the typology of violence to include all robbery and snatch theft, irrespective of where they occurred.' (Snatch theft is a 'sub-category of theft from the person', ibid.: 187). See also Hall *et al.* 1978, Gilroy 1987a, b, Keith 1997 for discussion of the social construction of 'mugging'.

(Russell 1998: 69). How extensive this phenomenon is in the UK context has not been investigated. However, it has been documented that *where the offender is not known*, white respondents, believing black people to be most commonly involved in crime, tend to ascribe their offences to black people (McConville and Shepherd 1992; Bowling 1999a: 210). Reviews of this field have argued that while some of the over-representation may be explained by mistakes in reporting and recording, it is unlikely to account for all of the over-representation of black people as offenders, particularly in relation to violent offences and robbery (Smith 1997a, b).

Based on the very small number of cases where the victims can identify their assailant, it appears from the British Crime Survey that many, but by no means all, personal crimes are *intra-ethnic*, that is, the victim and offender are from the same ethnic group (see table 4.2). The vast majority of white victims said that white offenders had been involved (88 per cent) with only a small proportion being committed by people of other ethnic origins (3 per cent black, 1 per cent Asian and 5 per cent 'mixed'). As FitzGerald and Hale (1996) point out, it is not surprising that so small a proportion of all offences committed against whites involve ethnic minority suspects because the latter make up little more than one-twentieth of the population at large and this is spread unevenly geographically. In most violent offences against ethnic minorities (51 per cent black, 62 per cent Asian), the offenders were also said to be white. This is also unsurprising because the general population is overwhelmingly white and because most people from ethnic minorities live, work and socialise in areas where white people are the majority. Once victimisation by white people is accounted for, the majority of black victimisation (42 per cent) is committed by other black people, while for Asians, 19 per cent is perpetrated by other Asians and 11 per cent by black people.

Some forms of violence – the most obvious example being *domestic* violence (between married or cohabiting couples) – are very likely to be intra-ethnic because of the pattern of family relationships between different ethnic groups. The Policy Studies Institute study of *Ethnic Minorities in Britain* estimated that only about 1 per cent of all partnerships in the population as a whole are 'mixed ethnic' (Modood and Berthoud 1997). Among ethnic minorities, around half of Caribbean men and one-third of women born in Britain have a white partner, compared with one in five British-born Indian and East African Asian men, and one in ten women. Hardly any Pakistanis or Bangladeshis have partners from white or other ethnic groups (Modood and Berthoud 1997: 30). These patterns of marriage and intimate relationships mean that domestic violence will be overwhelmingly intra-ethnic except for the more intermarried population of Caribbean origin (see also Southall Black Sisters 1989, Mama 1995, Patel 1997). To some extent the same must apply to violence in other social settings. Places of entertainment, except in cosmopolitan urban settings, are to a large extent still segregated in Britain, reflecting structurally patterned geographical settlement, employment, family and friendship formation, and different tastes in entertainment and socialising (see chapter 2).

Street robbery and 'mugging'

'Mugging' is a criminal label with no formal legal standing imported from the USA in August 1972, since when it has taken its 'own kind of stranglehold on the public and official imagination' (Hall *et al.* 1978: 5–6). The term – now used in the British Crime Survey questionnaire – is defined by Mayhew, Aye Maung and Mirrlees-Black (1993: 111) as comprising robbery (1.2 per cent of British Crime Survey offences) together with a proportion of the thefts from the person (2.9 per cent of BCS offences). This amounts to a very small proportion of all crime, but has consistently provoked media panics and public fears since the early 1970s. Of all offences, 'mugging' stands out as one which has consistently been portrayed as a 'black crime' (Hall *et al.* 1978: 333, Solomos 1988: 108–11; McConville and Shepherd 1992: 110–11; Bowling 1999a: 83–4, 213–14, cf. Pratt 1981). The legacy of this thinking is clearly evident today:

Box 4.1 Hypotheses proposed to explain black over-representation in robbery

- Robbery is related to poverty and social exclusion. The places where both robbery and black communities are concentrated have the lowest incomes, highest rates of school exclusion, under-achievement at secondary school and unemployment. They are concentrated into the most impoverished urban environments where recreational and other facilities are in shortest supply.

- Robbery is associated with the most demoralised sectors of the working class and should be explained not only as a product of unequal distribution of wealth and chaotic labour market practices but demoralising social relations and an individualistic ideology that characterises late capitalism.

- Many robberies among young people are very minor, involve little or no injury and should be considered 'adolescent bullying rather than violent crime' (McClintock and Gibson 1961). Robberies among young people are particularly likely to involve easily portable consumer items, such as mobile telephones.

- The socio-economic position of robbers is not 'desperate' – few are homeless, for example – so while money is the main object in street robbery, 'few people rob out of real need' (Burney 1990: 47). 'Street crime' mainly involves a small group of committed robbers and takes place within the 'group identity' of the 'so-called posses', the main motive for which is to gain money for stylish clothes and trainers in order to 'maintain a certain style of dress' (Burney 1990) and to pay for going out to bars and clubs and to pay for alcohol, cigarettes and cannabis (Savill 1994).

- Peer pressure contributes to robbery and, in particular, older brothers and friends are admired and emulated for toughness, especially if they have served a custodial sentence (Burney 1990: 53). Black young people gain self-esteem from the development of a specific youth cultural style, but this leads to too much concern with money and consumer goods which simply props up a commercial culture (Sewell 1997).

- Black young men commit robbery to get back at white society, a phenomenon that can be seen as a manifestation of 'black power' (Pratt 1981).

- Mass media images based on corporate branding aimed at youth culture derives its images from and celebrates 'street culture'. These flattering images of consumerist street style, often derived from black

> street culture and representations of the black male body. generate pressures to acquire greater levels of 'branding' success, regardless of the legitimacy of the means used (Webster 2001).
>
> - Black young people who are frequently stopped or arrested for crimes they did not commit may get to feel that because they are labelled as criminals, they may as well commit crimes (Burney 1990: 53).
>
> - Robbers have disproportionately suffered tragic or stressful circumstances such as parental separation, bereavement and family stress. An unpublished study based on young robbers in prison identified that many offenders of all ethnic groups had serious disruption at home and school, periods in residential care and the death of a parent (Jowitt, 2000).

> Black people are dangerous animals. I shouldn't say this, but when [a mugging] happens, I hate all blacks. I don't normally allow a black in this house. . . . If you say to me who are the first football hooligans, I would say the British; they were the ones slung out of Europe. You say to a black that mugging is a black crime, crash! That's a red rag to a bull. They won't have it.
> (McConville and Shepherd 1992: 110)

Data from the British Crime Survey indicates that half of the white victims surveyed were 'mugged' by other whites (see table 4.2). However, it is also striking that nearly one in three white victims of 'mugging' said the protagonist was black. Among the black respondents who said they were 'mugged', nearly six out of ten (58 per cent) said that it involved another black person while only 16 per cent said the perpetrator was white. Among Asians, again, more than half of those who said they had been mugged said that a black person was responsible (55 per cent), while 20 per cent were said to have been committed by whites and 10 per cent by Asians. These findings must be treated with extreme caution because of the small number of interviews on which they are based.

Explaining robbery has been a central concern of criminology throughout the history of the discipline and the questions of class and ethnicity have often formed part of the analysis. McClintock and Gibson's (1961) study of the 81 per cent increase in recorded robbery between 1957 and 1960, for example, found very few arrestees from Commonwealth countries, but did they find evidence of an over-representation of migrants from Ireland. More recently, a number of studies have examined the over-representation of black young men in recorded robbery (for example, Pratt 1981, Burney 1990, Barker *et al.* 1993, Savill 1994). However, these studies have a number of weaknesses that raise questions about their reliability and validity. Pratt's (1981) study was based on Metropolitan Police recorded data leaving the author only to speculate about various possible explanations from genetics to relative deprivation. Burney's (1990) study was based on police records and interviews with victims and probation officers who had robbers in their caseload. The only study that actually included interviews with robbers is a small-scale survey conducted for a master's dissertation in police studies (Savill 1994). Despite the limited nature of the studies, they do raise a set of hypotheses to be explored in future research based on interviews with the offenders themselves (see box 4.1)

Homicide

The Home Office has published official statistics on the ethnicity of homicide victims and suspects (as recorded by the police) since 1997 (Home Office 1997, 2000). Homicide figures are generally thought to be more robust than many statistics on offending because they are few in number, most likely to be reported or discovered by a third party, and more extensively investigated than other offences. Nonetheless, murder statistics share the weaknesses of other official records. In cases of violent death, for example, accidents and suicide have to be distinguished from homicide. There is clearly scope for making errors in this judgement, and there is some evidence that mistakes have been made. In a number of recent *causes célèbre*, there has been disagreement between police officers investigating and the families of victims about whether the death was the result of suicide or an accident (the police view) or murder (the view of the families in each case).

Ricky Reel went missing after being separated from a group of friends in the wake of a racist attack in Kingston, West London, and his body was discovered later in the River Thames. The initial conclusion drawn by the police was that Ricky had accidentally fallen into the river, but, after a long-running campaign on the part of the Reel family, the police reinvestigated his death, pursuing the possibility that it was a racist murder. An inquest recorded an open verdict. In the case of Michael Menson, investigating police officers reached the conclusion that the black musician had committed suicide by setting fire to himself. It transpired that detectives had not conducted basic forensic analyses or interviewed Menson before he died in hospital several days after his attack. A reinvestigation led to the discovery that Menson had been targeted by a group of young men in a car who had poured or sprayed accelerant on to his clothing and set him alight. The suspects were convicted of murder.

Notwithstanding these tragic failures, homicide data do not generally suffer the well-documented problems of definition and categorisation that afflict other offences. For example, deciding whether a violent incident should be categorised as 'common assault', 'actual' or 'grievous' bodily harm depends on subjective judgement to a much greater degree than homicide. Similarly, the offences of 'robbery', 'theft from the person' and 'pick-pocketing' are subject to narrow subjective distinctions.

The recording and categorisation of these crimes will commonly be much less closely investigated than a suspicious death. Nonetheless, in common with many other criminal justice statistics, the ethnicity of both victim and suspect are categorised by the police and must still be treated with caution. It should be remembered also that homicide is a relatively rare event, amounting in England and Wales to an average of 630 per year between 1996 and 1999 (Home Office 2000c: 16).

In most homicides a suspect is identified, but this is less common for black victims. In fact, no suspect was detected by the police in 28 per cent of homicides where the victim was African/Caribbean, compared with 11 per cent where the victim was either white or Asian (see figure 4.4). One reason that suspects involved in the murders of black people are less likely to be identified is the circumstance of the case. Black victims are much more likely to have been shot and homicides by shooting are, generally, much more likely not to have suspects identified. Other possible reasons that suspects are less likely to be identified in murders of black people include a lack of trust on the part of black communities leading to a lesser willingness to provide evidence to the police and lack of interest or effort on the part of the police investigating these cases (see chapter 6).

In the majority of recorded homicides the victim and suspect were known to one another. In just over 60 per cent of cases involving white victims, the suspect was a spouse, lover, other family member or someone else known to the victim. This was also true for 44 per cent of black victims, 69 per cent of Asian victims and 55 per cent for victims of other ethnic origin. It should be noted that, in the case of black victims, the fact that the suspect is unknown in nearly one in three cases makes it difficult to interpret these results. In cases where there is no suspect, it is obviously most likely that this person is unknown to the victim, or at least they are less likely to be very close. Where suspects were identified, the pattern is very similar to that of violent crime reported to the British Crime Survey, supporting the main contention that the majority of homicides are intra-ethnic. Thus, 94 per cent of whites, 59 per cent of blacks and 66 per cent of Asians were murdered by someone from the same ethnic group (see figures 4.5a and b).

People from ethnic minorities are at greater risk of homicide and also of being suspected of murder than would be expected by their number in the population, and this is most marked for black people. About 10 per cent of murder victims and suspects in England and Wales were black (compared with 2 per cent of the general population) and 6 per cent were Asian (compared with 3 per cent of the general population). As with violent crime more generally, this pattern may be partly explained by the demographic profile of the ethnic minority population, a contention that will be explored in more detail later in this chapter.

There has been an increasingly vocal concern expressed about 'black-on-black' violence, and murder in particular. There is no doubt that the very public nature of some of these crimes, and those involving firearms

Offending and victimisation 97

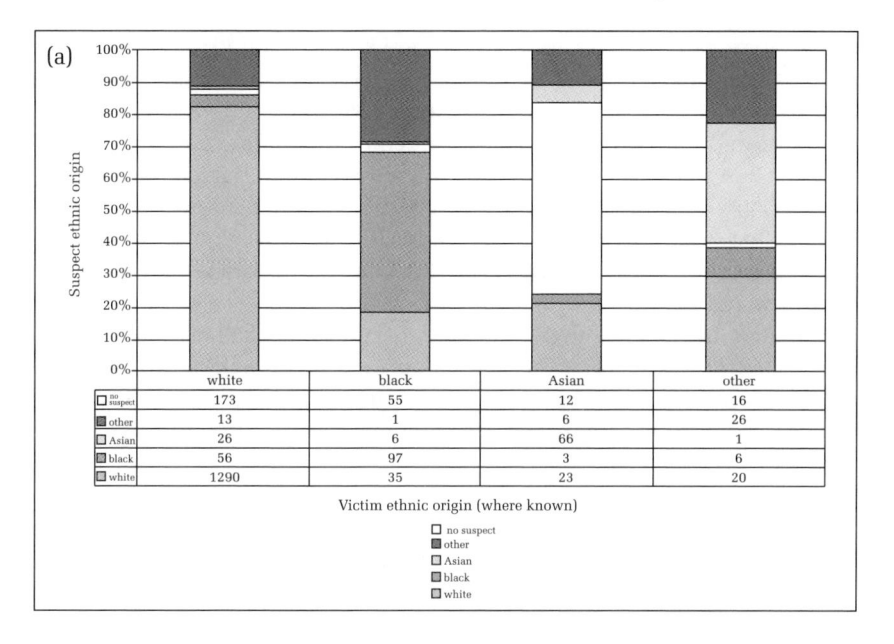

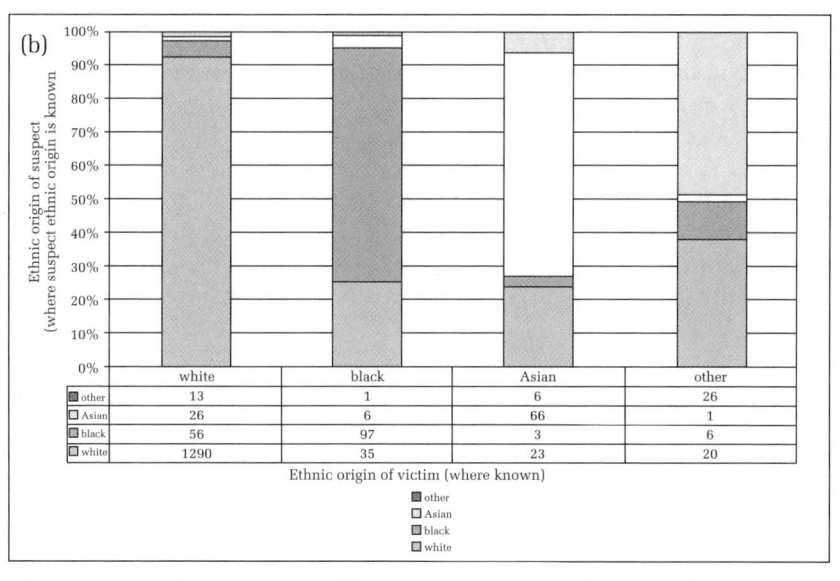

(a)

	white	black	Asian	other
no suspect	173	55	12	16
other	13	1	6	26
Asian	26	6	66	1
black	56	97	3	6
white	1290	35	23	20

Victim ethnic origin (where known)

(b)

	white	black	Asian	other
other	13	1	6	26
Asian	26	6	66	1
black	56	97	3	6
white	1290	35	23	20

Ethnic origin of victim (where known)

Figures 4.5 a & b Ethnicity of homicide victim by ethnicity of principal suspect
Source: Home Office s. 95 report 2000)

in particular, have caused a great deal of consternation within the black community and beyond. Media reports have focused on 'black-on-black' shootings, often occurring in shopping centres and residential areas, and these have been reported in Birmingham, Leeds, Manchester and in numerous locations in London including Harlesden and Hackney.[3] High-profile operations – such as Operation Trident, in the Metropolitan Police, have been set up directly to target serious offenders of Caribbean origin thought to be responsible for much of this violence.[4]

The scale of 'black-on-black' homicide – judging from figures for 1997–2000 – is not as extensive as may be imagined, however. In that three-year period, 97 murders were known to be 'black-on-black' crimes out of a total of 2003. Although these account for seven out of ten murders of black people, they account for about 5 per cent of all murders in England and Wales. Nonetheless, the pattern of black-on-black homicide is a cause for concern. These murders are much more likely to involve a stranger and also to be a shooting – 37 per cent of black victims were shot dead, compared with 5 per cent of whites and 11 per cent Asians.

Self-report studies

The self-report method assumes that 'real' rates of offending are 'knowable' and that some attempt should be made to estimate patterns of offending unbiased by the attrition and selection process inherent in the production of official statistics, and which gets past the limitations of victims' descriptions.

These studies are similar to victimisation surveys: first some general questions are asked about the respondent's social and economic situation and then they are asked to describe any offences that they themselves have committed, irrespective of whether these came to the attention of the police. Usually respondents are shown a list of dishonest and violent acts and are asked to say which ones they have ever committed (see box 4.2).

---

[3] This phenomenon has received little scholarly attention (Murji 1999), but there has been extensive press coverage, for example: 'Dealing out Death on the Streets', Justin Davenport, *Evening Standard*, 27 May 1997; 'Gangsters make another killing', Duncan Campbell, and 'Life for Shotgun Murderer', Vivek Chaudhary, *Guardian*, 15 November 1997; 'Yardies Shoot 3 in a Day', *Evening Standard*, 26 April 2000; 'Enough is Enough: Martin Luther King's words used in police "stop the violence" campaign as gun crimes soar', *Voice*, 22 May 2000 pp. 1–3; 'Police Set Sights on Yardies' Gun Dealers: Special Report on Gun Violence in Britain', Stephen Morris, *Guardian*, 8 January 2001.

[4] Trident is 'the current Metropolitan Police service response to the gun crime occurring within some identified Black communities in London'. It has a staff of 200 and has the aims of 'increasing community confidence, reduce the fear of crime and bring to justice those persons involved in drug-related violence, including shootings, within the Black communities of London thereby making it a safer city' (Metropolitan Police Service: '*Operation Trident*' leaflet).

> **Box 4.2 Self-report offending questionnaire**
>
> Sometimes people take things away from others, without the intention of returning them. Now, we would like to know if you have ever done something like that. Of course all your answers will be treated in strict confidence.
>
> (1) no (2) yes Did you ever take away a bicycle, moped or motorcycle?
>
> (1) no (2) yes Did you ever take away a car?
>
> (1) no (2) yes Did you ever steal something out of or from a car?
>
> (1) no (2) yes Did you ever snatch from a person a purse or a bag?
>
> *Source*: International Self-Report Delinquency Questionnaire. See Junger Tas, Terlouw and Klein (1994)

The technique relies upon the honesty of interviewees to reveal their dishonest, violent and disorderly behaviour. This obviously raises methodological objections to which we return later in this chapter. Despite their limitations, self-report studies provide information on crime and criminals that can be gathered using no other method. We have already noted the strengths and weakness of recorded crime data and of victimisation surveys. What neither of these two sources provides is information – directly from the participants themselves – about offending behaviour, the personal and social characteristics of offenders and the factors that correlate statistically with offending. Self-report surveys have produced some controversial findings. In particular, they have suggested that class and race differences usually observed in official records are either absent or much reduced in self-reported offending.

British self-report offending studies paid no attention to the question of ethnicity until the Home Office study *Young People and Crime* (Bowling, Graham and Ross 1994, Graham and Bowling 1995). Based on a sample of 1,700 14–25 year olds and a random sample of 800 young people from ethnic minority communities, this study found that white and black respondents had very similar rates of offending (44 per cent and 43 per cent respectively), while Asian respondents – Indians 30 per cent, Pakistanis 28 per cent and Bangladeshis 13 per cent – had significantly lower rates (see table 4.3). The pattern is broadly consistent for both property, expressive and violent offences. The second sweep of the self-reported offending survey, now incorporated into the British Crime Survey, produced very similar findings (Flood Page *et al.* 2000).

The British Crime Survey has included reported drug use since its inception in 1982 (see table 4.4). The general picture, consistent across each of the studies, is that rates of drug use tend to be roughly similar

Table 4.3 Young people (aged 14–25) who said that they had 'ever' committed a specified list of criminal offences (per cent)

Offence	White %	Black %	Indian %	Pakistani %	Bangladeshi[3] %
Property offences	39	38*ns*	25*	24*	12*
Violent offences	19	25*ns*	13*ns*	18*ns*	7*
Expressive offences[1]	22	21*ns*	12*	16*	7*
All offences[2]	44	43*ns*	30*	28*	13*
Number interviewed	1,500	202	208	205	104

Source: Graham and Bowling (1995: 15 table 2.3)
Notes: [1] Graffiti, vandalism and arson
[2] Excluding drug use
[3] 'Other Asian' and 'other' ethnic groups were excluded from the analysis.
ns = non significant at $p < 0.05$; *$p < 0.001$. Tests of statistical significance between white respondents and ethnic minority respondents assess the extent to which results could have occurred as a results of random fluctuations in the data. Non-significant results indicate that apparent differences are insufficiently robust to be relied upon.

among white and black respondents, and rather lower among those of Asian origin. What is striking about these surveys is not that rates of drug usage among ethnic minorities are particularly low, but that rates of usage among the white *majority* population are strikingly high. Because black and Asian people make up a small minority of the general population, and because their likelihood of ever using drugs is lower than whites, the overwhelming majority – 95 per cent at least – of the estimated 6 million drug users in England and Wales are white.

What can account for the fact that these figures depart so strikingly from the popular stereotype of black people as the predominant drug-using group in Britain? There is evidence that there has been an historical change in patterns of drug use. The British Crime Survey analysis by Ramsay and Percy suggest that African/Caribbeans in the 30–59 age bracket had slightly higher rates of drug use than whites: 25 per cent compared with 22 per cent. Among those aged 16–29, the picture was reversed: 34 per cent of blacks compared with 43 per cent whites had tried drugs in the previous year. Based on these results, they conclude that the picture of black people having the highest levels of drug use is 'passing into history' (1996: 59).

Problems with self-report offending data

The consistent findings from self-report drug use and offending surveys add weight to the argument that official crime data exaggerate the extent of offending among ethnic minority communities. However, there are

Table 4.4 Respondents 'ever taken' cannabis, by ethnic origin (per cent): Home Office funded self-report studies 1992–8

	White	Black	Asian Indian	Asian Pakistani	Asian Bangladeshi	Number interviewed
1992 BCS (Mott and Mirrlees-Black 1995) all ages	24	26		7		2,370
1992 Four Cities Survey, (Leitner, Shapland and Wiles 1993)						
Bradford main sample (all ages)	14			3		1,004
Bradford booster sample (aged 16–29)	42			9		231
Lewisham main sample (all ages)	23	25		–		1,139
Lewisham booster sample (aged 16–29)	51	34		–		233
1994 Young people and crime (Graham and Bowling, 1995) aged 14–25	34	22	18	10	6	2,237
1994 BCS (Ramsay and Percy 1996) aged 16–29	34	27	13		12	3,377
all ages	21	23	7		9	11,167
1996 BCS (Ramsay and Spiller 1997) aged 16–29	38	26	18		11	3,676
all ages	23	18	10		8	12,618

weaknesses in the self-report method that have implications for the attempt to make comparisons between different ethnic groups. Minor offending lends itself more easily than serious offending to measurement in self-report surveys. Perhaps acts of minor violence and petty theft are evenly spread across all ethnic groups, while the most serious forms of offending – like wounding and robbery – are more concentrated among particular groups. Although offending is widely spread across the population (one in three men and one in 12 women will be convicted of a crime before they are 40 years old), the most serious, high-frequency and persistent offenders comprise only a tiny minority of the population. The most at-risk populations (for example, those in the custody of the prison service or local authority secure units, in care homes, the homeless and those who are never at home to answer surveys) are either indirectly 'under-sampled' or deliberately excluded from such surveys.

Response rates in *Young People and Crime* were slightly *higher* among ethnic minority groups than whites, showing no great reluctance to participate in the survey. However, ethnic minority respondents had generally lower rates of completion of the sections on drug use and offending, a tendency also found in the British Crime Survey analysis of drug use. This raises the question of why people refused or otherwise failed to answer questions on drug use and offending. Did they see the question as irrelevant or were they unwilling to admit these activities? If the latter were the case, the ethnic minority sample would be skewed towards a less delinquent population than the white sample. Although we cannot answer this question based on British data, attempts to compare the validity of the method among different ethnic groups have been made in the USA and the Netherlands.

Hindelang, Hirschi and Weis (1981) reached the view that the self-report method is appropriate for 'white, in-school, not seriously delinquent population' and 'least valid among those who are black, male and officially delinquent' (Coleman and Moynihan 1996: 56). In Hindelang, Hirschi and Weis's study, the latter group were three times less likely than others to admit to researchers offences already known to the police. This question of differential validity – which seriously undermines attempts to assess ethnic differences in offending – was addressed in a study comparing self-reported offending rates among young people in the Netherlands who were of 'indigenous' Dutch, Surinamese, Moroccan and Turkish origin (Junger 1989; see also Bowling 1990, Junger 1990). On the basis of back-checking self-reports against 'official police contacts', Junger concluded that respondents of Turkish and Moroccan origin were much less likely to admit delinquency than those of Surinamese origin or the 'indigenous' (that is, white) Dutch. The study had numerous conceptual, methodological and analytical weaknesses, but the most fundamental problem with validating self-report data against arrest or 'police contact' data is that the latter is not, itself, an acceptable measure of delinquency (Bowling 1990: 484–6). Arrest data are bound to *exclude* the vast majority of offences which are undetected and, as a consequence, nothing can be said about the validity of the self-reported offending among those who have had no contact with the police. In other words, this method of 'validation' does not resolve the problem of measuring the extent of *undetected* offences. Second, arrest data may *include* contacts that have been incorrectly defined as criminal. As Junger (1990) herself pointed out, it could be that 'because blacks are more often unjustly arrested; considering themselves innocent, they will tend not to mention the "delinquent" behaviour that has made them known to the police' (Junger 1989: 274, citing Elliott 1982).

Assessments of differential validity focus attention on a more general weakness in self-report studies. For example, in Junger's (1989) study only a small proportion of respondents *of all ethnic origins* admitted offending behaviour, or having contact with the police. Even among white Dutch only 38 per cent of respondents admitted having contact with the police in the previous year (compared with, respectively, 28 per cent, 20 per cent and 9 per cent of those of Moroccan, Surinamese and Turkish origin). Although admission rates in this study vary by ethnic group, this must be seen in the context of an overall unwillingness to admit offences to the interviewers. It may be acceptable to find that 10–20 per cent of respondents fail to admit known offences (or known contacts with the police), but what should be made of a method of estimating offending where 'concealment' rates varied from 62 per cent to 91 per cent? This magnitude of concealment casts doubt on the validity of the method because differences or similarities in rates of self-reported offending can always be countered by the charge that such results are, themselves, due to a greater degree of dishonesty among ethnic minorities. This is a double-bind from which there is no escape.

Self-report data cannot, with any finality, resolve the question of whether or not there are differences in offending rates between social groups. As Junger (1990: 493) put it, we have 'no confidence in either self-report or arrest data' in establishing ethnic differences in offending. But it would be a dangerous error to conclude by default that 'arrest data probably provide the best indicator for comparing criminal involvement between ethnic groups' (Junger 1989: 273). Judgements about the validity of arrest data can only be made against an independent criterion. Indeed, without examining police practices, a 'discrepancy' between police contact data and self-reported offending suggests a *prima facie* case that arrest data are an *invalid* measure of delinquency. As Bowling argued:

> even with perfectly equitable police officers, the relationship between 'all crime' and arrests will not be linear. There will be certain types of crime (such as that which is easily solved or which is revealed by the police themselves) in which arrests are more often made. There will be certain locations (such as those with a reputation for 'criminality') in which the police will focus their activity. And there will be social groups (such as those

most often on the street, those who live in the most policed locations, those who are easily identifiable and who are the focus of proactive policing) who will more often come into contact with the police.

(1990: 487)

As we show in chapter 6, it is apparent that police officers are not 'perfectly equitable'; on the contrary, there is good evidence that individual, cultural and institutional racism have the consequence of focusing police activity and criminalising decisions on to some groups and not others.

It is clear that there are fundamental problems in assessing the 'real' rate of offending, comparing one ethnic group with another, perhaps even making such an enterprise unworkable (Keith and Murji 1993: 118). Partly because of these difficulties and partly in a spirit of shallow pragmatism, some authors have adapted the approach of 'taking "black criminality" as given and then apologising for it on the grounds of racial deprivation' (ibid.: 116–18). This, according to Keith and Murji serves to reify – to fix and 'naturalise' – images of black people as criminal. Others, as we have described above, focus exclusively on discrimination and the social construction of black criminality.

Controlling for demographic and social factors

One further problem with analysing official statistics and victimisation surveys is that factors other than ethnicity *per se* may contribute to the greater risks of victimisation, offending and coming to the attention of the authorities. As the British Crime Survey authors put it, higher risks of violent crime and household property theft for minority groups are 'rooted in demographic, social and area factors known to be related to greater vulnerability to crime' (Mayhew, Aye Maung and Mirrlees-Black 1993: 87).

Data from the 1991 Census, and more recently from the Labour Force Survey, show that the ethnic minority communities are, in general, younger than the white majority, though this differs markedly for specific groups (see chapter 1). In the 1988 British Crime Survey, for example, 25 per cent of the white people sampled at random were aged 16–30, compared with 44 per cent of African/Caribbeans, 37 per cent of Indians, 47 per cent of Pakistanis and 40 per cent of Bangladeshis. Partly for sampling reasons, and partly because of the history of patterns of migration and settlement, the British Crime Survey also found that while African/Caribbeans and whites were split more or less 50/50 by sex, males formed between 56 per cent and 64 per cent of the Asian samples. These demographic data would suggest that significant demographic differences between black, white and Asian populations account, in part, for the differences in risks of offending, victimisation and contact with the criminal justice system. Since ethnic differences in the age structure of the population are not a direct product of discrimination, age and sex need to be controlled so that like can be compared with 'like'.

The ethnic minority population of England and Wales clearly differs from the white population in terms of its demographic profile and there are also some striking differences in its social and economic profile. Again, a more fine-grained description of offending and victimisation qualifies the 'headline' risk rates. For example, crime rates differ by geography (especially between urban and rural areas), and even within areas that are similarly urbanised, the most disadvantaged areas tend to have the highest rates. Ethnic minority populations live overwhelmingly in urban areas and in the most impoverished of those areas. For example, while only 17 per cent of the white people sampled in the 1988 British Crime Survey lived in 'inner-city' areas, this was true of 40 per cent of Asians and 70 per cent of African/Caribbeans. More importantly for the current discussion, white people were much less likely to live in areas where there was a high risk of crime victimisation than their black counterparts. It is clear that the 'geographically disadvantaged' position of black and Asian communities places them at risk of offending as well as victimisation. Is it reasonable to 'control' for this as a neutral fact, since these patterns are the result of racial discrimination in employment and housing markets (See chapter 2 pp 44–51).

People from ethnic minorities are also at greater risk of victimisation because of the types of employment in which they are concentrated (for example, health service, public transport, catering and low-status work involving regular contact with the public). Ekblom and Simon's (1988) study of crime against Asian-run small shops found that 80 per cent had experienced some form of crime, including 33 per cent who had windows smashed, 28 per cent who had suffered threats, 27 per cent who were verbally abused and 24 per cent who had experienced snatch thefts from their till (Ekblom and Simon 1988). Aye Maung and Mirrlees-Black found that, although levels of verbal abuse against workers were similar for African/Caribbeans and whites, when ethnic minority workers were verbally abused about half the incidents involved racial insults (1994: v).

This analysis suggests that higher than expected rates of offending, victimisation and contact with the criminal justice process among ethnic minorities are less striking when comparisons are made among ethnic minorities and whites sharing similar social and economic conditions, but is it justifiable to compare 'like with like'? Does it make sense – when attempting to assess risks of crime among different ethnic groups – to 'control' for such factors as area of residence, income, class, etc? Is it justifiable to compare only between 'similarly placed' black, white and Asian people? Or does the social fact that, typically, they are not 'similarly placed' make such comparisons unhelpful? In our view, the answer to this is 'it depends'. That is, *some factors* should be taken account of in *some circumstances*; the key question being to what extent is the factor being 'controlled for', even in part, itself the result of racial discrimination? For most purposes it is clearly necessary that comparisons are made between groups of the same age and sex. In some circumstances it is appropriate to discuss people who live in the same areas and hold the same jobs; in other circumstances it is not. We take our cue from Susan Smith who warns that

> attempts to isolate the contribution of race, or racial discrimination ... by filtering out the contribution of class, housing tenure, language, education and so on ... make a theoretical error by trying to take away the very factors through which race is constituted [and] an empirical error by inferring the extent of racial discrimination without exposing the policy mechanisms and institutional practices that are responsible for it.
>
> (Smith 1989: 22)

Conclusion: searching for a chimera? The end of the road for attempts to uncover the 'real' rate of crime among different ethnic groups

Rather than hoping that the question of ethnic differences in offending can be resolved by empirical data or prioritising one form of data over another, it seems more sensible to observe that different things are being 'measured' at each point. Official data measure, with reasonable accuracy, the product of the actions of criminal justice agents – to stop/search, arrest or imprison – but they cannot measure crime, 'out there' as it were. Victims' reports of those who offend against them show that offending and victimisation are largely intra-ethnic. However, because most crimes are committed by people who are unknown to (and largely *unseen* by) their victims, we have no way of knowing about 'volume' property crime except self-report studies based on offenders' own admissions. These attempts to discover a 'real' rate of offending among different ethnic groups produce a picture that contradicts criminal justice records, echoing the official view of 30 years ago that the African/Caribbean crime rate is much the same as that of the 'white' population and the rate for Asians is very much lower. Self-report surveys, like all methods, have flaws and at best are only getting part of the picture. The ultimate conclusion of our analysis of different ways of estimating 'ethnic differences' in offending is that there is no conclusive way in which this can be done. As Keith has put it:

> it is impossible to conceive of an objective empirical reality of 'Black crime' which can be investigated by social research. This is because criminality, a chameleon concept defined by the histories of legal whim and political fashion, is at once both social reality and emotive myth. Clearly, demographically concentrated both in social areas and economic classes structured by material deprivation, it is no surprise to find individuals from migrant minority backgrounds committing individual crimes. But this does not mean that 'Black crime' can be reified, subjected to scrutiny as a subject category in its own right, without reference to the broader social, political and moral context in which such scrutiny occurs.
>
> (Keith 1993: 278)

We may have to accept that we have reached a theoretical and methodological dead-end in the endeavour to answer: 'what is the "real" rate of offending among different ethnic groups?' It may, in any case, have been the wrong question. Criminalisation cannot be understood without an analysis of the routes by which people reach imprisonment; neither can the progression from deviant citizen to imprisoned criminal be understood without an analysis of policing practice, the operation of the courts and the experience of life behind bars. We examine the criminal justice process in chapters 6, 7 and 8. Before doing so, we turn our attention to ethnic minority communities' experience of racist violence.

Chapter 5

Racist violence

Although it has been observed that most crime in England is committed – unsurprisingly – by the white majority community, popular concern and scholarly attention have focused on the disproportionate rates of arrest and imprisonment among minority communities. As Russell (1998) suggests, a preoccupation with such concepts as 'black criminality' and 'black-on-black' crime has tended to obscure the extent of 'white-on-white' crime or 'white-on-minority' violence, to the extent that the very terms seem odd. A further consequence of the narrow focus of the 'race and crime debate' is that, until recently (and with some notable exceptions), criminologists have tended to ignore racist violence; that is violence specifically targeted against ethnic minority communities and incidents that are aggravated by racism and racial prejudice.

Historical research shows that ethnic minority communities have been the targets of verbal abuse, harassment and physical attacks – including crowd violence and murder – throughout their history in Britain (see Fryer 1984, Panayi 1996, Bowling 1999a). In the 1960s and 1970s, documentary evidence of its extent and nature was collected and published by community-based organisations around the country (Institute for Race Relations 1979, Bethnall Green and Stepney Trades Council 1978, Commision for Racial Equality 1979, Campaign Against Racism and Fascism 1981). This evidence, and the campaigns built to support the families of racist violence, led slowly to a recognition that racist violence was a serious problem facing minority communities (see Home Office 1981, Institute of Race Relations 1987). In the 1980s, public concern about racist violence increased in the US[1] (Hamm 1994), continental

---

[1] Of the recent cases in the US, the murder of James Byrd stands out as the epitome of a racist crime. On 7 June 1998, John William King, Shawn Berry and Lawrence Brewer, three roommates, were out driving when they encountered James Byrd hitchhiking. After offering him a lift, the three then beat Byrd unconscious, stripped him and chained him to the back of their pick-up truck

Europe[2] (Bjørgo and Witte 1993) and Britain (Bowling 1999a) which led to the development of new directions in research and public policy. During the 1990s, as a result of a number of well-publicised incidents, this concern about racist violence was heightened in numerous places. (See Macpherson 1999, and also Cathcart 1999, Norton-Taylor 1999, Bowling 1999a).

Above all, the murder of Stephen Lawrence and the subsequent police investigation has come to represent the experience of many victims of racist violence in Britain. Rather than being an isolated case it is entirely consistent with the extensive empirical and documentary evidence gathered over the last four decades. The remainder of this chapter reviews the literature on racist violence in England and points tentatively towards some explanations for the patterns that emerge. We also examine some of the individual, community and statutory responses that have developed.

The extent and nature of racist victimisation

In the 1980s the police and Home Office began to keep records of 'racial incidents' since when they have increased sharply (see figure 5.1). Recorded crime statistics are, as is well known, an unreliable and sometimes misleading measure of actual experiences of crime (Coleman and Moynihan 1996). Such statistics are even less useful as a means of capturing the process of victimisation or the experience of being safe or unsafe. Nonetheless, they remain one of the most frequently cited measures of crime and police effectiveness and deserve critical scrutiny. Between the year ending March 1998 and March 1999, recorded racial incidents in England and Wales increased by two-thirds from 13,878 to 23,049 and then doubled to 47,814 in 1999/2000. By any standard, this is a remarkable increase and one that has been interpreted in conflicting ways. One view is that this indicates a serious increase in the extent of violent racism. Another view is that the rise in recorded incidents reflects an increasing

---

and dragged him for two and a half miles until his head and right arm were ripped from his body. At the subsequent trial, it was found that King had been involved, for some years previously, in racist extremism and was tattooed with Nazi SS symbols and a depiction of a black man being lynched. All three men were found guilty. King and Brewer were sentenced to death by lethal injection while Berry – who had no history of racist activities – was sentenced to life in prison without the possibility of parole for 40 years.

[2] In the early 1990s in Germany, for example, there was a spate of arson attacks against asylum seekers' hostels and the homes of people from ethnic minorities. Of these crimes, the most atrocious was an arson attack on 23 November 1992 in Molln by two neo-Nazi skinheads in which three members of the Arslan family, of Turkish origin, were burned to death (Hamm 1994).

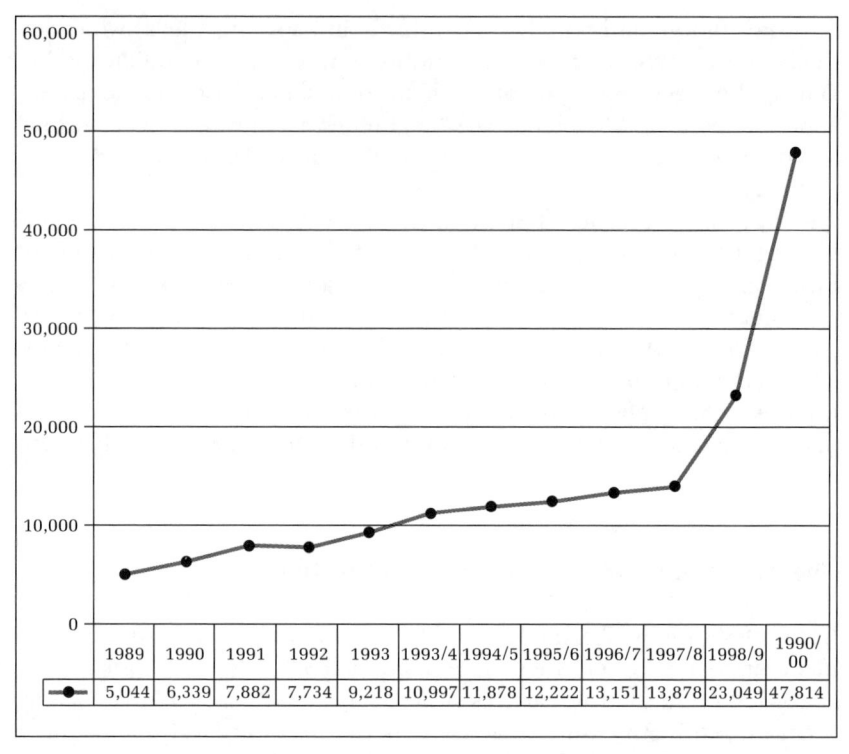

Figure 5.1 Racist incidents recorded by the police, England and Wales 1989–2000
Source: Home Office s.95 report

1989	1990	1991	1992	1993	1993/4	1994/5	1995/6	1996/7	1997/8	1998/9	1990/00
5,044	6,339	7,882	7,734	9,218	10,997	11,878	12,222	13,151	13,878	23,049	47,814

willingness on the part of victims to report incidents and for police officers to be more compliant in recording them. The police may feel that the statistics show some hope that confidence is returning, but they are probably not much comfort to actual or potential victims, who might reasonably conclude that, at best, they face no lesser risk of victimisation today than they did two years ago (Institute of Race Relations 2001). The 'campaign' of nail bomb attacks by David Copeland and new instances of serious racially aggravated crime being reported in the media mean that the fear of racist violence has probably not diminished (see box 5.1).

Recent Home Office Research has shed some light on patterns of racially motivated incidents recorded by the police (Maynard and Read 1997). Based on a survey of all police forces in England and Wales, the authors found that there was wide variation in what was actually recorded and counted as racially motivated (see also Sibbitt 1997, Bowling 1999a). Where the type of crime was known 38 per cent of incidents comprised verbal abuse, 21 per cent assault and 20 per cent damage to property. Only 2 per cent were recorded as serious crime. However, where racially motivated incidents are recorded as serious crime – such as 'grievous

> **Box 5.1 Nail bombs in London, 1999**
>
> In April 1999, David Copeland detonated bombs in Brixton, Brick Lane and Old Compton Street, Soho, the best-known centres of, respectively, black, Asian and gay communities in London. In the bombing of the Admiral Duncan pub in Old Compton Street 79 people were seriously injured and John Light, Nick Moore and Andrea Dykes (who was pregnant at the time) were killed. Copeland was recognised by one of his co-workers from CCTV images shown on television and he was arrested within hours of the Soho bomb. When police officers went to his home they found two swastika flags on the walls of his room, a collection of Nazi memorabilia, bomb-making equipment and his membership card of the far right National Socialist Movement. During interviews with the police he admitted that he had specifically chosen the targets of his nail bombs to spark a racial war that would cause white people to vote for the British National Party. He told police that he was a Nazi who believed in a white master race, that he did not like black or Asian people and that he wanted them out of the country. He said that he thought the British people had a right to ethnic cleansing, 'like the Serbs'. It later transpired that Copeland had a long history of involvement with racist extremism including the British National Party (*Searchlight*). On conviction he received six life sentences.
>
> *Sources*: *Evening Standard*, 5 June 2000.
> *Guardian*, 6 June 2000.
> *Job*, 30 June 2000.

bodily harm' or murder – they are frequently not recorded as racial incidents. Their categorisation as a specific type of serious crime overrides and negates their definition by the police as 'racial' (see also Bowling 1999a: 151–4). To some extent this was what happened in the Stephen Lawrence murder.

The police forces that record the largest number of racially motivated incidents tend to be in metropolitan areas where there are significant ethnic minority communities. After calculating the number of racially motivated incidents per 1,000 ethnic minority population, however, Maynard and Read (1997) found that three provincial forces in the north of England had the highest victimisation rates of 14 or more per 1,000 black or Asian population. Differences in reporting and recording practices dog attempts to make comparisons of the extent and nature of racist violence across time and space. Nonetheless, this finding supports earlier research showing that where people from ethnic minorities make up only a small proportion of the local population, they are at greater risk of victimisation than their counterparts in cosmopolitan areas of towns and cities (see Smith 1989, Hesse *et al.* 1992, Sampson and Phillips 1992, 1996, Bowling 1999a).

Survey estimates of racist violence

Like any other form of crime, racial 'incidents' recorded by the police reflect only a small proportion of all those that occur – thus concealing the so-called 'dark figure'. In order to overcome the inadequacies of police records, a number of local crime surveys since the early 1980s have attempted to make quantitative estimates of racist violence. Each of these have identified low levels of reporting to the police (see, for example, Brown 1984; Jones, Maclean and Young 1986). In Bowling's study in the London Borough of Newham, 21 per cent of black women, 19 per cent of Asian men, 18 per cent of Asian women and 17 per cent of black men had experienced some form of racist victimisation (1999a: 196). A small proportion of white people – 8 per cent of men and 7 per cent of women – also said that they had been racially victimised (ibid.). In this locality no more than 5 per cent of racial incidents were recorded by the police (ibid., see also Saulsbury and Bowling 1991).

Every sweep of the British Crime Survey (1988 to 1996) has found that more than one-third of assaults directed against Asians and blacks were thought by respondents to be racially motivated, as were about half of the incidents involving threats. The use of racist language was the main reason given by both black and Asian respondents for thinking that the incident was racially motivated. Using British Crime Survey data for 1988 and 1992 combined, FitzGerald and Hale (1996) found that of a national sample, 4 per cent of blacks, 5 per cent of Indians and around 8 per cent of Pakistanis and Bangladeshis had been the victims of racially motivated offences in the previous year. Extrapolating from British Crime Survey victimisation rates, the Home Office calculated that there were about 143,000 incidents of crime and threats against black and Asian people which were thought to have been motivated by racism in 1997 (Percy 1998, see also Aye Maung and Mirrlees-Black 1994). This represented 15 per cent of the estimated total of 984,000 incidents against them altogether. Around 41,000 of these incidents were *reported* to the police, compared with the 12,222 *recorded* by the police that year. Expressed as a proportion, 29 per cent of the incidents are *reported to* the police, and about 8 per cent are *recorded by* the police.

The most recent British Crime Survey indicates that the number of incidents considered by the victim to have been racially motivated fell from 382,000 in 1995 to 280,000 in 1999 (Home Office 2000c: 49). Taking only those incidents directed against ethnic minorities, the number of racially motivated incidents rose from 130,000 to 143,000 between 1991 and 1995 and then fell to 98,000 in 1999 (Aye Maung and Mirrlees-Black 1994, Percy 1998, Home Office 2000c). These findings lend weight to the view that the recent sharp rise in police recorded incidents reflects increases in public reporting and police recording practices (Home Ofice 2000c: 49, cf. Institute of Race Relations 2001: 13).

The process of racist victimisation and its impact

Estimating the 'real' extent of violent racism is an exercise fraught with conceptual and methodological problems (Bowling 1993a, 1999a: 150–68, Hesse *et al.* 1992). Not only is the attempt to count so many complex events occurring across time and space difficult, it is in some ways misconceived. Considering the patterns of intimidation and harassment that provide part of the context for serious violence, it becomes clear that the issues of safety and perceptions of safety cannot realistically be 'measured'. Feminist research on violence against women has also observed that the experience of sexual assault or domestic violence can be better understood as a continuum, connecting 'everyday' abuse with extreme acts of violence (for example, Kelly 1987, Stanko 1990). Similarly, conceiving of violent racism as a process allows connections to be made between the racist abuse at one end of the spectrum and murder at the other. Studies have confirmed the pattern of repeat victimisation among victims of racist violence (for example, Sampson and Phillips 1992, Phillips and Sampson 1998).

This context also helps to explain fear of crime within ethnic minority communities (Genn 1988, Pearson *et al.* 1989, Feagin and Sikes 1994, Bowling 1999a). On a number of dimensions, people from ethnic minority communities are more fearful than those from white communities, and this is particularly the case in relation to fear of violent racism. The British Crime Survey probes further to attempt to measure people's perceptions of safety and unsafety. Percy (1998) shows that on the street, and especially at home alone at night, people from ethnic minorities feel less safe than white people and it seems likely that feelings of 'unsafety' affect individual freedom of movement. For example, people from ethnic minorities (Pakistanis and Bangladeshis in particular) avoid going out at night through fear of crime, avoid walking near certain types of people, are always accompanied when walking out after dark and avoid certain places or events (such as football matches, nightclubs, theatres or pubs) because they fear crime or violence (see chapter 4). Although the relationship between fear, crime and victimisation is a complex one, fear of 'ordinary crime' among people from ethnic minority communities is fundamentally shaped by their *fear of racist victimisation*. Although this is not a frequent occurrence for most people, pernicious racist abuse does sometimes precede extreme acts of violence, as exemplified in the case of Stephen Lawrence. This experience provides a backdrop to the lives of many people from ethnic minorities in Britain today.

Police records and victimisation surveys, already referred to, are the two most common methods of quantifying the extent of violent racism. Although this measurement has its value, alternative sources often enable richer and more meaningful information to be collected. Among these alternative sources are qualitative techniques (for example, Chahal 1999); case studies employing mixed methods (for example, Bowling 1999a);

journalistic accounts (for example, Rose 1996, Bufford 1991); records of local monitoring groups (for example, Newham Monitoring Project 1991); and public inquiries, such as that carried out by Macpherson (1999) into the events surrounding the murder of Stephen Lawrence (see also Hesse *et al.* 1993, Institute of Race Relations 2001). Indeed, like sexual harassment and domestic violence against women, the issue of racist violence emerged on to the public agenda only as a result of the work of activists campaigning for victims' rights who drew, for their evidence, on case studies and documentary methods. There are, of course, some methodological limitations to using these sources. Journalistic accounts may be unrepresentative while reports of monitoring groups are, by nature, partisan. Nonetheless both are often richer, more detailed and more contextualised than academic sources. Similarly, public inquiries provide the opportunity to learn about the way in which individuals and organisations think about problems. By documenting the collective experience of thousands of people who have experienced such racist violence, greater insight into the victims' perspective has been gained.

We can now say with confidence that racist violence affects a considerable proportion of the ethnic minority communities on an enduring basis, that serious and mundane incidents are interwoven to create a threatening environment which undermines their personal safety and freedom of movement. What is now required is a shift away from the victimological perspective to an analysis of the characteristics of offenders, the social milieu in which violence is fostered, and the process by which it becomes directed against people from ethnic minorities.

Racist offending: from profiling to explanation

The focus on victims has tended to obscure the importance of researching racist offenders. Moreover, there has been a reluctance to examine racist offenders partly, perhaps, because it risks appearing to 'understand' racist behaviour rather than simply to 'condemn' it (Rose 1996: 73–86, Bowling 1999a: 306). Racist offenders have no allies in the political mainstream – doubly condemned because of their violence and their racist expressions. Police and politicians rarely get beyond epithets – 'yobs', 'louts' and 'thugs' – to describe such offenders. Even criminologists have frequently opted for shallow 'theoreotyping', constructing academic theories out of common stereotypes (Rose 1996, Pitts 1993, Bowling 1999a: 305). There has been a renaissance in research on offending and offenders in recent years, but there are still few studies that seek to explore racist offenders' backgrounds, experiences and motives (see, for example, Bufford 1991 and Webster 1997). And yet, examining the offender's perspective is critical for developing ways of responding to violent racism.

Until recently, our knowledge of racist offenders relied principally on information from the victim. Victims' accounts suggest that most of the people committing acts of violent racism are men and are young adults – aged between 16 and 25 – though young children and older adults have been reported (Mayhew, Elliott and Dowds 1989, Aye Maung and Mirrlees-Black 1994, Sibbitt 1997, Bowling 1999a). Aye Maung and Mirrlees-Black (1994), using 1992 British Crime Survey data, found that three-quarters of Asian victims of violent incidents (wounding, common assault and robbery) and threats involved more than one offender and two-fifths involved four or more. Nine out of ten Asian council tenants surveyed by Bowling (1999a) who had been victimised were attacked by more than one offender. In instances of violence or threats reported to the British Crime Survey, which were thought to be racially motivated, victims nearly always cited white offenders.

Sibbitt's (1997) qualitative study of the perpetrators of racist harassment adds the socio-economic dimension to this profile, using police records, case studies and interviews. Sibbitt found that the perpetrators' racist views were shared by the communities to which they belonged, and offenders saw this as legitimating their action. Thus, wider communities not only 'spawn' perpetrators but they reinforce their behaviour by not condemning it. Sibbitt argues that united attitudes towards ethnic minorities serve to focus individuals' grievances and sense of injustice on an external scapegoat. Frequently, racist offenders react to what they see as preferential treatment or access to scarce social and economic resources, such as housing, employment and education. This is epitomised in the comment made by a woman cited in Sibbitt (1997: 102): 'They refuse to learn English – the kids have to get a special teacher in. *My son could do with a special teacher, but he won't get it, will he?*'

The evidence that violent racism is concentrated in areas of multiple deprivation points to the relevance of economic and social factors. However, *per capita* rates of victimisation suggest that racist violence also afflicts rural, suburban and relatively prosperous areas as well as blighted inner-city locales (see also Husbands 1993). Moreover, the evidence for a relationship between economic changes and violent crime in general is mixed. Field (1990) found that violent crime increases during periods of *increased* consumption and declines during periods of economic downturn. The economic scapegoating of ethnic minorities is one of five main theoretical approaches to explaining why ethnic minorities are the targets of violence, directed against individuals, their homes, places of worship or entertainment, and at other aspects of social and cultural life.

A second popular explanation contends that levels of hostility and violence are related to the size of the minority population, or to increases in its size over a short period of time (Bjørgo and Witte 1993). In 1958, for example, riots in Nottingham and Notting Hill were said by Labour and Conservative politicians to have been caused by the arrival of 'too many' black people, which caused resentment among the 'indigenous' white population resulting in a violent backlash. The 'upsurge' in racist violence in Germany in the early 1990s was blamed directly by many commentators on the arrival of a 'flood' of asylum seekers. In our view, this reasoning is flawed for several reasons. Historically, minority populations have come under attack in Britain even when their numbers were tiny – in the thousands or even mere hundreds, as was the case for the riots of 1919 (Jenkinson 1996). In Britain today, racist violence is also prevalent where black and Asian people make up only a small minority – sometimes only 1 or 2 per cent – of local populations. The 'numbers thesis' also fails to explain violence against Jewish people, their property, places of worship and burial, who comprise 0.5 per cent of the UK population. Although actual numbers, or even increases in numbers, may not provide an explanation for violent racism, it may be that the *meaning* attached to these changes does. Research has indicated that racist violence is common in neighbourhoods where black and Asian people make up a small but *increasing* minority of a neighbourhood and where community attitudes define this as a problem. Authors including Husbands (1982), Smith (1989) and Hesse *et al.* (1992) point to the relationship between racist victimisation and white territorialism and exclusionism. White neighbourhoods may be maintained as '[t]he prospect of violent intimidation is a strong disincentive to black households who might otherwise wish to move away from the poor properties in which they are overrepresented' (Smith 1989: 161–2).

The attempt to explain the extent of violent racism as a reaction to 'the numbers' is consistent with the assumption that policies to reduce the number of immigrants would reduce the extent of violence targeted against them. However, the empirical evidence from several contexts suggests that racist violence has increased dramatically *after* governments have advocated or implemented measures to restrict immigration and asylum. Among the periods of most ferocious racist violence in the UK was 1981 in the immediate aftermath of the 1981 Nationality Act which only ended 'primary immigration' from former colonies in the Caribbean and Africa and also severely restricted the rights of dependants to join families settled in Britain. In Sweden, a wave of racist violence started in May 1990 five months after the government tightened its liberal asylum policy (Bjørgo and Witte 1993: 7; Bjørgo 1993). In Germany, racist attacks and riots intensified dramatically after the government initiated a debate on reducing the numbers of asylum seekers coming into Germany (Bjørgo and Witte 1993: 7–8, Atkinson 1993).

Theories of culture comprise a third approach to explaining racist violence. Common in media representations of racist violence are depictions of racism as an aspect of 'national character'. Goldhagen argues that the holocaust in Germany must be seen as a specifically German phenomenon, rooted in the pursuit of 'German national political goals' (1996: 7). His approach is to 'explain the culture's constitution, its idiosyncratic patterns of practice, and its collective projects and products' (1996: 15).

England's history of racism is very different from Germany's. However, the history of chattel slavery, colonialism and support for South African apartheid, as well as the configuration of contemporary racism, might suggest that racist violence has a specifically English cultural variant.

A fourth approach draws on the evidence that racist violence is associated with the consumption of alcohol, either as a direct result of intoxication (by lowering inhibitions) or in the social context of drinking, such as crowd behaviour after bars have closed (Tuck 1989, Field 1990: 8). Although it seems likely that alcohol can be seen as a contributory factor, the 'drunken pranks' explanation is frequently used to suggest that incidents are unconnected with racism. Some police officers have gone to ridiculous lengths to redefine racist incidents as merely drunken hooliganism (see Graeff 1989: 131, Pearson *et al.*, 1989: 128). Nonetheless, heavy consumption of alcohol is a typical trait in diverse forms of violent racism. Anti-Jewish pogroms in Russia at the turn of the century (Klier 1993: 133–5), riots against Italian immigrants in France in the 1890s; numerous instances of racist violence in Britain, fire bombings of asylum centres in Scandinavia and Germany in the 1990s, all appear to have alcohol as a contributory factor (Bjørgo 1993: 35–6, 41–2). However, the finding that offenders are often under the influence of alcohol can be misinterpreted to mean that no further explanation is necessary. Alcohol should be seen as only one means for overcoming inhibitions once a situation arises. As Bjørgo and Witte (1993: 10) put it, 'even if an act of violence is perpetrated under the influence of alcohol, this certainly does not mean that it may not also be influenced by racist motives'.

Although the activities of extreme right-wing organisations[3] and their links to ordinary communities are well documented in numerous contexts, this fifth theoretical approach has rarely been used to analyse the experiences of ethnic minority victims in the UK. It is evident that many aspects of the ideology, language and practices of explicitly racist or extreme right-wing groupings are shared in common across Europe and the US. Lööw (1993), for example, interviewed members of the Swedish 'white power networks', and found that the language used within these networks is a mixture of national socialist terminology of the 1930s and the contemporary code of the Ku Klux Klan and other American white supremacist groups. Themes identified by Lööw in Sweden – including a belief in 'ZOG (Zionist Occupational Government)', denial of the Nazi holocaust, defence of the 'white race' against its 'enemies' (communists, homosexuals, Jews, immigrants and anti-racists) – appear to be common to similar organisations in other Scandinavian countries, and in Germany,

---

[3] There are numerous such groups including National Front, Column 88, British National Party, Combat 18, the Ku Klux Klan, White Aryan Resistance, etc.; Choice; English Solidarity; International Third Position (see *Searchlight*, CARF, etc.)

the USA and Britain (Kaplan and Bjørgo 1998). The similarity between these organisations is uncanny: and at their centre is a notion of a specifically *European* superiority and supremacy (ibid.).

In several different national contexts there appears to be a relationship between the most extreme forms of racist politics and the manifestation of both explicitly racist attacks and apparently *apolitical* acts of violence directed at ethnic minorities. It seems that politically motivated racists are able to influence – directly and indirectly – groups of young people who hold 'anti-immigration' views or are in some other way sympathetic to racist ideology. Although international neo-Nazi groups appear to have

---

Box 5.2 Racism on the Internet

The emergence of the Internet has begun to transform the rules of engagement in the marketplace of ideas. The new 'virtual' world of cyberspace is accessible globally, and many 'hate groups' have embraced this new technology as a tool to disseminate racist ideology. The Internet has facilitated previously unconnected people, to construct, through its speed and freedom, 'virtual' communities. In short, it brings together multifarious 'subjects' with a shared interest in white supremacy that transcends not only regions, but national borders and physical continents.

Some implications of this are clear: not least the undoubted potential of the Internet to promulgate a very 'big' message. Tied to this is the Net's capability to expedite links both formally and informally between groups and individuals across the globe. These capabilities are not inconsequential. The Internet is used by millions, and is increasingly found in homes, which means that racist messages are able to penetrate to Internet users of *all* ages. This seems an intended ploy by some racist groups; the 'race hate' website *Stormfront*, for instance, has a web page specifically for 'Stormfront Kids'.

Concerns relating to racism on the Internet may have already begun to be realised. In July 1999 Benjamin Smith went on a weekend shooting spree, killing two and wounding nine others in Chicago, USA. Significantly, Smith belonged to the *World Church of the Creator*, a white supremacist organisation that utilised the Internet heavily to disseminate its message. Following the shootings the group has dismantled its web page. Racism on the Internet raises a plethora of challenging policy issues, most poignantly questions concerning the policing of the Net, which, as yet, has not been regulated and perhaps cannot be controlled. (Thanks to Alex Campbell)

For further reading see: Back, Keith and Solomos 1998. 'Racism on the Internet: Mapping Neo-Fascist Subcultures in Cyberspace', in Kaplan and Bjørgo (1998).

little centralised leadership or hierarchy, they do co-operate in a number of ways Erik Jensen (1993). The British National Party, for example, has participated with German neo-Nazi groups in paramilitary training. One crucial medium for spreading racist ideas and inciting violence is 'Oi-music' with extremely brutal, racist and violent lyrics and its associated youth culture. A recent development is the use of computer networks by neo-Nazi organisations and looser networks of racist supremacists. Internet newsgroups exist where racist ideology can be disseminated, Nazi memorabilia purchased and distributed, and information on bomb making, 'hit-lists' and hate campaigning circulated (see box 5.2).

One final approach to explaining racist violence that deserves a mention is a theory proposed by Beck and Tolnay (1995) which integrates some of the elements set out above. Their thesis is based on an analysis of violence towards African/Americans in the era of the white lynch mob and can be expressed as a formula. Beck and Tolnay argue that the potential for racist violence is the product of the extent of racist ideology, the permissiveness of the state response to racist violence and competition for scarce resources (such as economic wealth, political power and social status). If each of these necessary factors are present, all that remains is some form of 'triggering event' to lead to an outbreak of anti-black violence.

Responses to racist violence

Individual and community self-defence

Although survey research has focused on fear of crime, the most commonly reported reaction to crime is anger. Bowling's survey in East London for example, found that 70 per cent of the victims of racist violence felt anger, compared with shock (44 per cent), while comparatively few (27 per cent) felt fearful (1999a: 216). The personal experiences of racist violence are so diverse, however, that it would be difficult to describe the ways in which individual people, families and communities have sought to shield themselves from victimisation. At the most personal, measures have included moving away from more spacious or well-maintained property in localities where racist violence is prevalent to safer areas where property is poorer, and other strategies to avoid situations where 'trouble' may be found, such as particular pubs, or a particular area on football match days. Individuals also put in place situational crime prevention measures, such as shatterproof glass and fireproof letterboxes, to reduce the impact of violent racist victimisation (Bowling 1999a: 222).

In response to a collective experience of victimisation, communities have also acted together in self-defence. In the 1958 racist riots, black transport workers provided escorts to and from places of employment (Fryer 1984). In response to racist assault in the 1970s and 1980s youth movements were formed to oppose racist organisations, such as the

National Front, who were staging provocative marches through areas of ethnic minority settlement. These grew in the 1980s into a strong self-defence movement, focusing on racist attacks and racism in policing, and were linked politically to the anti-racist movement (Sivanandan 1982, Newham Monitoring Project 1991, Institute of Race Relations 1987).

The state response

Witte (1996) argues that the state response to racist violence has been very similar in France, the Netherlands and Britain. At first, governments ignored the problem entirely or denied the racist nature of the violence. When this was no longer possible because of the extent of demands among ethnic minority communities for protection, racism became linked with questions of 'immigration' and 'integration' of victimised communities while racial prejudice and violence are seen as 'side effects'. Because migration was seen as the dominant topic, state responses largely consisted of migration-*restricting* policies (such as the Nationality and Immigration Acts (Solomos 1993)) – what Witte refers to as 'excluding recognition' – and simultaneous anti-discrimination policies (such as the Race Relations Acts 1965, 1968 and 1976). The resulting 'two-faced' state response is a result of being caught between 'pressures from racist sentiments, parties and ideologies and pressures from anti-racism movements and ideologies' (Witte 1996: 201–3).

The British state officially recognised racist violence as a specific social problem in November 1981, with the publication of the Home Office report, *Racial Attacks* (Home Office 1981). Until then racially motivated attacks and harassment did not officially exist, nor was there a publicly stated police or government policy to deal with it. Two years later, this situation began to change. A range of governmental agencies – among them the House of Commons, Home Office, Metropolitan Police, Association of Chief Police Officers and the Greater London Council – each elevated racist violence to the status of 'urgent priority' (see Bowling 1999a, chapter 3). The subsequent years have seen a rapidly increasing policy debate about ways of tackling racially motivated crime. This has focused on policing, the 'multi-agency approach' and new legislation.

Racist crime and the law

Racist crime and harassment can be approached from a variety of legal angles. Section 70 of the Race Relations Act 1976 created a new offence of 'incitement to racial hatred' by enacting a new section (5A) of the 1936 Public order Act.[4] Prosecutions for this offence can only be instituted with

---

[4] Now consolidated by sections 18–23 of the 1986 Public Order Act.

the consent of the Attorney General and this has been a rare occurrence. A person commits an offence under the Act if he publishes written matter which is 'threatening, abusive or insulting ... where "having regard to all the circumstances, hatred is likely to be stirred up against any racial group in Great Britain by the matter or words in question" '. Under the 1965 Race Relations Act, proof was required of an *intent* to stir up racial hatred. Under current provisions, it is sufficient that the accused action was *likely*, in *all circumstances* to stir up racial hatred, an objective test.

Acts such as murder, assault and criminal damage are criminal offences and can be, and are, prosecuted as such, irrespective of racist 'motive' or 'aggravation'. There has, therefore, been a great deal of debate, which remains still, even in light of the passage of the Crime and Disorder Act 1998, as to whether there should be specific racially aggravated criminal offences. The judiciary has always enjoyed sentencing discretion and does have the option of sentence enhancement if they believe that the offence was motivated by racial hatred. This was never seen as particularly controversial. However, actually enshrining within the law specific offences with greater sentences because of their racial motivation is very different, and there are several arguments for either side of the debate.

It is arguable that the harm that racially motivated offences cause is much higher both to the individual victim and to their community. Actually being targeted for an attack because of a particular characteristic is very different to a victim being picked at random. This obviously creates feelings of hostility and tension, which would not be found in an 'ordinary' attack, making both the victim and the community feel vulnerable to future attacks. The higher sentence imposed on a racially motivated perpetrator may, therefore, be justified on utilitarian or consequentialist grounds, in that it is necessary to try and prevent future, greater harm. There is also a strong element of premeditation involved in crimes which have specific targets, and as the criminal law is intended to punish those who can be held morally culpable it may be that a higher moral culpability deserves a higher sentence.

A counter argument is that more severe punishment for these offences could lead to further victimisation of minority communities. These laws have emerged from the recognition that the state was failing to protect minority communities from widespread racist violence. This is not to deny that white people are sometimes the victims of racism nor that people from minority communities commit crimes against members of the white majority. It is clear that some crime is simply inter-ethnic (see chapter 4) and the question of attributing motive is notoriously complex. Nonetheless, the laws are intended to offer 'special protection' to people from black and Asian communities who are most frequently targets of white racism and are uniquely vulnerable to its impact. Some critics have argued that while such protection can be justified in principle, it could provoke a 'white racist backlash', particularly among those who already hold racist views or believe that minorities get preferential treatment.

There is the further possibility that the notions of racist motivation or aggravation are flexible enough to cast a wide spectrum of incidents involving people from ethnic minority communities (as both victims and suspected offenders) as 'racially aggravated'. It would be a cruel irony if laws against racism were used disproportionately against those whom they were intended to protect.

After years of high-profile cases involving racism in every aspect of British life it is clear to see why the state would want to be seen to be combating racism and enforcing justice. Unfortunately, laws in this area may be more symbolic than substantive. The Labour government pledged to make racially motivated crimes specific offences and did so with the Crime and Disorder Act 1998. Section 28 sets out the definition of 'racially aggravated', saying that an offence is racially aggravated if the offender 'demonstrates towards the victim of the offence hostility based on the victim's membership (or presumed membership) of a racial group' either 'immediately before or after' committing the offence, or if the 'offence is motivated (wholly or partly) by hostility towards members of a racial group based on their membership of that group'. Sections 29–32 state the offences which can be racially motivated, these are respectively: assaults under the Offences Against the Person Act 1861, Criminal Damage, Public Order Offences from the 1986 Act and harassment from the Protection from Harassment Act 1997.

The debate as to whether these aggravated offences should exist still continues and is likely to do so for some time. The Crime and Disorder Act 1998 has not been in place long enough for there to be any substantial research undertaken on its effect. Racist violence is obviously an area where something needs to be done and initiatives taken, but it remains to be seen whether such laws improve or exacerbate the situation or have no effect at all (Malik 1999, Institute of Race Relations 2001). Of course any law is only as effective as the mechanisms with which it is enforced, which leads us to a consideration of the police response.

The police response

A long string of reports on the police response to ethnic minorities in general and to the victims of violent racism have been highly critical of their treatment by the police (see Bowling 1999a for a review).

Early studies indicated that 'the police do not do enough to detect the everyday crimes that affect ordinary people' and went further to say that reporting crime sometimes invited police harassment, such as rough treatment, inappropriate questioning and immigration checks (Institute of Race Relations 1987). Such allegations continue to be made against the police today (Macpherson 1999).

The British Crime Survey found that satisfaction with the police response is significantly worse in dealing with reported racial incidents than with incidents in general (Percy 1998). In Bowling's (1999a) study of an area with a high rate of victimisation, just under one in ten people who reported to the police said they were very satisfied with the way in which the police handled the matter, while only 44 per cent were very or fairly satisfied. This contrasted sharply with comparable 1988 British Crime Survey figures of 22 per cent and 60 per cent respectively. This suggests that victims of racial incidents are much less likely to be satisfied with police service than victims of crime in general. The most common complaint among those who are dissatisfied with the police response was that the police did not 'do enough', that they failed to keep the victim informed and that they seemed not to be interested (Bowling 1999a: 235–8). Some respondents were very critical of the police response, pointing specifically to what they saw as police prejudice against blacks and Asians. One commented, 'They don't get the offenders. And if they catch them they don't charge them. If I was to offend someone like this the police would harass me instead of turning a blind eye which is what I feel they do in the case of white offenders. And the offenders feel they can do anything they like as they are always let off' (Bowling 1999a: 237). The same study found that only a very small minority – as few as 5 per cent – felt generally very satisfied with the way in which racist harassment was dealt with in their area and less than one-third were at all satisfied. This picture resonates with the documented experience of minority communities.

It is clear that the police continue to deny that racist violence is a problem and are, in practice, frequently unwilling to acknowledge the possibility of racist motives for many attacks even in the face of strong evidence. This can, in part, be explained by racist stereotyping by individual officers who define ethnic minorities as potential offenders rather than as potential victims. This was the experience of Duwayne Brooks in the aftermath of the murder of his friend Stephen Lawrence. There is evidence of widespread racist assumptions, prejudice and stereotyping in the culture of the police organisation too. As Bowling (1999a: 248–56) documents, some police officers empathise with the white man who 'resents having *his* area taken over', sympathise with white 'yobs' who feel that 'the system' which should be working for *them* is working also for black and Asian communities. Some think it is 'despicable' when Asian people speak their mother tongue, and believe that 'failing to adapt' to English customs (wearing traditional clothes, for example) renders them both 'threatening' and 'vulnerable'. These racist attitudes and prejudices are clearly reflected in the behaviour towards black and Asian victims, witnesses, suspects, employees and the general public.

The multi-agency partnership approach

One of the central planks of government policy on racist victimisation throughout the 1980s and 1990s was the 'multi-agency', or 'partnership approach' now mandatory under s.5 of the 1998 Crime and Disorder Act. The origins of this approach lie in the history of post-war British rational scientific management and grew partly from the belief, which strengthened during the 1970s and 1980s, that the police alone could not be expected to reduce crime (Weatheritt 1986, Bowling 1999a: 101–49, Crawford 1999). Since complex social problems like racism and violence are rooted in such contextual factors as housing, education and the consumption of alcohol (and its licensing), a multi-faceted approach involving the police, local government, community organisations, schools and other social institutions was called for. Despite the intuitive appeal of this idea, however, the research on the effectiveness of the multi-agency approach has been equivocal at best, and damning at worst (see, for example, Rein 1983, Weatheritt 1986, Bowling 1999a: 140–5). A multitude of problems beset attempts to develop a multi-agency approach to racist violence. Two Home Office funded projects, set up to develop the approach, both fell well short of their stated goals (Saulsbury and Bowling 1991, Bowling and Saulsbury 1993, Sampson and Phillips 1992, 1996, Phillips and Sampson 1998). Both studies identified major differences in the way in which organisations defined and understood the problem, a denial of the extent and nature of the problem, that victims were blamed for failing to 'integrate', and that there was a reluctance to investigate or take action against perpetrators for fear of a white backlash. Ethnic minorities who experienced violent racist victimisation were not defined as victims, were blamed for their own victimisation, and were informed that inaction against offenders was the most appropriate statutory response.

England and Wales after the Lawrence Inquiry

The inquiry into the murder of Stephen Lawrence brought to light many of the issues central to this chapter. It demonstrated that black and Asian people in Britain are specifically targeted for 'everyday' and politically organised racist violence and that this enduring experience of being under attack fundamentally affects how ethnic minority communities think, feel and act. The inquiry demonstrated that racist violence undermines their *sense* of security as well as their actual safety; it curtails their freedom of movement, including their ability to visit certain localities; it affects fundamental life choices, such as where to live and work. Calls for protection by black and Asian communities have typically been met with denial either that a problem existed, that it bore any connection with racism, or that there were weaknesses in the subsequent police response. The Lawrence Inquiry brought to light evidence that police are 'racism-blind', or have a world view which favours racist offenders over black and Asian communities. Ultimately, it demonstrated the failure to meet the requirements to do justice, to be fair, and to ensure community safety.

The murder of Stephen Lawrence seemed to demonstrate the emptiness of the claim that the police and criminal justice system offered equal protection irrespective of race or ethnic origin. The main suspects – who had a history of extreme violence – committed a brutal murder and were then able to get away with it with impunity. Despite the exertion of a great amount of effort, police investigators were unable to collect sufficient evidence to put a case before the court. The Lawrence Inquiry's acknowledgement that the initial investigation was 'marred by a combination of professional incompetence, institutional racism and a failure of leadership by senior officers' was symbolically important (Macpherson 1999: 46.1). Even more significant was the empirical and documentary evidence that the Lawrence Inquiry unearthed and exposed to public view. As Jack Straw, the Home Secretary, commented, in presenting the inquiry report to the House of Commons, it had 'opened all our eyes to what it is to be black or Asian in Britain today'. A renewed commitment to tackling racist crime, to ensuring that ethnic minority communities are properly served and protected, and to a new era of 'anti-racist policing' are grounds for optimism about the future. Stephen Lawrence will be remembered as one of at least 90 victims of racist murder over the past four decades in Britain. But if his death is to mean more than this, the police – the subject of the next chapter – must be fair and accountable and protect the fundamental human rights to life, liberty and security.

Conclusion

Racist violence provides an example of the impact of direct, individual racism. Frequently, members of extreme racist organisations have set out specifically to maim or kill people from ethnic minorities. However, racist violence cannot be seen only as the madness of individual hooligans, 'inexplicable', mindless or, even, simply 'politically motivated'. Racist violence is a much broader phenomenon that includes violence perpetrated by individuals and groups of youths in contexts where the implicit 'goals' are shared among a much broader section of the English population. Research on prejudice and racism among 'ordinary', non-violent white people suggests that some share the goals of the perpetrators of racial harassment, for example discouraging people from ethnic minorities to move into 'their' neighbourhood (for example Husbands 1983, Hesse *et al.* 1992), even if they do not agree with the means (that is, violence) which is used to achieve this (for example, Foster 1998).

The problem of violent racism, therefore, is not simply a matter of racist individuals, but a wider racist culture, which defines people as problematic, 'threatening' and (simultaneously) vulnerable. Taking a still broader view, racist culture does not exist in a vacuum but is formed, transformed and reformed in a specific social context. Racism is the result of the politicisation of competition for scare resources. Where class relations dominate the way in which goods (as well as 'bads') and services are distributed, race divides people who would otherwise find themselves in more or less the same material conditions. In short, the over-victimisation of ethnic minority communities through violent racism in particular is the result of individual action, cultural racism and the indirect impact of structural forces.

If the absence of racist crime, or even reducing it to tolerable levels, is too stringent a criterion against which to evaluate the effectiveness of the police and criminal justice system, then perhaps 'visible activity' is more reasonable. We should perhaps be encouraged if more is being done, and there are certainly grounds to believe that enforcement has increased sharply. In London, the number of 'intelligence reports' submitted by police officers has increased geometrically, while the number of arrests increased from around 100 per month in 1998 to an average of more than 400 per month in 2000. This enforcement activity has been welcomed after the denial and inactivity that characterised the state response to racist violence in the 1980s and early 1990s, but there remains evidence that the response is still far from effective in providing protection from victimisation. It is too early to say what impact the escalation of enforcement will have on the extent and nature of violence, assuming that such an assessment is possible given the limitations of the data.

The cases of David Copeland and Robert Stewart (see chapter 8) make it clear that we need to give more thought to the penology of racist violence. The dominant, if implicit, philosophies behind the punishment of racist offenders have been denunciation and retribution emerging within a broader politics of punitiveness. The expression of moral outrage in response to offenders seen (literally) to have got away with murder has led many to the view that 'more must be done.' This 'more' has been interpreted largely in punitive terms, including the introduction of penalty enhancements in the form, for example, of the racially aggravated offences in the Crime and Disorder Act 1998[1] and increased levels of enforcement described above.

Utilitarians clearly hope that 'locking up racists' serves to deter, or incapacitate sufficient offenders to reduce the extent of victimisation. However, it must be remembered that punishment often fails to achieve its stated ends and often has unanticipated and unwanted consequences. Punishments perceived to be unfair can result in both defiance and the confirmation of deviant identities which lead in turn to increased rather than decreased levels of offending. Many criminologists and criminal justice practitioners have pointed to the contradictions between the *intention* of policing and the criminal justice process and its actual *effect* on the problems it is intended to (re)solve. These contradictions, which may be even more acute than in other cases, seem to have been forgotten when people are accused or convicted of racist offences (see Rose 1996). The

---

[1] Maleiha Malik, 'Racist Crime' (1999 62 *Modern Law Review* 409 and 416–419).

potential to confirm criminal or racist identities, to forge new violent or racist associates while in custody is more likely for these individuals (see Gordon 1984).

The question of preventing re-offending or rehabilitation among people imprisoned or on probation orders for offences aggravated by racism has hardly been broached by criminological theorists or criminal justice practitioners. Programmes directed at challenging violent racist behaviour are in their infancy and few, if any, have been properly evaluated. The tragedy of Zahid Mubarek's murder while in prison custody (see chapter 8) is also a reflection of the failure of the prison service to respond effectively to offenders convicted of racist offences in past decades. The overwhelming approach seems to be no more imaginative than warehousing offenders. Not only do prison-based programmes for this challenging group not exist, but their content has yet to be envisioned by prison or probation officers or, indeed, criminologists. This observation raises a further unresolved issue of what is to be done with convicted racist offenders when they are released from prison. In the cases of Stewart and Copeland, this is a bridge that will be crossed only in the distant future. But the question remains: does the murderer who is also a committed racist pose a danger to society that is qualitatively different from an 'ordinary' killer?

Even though levels of enforcement have increased dramatically over the past two years, there is no evidence that the problem of violent racism is being brought under control. We must ask ourselves whether a neo-classical response to racist violence based on 'zero tolerance', intelligence-led enforcement, arrest and punishment is likely to produce a safer society when offenders are simply propelled through the criminal justice process and back into society either immediately or after a spell in prison. This leads to the bigger question of whether populist punitiveness is any more viable a philosophy of punishment in this sphere than it is elsewhere. We think there is need to envision a much broader response that can mobilise communities and social institutions to challenge racist and violent behaviour and which seeks to do justice to both victims and offenders in ways that genuinely enhance community safety.

Chapter 6

Policing

People come into contact with the police in a variety of situations: as victims of crime, as witnesses, as informants, when they report crime, disturbances or disorder, because they seek information, or when suspected of committing an offence. In this chapter we examine historical and contemporary accounts of policing and ethnic minorities experiences of policing. Exploring the dynamics of the police–community relationship can assist in explaining ethnic minority attitudes towards the criminal justice system as a whole. This, in turn, helps us to understand decisions made throughout the criminal justice process, and to contextualise differential outcomes at key points in the process.

Police deployment and targeting

The conflicts between the police and African, Caribbean, and to a lesser extent Asian youth during the 1970s and 1980s in particular occurred in the context of a perception of 'over-policing' neighbourhoods where ethnic minority communities are concentrated (Gordon 1983: 24–50). The experience of over-policing has been consistently reported in community accounts of policing. The first such study, conducted by Hunte (1966) for the West Indian Standing Conference, found that:

> It has been confirmed from reliable sources that sergeants and constables do leave stations with the express purpose of going 'nigger hunting'. That is to say, they do not get orders from superiors to act in this way, but among themselves they decided to bring in a coloured person at all cost.
>
> (1966: 12)

A similar picture was painted in a series of reports in the 1970s.

For example, a study of 34 African/Caribbean men in Birmingham by All Faiths for One Race (1978) found that more than one-third recounted personal experiences of at least one incident of police harassment or brutality which they had experienced and half mentioned an incident relating to a close friend. Many specifically accused the police of acting and speaking in a racially abusive manner which indicated that they thought black people were inferior, and the report concluded that racist tendencies among the police were widespread.

In a report drawing on their submission to the 1979 Royal Commission on Criminal Procedure, the Institute of Race Relations (1979, 1987) concluded that police officers demonstrated little regard for the civil liberties of black people. The authors pointed to oppressive police tactics such as mass stop and search operations, co-ordinated raids, the use of riot squads using semi-military equipment; continuous intelligence gathering and surveillance and the 'skilful use of the tabloid press to convey the police view to the wider public'. Police commanders were 'targeting' police resources, including the use of specialist units, into specific 'high crime areas', including what have become known as 'symbolic locations' – coded language for the centres of Britain's African and Caribbean communities: such as Toxteth in Liverpool, Moss Side in Manchester, Handsworth in Birmingham, St Paul's in Bristol, and Brixton, Notting Hill, Tottenham, Lewisham, Dalston and elsewhere in London (see also Newham Monitoring Project, Annual Reports, Keith 1993).

In addition to street stops (which we discuss in more detail below), places where African, Caribbean and Asian people gathered, such as clubs, were targeted by the police. These included the raid on the Black and White Cafe in Bristol, April 1980, Operations Condor, Broadlands and Trident in Brixton, between 1986 and 1987, the Broadwater Farm 'anniversary' raid on 12 August 1986, and the raid on the 'Rivers' disco in Newham. In 1987, Notting Hill Carnival was policed with riot control tactics involving armoured Land Rovers with gun ports. During February and March 1988, Operations Vulture and Falcon resulted in riot-clad police using sledgehammers on the Mangrove Club in Notting Hill. Housing estates with a large black population have also been targeted, classifying them as high risk in terms of their potential for disorder and with contingency plans to take control of the estate in the case of any disturbances. Estates such as Broadwater Farm and Ferry Lane in Tottenham, East Dulwich Housing Estate and Clapton Park Estate in Hackney, were subject to such policing on numerous occasions in the 1980s (Institute of Race Relations 1979, 1987). The same report also presented evidence of more pervasive, ongoing targeting that appeared to regard 'black areas as intrinsically criminal and black people a potential threat to public order'. This involved stopping vehicles 'often on a flimsy pretext', persistent stop and search on the streets, commonplace rude and hostile questioning accompanied by racial abuse, arbitrary arrest, violence on arrest, the arrest of witnesses and bystanders, punitive and indiscriminate attacks, victimisation on reporting crime, acting on false information, forced entry and violence, provocative and unnecessary armed raids, and repeated harassment and trawling for suspects (ibid.).

To what extent do proactive police initiatives such as targeted patrols and stop and search contribute to the process by which people of African and Caribbean origin are brought into the criminal justice process? Citing the higher than expected arrest rates of black people for 'other violent thefts' (snatches causing no injury) in London in 1975, Stevens and Willis (1979) question whether this reflects the likelihood that police officers are more likely to suspect black people of these offences. Similar results were found by Cain and Sadigh (1982) who also discovered that West Indians were much more likely to be charged as a result of police initiative than as a result of action by any victim. Hood's (1992) study of Crown Courts in the West Midlands found that among sentenced defendants, 15 per cent of those dealt with by the courts for drugs offences were black compared with only 3 per cent of Asians and 2 per cent of whites, and these were typically for small trades in cannabis. These offences almost exclusively came to official attention following proactive policing. Indeed, Home Office (2000c) statistics show that the most common reason for searching black and Asian people was for drugs. African/Caribbean defendants 'known to the police' were more likely than white and Asian defendants to be arrested 'on suspicion'. There are strong indications that black people have been brought into the criminal justice process more often because of proactive police practices over a period of 35 years.

Immigration policing

One of the most controversial areas of police targeting relates to the policing of 'immigration' and the people who are defined as 'immigrants'. During the 1960s and 1970s 'coloured immigration' was not only a potent political issue, but also one that framed the experiences of black and Asian people in a range of spheres including policing and criminal justice. Many research studies uncovered evidence that ordinary policing often involved checking immigration status, such as asking for passports, for instance when people from ethnic minorities reported crimes of which they had been victims.

The 1971 Immigration Act gives the police and immigration authorities considerable powers to detain and question those people who are suspected of being in breach of immigration law, such as entering illegally or overstaying terms of entry (see Gordon 1984). Gordon (1984) suggests that with the 1971 Immigration Act, the control of immigration began to shift from external border controls to 'internal controls', or 'pass laws', for people of African, Caribbean and Asian descent resident in Britain (Sivanandan 1982: 135). In the months following the implementation of the Act, numerous high-profile passport raids were conducted, amounting to a 'witch hunt' of African, Caribbean and Asian communities according to Gordon (1984). Immigration policing was a major source of suspicion and mistrust between the police and minority communities, and was even labelled 'sus 2' by the Institute of Race Relations (1987).

Despite the waning of the 'moral panic' about the arrival and settlement of African, Caribbean and Asian people in the UK after successively restrictive immigration and nationality legislation, the policing of immigration remains contentious today. The Joint Council for the Welfare of Immigrants (1995) reported that the police increasingly ask for identification documents and evidence of immigration status from black and 'foreign-looking' people they stop during routine traffic stops or as a witness to an accident or crime. For example, a person may call the police after being burgled and then be asked to prove their immigration status. There is evidence that policing immigration through 'internal controls' is intensifying. It is certainly the case that the number of people subject to enforcement action under the 1971 Immigration Act have increased sharply in recent years – from 3,200 in 1986 to 22,890 in 1999 (Jackson and McGregor 2000, see also Weber and Gelsthorpe 2000).

On 29 July 1993, Joy Gardner died as a result of the police restraint used on her while executing a deportation order.[1] Following this, a Home Office review of procedures in deportation cases where the police were involved concluded that all requests for police assistance made by the Immigration Service should be standardised to ensure that all relevant information was available to the police and immigration authorities. It also concluded that people should not usually be taken directly from their homes to an airport for departure on the same day, but that the police should still be used for escort and support duties. The use of mouth restraints was suspended permanently (Joint Council for the Welfare of Immigrants 1995: 241).

Police violence and deaths in custody

> The greatest fear most English people seem to have for their children, is that they'll be abducted or molested by paedophiles or something ... But I fear for my son's safety at the hands of the police. These people are supposed to protect us ... all of us. What am I supposed to tell him? Don't go out because the people we're expected to trust, the people governed to uphold the law, might kill you? What kind of life is that for a young man?
> (*Caribbean Times*, 3 April 1997)

It is an axiom of liberal analyses that the legitimate use of force is central to the role of the police. For commentators such as Bittner (1970), the

---

[1] Joy Gardner, a black woman of Jamaican origin, had overstayed her visa and was visited by the Alien Deportation Group. Her wrists were handcuffed to a leather strap around her waist, bound by a second belt around her thighs and a third one around her ankles. As she lay on the floor, 13 feet of adhesive tape was wound around her head and face. Mrs Gardner collapsed and died in hospital a few hours later (Chigwada-Bailey 1997: 34)

capacity to use legitimate, state-sanctioned force is the defining feature of the police organisation. The guiding principle is that police use of force must be essential (used as a tactic of *last resort*) and minimal (must be *no more than is needed* to prevent anticipated harm) (Uglow 1988). The use of force must also be seen as legitimate (justifiable to the public and with its consent) (Morgan 1989), and the police must be able to account for their actions (McLaughlin 1991).

There is a considerable amount of material which questions the extent to which the police have adhered to the principle of the 'minimum use of force' in their dealings with the African, Caribbean, Asian and other minority communities. Accusations by black people about extreme police brutality and deaths have been publicised in the ethnic minority press, in community campaigns, and in reggae music, such as Macka B's (1986) 'We've Had Enough' and Linton Kwesi Johnson's (1985) 'Sonny's Lettah' and (1998) 'Licence To Kill'. Despite the obvious strength of feeling among minority communities, the reader of criminological literature in the field has to work hard to find explicit references to excessive use of force, police violence or brutality. Among the exceptions is Graef's (1989) study which notes that it is extremely difficult to establish how widespread the excessive use of force might be. Many officers insist that they have only ever seen the police use violence in situations that are justified. Others acknowledge that there are a small number of 'cowboys' who occasionally use excessive force (Foster 1989). In some places, however, violence is reckoned to be 'standard practice' (Graef 1989: 229). For example, a Metropolitan Police inspector admitted that:

> in the years before the riots, the police in Lambeth treated the community with contempt. There were stories of people having their heads stuffed down the toilet and flushed. Whenever you went into the charge room there was blood on the walls. There were incidents that were just horrendous ... Brixton nick also had the reputation that if you went through the front door you came out the back with blood on your face. And that's not one bloke doing it, that was the norm. It almost gets to the point that it has to happen to maintain the nick's reputation.
>
> (ibid.: 234)

The issue of deaths at the hands of the police has been similarly absent in criminological discussions. Why this should be the case is unclear, though we are drawn to Sivanandan's comment that '[b]lack deaths do not have a good press, especially when they occur in the custody of our custodians. The media leads the public to believe that our guardians can do no wrong. Racism leads them to believe that blacks can do no right' (Institute of Race Relations 1991: 3)

The Institute of Race Relations (1991) paper, 'Deadly Silence: Black Deaths in Custody' documents 16 cases between 1969 and 1991 in which the death of a black person came about either through lack of care or through the use of oppressive control techniques. For example, in 1969 David Oluwale was found dead in a river after being beaten by the police and chased by them along its river banks. The officers involved were convicted of assault but cleared of manslaughter. Others have occurred during raids, such as the death of Cynthia Jarrett who was pushed, or fell, during a police raid on her home in 1985. The inquest returned a verdict of 'accidental death' which linked her death to the actions of the police, though not intentionally or recklessly (ibid.: 11).

Several black people have died while being arrested by the police. Clinton McCurbin died when, after resisting arrest for alleged use of a stolen credit card, he was held in an arm lock around his neck for several minutes. Witnesses said the police officer was 'practically strangling' McCurbin and that he was held in a choke hold for some time after he had stopped struggling. Immediately after his death, the police issued a statement that his death may have been a heart attack induced by drug abuse and it was also falsely stated that McCurbin had been a Rastafarian. Medical evidence from two pathologists found no traces of drugs or evidence of a heart attack, but concluded that his death had been caused by asphyxiation due to the obstruction of his airway. The Police Complaints Authority investigation recommended (and this was confirmed by the coroner) that no action should be taken against the officers. The inquest resulted in the ambiguous verdict of 'death by misadventure'.

For the Institute of Race Relations (1991), deaths in police custody are to be seen in the context of unequal treatment before the law. They note that there is a tendency to obscure information about what has happened and to create 'official misinformation' that explains the deaths as accidental, or a misadventure or 'even the fault of the victim, because of his or her behaviour, drunkenness, abuse of drugs, or mental or physical condition' (Institute of Race Relations 1991: 5). This characterisation shifts the focus of public attention away from what the police did to what the citizen did, or failed to do, and attention is 'deflected from police deviance to questions of the victim's deviance' (Kappeler *et al.* 1994: 164). There is convincing evidence that racist assumptions about 'dangerous', 'out-of-control' 'drug addicts' or 'schizophrenics' can lead police officers to overlook signs of physical illness which remain untreated and lead to tragic fatalities (Kappeler *et al.*, 1994, Chigwada-Bailey 1997, Institute of Race Relations 1991).

The deaths of Oluwasijibomi Lapite in December 1994 and Richard O'Brien in April 1994 by asphyxia during arrest have implications for the criminal investigation of police officers accused of killing suspects in their care, particularly where coroners' juries have returned verdicts of unlawful killing. The Director of Public Prosecutions was ruled against by the courts for not mounting a prosecution case against the police who were deemed responsible by coroners' juries for the two deaths. An inquiry, led by Gerald Butler QC, identified significant weaknesses in the decision-making processes of the Crown Prosecution Service, referring to the system employed by Central Casework in determining whether there should be a prosecution as 'inefficient and fundamentally unsound' (Butler 1999).

Three other recent fatalities while black men have been in the care of the police have provoked anger and outrage in black communities. In 1995, Brian Douglas died from a fractured skull after being hit with a police baton, while the death of Wayne Douglas from positional asphyxia provoked outrage in the local community (see also Spencer and Hough 2000). Likewise the death of Roger Sylvester in January 1999 has ensured that the issues of the stereotyping of black men as aggressive, violent and dangerously threatening, and the lack of a fully independent investigatory process following deaths in custody, have stayed on the political agenda.[2]

Table 6.1 Deaths in police custody by ethnic origin 1996/7 and 1998/9

	Number of deaths	%	% in arrested population in nine force areas[1] (England and Wales)[2]	% in general population
1996/7	**57**			
White	49	86	85 (92)	95
Black	7	12	6 (4)	2
Asian	1	2	7 (3)	3
Other	0	0	1 (1)	1
1998/9	**68**			
White	60	88	88	95
Black	2	3	7	2
Asian	3	4	4	3
Other	3	4	1	1

Sources: Cotton and Povey (1997) *Police Complaints and Deaths in Police Custody in England and Wales*; Home Office (1997a) *Race and the Criminal Justice System*; Home Office (2000c) *Statistics on Race and the Criminal Justice System*.

Notes:
1 Figures for 1996/7 are based on Table 3.3 Home Office (1997a) Race and the Criminal Justice System. The first column includes data for Bedfordshire, Hertfordshire, Lancashire, Leicestershire, Greater Manchester, Nottinghamshire, Thames Valley, West Midlands, and West Yorkshire police forces, where there are the highest ethnic minority populations. It excludes figures for the Metropolitan Police Service where data were not available.
2 The figures in parentheses includes data for 38 of the police forces in England and Wales – data were not included for the Metropolitan Police Service, Cheshire, Cleveland, Cumbria and West Mercia police forces, where ethnic origin was not recorded in more than 20 per cent of cases (Home Office 1997a: table 3.3).
3 Percentages do not necessarily sum to 100 due to rounding.

---

[2] (Roger Sylvester Campaign (see http://www.blink.org.uk/campaign/rogercampaign and http://www.gn.apc.org/inquest/briefings/sylvester2).

Operation Justice (launched in 1997 by Inquest, Liberty, National Assembly Against Racism, the Churches Commission for Racial Justice, Society of Black Lawyers, 1990 Trust, National Black Caucus and National Black Alliance) has similarly lobbied to challenge for reform in police practices which contribute to deaths in custody.[3]

For the UK as a whole, in 1996/7, 57 people died in police custody or 'otherwise in the hands of the police', an increase of 14 per cent on the previous year (see table 6.1). African/Caribbean people were six times more likely to die in the custody of the police than would be expected from their numbers in the population. The proportion of black deaths in custody was also significantly higher than the proportion of black arrests in 1996/7. Moreover, ethnic minorities make up the bulk of those who have died as a result of physical force (other than guns) by the police or because of the use of restraints (Inquest, 1996). More recent figures for 1998/9 show an increase in deaths in custody overall, but a lower proportion of ethnic minorities relative to the arrested population (see Home Office 2000c).

Attitudes towards the police

The history of interactions between the police and ethnic minority communities helps to contextualise victimisation survey data which have shed light on public-initiated encounters. Such sources tell us about how satisfied people were with the police response when they reported a crime and their perceptions of police (mis)conduct. Surveys also shed light on police-initiated contacts, such as stop and search. The British Crime Survey presents a 'consumer' perspective on police operations. Mayhew *et al.*'s (1993) 'overall police performance score' was based on five items reported by respondents: showing enough interest, not having to wait an unreasonable amount of time, showing enough effort, keeping the victim informed, being fairly or very polite, all of which contribute to public confidence in the police (Skogan 1990). Mayhew, Aye Maung and Mirrlees-Black (1993) found that for whites, the performance score was 3.5 compared with 2.6 for ethnic minority respondents. The same picture of a lower level of satisfaction with the police among ethnic minorities has emerged from the other British Crime Surveys and Gallup public opinion surveys (see Southgate and Ekblom 1984, Mayhew *et al.* 1989, Skogan 1990, 1994, Aye Maung 1995, Southgate and Crisp 1992).

Further insight into the attitudes of ethnic minorities towards the police comes from a series of local studies which have examined crime, victimisation and policing in urban areas (table 6.2). Although there are some differences between national and local surveys, black respondents

---

[3] (see http://www.blink.org.uk/campaign/justice).

Table 6.2 Attitudes towards the police

	White	African/Caribbean	Asian
The police do a very good job			
BCS 1988	26	16	16
BCS 1994	24	17	–
BCS 1996	22	16	19
BCS 1992 (12–15 year olds)[1]	64	44	57
The police do not treat all people fairly			
BCS 1992 (12–15 year olds)[1]	34	48	33
London[2]	26	62	36
Leeds[3]	65	70	38
Hammersmith and Fulham[4]	57	71	56
Islington I[5]	29	61	30
Willingness to inform the police about youths smashing up a bus shelter			
London[2]	83	68	81
Leeds[3]	66	48	81
Hammersmith and Fulham[4]	76	46	36
Islington I[5]	74	66	66
Islington II[6]	67	45	–

Notes:
1. Aye Maung (1995), $n = 1,051$, ethnic minority booster ($n = 299$). Response category included police doing a 'fairly and very good job'. Response category asked about the police treating young people less fairly.
2. Smith and Gray (1983), $n = 1411$, ethnic minority booster (n=1,009).
3. Jefferson and Walker (1992), $n = 271$ whites, $n = 370$ ethnic minorities aged 6–35 years.
4. Painter *et al.* (1989), $n = 1,315$, 86 per cent white, 9 per cent African/Caribbean, 2 per cent Asian, 3 per cent other ethnic minorities. Response category was the willingness to give evidence about youths smashing up a bus shelter.
5. Jones, Maclean and Young (1986), $n = 1,719$, ethnic booster sample ($n = 225$).
6. Crawford *et al.* (1990), $n = 1,621$.

are generally less satisfied with police action and perceive the police to be unfair to certain groups, and, not surprisingly, are less willing to co-operate with the police than white respondents (see also Spencer and Hough 2000, Chigwada-Bailey 1997). The findings with respect to Asians are more mixed, with less disapproval of the police than black and white respondents reported in some studies, whereas in others, Asians tend to hold views which put them between black and white respondents. The general pattern has been confirmed by the 2000 British Crime Survey which reported that twice as many black respondents (38 per cent), as white respondents, (19 per cent), could recall being 'really annoyed' by the behaviour of a police officer in the last five years; for Asian respondents the figure was 23 per cent. The main reasons cited by those interviewed were that the police had been rude, unfriendly, behaved unreasonably or had failed to do anything (Sims and Myhill 2001).

Similar responses were reported when people were asked about police misconduct. For example, in a survey of males aged 10–35 living in areas of Leeds which were of more than 10 per cent ethnic minority composition, black respondents were more likely than white and Asian respondents to agree broadly that 'there are quite a lot of dishonest policemen in Leeds' and 'it is best to avoid the police wherever possible' (Jefferson and Walker 1992). Black people were less likely than Asian and white respondents broadly to agree with statements such as 'the police try and help the community' and 'there are not enough police officers in Leeds at present'. The results of a mean disapproval score showed that blacks (7.4) were most disapproving of the police, followed by whites (6.3) and then Asians (5.7).

Some 29 per cent of black respondents believed that the police made up evidence 'very or quite often', compared with 24 per cent of white respondents and 8 per cent of Asians. Overall, Asians were less likely to report that they believed police misconduct to occur frequently compared with white and African/Caribbean respondents. In table 6.3, Jefferson and Walker's (1993) figures on the use of unnecessary violence by the police (according to respondents) is presented alongside those reported in local victimisation surveys, although the response categories

---

Box 6.1 Increasing trust and confidence in policing among minority ethnic communities: a ministerial priority for the police service for 1999/00 and 2000/01

Set up to respond to the recommendations of the Stephen Lawrence Inquiry, the police service are now required by the Home Office to: improve the reporting, recording, investigation, prosecution and prevention of racist incidents; achieve equal levels of satisfaction with the police across all ethnic groups; improve the performance and training of family and witness/victim liaison officers; undertake racism awareness training; implement policy directives on stop/searches; increase minority ethnic recruitment, retention and progression; and assess levels of complaints of racist attitudes and behaviour. The second annual progress report indicated progress on some of these criteria, particularly in developing community and race relations strategies, consultative mechanisms, understanding of racist incidents, and in initiatives for officer recruitment. Less had been achieved in the important areas of managing and supervising stop/searches, retention and progression of minority officers, and racism awareness training.

Source: Home Office (2001a)

Table 6.3 The use of unnecessary violence by the police: local studies

	White	Black	Asian
The police use unnecessary violence at police stations			
Often			
London[1]	12	37	13
Leeds[2]	9	12	1
Islington I (16–24 year olds)[3]	36	51	11
Hammersmith and Fulham[4]	14	34	19

Notes: 1 Smith and Gray (1983), $n = 1,411$, ethnic minority booster ($n = 1,009$).
2 Jefferson and Walker (1992), $n = 271$ whites, $n = 370$ ethnic minorities aged 16–35 years.
3 Jones, Maclean and Young (1986), $n = 1,719$, ethnic booster sample ($n = 225$).
4 Painter *et al.* (1989), $n = 1,315$, 86 per cent white, 9 per cent African/Caribbean, 2 per cent Asian, 3 per cent other ethnic minorities.

are not strictly comparable, since the response options varied in each of the studies. For more white and black respondents than Asians in the Leeds sample, these beliefs and attitudes towards the police came directly from personal experience, but it did seem that the positions adopted reflected both direct and vicarious experiences (knowing someone who had had these experiences).

Representations made by ethnic minority communities to the Stephen Lawrence Inquiry echoed the negative attitudes reported in these attitudinal surveys (Macpherson 1999). The response by the Home Office has been to establish a ministerial priority for the police for 1999/2000 to increase trust and confidence among ethnic minority communities (see box 6.1).

Stop and search

Concern about the equitable use of stop and search powers has been one of the most controversial issues in policing. From the perspective of young black men, and increasingly young Asian men in certain areas of the country, it is perhaps the most glaring example of an abuse of police powers (see, for example, Gordon 1983, Institute of Race Relations 1987, Newham Monitoring Project 1988, 1990, 1993, Roach Family Support Committee 1989, Spencer and Hough 2000). Indeed, the late Bernie Grant (NACRO 1997: 3), formerly Member of Parliament for Haringey said:

> nothing has been more damaging to the relationship between the police and the black community than the ill-judged use of stop and search powers. For young black men in particular, the humiliating experience of being

repeatedly stopped and searched is a fact of life, in some parts of London at least. It is hardly surprising that those on the receiving end of this treatment should develop hostile attitudes towards the police. The right to walk the streets is a fundamental one, and one that is quite rightly jealously guarded.

In 1994 Bernie Grant asked a parliamentary question that drew attention to Home Office data supporting what had been known for a long time, that black people were disproportionately stopped and searched.[4] Since then it has emerged that black men from all walks of life – including politicians, actors, lawyers and even policemen – have been repeatedly stopped and searched, often without justification and sometimes rudely.[5] Among those who have complained publicly about being stopped unjustifiably are the Conservative Peer, Lord Taylor of Warwick, John Sentamu Bishop of Stepney, Neville Lawrence and Trevor Hall adviser to the Permanent Secretary of the Home Office. Desune Coleman, the actor who played Lenny in *EastEnders*, said of his experience of being stopped forty times, 'It's happened to me so often I view being stopped by police as part of my driving life.' The journalist Darcus Howe concluded that, 'Too many police officers seem to think being black constitutes a "reasonable ground" for stopping and searching someone.'[6]

'Sus'

The use of stop and search powers is authorised under the Police and Criminal Evidence Act (PACE) 1984. Stop and search is also authorised under the Road Traffic Act, Misuse of Drugs Act 1971, Immigration Act 1971, Criminal Justice and Public Order Act 1994 and s.15 Prevention of Terrorism (Temporary Provisions) Act 1989, prior to which police operated under various general and local legislation (Brown 1997). Much has been written about these practices under these so-called 'sus' laws, where a person could be arrested under the 1824 Vagrancy Act (s.4 and s.6) for frequenting or loitering in a public place with intent to commit an arrestable offence. Documentary and empirical evidence pointed to the extremely heavy use of these powers against ethnic minorities, particularly young black people. Among numerous operations in the early 1980s was Operation Swamp 1981. For a week, 120 plain-clothes and uniformed police officers patrolled Brixton with specific instruction to stop and question anyone who looked 'suspicious'. In all, 943 people were stopped over the course of four days. Of these 118 were arrested, more than half

---

[4] PQF00343H, House of Commons, Priority PQ from Bernie Grant (Lab, Tottenham). See also *Home Office Research Bulletins* 15/94, 21/93, 15/92 and 14/91.
[5] *Time Out*, February 28, 2000
[6] *Time Out*, February 28, 2000

of whom were black. Among the 75 who were charged, only one was for robbery, one for attempted burglary and 18 for theft or attempted theft. Despite the public disorder which was triggered by this saturation policing, targeted patrols of a similar type continued to be used throughout the 1980s in neighbourhoods with significant ethnic minority populations (Keith 1993).

The Police and Criminal Evidence Act (PACE) 1984

Following public concern about police discrimination and particularly the work of such organisations as the Scrap Sus Campaign (1979), together with an acknowledgement by the police and the Royal Commission on Criminal Procedure (1981) that the provisions were too loose and lacking in accountability, the 1984 Police and Criminal Evidence Act was introduced. The Act permits the police to stop and search persons and vehicles where the officer has 'reasonable suspicion' that they are carrying stolen or prohibited articles.[7] The code stipulates that there must be an 'objective basis' for stopping an individual:

> reasonable suspicion can never be supported on the basis of personal factors alone without supporting intelligence or information. For example, a person's colour, age, hairstyle or manner of dress, or the fact that he is known to have a previous conviction for possession of an unlawful article, cannot be used alone or in combination with each as the sole basis on which to search that person. Nor may it be founded on the basis of stereotyped images of certain persons or groups as more likely to be committing offences.
>
> (Home Office 1997c: 3)

The police and government argue that the police need to use stop and search tactics to identify criminal offenders, even though Home Office research concluded that the tactic has an extremely limited impact on detection, disrupting the activity of those going out to commit offences or in its deterrent effect. Stop and searches undoubtedly provide intelligence which will inform subsequent police work (Miller, Bland and Quinton 2000, cf. FitzGerald 1999) but this falls outside of the spirit and letter of the Act.

There is official acknowledgement that stop and search powers must be regulated to safeguard the individual's right to privacy and against unnecessary intrusion by the state (Home Office 1997c). The inherent danger

---

[7] PACE Code of Practice (A) documents the powers available. The latest version which went into effect on 15 May 1997 also incorporates provisions on stop/search powers under s.60 of the Criminal Justice and Public Order Act 1994 (Home Office, 1997c). This permits the police, on the authority of a senior officer, to stop and search anyone where there is a 'reasonable belief that incidents involving serious violence may take place within a locality'.

lies in the extent of discretion which such powers allow. Despite attempts to make the use of discretion less arbitrary and to make police officers more accountable, research indicates that police officers tend to circumvent PACE requirements and rely on informal working practices, such as 'hunches' about suspicious individuals or those already known to the police (Brown 1997), which clearly has implications for the policing of ethnic minority individuals.

Young (1994) suggests three reasons why the legal regulation of stop and search powers does not prevent the abuse of discretion. First, police officers have to interpret the legal rules for which no amount of guidance could cover every eventuality. Second, the concepts 'reasonable suspicion' and 'consent' are vague and difficult to put into practice. Recent Home Office research has confirmed that there is considerable variation in police officers' understanding of the concept of 'reasonable suspicion' (Quinton, Bland and Miller 2000). In addition, stop and searches which are 'consented' to by suspects do not invoke the powers and protections afforded individuals under PACE. This is problematic because the concept of 'consent' is rather slippery, not least because suspects may be ignorant of their rights to refuse to be searched (Dixon, Coleman and Bottomley 1990). The third reason according to Young is that stop/searches occur outside the police station, and like many aspects of police work are therefore outside the purview of supervisory officers and 'the norms and working practices of the street level police officer take priority over outside regulation' (Young, 1994: 14).

Young rejects the central underpinning of the PACE guidelines – the idea that the police should suspect all citizens equally and democratically and not be biased by personal prejudice – as misguided and untenable. Police officers will inevitably consider the patterning of crime and offenders based on official crime statistics and will use this information to maximise the likelihood of getting an arrest. The problem with Young's position is that crime statistics are a product of the actions of the police and so serve only to reinforce existing prejudices about disproportionate involvement of specific ethnic minority groups in crime.

The consequences of the abuse of stop and search powers are wide ranging. It undermines ethnic minorities' confidence in the police, their willingness to co-operate by providing information about crime, and to co-operate with other aspects of the criminal justice process. The way stop and search powers are used by the police can also have ramifications for the proportion of ethnic minorities who become enmeshed in the criminal justice system, as Hood's research in the West Midlands has shown. Notwithstanding this, in 1999/00, only 13 per cent of PACE stop/searches resulted in an arrest (13 per cent, 17 per cent and 14 per cent for white, black and Asian suspects respectively), albeit with considerable variation across police force areas (Home Office 2000c).

Post-PACE research

One of the most consistent of empirical research findings in this field is that black people are disproportionately more likely to be stop/searched (and repeatedly so) by the police when compared with whites and Asians, judged against their representation in the general population. Official statistics produced have all confirmed this pattern (Home Office 1999d, 1998b, 1997a). The most recent national ethnic monitoring exercise for 1999/2000 found, with some force variation, that the number of searches of black people to be five times higher than for whites. Asians were stopped and searched by the police to a lesser extent than blacks, but it was still the case that the rates were almost always higher than for whites (Home Office 2000c).[8]

Ethnic monitoring of the provision under s.60 of the 1994 Criminal Justice and Public Order Act, where police officers can stop and search anyone where they believe serious violence will take place, has also shown that this power is being used disproportionately against ethnic minorities (Home Office 2000c). The limited data available on searches of premises and 'producers' (or HO/R1s (Home Office Road Traffic Forms) where individuals are required to produce their driving documents at their nearest police station) have followed the same trend as for street stops (see also Bucke 1997).

Disproportionate use of stop and search powers have also been found in the implementation of sections 13A and 13B of the 1989 Prevention of Terrorism Act, designed specifically to combat terrorism by the Provisional Irish Republican Army (IRA). Of the 13,760 people stopped under these powers in 1997/8, 7 per cent were African/Caribbean and 5 per cent Asian (Home Office 1998b:14).[9] Given that there are very few people of African, Caribbean or Asian origin who are suspected of being members of the Northern Ireland paramilitary organisations, these data suggest that in a two-year period about 6,500 people were unlawfully detained under this one power. Police officers with responsibility for policing the 'ring of steel' around the City of London, where these powers were concentrated, would concede that this is an example of direct discrimination in policing.

---

[8] FitzGerald and Sibbitt (1997), however, have warned that comparing stop/search rates with local population estimates may be misleading, especially at beat or division level. This is because stop/searches are often made of individuals who do not live within the beat or division that they are stopped in. Similarly, even at the force level, this method of comparison may be problematic because stop/searches are probably concentrated in a few areas across the force and not evenly distributed across the force area (see also Brown 1997). There is the additional problem with using 1991 Census data which is outdated and undercounts certain ethnic groups.

[9] In 1996/7 approximately 11 per cent of the 43,700 stops under s.13A and 13B of the Prevention of Terrorism Act were recorded as being of 'non-white' ethnic appearance (Home Office 1997a: 12). No figures are provided for the use of this power after 1998.

The picture of the use of stop and search has been supplemented with an observational study of police–suspect encounters in two divisions in London and one in Surrey in 1986/7. Norris *et al.* (1992) focused on stops where the person was suspected of an infraction. They found that police stopped blacks on speculative grounds more often than whites, in the hope that they would discover evidence of an offence. In only 44 per cent of stops of blacks was there an obvious enforcement reason for the stop, compared with 58 per cent of stops of whites. Further, in examining the dynamics of the encounter, Norris *et al.* reported that the police were less likely to act negatively in stops involving blacks (10 per cent) than those involving whites (27 per cent). Although an 'observer effect' could not be discounted, 40 per cent of African/Caribbean persons stopped had formal action taken against them by the police, while the figure was 31 per cent for whites stopped. The same pattern was observed by Bucke (1997) using data from the 1996 British Crime Survey.

Socio-demographic factors

Alongside categorical accusations of racism by many grassroots organisations, other reasons have been put forward to explain the differential stop rates of black people by the police. Jefferson (1993) has pointed to the role of sex, age and class in explaining the criminalising experiences of black people (see also FitzGerald 1993b, Reiner 1993). He suggests that African/Caribbean youth–police conflict is really better viewed as conflict between the state and the 'underclass' or the 'raggle taggle army of the dispossessed' which leads to the criminalisation of young blacks. In using the term 'underclass' he is referring to those whose unskilled labour is less in demand in post-industrial Britain – that is, the unemployed and the homeless, which will disproportionately include young black people. It is this group of the 'criminal other', according to Jefferson, who will be subjected to harsher treatment by the police.

Crime is more prevalent, or at least more visible, among young people and this does not escape the attention of police officers whose actions in turn must be seen in the light of, among other things, their 'working knowledge'. It is to be expected, therefore, that the police will conduct more stops of young people than older groups. This is relevant because as FitzGerald (1993) has observed, the age structure of ethnic minority populations is significantly younger than that of whites. This must be taken into account when assessing the prevalence of stop/search in white and ethnic minority populations, since they are inevitably more likely to be in the target group selected by the police.

The 1988 British Crime Survey analysis found that ethnic origin was a predictor of being stopped by the police, even once other factors, such as age, household income, employment status, occupation, type of housing tenure and area, vehicle access, gender, marital status, and age of leaving school, had been taken into account (Skogan 1990). This suggests that the patterns of stop/searches are explained by direct discrimination and the negative stereotyping of African/Caribbeans, but not necessarily Asians. FitzGerald and Sibbitt (1997) make the crucial point that:

> the police contribute to the large ethnic differences in the PACE data by virtue of their heightened suspiciousness of black people. This is pervasive and deeply entrenched; and it may significantly increase the chances of black people coming to the attention of the police relative to other groups.
>
> (FitzGerald and Sibbitt 1997: 66)

A small number of such examples were presented in research by Quinton, Bland and Miller (2000: 24) in their observations of police–public encounters. This pattern is exacerbated by constraints in the legal regulation of policing practices because of the minimal supervision of police officers when out on the streets.

Policing factors and 'working knowledge'

In addition to socio-demographic factors, such as gender, age, social class and marital status, and policing factors (such as between-force variation in the use of stop and search), FitzGerald and Sibbitt (1997) have highlighted the importance of several other factors which are important for understanding and interpreting the stop/search statistics and other data. Force objectives and policing priorities impact on the pattern of stop/search in different areas, especially in the context of targeted operations for specific offences. A second operational factor relates to the use of 'intelligence' about local 'villains' which will increase their risk of being stopped/searched when an incident occurs; however, this in itself may not be 'racially neutral'. Similarly, victim reports will direct police actions somewhat; thus, in one of the areas studied, robbery suspects were reported by victims to be black in over three-quarters of incidents, although, as we discussed in chapter 4, victim identifications are not always accurate.

A third factor is 'suspect availability'. The majority of stops occur in the afternoon, evening and night, and it is blacks who are most likely to be 'available' for stopping on the streets at these times (FitzGerald and Sibbitt 1997: 59), because of their higher levels of unemployment and school exclusions and going out in the evening. Building on this proposition, MVA and Miller (2000) assessed the pedestrian and vehicle populations in Hounslow, Greenwich, Ipswich, Chapeltown and central Leicester, in an attempt to overcome the inadequacies of dated census data and differences between available populations and resident populations. Using CCTV and street observers, the research found that across the five sites, on average white people were over-represented among those stopped and searched by the police, while Asian people were under-represented when rates were calculated on 'available' rather than 'resident' populations. The findings for black people were mixed; there was evidence of both under- and over-representation. This study emphasises the need for caution in assuming disproportionality when using outdated resident populations, but it also raises important questions about the neutrality of availability. As chapter 2 described, black pupils may be victims of direct discrimination when they are excluded from school, and racism undoubtedly contributes to unemployment patterns among ethnic minorities. Thus, 'being available' to be stopped and searched by the police may in itself be the result of indirect discrimination. It is also problematic that 'lifestyle factors', such as going out more frequently in the evening, should lead black people to be more often the subject of proactive policing than other ethnic groups (Modood and Berthoud 1997, Bourne, Bridges and Searle 1997).

FitzGerald and Sibbitt (1997) suggest that African/Caribbeans may be less likely to receive the benefit of police exercising their discretion for under-enforcement, because they and the police are influenced by their long-standing suspicion of each other which will increase the likelihood of the encounter being confrontational (cf. Norris *et al.* 1992). To this long list of factors which arouse police officer suspicion, Quinton, Bland and Miller (2000) have added other factors which police officers draw on from their experiential working knowledge, identified in interviews and patrol observations. These include clothing (such as baseball caps and hooded jackets), older cars (which might have vehicle defects), makes of cars which are commonly stolen, expensive cars (particularly those driven by ethnic minorities who were assumed not to be able to buy them legitimately), 'standing out' and engaging in 'suspicious activity' (such as checking out cars or avoiding eye contact), both of which could be related to ethnicity, and being out at certain times and in certain places.

Stop and search in the 1990s

A range of important issues emerge from the raft of research conducted in the wake of the Stephen Lawrence Inquiry which provides more in-depth insight into the use of stop and search in the 1990s. FitzGerald's (1999) study, conducted for the Metropolitan Police Service, for example, found public support for the idea that the police should have the power to stop, question and search someone they honestly suspect of being involved in crime (see also Her Majesty's Inspectorate of Constabulary 2000, Bowling 1999c). However, it is clear from the report that current practice is consistent with neither the spirit nor the letter of the law. The study found that the police use of section 1 PACE in London is frequently unlawful, sometimes conducted aggressively or rudely and has little or no impact on the crimes which are of most concern to the public, such as burglary and robbery. These findings are consistent with findings from the Home Office programme of research instituted following the Stephen Lawrence Inquiry (see Miller, Bland and Quinton 2000, Quinton, Bland and Miller 2000, Stone and Pettigrew 2000). FitzGerald's study found that 'reasonable suspicion' is frequently absent and, more importantly, the power is not even being used for the purpose of catching suspects, but for the purposes of 'gaining intelligence' or for 'social control' by

Box 6.2 The Tottenham Experiment

In an attempt to increase the understanding about the use of stop and search powers among police officers and the local community in Tottenham, an experiment was undertaken involving police officers issuing a leaflet to people stopped and searched informing them of the powers being used as well as their rights. An evaluation of the initiative was carried out by NACRO (1997).

In Tottenham, police records showed the use of police stop and search powers fell by 52 per cent during the lifetime of the project, while in the control area (Vauxhall) there was no reduction. While the decline appeared to have begun before the start of the project, when the police in Tottenham ceased to use the numbers of stop/searches as a performance indicator (with its associated competition between individual officers and teams), the leaflet may well have been partly responsible for this reduction. However, the over-representation of African/Caribbeans among those stopped and searched did not change. In the pre-leaflet 12-month period, around 44 per cent of those stopped and searched were African/Caribbean, as against their 24 per cent representation in the local Tottenham population. In the 12-month period where the leaflet was distributed, the average proportion of African/Caribbeans stopped and searched was 45 per cent. The same occurred in the control area.

The various police perspectives on the use of stop and search powers revealed some important indicators to explain the use of these powers. First, there was evidence of a backlash against external criticism of the use of stop and search powers. Second, police officers reported that they used their stop and search powers often in response to descriptions provided by a victim or witness. Thus, during the period August 1995 to May 1996, the victims of street robbery described suspects as being African/Caribbean in 81 per cent of cases in Tottenham, although, of course, stop/searches will also target those suspected of other crimes (see also FitzGerald and Sibbitt 1997 who describe similar police views on the use of stop/search and the collection of ethnic monitoring data. Some officers even advocated the use of stop/search statistics to demonstrate the greater criminality of African/Caribbeans). Previously, Young (1994) has suggested that police officers may be generalising the 'race-of-suspect' information to other crime types, such as burglary and drug offences. A selection of comments made by police officers of different ranks are presented (NACRO, 1997):

- It's a difficult division to police, as it can be a political area. But the stop and search leaflet in my opinion is a good idea. (PC)
- Public should be educated that stop and search is backed by the law and is not a 'tool of oppression'. (PC)

- Distribution of leaflets hinders stop. It's not law and is an unnecessary burden on the officers concerned. (Sergeant)

Of those surveyed who were stop/searched in the Tottenham experiment, two-thirds felt that the police had not been polite and courteous in their interaction, mirroring the findings from other studies. Around one-half of respondents had been given a reason for the search, but most felt that the reason did not justify the search. Of those also stopped before the leaflet experiment, none reported that the current stop had been different, and around one-fifth reported that the search was worse in some way than before. Only 28 per cent of the sample said that they had received a copy of the leaflet when they were stopped during the experiment, and, among these, few felt that it made any difference to their experience. A selection of comments made by the respondents included (NACRO 1997):

- It is silly to stop a driver to check whether they are the owner, unless reported stolen. (African/Caribbean female, age 21)

- The police seem to think that everyone who looks different is a criminal so they stop them. (White male, age 24)

- There was no need to search both of us as the driver had all his papers. (African/Caribbean male, age 24)

The respondents recommended improving the training of police officers to enhance their understanding of the communities they served, and to eliminate racist attitudes, and in order to emphasise that most African/Caribbean people were law-abiding. There was also a strong view among respondents that the police service should more clearly reflect the ethnic make-up of the surrounding community, a point we will return to later in the book.

Recording Stops and Searches: Piloting the Macpherson Inquiry Recommendations

Bland, Miller and Quinton's (2000) evaluation of piloting the recording of stops and attempts to improve public accountability encountered similar problems to those identified in Tottenham. Significant under-recording of stop and searches were the result of officer misunderstanding, concern about unnecessary intrusion in police–public encounters, confusion about which types of interaction were to be recorded and officer selectivity.

The impact of piloting different recording practices did not appear to affect rates of stop and search. That said, interviews with some police officers did suggest that the pilot had changed their 'mind-set', encouraging them to think more carefully about the reasons for stopping

> someone. Like in the Tottenham experiment, however, some officers were less than positive about recording stops and giving those stopped an explanation for why the power was being used. Similarly, public reflections on the way they had been dealt with by the police echoed the findings from the NACRO evaluation; most important was the attitude of the officer and the manner in which they were dealt with. As Stone and Pettigrew's (2000: 29) qualitative study noted '[t]here was a very strong perception that the way in which stops and searches are currently handled causes more distrust, antagonism, and resentment than any of the positive effects it can have'.
>
> *Source:* Walker, Spohn and Delone (1996: 140–2).

'disrupting', 'breaking up' or 'moving on' groups of young people. This, as FitzGerald points out, is unjustifiable in terms of PACE and the inference is that such stops are, therefore, unlawful. The main result is the harassment and disaffection of major sections of the public because each stop and search encounter leaves the person stopped less satisfied with police service delivery and less confident in the police (see box 6.2).

In 1997, the Metropolitan Police abandoned the use of stop and search as a 'performance indicator'. Prior to this police managers formally encouraged constables to conduct as many searches as possible, taking this as a measure of their productivity. Despite this policy shift, some operational officers believe it is still used by supervisors (see Her Majesty's Inspectorate of Constabulary 2000). Moreover, levels of stop and search continued afterwards to increase and to be disproportionately focused on London's ethnic minority communities.

Thus, the number of stop/searches per 1,000 ethnic minority population rose from 80 to 87 between 1996 and 1998. The fact that levels of recorded stop and search began to fall in the spring of 1999 suggests that the policy decision taken in 1997 had begun to be implemented following briefings given in the wake of the publication of the Lawrence Inquiry findings. Moreover, concerns about the declining use of stop/search for ethnic minorities in the wake of the Lawrence Inquiry are not easily borne out by the statistical evidence (see FitzGerald 1999). Home Office (2000c) statistics show that in 1999/2000 the fall in the number of recorded stops was lower for black people in London and in England and Wales (35 per cent and 10 per cent), than it was for other ethnic groups (40 per cent and 14 per cent).

Arrest

Only a small minority of arrests – 8 per cent of all ethnic groups in 1999/2000 – result from a stop and search by the police (Home Office 2000c). Although this figure is slightly higher for black and Asian people, it is clear that most arrests result from reactive behaviour by the police following notification of an offence by a member of the public (see Mawby 1979, Steer 1980, Bottomley and Coleman 1981). Under PACE, the police can arrest an individual when they have reasonable grounds for suspicion that they have committed an offence. As Brown (1997: 55) notes, however: '[a]s a non-legal factor, race should have no bearing on the decision to arrest'.

Arrest statistics published by the Home Office (2000c) show that in 1999/2000 the number of black people arrested was on average four times higher than white people, relative to their numbers in the general population (see chapter 4). The arrest rate for Asians was also higher than it was for whites. The pre-PACE (Stevens and Willis 1979, Smith and Gray 1985, Phillips and Brown 1998, Home Office 1989a) and post-PACE studies have reported the same findings. Typically the breakdown according to offence type mirrors that observed among those imprisoned, with a marked over-representation of whites among those arrested for burglary and criminal damage (amounting to 17 per cent and 18 per cent of recorded notifiable offences in 1999/2000). There was an over-representation of both black and Asian people arrested for fraud and forgery and drugs, which represented 6 per cent and 2 per cent respectively of recorded notifiable offences in 1999/2000 (see Home Office 2000c, Povey, Cotton and Sisson 2000).

The statistics indicated a significant over-representation of blacks arrested for robbery, Although this is a crime which causes serious public concern, it accounted for only 2 per cent of recorded notifiable offences in 1999/2000. What is apparent from the local research conducted to examine ethnic monitoring is that arrests are more likely for certain offences and that forces typically depend on arrests to 'clear up' robbery offences and meet locally or force-set targets (FitzGerald and Sibbitt 1997). A cynical interpretation would suggest that these offences are being targeted because they are more likely to lead to the arrest of black suspects and can justify 'excessive' stop/search; alternatively, it could reflect objectives to prioritise violent crimes over property crimes in recognition of public anxieties. It is also possible that personal thefts by African/Caribbeans are more likely to be recorded as robbery, even in instances where no violence is involved (Blom-Cooper and Drabble 1982).

Outcomes following arrest

Arrest marks the first stage of the criminal justice process and the initial decisions about whether an individual enters the formal criminal justice system. The decisions to charge and prosecute are taken while the suspect is detained in police custody. Therefore, an examination of arrest outcomes can shed some light on the police processing and treatment of ethnic minorities. Are ethnic minority arrestees more or less likely to be charged with a criminal offence by the police than their white counterparts?

The decision to charge a suspect with an offence requires that there is sufficient evidence to do so. However, it is not the only option available to the police. They may decide to caution the suspect, or release them without charge either because they lack evidence or because a charge is not in the public interest. The option of cautioning is only available where: (a) the suspect admits the offence for which they have been arrested, and (b) they consent to being given a caution and (c) where the circumstances of both the offence and the offender are such that a caution is considered appropriate by a police officer.

In order to assess the equity of the police decision to charge/caution or take no further action against a suspect, it is necessary to consider legal factors, such as the strength of the evidence and admission of the offence. The type and seriousness of the offence will also be influential, although the way in which offences are categorised may, itself, be affected by discriminatory decision-making processes. Blom-Cooper and Drabble (1982) have speculated that young and inexperienced police officers in Brixton in the early 1980s were categorising all thefts from the person as 'other violent thefts', thus making them appear more serious in nature, and increasing the likelihood of being charged after arrest. The age of the suspect is also relevant, since there is a presumption in criminal justice policy in favour of cautioning juveniles in order that they be diverted from the criminal justice system.

In Phillips and Brown's (1998) study, researchers based in the custody areas observed those arrested at ten representative police stations in England and Wales in 1993/4. African/Caribbeans were more likely to be arrested than would be expected by their representation in the local populations, even at stations covering areas with smaller ethnic minority populations. The picture for Asians was less clear-cut, with both evidence of under- and over-representation depending on the location of the police station. Since arrested suspects were observed during their time at the police station, it was possible for the researchers to examine the extent to which factors, such as requesting legal advice and admitting the offence during police interviews, occurred differently for each ethnic group. This is important because it links to findings from research in courts that have

Box 6.3 Mistaken identity?

The operation of identity parades has come under scrutiny in recent years with two police forces being admonished by the courts for failing to provide a line-up of people 'matched' with the ethnic origin of the suspect to participate in identity parades. In a recent case, Gloucestershire police officers used make-up and wigs for men appearing as Rastafarians in a line-up.

Guardian, 19 August 1997

suggested that black people tend to distrust the criminal justice system and that this is reflected in their tendency to seek legal advice while at the police station. Indeed, it was the case that both blacks (51 per cent) and Asians (44 per cent) were more likely to seek legal advice than their white counterparts (35 per cent), confirming the pattern identified by Hood (1992) and Bucke and Brown (1997). It might also be the case that those suspects who distrust the police or feel they have been subjected to discriminatory treatment may more frequently deny the offence, which would in turn reduce their likelihood of being cautioned by the police rather than prosecuted. Phillips and Brown (1998) found that while 58 per cent of white suspects admitted the offence for which they had been arrested, only 44 per cent of blacks and 48 per cent of Asians did so.

In their study of the revised PACE codes of practice, which allow inferences to be drawn from a suspect's exercise of their right of silence, Bucke and Brown (1997) reported that African/Caribbeans were significantly more likely to refuse to answer some or all questions during police interview than their white and Asian counterparts. The question which none of these studies can address, of course, is the extent to which an unwillingness to admit offences or to answer police questioning is an indication of a reluctance to 'own up' to offending or an indication that the suspect is innocent of the alleged offence (see box 6.3).

Although comprehensive data on arrest outcomes is not yet available nationally, ethnic monitoring of police cautioning of notifiable offences by the Home Office (2000c) has shown that there are marked differences in the cautioning rates in 1999/2000 for white (16 per cent) and Asian suspects (15 per cent) compared with black (11 per cent) suspects. However, these data have not been able to take into account factors such as offence type, seriousness and order, force variation in cautioning practices and differences in admission of the offence and offender remorse.

Box 6.4 Grassroots action: an example

As community organisations have become aware of the over-representation of people among those arrested and detained by the police, initiatives have emerged to inform individuals of their rights while in police custody. One such initiative based in Sheffield, the Black Justice Project, operates a 'Help on Arrest Scheme'. Ethnic minority volunteers are available on a 24-hour basis to provide rights advice to suspects (in police cells if necessary), and they will contact suspects' families, friends or solicitors if required. When an ethnic minority suspect is arrested, the South Yorkshire Police hand out a leaflet advertising the services of the Black Justice Project (1995). Britton's (2000: 648) qualitative research of a Help On Arrest Scheme suggests that they may be viewed critically by police custody staff, who perceive them to be 'special treatment' for black people, an 'unacceptable form of positive discrimination'.

Phillips and Brown (1998) found that the final outcome of the arrest process did not appear to be related to the ethnic origin of the suspect. The same proportion (59 per cent) of white and black suspects were charged by the police, compared with 54 per cent of Asians. Thus, on the face of it, there appeared to be no evidence of discriminatory practices by the police. However, blacks (16 per cent) and Asians (14 per cent) were significantly less likely to be cautioned than white suspects (19 per cent), probably because they were less likely to admit the offence.

Although ethnic origin was not a significant predictor of the decision to take no further action, the real test is with Crown Prosecution Service (CPS) decision making. Set up to take over the prosecution of cases from the police, the CPS provide the acid test of whether cases stand a realistic prospect of conviction if they proceed to court and whether prosecution is in the public interest. Since the charged suspects in the Phillips and Brown (1998) study were followed through to the CPS review process, we return to this in the following chapter.

Police processing of juveniles

Criminal justice policy has, throughout most of the twentieth century, and certainly since the 1969 Children and Young Persons Act, worked on the principle that diversion from court proceedings is the most appropriate way to deal with juveniles and young offenders in order to reduce their chances of committing further offences, by avoiding the stigma of prosecution and the associated difficulties of having a criminal record or serving a custodial sentence. Police cautioning – a stern lecture delivered by a police officer – has provided the means for diverting many young people from the formal criminal justice system, with a multi-agency input into this process. The use of cautioning varies widely in different areas and by officers within the police, reflecting its discretionary nature (Evans and Wilkinson 1990). This may have considerable implications for its use among black and Asian juveniles when compared with their white counterparts.

Landau's (1981) pioneering study aimed to discover whether the police immediately charged or referred cases to a multi-agency forum, then known as the 'juvenile bureau', for their consideration.[10] The juvenile's previous record was found to be the most important factor relating to the police decision, but area differences were also apparent, and these interacted with offence type to produce more severe outcomes for certain young people. Ethnic origin was significantly related to the police

---

[10] These decisions were made in respect of 896 white juveniles and 548 black juveniles in five divisions in the Metropolitan Police District between October and December 1978.

decision to charge immediately, over and above the effect of previous record, but only in interaction with offence type. Thus, black juveniles who were arrested for violent crime, burglary, public order offences and other offences (including 'sus') more frequently faced an immediate charge than their white counterparts. Where the offence was theft, white and black juveniles were treated in a similar fashion. Moreover, black first-time offenders appeared to be more harshly treated than white first-time offenders.

In a follow-up study, Landau and Nathan (1983) examined the second stage of police decision making, where the juvenile bureau recommends that the police charge, caution, or take no further action. At that time, juvenile bureaux which received a referral would typically consider the juvenile's alleged offence and their background before deciding upon the most appropriate course of action. This would include a home visit, as well as contact with social and educational welfare services. Landau and Nathan found that white juveniles were much more likely to be cautioned than their black counterparts, even when previous record and offence type and seriousness had been controlled for (see also Tipler 1989). This pattern was particularly evident where the offence was public order, a motor vehicle offence or violence against the person. Only in traffic offences did black juveniles fare better than their white counterparts.

Although information on background characteristics was somewhat limited, the data did show that black juveniles were more likely to come from disrupted families (that is, those affected by divorce, separation, death, illness, prison and paternal unemployment) or to be 'latch-key kids' than white juveniles. These features may well have explained the police decision to charge these juveniles. This type of decision making can be viewed as indirect racial discrimination where apparently neutral decisions have a negative impact on ethnic minorities because of racial disadvantage. Similarly, Landau and Nathan (1983) recognised the importance of 'substantive non-legal variables', such as degree of parental control, which operated to produce more punitive outcomes for ethnic minority juveniles (see also FitzGerald and Sibbitt 1997: 79.)

These studies provide useful information about the police decision to refer an individual to the juvenile bureau, and the decision to charge or caution a juvenile suspect. However, they do not take into account one of the most important criteria for a caution: admission of the offence. In a more recent study carried out on behalf of the Commission For Racial Equality (1992), data was collected by the Avon and Somerset Constabulary on the final dispositions of 978 juvenile cases in Bristol during September 1989 and August 1990. In Bristol, 51–57 per cent of ethnic minority and 34 per cent of white juveniles were prosecuted. This was linked to the former group's greater likelihood of being arrested for more serious offences, and partly the result of them having a higher number of previous convictions. While no percentages are presented in the report on these two variables, this study did show that only 37 per cent of black juveniles admitted the offence and thus would have been eligible for a caution, compared with 62 per cent of their white counterparts. Whether this indicates innocence and a distrust of the police or an unwillingness to admit participation in an offence is not clear.

Similarly, research by the West Midlands Joint Data Team (1996) found lower rates of cautioning for Asian juveniles, with similar cautioning rates for black and white juveniles, when legal factors, such as offending on bail/warrant, admission of the offence and divisional policy, were taken into consideration. However, black/white differences remained in some areas in the West Midlands force, and there was not a breakdown of offence by type (cited in FitzGerald and Sibbitt 1997: 81). Further analysis of the data collected during the Metropolitan Police CRE (Commission for Racial Equality) project found that in London in 1993 cautioning rates were similar for white and black juveniles for the offences of theft and burglary, for cases where the offence was admitted and the juvenile was a first-time offender. However, for robbery black and Asians were less likely to be cautioned than whites under the same circumstances, although the numbers in the sub-samples were too small to enable meaningful comparisons (FitzGerald and Sibbitt 1997). Phillips and Brown's (1998) study suggests that the black juveniles are far less likely than white or Asian juveniles to have their cases referred to inter-agency panels, even after controlling for their lower admission rates. Future research in this area which includes details of the decision making of multi-agency juvenile panels is essential to test these findings further, and to consider the role of direct and indirect discrimination.

Police remand

The police also have at their disposal the powers to remand a suspect in custody after charging, or they may bail them to appear in court at a later date. The power to remand in custody exists to maximise the chances that the defendant will appear at court, that they will not reoffend or interfere with the administration of justice. The Criminal Justice and Public Order Act 1994 further extended these powers in relation to bail, allowing the police to impose bail conditions on defendants to ensure their appearance in court while releasing them from custody.

Walker's (1989) study of 27,000 male defendants prosecuted in London magistrates' and Crown Courts in 1983 (to which we return in the next chapter) also collected data on police remands. Among 17–20 year olds and 21–5 year olds, black suspects were significantly more likely to be held at the police station prior to court than either white or Asian suspects, though no information was available on the reason for the police decision to refuse bail. Phillips and Brown (1998) found the refusal of bail to be related to the ethnic origin of the suspect, even once offence type and previous convictions had been taken into account. Some 26 per cent of white suspects in their study were refused bail, compared with 35 per cent of black and 34 per cent of Asian suspects. In contrast, Bucke and Brown (1997) have suggested that the higher rate of detention after charge for black people in their study was the result of their offence profile, with more having been charged with drugs, robbery and burglary offences. The interaction of 'race' with these factors further complicates this picture. As we have mentioned before, seriousness of the offence may reflect 'overcharging' practices, and homelessness itself results from social and economic disadvantage which disproportionately affects ethnic minorities.

The importance of police remand should not be underestimated since the decision made by the police with regard to bail has implications for how the defendant fares at court. It is likely that the courts will follow the lead of the police in deciding whether a defendant should receive court bail later on in the criminal justice process (see Burrows, Henderson and Morgan 1995, cf. Walker 1988). As will be seen in the next chapter, being remanded in custody by the courts is a significant factor in the defendant receiving a custodial sentence if convicted. Future research must examine police remand decisions since this is likely to have a cumulative effect on the experiences of individuals accused of crimes.

The extent to which discriminatory processing of blacks by the police contributes to their over-representation in sentenced and remanded prison populations cannot be easily assessed with the disparate information currently available on the criminal justice process. We return to this question once we have examined prosecution and considered the role of indirect discrimination in diversion from court and custody in chapter 7. Suffice to say here, it seems likely that police stereotyping of blacks and Asians (albeit in a distinctively different way) during police processing (Phillips and Brown 1998) contributes to fewer black juveniles having their cases referred to multi-agency juvenile panels and their markedly lower rate of being granted police bail.

Explaining discrimination in policing

Having set out the empirical evidence relating to the policing of ethnic minority communities and their entry into the criminal justice process in comparison with their white peers, we now turn our attention to the ways in which evidence of discriminatory conduct has been explained by criminological researchers and theorists. There is a bewildering array of different theories of policing based on individual, cultural and structural perspectives.

The 'bad apple' thesis

Racial prejudice and discrimination in the police service have traditionally been formulated as a problem of a small number of racist police officers' individual actions. Racism, in these accounts, is described principally as a personal attribute. For example, Lord Scarman (1981/6: 105) pointed to the 'ill-considered, immature and racially prejudiced actions of some officers in their dealings on the streets with young black people'. In his view, racial prejudice was not to be found among senior police officers, and he thought it uncommon even among more junior officers. For Scarman, the answer to allegations of police racism was to check recruitment into the police service through 'scientific means' alongside training, supervision and discipline. One early study examined the individual psychology of police officers, arguing that they tend to be more 'authoritarian' than similarly placed people in other professions (Coleman and Gorman 1982). The approach based on individual behaviour is appealing, as Scarman indicates, because the obvious solution is to ferret out the 'bad apples' who have sneaked into the barrel and prevent any more from getting in. However, it has been criticised because it takes insufficient account of the extent to which individual prejudices are shared within the police organisational culture and the extent to which these are shared by the wider society and fails to place police work in its structural context (Keith 1993, Cathcart 1999).

The 'reflection of society' thesis

The 'bad apple' thesis is linked to a second explanation which is that because the police service is a cross-section of society some police officers are more likely to be racially prejudiced than others (Scarman 1981/6: 106, see also Keith 1993). This 'bad apple' theory goes further than others to argue that if white people in the general population hold prejudices against African, Caribbean and Asian people, this will be reflected in the attitudes, prejudices and presuppositions of the force as a whole. Scarman accepted the premise, but roundly rejected the 'cross-section of society' as a defence of discriminatory practice:

> The police cannot rest on the argument that since they are a cross-section of society some officers are bound to be racially prejudiced. Senior Metropolitan Police officers accept this. They recognise that in this respect, as in others, the standards we apply to the police must be higher than the norms of behaviour prevalent in society as a whole.
>
> (Scarman 1981/6: 106)

More recently, Her Majesty's Chief Inspectorate of Constabulary (1997) published a 'thematic' inspection looking specifically at community and race relations policies and practices within the police service (see also Her Majesty's Chief Inspectorate of Constabulary 1999). The conclusion of the report echoes much of what was said in the earlier period about racism in wider society and its 'reflection' in policing.

> Racial discrimination, both direct and indirect, and harassment are endemic within our society and the police service is no exception ... There was continuing evidence during the Inspection of inappropriate language and behaviour by police officers, but even more worrying was the lack of intervention by sergeants and inspectors. This was reinforced during the observation of assessment panels for promotion to sergeant and inspector where potential supervisors demonstrated a reluctance to challenge colleagues who indulge in racist 'banter' and racist behaviour.

The 'canteen culture' thesis

A third approach is what Keith (1993) refers to as 'pathology sociology', which relies exclusively on an analysis of the subcultural aspects of policing. Like any other organisation, the police service consists of a distinctive range of organisational cultures. These cultures are marked by specific languages, rituals, values, norms, perspectives and craft rules. Cultures change over time and differ from one force to the next – or even from one police station to the next (Foster 1990) – they differ by rank (Reiner 2000), and between specialisms such as community police (Holdaway 1983, Fielding 1995), and detectives (Hobbs 1988). Despite these variations some specific cultural themes can be found to run through the police service because they are a response to constant problems and pressures faced by individuals carrying out the policing function (Reiner 1992). The 'core characteristics' of the police working culture are a sense of 'mission', pragmatism, a thirst for action, cynicism, pessimism, suspicion, isolation from the public and solidarity with other police ('them' against 'us'), conservatism, machismo, authoritarianism (Coleman and Gorman 1982), and racial prejudice (Reiner 1992, Graef 1989, Holdaway 1983, 1997).

According to Reiner, 'cop culture' is crucial to an analysis of what police do because the rank-and-file officer defines what policing means on the street. Unlike other organisations in which autonomy and discretion are greatest at the most senior levels, policing is characterised by the increasing discretion towards the lower ranks (Reiner 1992, Wilson 1968). Although criminal law and criminal procedure do provide certain constraints for police action, laws governing police behaviour are 'permissive' in the sense that they do not purport to determine practical policing. This leaves 'considerable leeway for police culture to shape police practice in accordance with situational exigencies' (Reiner 1992: 108).

Among the cultural characteristics of interest to the present discussion is the use of specific stereotypes and ways of classifying the public, and specifically racial prejudice (Reiner 2000: 98–100, 115–21). In general, Reiner argues that black and Asian people are likely to be seen as 'police property' – lower status, powerless groups whom the dominant majority see as problematic and distasteful. According to Reiner, the police believe that the majority of the public give them 'permission' to deal with ethnic minorities, along with vagrants, alcoholics, the unemployed, deviant youth, gays, prostitutes and political radicals as though they were their 'property' and turn a blind eye to the manner in which this is done (Choong 1998). When ethnic minorities call upon the services of the police they are seen, along with other marginal groups, as 'rubbish' – people who make calls on the police which are seen as messy, intractable, unworthy of attention, or the complainant's own fault (Reiner 2000, Smith and Gray 1985).

Evidence for the stereotyping of African/Caribbean and Asian people by the police has come from a number of research studies. In a study conducted two decades ago, Smith and Gray (1983) found that 'racial prejudice and racialist talk ... [were] pervasive ... expected, accepted and even fashionable'. Moreover, this was not something restricted to constables, but was to be found throughout the ranks. Smith and Gray's work was confirmed by Holdaway's (1983, 1997: 78) 'insider account' of the routine negative views of black people. Most shocking was the persistent use of racist terms such as 'coon', 'wog' 'nig-nog', 'spade', 'sooty', 'satchie', 'monkey' and 'nigger' that Holdaway describes as 'common verbal currency among the lower ranks'. There are also specific, and quite different, stereotypes attaching to Asians and black people. Cain (1973) found that Asians tended to be regarded as devious, liars and potential illegal immigrants. As a police officer in Graef's (1989: 131) study put it: 'That's a problem with Asians: they make so many allegations that are totally a pack of lies.' Black people by contrast are thought prone to violence or crime, incomprehensible, suspicious and hard to handle (cited in Reiner 1992). Officers interviewed by Graef saw African/Caribbean people as 'naturally excitable', aggressive, 'lacking brainpower', 'anti', drug users, troublesome and 'tooled up' (Graef 1989).

While such attitudes were not held by each and every individual officer, there is patchy evidence that they remain pervasive and accepted. Bowling (1999a) found that police officers saw racism as a 'natural' and inevitable resentment of ethnic minorities in what had been at one time 'white areas'. One source of this resentment was the existence of racial equality or equal opportunities policies. This natural resentment, it was suggested, would lead to spontaneous expressions of violence. Police officers of all ranks expressed views that reflected the logic of white territorial ownership of the locality and its resources. The areas 'belonged to' the white community – it was 'theirs' – while ethnic minorities were seen to be 'taking over'. It is not that the police condoned racist violence but they clearly identified with the viewpoint of the white community, seeing their resentment and its expression in violence as 'natural' and understandable. Few interviewees questioned this territorial logic, or expressed the view that the ethnic minorities had an equal right to live in the locality. A related view was that an inevitable conflict between the cultural practices of whites and ethnic minorities was the cause of racism. This viewpoint relied principally on stereotypes of African/Caribbeans liking loud music and Asians cooking smelly food. Again, the dominant view was that 'our' culture was being rejected, 'their' customs, language, food and dress were unacceptable and resentment was the natural outcome. Thus, racist violence was not a consequence of racial prejudice, but of the rejection of the English language and failure to adapt to English customs, diet and style of dress. This, seen as a failure to 'accept' Englishness, made ethnic minorities at once threatening and vulnerable to attack (Bowling 1999a).

Reiner, in his study *Chief Constables*, found that race was spontaneously mentioned more often than any other social division in society and mentioned frequently in other contexts (Reiner 1991: 204–10). Although a number of the 'younger and better educated chiefs and those in the metropolitan areas' discussed 'race' without invoking negative stereotypes, most did. As Reiner (ibid.: 207) puts it, the standard view was to regard the presence of black people, or sometimes 'foreigners' more generally, as problematic for the police. They tended to be seen as crime-prone, disorderly, argumentative, irrational, 'likely to be carrying drugs or dangerous implements, noisy, and responsible for the antipathy held towards them'. One chief, on seeing a 'coloured man' walking down the road said 'Hello! What's that? Give us a few more of those and we'll have problems here' (ibid.: 205).

As Keith (1993) correctly points out, however, there is a danger that ethnographic research which is frequently 'under-theorised' culminates in cultural generalisations of junior officers which either provides a rhetorical let-off for their senior colleagues or a convenient scapegoat for analysis of police–black antagonisms. Certainly, although it is not irrelevant, the subcultural theme is inadequate as the sole explanation of police racism. Nonetheless, charting the facets of police occupational culture is a crucial component of police practices *vis-à-vis* black and Asian people.

The 'institutional racism' thesis

The Scarman Report is taken by many as the classic defence against the allegation that 'Britain is an institutionally racist society'. The report actually suggests two contrasting definitions:

> If, by [institutionally racist] it is meant that it is [1] a society which knowingly, as a matter of policy, discriminates against black people, I reject the allegation. If, however, the suggestion being made is that [2] practices may be adopted by public bodies as well as private individuals which are unwittingly discriminatory against black people, then this is an allegation which deserves serious consideration, and, where proved, swift remedy.
>
> (1981/6: 28, numerals added)

First, then, Scarman rejected the notion of an explicit 'knowing' policy of discrimination; what might be termed 'direct' discrimination under the 1976 Race Relations Act. It is possible to see how Scarman felt able to reject this allegation. With the notorious exception of immigration law, there are few examples of British government policy in the early 1980s which explicitly and formally denied specific rights on the basis of race in the way of apartheid South Africa, Jim Crow USA, or even Britain in the era of 'colour bar', during the inter-war years. Scarman's second definition refers to the 'unwitting' (that is, unintentional) discrimination found in the practices of public institutions; this might be termed 'indirect discrimination' under the 1976 Act. Here Scarman accepted both the possibility that such 'unwitting discrimination' could exist and the need for 'swift remedy' where it was proven. Studies at the time provided ample evidence that people from ethnic minorities were discriminated against in a variety of different settings including housing, employment and education (for example, Smith 1977, Brown 1984). In policing terms, Scarman admitted that 'some officers ... lapse into an unthinking assumption that all young black people are potential criminals', stereotyping in a way which was supported by research conducted at the time (for example, Smith and Gray 1983) and which resonated with the wider concerns about police attitudes and behaviour in general and towards people from ethnic minorities in particular (Home Office 1981, House of Commons Home Affairs Committee 1982).

However, the Lawrence Inquiry took a different view. It considered the evidence of a range of different forms of indirect discrimination – including stereotyping Stephen Lawrence and Duwayne Brookes at the scene of the murder, patronising behaviour towards the Lawrence family, as well as stop and search powers targeted against young people from ethnic minorities. Formally at least, the problem of institutional racism has been recognised by ACPO and the Home Office. As the Home Secretary commented, when the Lawrence Inquiry was published:

> [t]he inquiry found that, on that definition, institutional racism exists within ... both the Metropolitan Police Service and in other Police Services and other institutions countrywide. ... That is a new definition of institutional racism, which I accept – and so does the Commissioner. The inquiry's assessment is clear and sensible. In my view, any long-established, white-dominated organisation is liable to have procedures, practices and a culture that tend to exclude or to disadvantage non-white people. The police service, in that respect, is little different from other parts of the criminal justice system – or from Government Departments, including the Home Office – and many other institutions.

Even John Newing, then President of ACPO and Chief Constable of Derbyshire, wrote to the inquiry saying:

> I define institutional racism as the racism which is inherent in wider society which shapes our attitudes and behaviour. Those attitudes and behaviour are then reinforced or reshaped by the culture of the organisation a person

works for. In the police service there is a distinct tendency for officers to stereotype people. That creates problems in a number of areas, but particularly in the way officers deal with black people. Discrimination and unfairness are the result. I know because as a young police officer I was guilty of such behaviour.

(Macpherson 1999: paragraph 6.50, pp. 31–2)

Contextual discrimination: social structure, institutional cultures and operational practices

There is an argument that racist ideas, *as ideas*, are neither dangerous nor worrisome. In this line of thinking, ideas found in documents or speech and are, in themselves, harmless. Opposing this are the views that (1) the creation and distribution of those words is a form of hostile action, because the words themselves can cause harassment, alarm, distress and other harms and (2) they are dangerous and harmful because of the acts that they inspire. The relationship between thought and action is clearly complex. As Stuart Hall *et al.* (1998) put it:

> The chain which connects racial attitudes to racial conduct is complex, but consistent. Our basic attitudes *do* influence how we behave. Where possible, we attempt to bring our conduct in line with our attitudes. Training, professionalism, policy directives, procedural guidance, managerial supervision, accountability and the monitoring of conduct are some of the ways in which organisations seek to interrupt and break the otherwise automatic link between attitudes and behaviour and attempt to instil more reflexive attitudes towards practice. However, these efforts often appear remote from the day-to-day tasks and well-established routines. Well-formed prejudices and institutional attitudes are deeply based and emotionally held in place; the culture of organisations is notoriously difficult to shift.
>
> (1998:6)

Smith and Gray's (1983: 109) study provides ample evidence of racist behaviour 'in private':

> our first impression ... was that racialist language and racial prejudice were prominent and pervasive and that many individual officers and also whole groups were preoccupied with ethnic differences.

However, they did not observe explicitly racist conduct on the street:

> on accompanying these officers as they went about their work we found that their relations with black and brown people were often relaxed or friendly and that the degree of tension between them and black people from day to day was much less than might have been expected from their own conversation or from accounts in the newspapers and on television.

This apparent conflict between attitudes and behaviours supposed by Smith and Gray (1985: 403) may be summarised by one of their interviewees who commented that:

> I freely admit that I hate, loathe and despise niggers. I can't stand them. I don't let it affect my job though.

It is the simplistic and flawed conclusion, based on the idea that thought and action are entirely separable, which leads them to the conclusion that police subcultural racism has no impact on the treatment of ethnic minority communities.

Although observational research has rarely revealed the use of racist language or behaviour in street encounters between police and ethnic minorities, the racist expressions (documented in the canteen) mirror almost exactly the experiences documented by black and Asian communities and the evidence produced by covert methods, such as the incident tape recorded by Malkjitt Natt (see Holdaway 1996: 72–3). The missing connection between police attitudes, verbal expressions of hostility and actual behaviour towards ethnic minorities is routine police conduct *unobserved* by social scientists or other third parties (cf. Phillips and Brown 1997). Contrary to Smith and Gray's (1985) conclusion, it is clear that racist thoughts are reflected in racist utterances (irrespective of who hears them) and these utterances contain racist stereotyping which suggest a course of action. As social psychological research shows, attitudes do ultimately affect the way in which people behave, even if the link is complex, indirect and does not apply in every instance. The point is, as Hall *et al.* suggest:

> There is no automatic or straightforward link between racially prejudiced attitudes and language and discriminatory or differential behaviour. Given the contingent nature of stereotyping, the complexities of police–public interactions and the broad discretionary powers enjoyed by officers, it is often difficult to establish whether it is 'race' rather than a multitude of other factors that triggers a police action. Researchers have witnessed many officers treating black people with considerably more courtesy and respect in the course of operational duties than individual and group attitudes would have suggested. Nonetheless, there is a consistency in the pervasive nature and expression of racial stereotypes and their influence on police expectations and behaviours in numerous incidents.
>
> (Hall *et al.* 1998: 9)

Her Majesty's Inspectorate of Constabularly (mainly comprised of recently retired chief officers and a staff of serving police officers) concluded after conducting a 'thematic review' of 'community and race relations' in English police forces in 1997 that there is '*a direct and vital link between internal culture in the way people are treated and external performance*' Her Majesty's Inspectorate of Constabulary (1997: 18) Accounts of racist banter, discrimination and its effects within the organisation were 'directly' and 'vitally' linked with the 'number of accounts from members of the public of racist behaviour by police officers'. They conclude that, 'Even if the majority of the accounts are dismissed as either the products of third-party articulation or even exaggeration, a picture still emerges of pockets of wholly unacceptable racist policing' (ibid.).

Police governance

The ability to explain and justify their actions to the public determines the extent to which the police and their use of coercion are judged legitimate and are the basis for the British tradition of 'policing by consent' (McLaughlin 1991, 1994, Morgan 1989, Reiner 1992). Systems of accountability are also one of the key mechanisms that have been proposed for reducing the extent of discrimination. It is when there are actual abuses of police power – such as the use of excessive force, false allegations or tampering with evidence – that issues of police accountability come to the fore. However, it goes much further than this, encompassing the routine contacts between the police and members of the public in their capacities as victim, suspect or witness.

It is a central plank of orthodox legal theory that the police are, first and foremost, accountable to the law. However, the 'rule of law' is an abstract concept that must be related to its expression *in practice* to be meaningful. Gilroy and Sim (1987) argue that law, police and court action cannot be separated. Rather than being directly accountable to the law, the existence of discretion means that the law is permissive (see also Grimshaw and Jefferson 1987, Lustgarten 1986). The law defines when a police officer may act, but cannot direct a police officer to act or act in a particular way in a given instance (Lustgarten 1986), nor does it act as a control on police activity during encounters with the public (Gilroy and Sim 1987). In practice, the law is frequently used as a resource by the police to achieve police defined goals (Holdaway 1983, Gilroy and Sim 1987). For example, although the police may only stop and search someone under PACE if they have 'reasonable suspicion' that an offence is being committed, as we have seen this is so permissive a concept that, *in practice*, the police can stop and search anyone in almost any circumstance. Moreover, some laws are constructed in such a way that they systemically disadvantage people from ethnic minorities. Successive immigration laws, for example, have systematically stripped many African, Caribbean and Asian migrants of the right of entry and abode and the ability to keep families intact. Through targeted immigration policing, ethnic minority communities are disadvantaged by legitimising colour as a basis for suspicion.

It has been argued that structures of police governance should reflect the demographic characteristics of the community being policed. However, ethnic minority communities are under-represented among chief police officers, middling or senior ranks of the Home Office and in police authorities (Jones and Newburn 1997). The idea of policing by consent is compromised if systems of accountability fail to reflect the diversity of the population. This 'democratic deficit' has long been recognised and attempts have been made to increase the responsiveness of the police to minority communities. Specialist 'community relations departments' have existed since African, Caribbean and Asian populations were first perceived to present a 'community relations problem' for the police from the late 1950s onwards (see Pope 1976, Roach 1978). Scarman specifically cited a failure to consult and inform communities as a cause of the 1981 riots. However, the 'Police Community Consultative Groups' (PCCGs),[11] recommended by Scarman, are widely viewed by police and public alike to be ineffective (Morgan 1989). Current arrangements offer few opportunities for local communities to exert any control over the police organisation, nor it seems, were they intended to (ibid.). Recent changes under the 1998 Crime and Disorder Act require community consultation in co-operation with local authorities and the police. This also requires consultation of the 'hard to reach' groups under s.6 of the Act. However, consultation does not amount to accountability (Bridges 1982) and consequently those who get involved will probably find, like the earlier generation, that their participation is of 'marginal importance to the principal areas of police activity' (Commission for Racial Equality, 1991: 30). The deficit in legal and political accountability is unlikely to be redressed by the creation of new systems of 'consultation'.

In recent years there has been a shift away from political accountability towards 'financial' and 'managerial' accountability (Jones and Newburn 1997: 12). Managerialist reforms emphasise effectiveness, efficiency, information about 'performance outputs' and defines participation in terms of consumers' purchasing services. As Jones and Newburn put it, policing in this formulation, is incorrectly presented as a politically neutral 'technical exercise', the output of which can be measured and thus its performance judged (ibid.: 15). Much lesser emphasis is placed on responsiveness to elected bodies, direct participation or equity. Consequently, formal democratic institutions play an even more limited role in the development of policy or changing criminal justice practice.

Complaints procedures

The process by which the public can formally complain about instances of error and misconduct is the 'touchstone' of police accountability. It is through this process that the police may be called upon to explain and account for allegations of misconduct and impropriety, and, where necessary, make amends for injury and deaths arising from the use of force. If the most serious cases are not dealt with in a way that satisfies the 'consumer' of police services and coercive powers, it is unlikely that the police can be accountable for other aspects of their conduct. First put on

---

[11] PCCGs or 'Scarman Committees' were formalised in s.106 of the Police and Criminal Evidence Act 1984, and consolidated in s.96 of the Police Act 1996 (see Keith 1988, 1993, Jones and Newburn 1997).

a statutory basis in 1964, the Police Complaints Authority[12] is not a completely independent system, but supervises police officers from another force area who conduct the investigation.

The way in which complaints by African, Caribbean and Asian people against the police have been handled has been the subject of much criticism (Institute of Race Relations 1979: 87). The first study in this area found that ethnic minority groups were much more likely to complain of misconduct than would have been expected from their numbers in the population but complaints made by black and Asian people were also significantly less likely to be substantiated (Stevens and Willis 1981). The report noted that these results might be explained by the fact that complaints of assault, particularly in the police cells after arrest, were more common among black complainants and that these types of allegations generally had a low substantiation rate.

The Police Complaints Authority does not provide breakdowns of complaints against the police by ethnic origin, but since 1990 has collected separate figures for complaints of racially discriminatory behaviour by police officers. In the first full year of recording (1991), there were 49 such complaints, which have increased 12-fold in a decade to 579 in 2000 (Police Complaints Authority 2000: 18). The substantiation rate for all complaints is about 2 per cent, while that for allegations of racially discriminatory conduct is substantially lower. The Police Complaints Authority notes that there are difficulties in substantiating these complaints, many of which allege incivility or the misuse of stop and search powers: 'in the former case, officers are unlikely to use offensive or racist language in the presence of independent witnesses. In the latter, it is difficult to prove beyond reasonable doubt that the complainant was picked out specifically because of his or her racial origin' (Police Complaints Authority 1997: 52). In 1996/7 a total of four officers were found guilty of racially discriminatory behaviour and were either dismissed or resigned from the service and a fifth resigned before the disciplinary hearing (ibid.). The police complaints process has been widely criticised from both within and outside the service. The British Social Attitudes survey notes that there is 'near universal support' that a new, properly independent body should be set up to investigate complaints against the police (Tarling and Dowds 1995).

---

[12] A formal complaints procedure was first put on a statutory basis in 1964, and modified by the 1976 Police Act. After much criticism of the way in which the system was working, particularly in the 1979 Royal Commission, the Police Complaints Board was transformed into the Police Complaints Authority (PCA), established under s.83 of the Police and Criminal Evidence Act (1984), and subsequently modified under the 1996 Police Act (s.103 (3)).

Redress through civil litigation

Perceived and actual ineffectiveness in the police complaints procedure and 'fear of themselves being criminalised or harassed' (Institute of Race Relations 1987) have led victims of alleged police misconduct increasingly to forgo the official complaints procedure and instead to take civil court proceedings for damages against the police. The use of the civil courts has increased dramatically over the past two decades. In London in 1979, only seven cases against the Metropolitan Police were heard, resulting in damages of only £1,991 being paid; in 1986, there were 126 cases heard, resulting in damages to victims of £373,000 (ibid.: 86). By 1994/5 in the Metropolitan Police this had leapt to 731 threatened actions, and 1,000 in 1996/7 (Metropolitan Police 1997: 83), while damage payments tripled from £1.3 million in 1994/5 to £3.9 million in 1999/2000 (Metropolitan Police 2001).

Conclusion

In recent years, the political language of 'zero tolerance' has encouraged police officers to focus more of their activity on 'stop and search'. The result is that the use of such powers has increased sharply. During 1997/8, the police stopped and searched just over a million people or vehicles in England and Wales, over nine times the number in 1986, the first year of the legislation. Because of police targeting, increasing rates of stop and search impact disproportionately on ethnic minority communities. Even taking account of the declining use of stop and search in 1999/2000, the per 1,000 population rates are 19 for whites, 95 for blacks, 37 for Asians and 13 for those from other ethnic groups (Home Office 2000c). One result of an increased level of coercive policing is the undermining of public trust towards the police and the creation of tension and resentment. It is clear that the use of proactive policing techniques, such as aggressive saturation policing and the extensive use of stop and search alienates people from all communities. These practices are influenced by racist stereotyping by the police, which may be reciprocated with hostility and leads to dissatisfaction. As we will see in subsequent chapters, the 'over-policing' of ethnic minorities provides part of the explanation for the over-representation of black people in the prison population.

The evidence reviewed here suggests a widespread tendency for black and Asian communities to receive greatly inferior treatment by the police (cf. Smith 1994: 1091). In general terms ethnic minority communities are considered to be 'suspect populations' in a way which transcends their class position and is defined specifically by police officers in terms of 'racial' characteristics as individuals and as a collective. Moreover, the apparent resistance of some police officers to commit themselves to equal opportunities does not bode well for ethnic minority communities in the future. The extent to which the reform process set in train by the Stephen Lawrence Inquiry will affect policing practice remains to be seen.

Chapter 7

Prosecution and sentencing

By the end point of the criminal justice process people of African and Caribbean origin are strikingly over-represented in remand and sentenced prison populations. Some evidence which enables us to explain this has emerged in the previous chapters on policing. Research indicates that the police do target some ethnic minority groups and that this may have the effect of drawing them in through the 'gates' of the criminal justice system disproportionately either to their numbers in the population or to their involvement in crime. In this chapter we turn our attention to a series of questions which have been raised about the treatment of ethnic minorities in the prosecution and sentencing process. Clearly, the central issue concerns sentencing disparities that lead to an over-representation of ethnic minorities in prison. Given this 'criminological fact', our guiding framework demands that we ask whether the empirical evidence indicates direct or indirect discrimination against ethnic minorities in the organisational policies and practices of the Crown Prosecution Service and the courts. We also seek to build up a picture of the differential experiences of ethnic minorities in an attempt to explain how these contribute to their treatment within criminal justice processing as a whole.

The decision to terminate or prosecute cases

It is not only people that receive a police caution that may be diverted from prosecution. Once a suspect has been charged with an offence at the police station, their case file is sent to the Crown Prosecution Service (CPS) in order that they can make the decision about whether to proceed to court with the case or to *terminate* the case – in which case the defendant does not have to attend court and face criminal charges. Prosecutors have to consider whether there is a 'realistic prospect of conviction' based on the strength of evidence against the suspect. If the evidence is judged to be strong enough, crown prosecutors then have to decide whether it is in the public interest for the case to proceed (Crown Prosecution Service 1994). This will depend on factors such as the seriousness of the offence, whether the defendant was central or peripheral to the offence, and the willingness of the victim to participate in the prosecution process.

Phillips and Brown's (1998) prospective study of a sample of persons arrested at ten police stations in England and Wales then tracked them as they progressed through the criminal justice process. It is one of only two studies which allows an examination of CPS decision making in cases involving ethnic minority defendants. In the Phillips and Brown research in only 40 per cent of cases was the ethnic origin of defendants known by crown prosecutors, a finding similarly reported by Crisp and Moxon (1994). Thus, on the face of it, the extent to which there was scope for crown prosecutors to discriminate knowingly against defendants on the basis of ethnic origin was rather limited by the fact that in the majority of cases this information was not available. However, Phillips and Brown reported that the termination rate for cases according to the ethnic origin of the defendant was as follows: 12 per cent for white defendants, 20 per cent for African/Caribbean defendants, and 27 per cent for Asian defendants. Being of ethnic minority origin predicted an increased chance of case termination by the CPS, taking into account type and seriousness of the offence and whether the defendant had previous convictions. This pattern of results has been similarly found in Mhlanga's (1999) more recent study of CPS and court decision making at 22 CPS branches in cases involving defendants aged under 22 years in 1996. Case termination rates were higher for black (17 per cent) and Asian defendants (19 per cent) than for white defendants (13 per cent (see Barclay and Mhlanga 2000)). Limited support for these findings also come from Home Office (2000c) statistics for 1999 which showed higher termination rates for black defendants compared with white and Asian defendants in five police force areas.

These findings strongly suggest that the CPS in contrast to the police does not treat ethnic minorities, particularly African/Caribbeans, more harshly than whites, even if this is not reflected in the final outcome at the police station. A presumption of guilt may be being selectively applied by police officers in the case of African/Caribbean and Asian suspects, reflecting negative stereotyping and racist practices. In particular, these findings highlight the inadequacy of research approaches that study one stage of the criminal justice process in isolation.

Bail and remand decisions

Before the defendant is tried in court, decisions are made about whether they should be remanded in custody or bailed to appear at court when they have been charged with an offence at the police station. This type of bail has already been discussed in the previous chapter, which showed that African/Caribbeans were less likely to be bailed to appear at court by the police. Here we consider the granting of bail during the prosecution and sentencing process, which is closely related to decisions made by the police at the police station. A magistrate can decide to remand in custody or bail a defendant before and during trial at any hearing – and on conviction – before sentencing (Barclay 1995). This is a critical decision point in the criminal justice process, since studies have demonstrated that those defendants who are remanded in custody pre-trial subsequently are more likely to receive a custodial sentence if found guilty (see, for example, Hood 1992). This is probably because being remanded in custody will prevent the defendant from being shown in a positive light, so they will not, for example, have been able to demonstrate regular employment or a smart physical appearance (ibid). Regular access to a solicitor may also be more limited for the remanded defendant and the tracing of witnesses may also prove more difficult.

In attempting to assess whether the decision to convict is made with reference to the 'race' of the defendant, Walker's (1989) study, of males aged 17–25 in 1983 in London, found that in two-thirds of cases, which were not dealt with immediately, African/Caribbeans were significantly more likely than whites and Asians to be remanded in custody at the magistrates' courts, and this was clearly related to the police decision on remand in custody/bail for suspects at the police station (see chapter 6). What is not clear from these analyses is whether the higher remand rate for African/Caribbean defendants was related to legally relevant factors, such as prior failure to appear at court, or other circumstances which will likely lead to a custodial remand. Bail may be denied where the defendant is homeless, and thus unable to demonstrate community ties, as this may be regarded by the courts as a possible indicator that the defendant will abscond (Commission for Racial Equality 1990a). In other words, ethnic minorities may be especially likely to fall into the category of those for whom a remand in custody is likely. A consequence of social inequality is that African/Caribbeans suffer indirect discrimination where homelessness, unemployment and disrupted families, which adversely impact on ethnic minorities, influence 'legally neutral' decisions.

> These characteristics of the penalized population are so often the very characteristics we are building in to various formalised decision-making criteria, adherence to which we take as evidence that we are dispensing impartial criminal justice.
>
> (Hudson 1993: 164)

There is also some evidence that psychiatric remands are more frequently made in cases involving African/Caribbean defendants. In an exploratory study of the psychiatric remand process in 70 cases in one magistrates' court, Browne (1990) found that while 13 per cent of white defendants were remanded on psychiatric grounds by the courts, the figure was much higher for African/Caribbean defendants (37 per cent). The higher rate for African/Caribbean defendants was often the result of previous contact with psychiatric services prior to the court appearance, a factor which is itself not necessarily 'racially neutral' (Browne 1997). It could also be due to the greater likelihood of decision makers as seeing African/Caribbean defendants as 'dangerous', a factor which may also be relevant in cases not involving psychiatric assessments.

Brown and Hullin (1992) studied contested bail applications which came before the Leeds magistrates' court during a six-month period in 1989. Even when the analysis took into account previous failures to surrender to bail, likelihood of reoffending (criminal record was used as a proxy), and offence type and seriousness, this pattern remained. A more comprehensive analysis of the remand decision in Crown Courts was undertaken by Hood (1992) in his study in the West Midlands in 1989 and Hood, like Walker (1989), found evidence that African/Caribbean defendants faced a greater likelihood of being remanded in custody pre-trial than their white counterparts. This was the case even once other factors, such as whether the defendant had breached a court order, and home and lifestyle, had been controlled for (see also Lewis and Mair 1988, Ekwe-Ekwe and Nzegwu 1995, Todd 1996). A look at the use of bail and supported lodging is also warranted, since these provide temporary residence, particularly for those defendants who are without permanent accommodation (Commission for Racial Equality 1990a). Nationally, ethnic minority referral rates to probation hostels exceed what might be expected from representation in the general population (Home Office 2000c). This contrasts with the picture from local studies which have found that bail hostels are rarely used by those of African/Caribbean and Asian descent because they are rarely referred to them (Ekwe-Ekwe and Nzegwu 1995, Todd 1995).

The final outcome of a case is also relevant to the bail/remand decision, since some defendants who are remanded in custody while they await trial will eventually be acquitted, and there is some evidence that this is especially true of ethnic minority defendants. For example, in the answer to a parliamentary question presented by John Patten in 1987, it was reported that in 1986 4 per cent of white defendants remanded in custody pre-trial were found not guilty or were not proceeded against, compared with 8 per cent of African/Caribbeans, 7 per cent of Asians and 7 per cent of defendants of other ethnic origins (Hansard 1987). The balance of the evidence points to a 'race' effect in the remand/bail decision, which is of great significance not only because of the independent effect that this has on sentencing outcomes, but also in terms of the deprivation of liberty for ethnic minorities, particularly those of African/Caribbean origin. These findings are reflected in the greater African/Caribbean over-representation in the remand population (see chapter 8).

The prosecution

Little research has been able to document the way in which the prosecution presents its case. An attempt to rectify this was made in a small-scale study of the influence of 'race' and unemployment in drug trafficking trials at a Crown Court in London. Kalunta-Crumpton (1996) has referred to processes of 'claimsmaking' occurring during her study of 27 trials involving 15 African/Caribbean and 16 white defendants. It is argued that the prosecution present comparable cases differently according to the 'race' of the defendant, using ideologies and stereotypes to establish a link between African/Caribbean unemployment and criminality. Kalunta-Crumpton (1996: 186) suggests that the prosecution use awareness about unemployment and poverty, disproportionately affecting African/Caribbean communities to strengthen their cases when prosecuting African/Caribbean defendants, but when white defendants are in similar socio-economic circumstances, this claim is not used, thus reinforcing stereotypical images of 'race', crime and drug dealing. Future research must attempt to study these aspects of the prosecution process in a comprehensive way.

Acquittals

We know very little about whether the 'race' of the defendant influences the decision of the magistrate to convict or acquit. Two early studies which have looked at acquittals both found negligible differences in the acquittal rates for white and ethnic minority defendants (Walker 1989, Home Office 1989b). Conversely, Barclay and Mhlanga's (2000) research with defendants aged under 22 years reported higher acquittal rates for both black and Asian defendants at the magistrates' court, including for contested trials. The same pattern was reported in the first publication of ethnic monitoring data for 1999 (Home Office 2000c, see also box 7.1).

The sentencing process

Public perceptions

We will begin our review of sentencing research with a quote which sums up the gulf between the personal experiences of ethnic minorities in the criminal justice system and that uncovered through empiricist criminology (see also Chigwada-Bailey 1997). Shallice and Gordon (1990: 31) have observed:

> In Britain, there seems to be an absolute discrepancy between the findings of researchers that there is no evidence of differential sentencing on racial

Box 7.1 Miscarriages of justice

Alleged and proven miscarriages of justice have also caused consternation in ethnic minority communities, including those involving those originally convicted of murder at Broadwater Farm, and the cases of Ivan Ferguson, the Cardiff Three and the M25 Three.

A recent example

In January 1998, the West Midlands police agreed to pay out £200,000 in damages after admitting that a miscarriage of justice occurred in the case of George Lewis (*The Times*, 20 January 1998: 9). He was imprisoned from 1987 to 1992 after being beaten by police officers and convicted on the basis of a false confession to two armed robberies and a burglary. According to his solicitor, after being falsely arrested at home, he was racially abused, punched and headbutted. During his ordeal, Mr Lewis was also threatened with a syringe as he was questioned at the police station. At his 'retrial', the Crown Prosecution Service offered no evidence against him.

grounds in the courts and the large numbers of people who readily assert the opposite, largely (though not unimportantly) on the basis of anecdotal, personal and collective experience.

There is some evidence that the population in general do not believe in the fairness of the judicial system. Tarling and Dowds (1995) used a simulated case in which two people – one black and one white – were charged with a crime that they did not commit. The survey conducted in 1994 asked which had the greater chance of being found guilty. Four per cent thought that a white person would be more likely to be found guilty, while 44 per cent believed that a black person would be more likely to be found guilty, while 49 per cent indicated that they thought that both would have the same chance of being found guilty. Almost half questioned thought that a black person would suffer a miscarriage of justice, which Tarling and Dowds (1995: 207) called 'something of an indictment of the criminal justice system'.

More recent evidence suggests a more complex picture concerning perceptions of fairness and justice. The 2000 British Crime Survey has recently looked at levels of confidence in the criminal justice system among the main ethnic groups. A higher proportion of black and Asian respondents than white respondents were very or fairly confident in the criminal justice system's ability to bring people to justice, deal with cases promptly and efficiently and meet the needs of crime victims. Where black respondents were less confident of the criminal justice system was in its respecting of the rights of suspects and treating them fairly, a finding consistent, although not directly comparable with, that of Tarling and Dowds's (1995) earlier research. Somewhat surprisingly, black and Asian respondents made more favourable judgements than white respondents about magistrates, the probation service, the CPS, judges and youth courts, assessing them as doing a good or excellent job. In contrast, ethnic minorities were less convinced than their white counterparts that the police and prison services were performing to this standard (Mirrlees-Black 2001).

Public perceptions are informed by several factors, including direct experience of the system as victims, suspects, witnesses and jurors, vicarious experiences and through the media. There is little empirical evidence about the qualitative nature of processes of prosecution and sentencing and how these impact on ethnic minorities as the remainder of the chapter reveals. Even the documentary evidence of racist comments by court personnel is now rather dated. Gordon (1983: 96), for example, cites a case reported in the *Guardian* in 1978 where a senior magistrate offered to pay for the repatriation of a black defendant who appeared before him for non-payment of a fine. More recently, press reports have reported derogatory remarks about ethnic minorities being made by judges: in one example Leeds solicitor Ruth Bundey recalled 'a particular judge dealing with a Nigerian applicant for bail, whose name he didn't seem able even to contemplate pronouncing, and I heard the judge say that perhaps the only possible reason that could be advanced for granting this man bail was that he might, as a result, return to Nigeria' (*Independent*, 1 March 1991: 21). In April 1999 an Old Bailey judge was alleged to have made a joke in an after dinner speech to the Criminal Bar Association which contained racist, sexist and homophobic remarks (*Guardian*, 28 April 1999). The critical question remains: Do such racist attitudes by some court personnel result in racial discrimination against ethnic minority defendants who appear before the court?

Data sources and analyses

Before we take a look at the quantitative empirical research evidence, it is useful to outline the data sources and types of analysis available to social researchers wishing to examine the influence of ethnicity and racism in sentencing outcomes. Official statistics do not provide the usual starting point for criminological enquiry here since the Home Office annual publication 'Criminal Statistics' does not provide a breakdown of sentencing by ethnic origin of the defendant. For this reason, our knowledge relies on the findings from empirical research studies, which are frequently – although not always – based in one location, typically a large metropolitan city. Consequently the results may not apply to other locales, but by considering the findings of multiple local studies, we can assess the extent to which they are in accordance with each other, thereby increasing our confidence in their reliability (Yin 1989).

The number of ethnic minority respondents in the sample, and whether the experiences of African/Caribbeans are distinguished from those of Asians, is also important for interpreting research findings. This is a critical point because, if one ethnic group is treated more harshly than whites while another is treated more leniently, the combined 'ethnic minority' group will appear to be more similar to whites than is really the case. An 'Asian' subsample is also inadequate for exploring differences among Indians on the one hand, and Pakistanis and Bangladeshis on the other, who may be dissimilar in various ways, including, most importantly, socio-economic status (see FitzGerald 1993b and FitzGerald and Marshall 1996). Unfortunately, no studies of sentencing to date allow such a refined analysis. Indeed, many of the studies reviewed in this chapter were unable to present detailed analyses of Asians as a group because of their small numbers in selected samples.

In the introductory chapter to this book we noted that proportionately more ethnic minorities were imprisoned and that their custodial sentence lengths were longer than for their white counterparts. If the court decided to imprison an African/Caribbean first offender but impose a fine on a white first offender, assuming the case was similar in all other respects, we would conclude that the court's actions were directly discriminatory, because they were using 'race' (whether or not this was intentional) in deciding sentence. However, *legal factors* could also explain these disparities. For example, a defendant who is charged with a property offence at the magistrates' court, but who has three previous convictions, can be expected to receive a harsher sentence (although not necessarily custodial) than a first-time offender. If it were the case that ethnic minorities are more likely to be repeat offenders, this could in itself explain the greater likelihood that they will receive a custodial sentence. Other legal factors include the seriousness of the offence, defendant plea (which can invoke a sentencing discount) and previous highest sentence.

There may, however, be confounding effects which complicate this picture. For example, although the defendant's criminal history (previous convictions and previous highest sentence) could legitimately influence sentencing outcomes, these legal factors may not be 'racially neutral'. In chapter 6, for example, we commented on how proactive policing practices and 'overcharging' can lead to African/Caribbean offenders being more likely to be arrested and charged than their white and Asian counterparts, and to be charged with offences which are more serious in nature than reflected in the offence itself. This means that 'seriousness of the offence' and 'previous convictions' may already be 'racially loaded' although they can be seen as legal factors which may legitimately influence sentencing outcomes. Finally, there are *extra-legal* factors that have been shown to influence sentencing practice, which are in turn closely associated with 'race'. For example, magistrates and judges consider the employment status of defendants when deciding whether to impose a custodial sentence: those in employment are more likely to have a non-custodial sentence imposed on them. Because people from ethnic minorities suffer higher levels of unemployment than whites (Jones 1993, Modood and Berthoud 1997), this may have an indirectly discriminatory impact on sentencing outcomes. Disentangling the effects of direct discrimination (the use of extra-legal factors) and indirect discrimination is a complex task, and not one which has been accomplished satisfactorily to date.

Sentencing in the magistrates' court

Once an individual has been convicted of an offence, magistrates decide on an appropriate sentence. This is accomplished by using the statutory framework established in the Criminal Justice Acts of 1991 and 1993, where magistrates have a duty to impose a sentence which is 'commensurate with the seriousness of the offence or offences committed by the offender' (Barclay 1995: 20). The magistrate will also take into account any aggravating circumstances (which may increase the severity of the sentence) or mitigating factors (which may reduce the severity of the sentence). In addition, Pre-Sentence Reports (PSRs, previously called Social Inquiry Reports or SIRs) provide details of the social context of the crime as well as the circumstances of the offender. These are used in the mitigation speech by the defence lawyer to help the court understand why the defendant committed the offence (Barclay 1995). They are most likely to be prepared where the defendant pleads guilty.

Pre-Sentence Reports (PSRs)

PSRs are prepared by a probation officer and contain information on the character, personality, social and domestic background of the defendant, as well as information on their educational and employment record. The report will also include an assessment of the impact of the crime on the victim, and the risk of reoffending (Barclay 1995). Therefore, the extent to which PSRs are prepared, their content, style and recommendations on sentencing options, may also have a bearing on the outcome at court. The research studies that have compared those written on white and ethnic minority defendants have produced rather mixed findings.

Using data collected on adult defendants tried for offences (excluding summary offences) in two magistrates' courts in West Yorkshire, Mair (1986) reported a higher proportion of reports being written for African/Caribbean defendants, presumably because they faced an increased risk of custody because they were convicted of more serious offences. The same finding was reported by Shallice and Gordon (1990) who observed the sentencing process for defendants who pleaded guilty in four London courts. Conversely, Hudson's (1989) survey of over 8,000 sentencing decisions in 14 magistrates' and Crown Courts in the Greater

London area reported that African/Caribbeans were less likely to have reports written on them, while Crow and Cove (1984) did not find a difference between the ethnic groups in this respect. A sample of 484 PSRs from 10 probation services examined by Her Majesty's Inspectorate of Probation (2000) reported the same findings as Hudson. The reports for white offenders were also more likely to assess adequately the context of the offence, the offender's culpability and social circumstances, than was the case in reports written for black offenders. Significant differences were identified in the assessment of risk: there was a failure to comment on the management of risk in the majority of PSRs prepared for black offenders.

As to the narrative content of reports, references to the 'race' of the defendant by individual probation officers were observed by Whitehouse (1983). She found that some SIRs (predecessors to PSRs) attached negative expressions to aspects of African/Caribbean culture, home and family life and economic circumstances, and this influenced recommendations to the court. Alternatively, Waters (1988) has argued that 'race' is largely marginal to the content of SIRs. Similarly, Gelsthorpe (1992) found no evidence of racial discrimination in report writing by probation officers in three areas; the reports did not contain racist language, or statements using stereotypes, or negative accounts of ethnic minorities' social and cultural backgrounds. Where Gelsthorpe did highlight the potential for discrimination was in the use of home visits in preparing reports. She suggests that concerns for officers' safety prevented them undertaking home visits with ethnic minorities, although this would not necessarily determine the sentencing recommendation. The recent inspectorate report on ten probation services reported that 16 per cent of PSRs written on black offenders and 11 per cent on Asian defendants reinforced stereotypical attitudes about race and ethnicity (Her Majesty's Inspectorate of Probation 2000).

In terms of the sentencing recommendations made by probation officers in PSRs/SIRs, Crow and Cove (1984), Mair (1986) and Shallice and Gordon (1990) all found that these did not appear to differ according to the 'race' of the defendant. These studies found that probation officers were no less likely to recommend alternatives to custody in cases involving African/Caribbean or other ethnic minority defendants. In fact, Voakes and Fowler (1989), in their study of SIRs written by Bradford probation officers for magistrates' and Crown Court adult cases, reported a higher proportion of positive recommendations made in cases involving African/Caribbean defendants compared with white defendants, with Asians having the least positive number of recommendations (see also Gelsthorpe 1992). However, Voakes and Fowler did note that there was a significantly larger proportion of 'nil' reports (with no sentencing recommendation) prepared for African/Caribbean defendants (18 per cent) and Asian defendants (23 per cent) compared with white defendants (11 per cent). National Probation Service statistics for 1995/6 reported the same finding (Home Office 1996c). On the balance of the

Table 7.1 Main studies of sentencing in the magistrates' court

Study	Location date	Type of court	Sample size	Method	Immediate custodial sentence Whites	Immediate custodial sentence A/C	Immediate custodial sentence Asian	Sentence length	Main sentences Whites	Main sentences A/C	Main sentences
Crow and Cove (1984)	England 1983	4 juvenile 3 magistrates' 2 Crown Courts	536 White 124 Afr/Car 125 Asian	Comparison	12%	11% (and Asian)		–	26% 7% 9% 5%	27% 12% 6% 7%	Fined Discharge Probation Com. Service
Mair (1986)	West Yorkshire 1983/4	2 magistrates'	126 White 127 Afr/Car 62 Asian[1]	Comparison	7%[2]	5%	5%	–	51% 13% 12% 7%	53% 11% 6% 8%	Fined Discharge Probation Com. Service
Hudson (1989)	London 3 years	14 magistrates' and Crown Courts	8,000+ decisions	Matching on: Victim age Offence Circumstances	Assault: 50%	75%	–	–	14% 10% 3%	23% 14% 7%	Con. Discharge[2] Probation Com. Service
Walker (1989)	London 1983	All magistrates' (and Crown Courts – see table 7.2)	17–25 year males 3,477 White 2,273 Afr/Car 244 Asian	Comparison	17–20 year olds:[3] 11% 21–25 year olds:[3] 9%	13% 12%	6% 7%	No difference	55% 6% 6%	55% 3% 4%	Fine Probation Com. Service
Home Office (1989b)	London 1984/5	All magistrates'	82,363 White 19,077 Afr/Car 3,811 Asian	Comparison and Matching	10%	11%	6%	No difference	46% 9% 5%	45% 8% 5%	Fine Probation Com. Service
Shallice and Gordon (1990)	London 1985	4 magistrates'	1,189 White 1,190 Afr/Car 136 Asian	Comparison	7%	7%	6%	–	54% 9% 4%	44% 14% 8%	Fine Probation Com. service
Brown and Hullin (1992)	Leeds 1988	All magistrates'	3,354 White 215 Afr/Car 119 Asian	Comparison Afr/Car	8%	5%	0%	–	66% 10% 8%	64% 7% 7%	Fine Probation Com. Service

Notes:
[1] 50 African/Caribbean and 50 white defendants were also matched on the basis of age, sex, charge, number of previous court appearances, and most serious previous disposal. The same exercise was carried out with another 50 white and Asian defendants. This produced the same pattern of findings on sentencing outcomes.
[2] Sub-sample of theft cases; defendants matched on single charge, unemployment, previous convictions and value of property stolen.
[3] Percentages are rounded.

Box 7.2 Interpreters

The Nuffield Foundation Project (1993) was set up in recognition of the European Convention on Human Rights which states that those charged with a criminal offence must be informed of the accusation against them in a language they understand and to be further assisted in court by an interpreter if necessary. In addition, Corsellis (1995) has noted the importance of non-English speakers and those whose backgrounds are different, learning about the role of court officials, including, for example, probation officers and court clerks who explain the trial election procedure. Despite this, the Nuffield Foundation Project, through its National Court Survey, reported a lack of co-ordination and organisation of local interpreting services. Moreover, the quality and competence of interpreters varied greatly. The study also found that only 14 per cent of Crown Courts and 6 per cent of County Courts reported that they displayed leaflets relevant to court business in other languages, particularly South Asian ones.

evidence, it is difficult to comment on the extent to which PSRs may or may not be written for ethnic minority defendants, but there is some consistency in the reported findings concerning probation officers not presenting a sentencing recommendation to the courts in more cases involving ethnic minorities than whites. This may leave magistrates free to impose a more severe sentencing option in these cases. Another aspect of the prosecution process which has implications for equal access to justice is the use of interpreters, referred to in box 7.2.

Table 7.1 summarises the main findings from studies of sentencing in the magistrates' courts. Most of the research studies have found little or no difference in the proportion of white and African/Caribbean defendants sentenced to immediate custody, or in custodial sentence lengths (see also limited ethnic monitoring data for 1999: Home Office 2000c). The same finding was reported by Jefferson and Walker (1992), whose study tracked cases of white, African/Caribbean and Asian suspects from arrest to sentencing. In addition to analysing court records, a researcher was present during 135 magistrates' court trials. Jefferson and Walker found no evidence of discrimination; cases were typically dealt with in a routinised and bureaucratic way. Notwithstanding this, interviews with solicitors revealed that they perceived that some differential treatment of ethnic minorities in the court process existed. The police were particularly criticised for harassment, although the courts were broadly seen to be fair and even-handed. A lower custodial rate for Asians, when compared with white and African/Caribbean defendants, was observed in the Home Office (1989b) study and those by Walker (1989) and Brown and Hullin (1992).

As for other sentencing options, Hudson (1989) and Shallice and Gordon (1990) have argued that African/Caribbean defendants receive more supervisory non-custodial sentences than similarly placed whites, even though their previous criminal history does not presuppose these harsher and more restrictive sentences. This has the effect of moving them higher up the sentencing 'tariff' which means that subsequent offending is more likely to result in a custodial sentence. It also means more African/Caribbean defendants are under the control of the Probation Service. Again table 7.1 shows the picture is mixed when supervisory orders, such as probation and community service, are compared with less severe sentences, such as discharges and fines.

Committals

So far we have only discussed the findings from sentencing studies in the magistrates' court, but the business of the lower courts also includes making decisions about the mode of trial and filtering cases through to the Crown Court. Many serious offences, such as robbery, are defined as 'indictable only', which means they cannot be tried by magistrates; instead defendants must be tried by jury in the Crown Court. Offences which are not indictable are categorised as either 'triable-either-way' offences, which means that cases can be heard in the magistrates' or Crown Courts (for example, theft from a motor vehicle), or as 'summary only', which are typically the least serious ones (for example, criminal damage below £5,000), and these can only be tried in the magistrates' courts.

There are two other ways in which cases reach the Crown Court. Where the defendant is charged with a triable-either-way offence they may elect for their case to be heard in the Crown Court. Alternatively, magistrates may decline jurisdiction (often on the advice of the CPS) in certain cases where they consider their sentencing powers to be insufficient in contrast to those of the Crown Court. In cases which are tried in the Crown Court, a convicted defendant is likely to face a harsher sentence than they would have done had they been convicted in the magistrates' court and sentenced there (Hedderman and Moxon 1992). Therefore, if the CPS and magistrates recommend more African/Caribbean defendants to be committed for trial at the Crown Court, this may demonstrate unequal treatment, which may in turn lead to a more punitive outcome for the African/Caribbean defendant. If the recommendation is made solely on the basis of the defendant's 'race', this would demonstrate direct racial discrimination. Unequal treatment which occurs at one stage of the criminal justice process, but which has a further detrimental effect in terms of outcome at a later stage of the criminal justice process, can be seen as an example of *cumulative disadvantage*.

The statistical and research evidence has been uniformly consistent in documenting higher committal rates for ethnic minorities, particularly African/Caribbeans, which means that even before sentencing decisions are made, African/Caribbeans overall face a greater possibility of a more severe sentencing outcome if found guilty than their white counterparts, by virtue of being tried in the Crown Court rather than the magistrates' court. Findings from research studies have been rather mixed on whether this is because more ethnic minority defendants elected for Crown Court trial or because magistrates were more likely to decline jurisdiction (Walker 1989, Home Office 1989b, Jefferson and Walker 1992, Shallice and Gordon 1992, Brown and Hullin 1992).

Outcomes at the Crown Court

It is not immediately apparent why African/Caribbeans would be more likely than other ethnic groups to elect for Crown Court trial, especially when the sentencing outcomes on conviction are likely to be more severe. It can be speculated, however, that their mistrust of the criminal justice system as attested to in individual and community accounts may explain this pattern. It is possible that African/Caribbean defendants are more prepared to risk their 'fate' at the hands of ordinary citizens through the jury system than by agents of the criminal justice system, that is, magistrates. Certainly their rates of acquittal are higher there, although this is related to offence type and court location, and is also due in part to their greater likelihood of pleading not guilty than white defendants (Walker 1989, Home Office 1989b, Hood 1992, Phillips and Brown 1998, Barclay and Mhlanga 2000). The Home Office (1989b) analysis of indictable cases in London in 1984/5 found no overall differences in the acquittal rates according to the ethnic origin of the defendant, but this masked considerably higher acquittal rates for African/Caribbeans and Asians compared with whites for criminal damage, and to a lesser extent, robbery and motoring offences.

Similarly, Hood's (1992) study (which will be discussed in detail below) found there was no difference in the larger courts (Dudley and Birmingham) in the proportion of white and African/Caribbean defendants (both 9 per cent) acquitted, but the rate was higher at around 16 per cent for Asians, broadly confirming the findings in the magistrates' courts. At two of the other courts, the combined acquittal rate was much higher for African/Caribbeans (15 per cent) and Asian defendants (18 per cent) than white defendants (7 per cent). Higher acquittal rates for young black and Asian defendants (aged under 22 years) compared with their white counterparts was also reported in Barclay and Mhlanga's (2000) research.

These patterns must raise questions about the weakness of the evidence in some cases involving ethnic minorities, and suggests that perhaps the police acted hastily in charging the suspects at the police station. This

Table 7.2 Main studies of sentencing in the Crown Court

Study location	Immediate custodial sentence White	African/Caribbean	Sentence length	Sample size	Method
McConville and Baldwin (1982) Birmingham London 1975–9	*Guilty pleas in Birmingham:* 48% *Not Guilty pleas in Birmingham:* 59%	46% (Afr/Car and Asian) 66% (Afr/Car and Asian)		272 Whites 272 African/ Caribbean/Asian	Matching[1]
Walker (1989) London 1983	*17–20 year olds:*[2] 49% *21–25 year olds:* 52%	50% 52%	*21 year olds+:* 243 days Whites 283 days African/ Caribbeans	*17–25 year males:* 2,229 Whites 990 African/ Caribbean	Comparison
Home Office (1989b) London 1984/5	51% 50% (Asian)	57%	*21 year old+ males:* 17.1 months Whites 18.1 months African/ Caribbeans 35.5 months Asians (mainly drug trafficking)	22,377 Whites 6,834 African/ Caribbean 1,193 Asian	Comparison
Moxon (1988) 18 areas 1986/7	38%[2]	36%[2]	—	1,824 Whites 1,825 African/ Caribbean 93 Asian	Matching on: Theft and Handling Criminal record

Notes:
1 Cases were matched as closely as possible on the basis of the following characteristics: sex, age, type of offence, number of counts, criminal record, length of previous custodial sentence, pre-trial bail status and plea. However, the influence of 'race' on sentencing outcome may have been hidden by the combining African/Caribbeans and Asians in the same sub-sample.
2 Includes partially suspended sentences.

might also be influenced by a weakness of evidence in relation to charges. If the police or CPS are 'over-charging' black defendants, this may lead them to want to contest them more often. Despite these findings, Smith (1997a) has argued that *overall* the acquittal rates between the ethnic groups do not vary very much, which in turn indicates the absence of massive bias at earlier stages of the criminal justice process. Alternatively it would seem reasonable to suggest that the variations in acquittal rates between ethnic groups according to the court dealing with the case and the offence charged is an example of *contextual discrimination*, where discrimination occurs in certain locations and circumstances but not in others.

The finding of a higher rate of not guilty pleas among African/Caribbeans, while probably influencing their higher acquittal rate, is also somewhat double-edged, since sentencing discounts are not available to those pleading not guilty if they are convicted (Hedderman and Moxon 1992). Understanding why African/Caribbeans are significantly more likely to plead not guilty is clearly an area where further research is required. The possibility that they may more frequently have been over-charged by the police, and therefore plead not guilty in order to protest their innocence or to secure a reduction in charges, should not be overlooked.

Table 7.2 outlines the key findings from the small number of studies of sentencing in the Crown Court. These studies have not always found differences which are related to the 'race' of the defendant, although they have tended to lack methodological sophistication. Logistic regression allows the researcher to sort out the independent effects of variables and to assess the strength of each factor in predicting a particular outcome (for example, a custodial sentence). As we mentioned earlier, however, it is also important to recognise that any type of analysis must take account of confounding effects whereby legally relevant factors, such as criminal history, may themselves be the product of discriminatory decision-making at earlier stages of the criminal justice process.

Roger Hood's (1992) landmark study of sentencing at the Crown Court in the West Midlands is still the only one to date which employed logistic regression analysis to examine differences in the sentencing of adult white and ethnic minority convicted defendants. In the section on juvenile justice we will review the work of Mhlanga (1997) which also utilised multivariate techniques to study case outcomes. The pioneering research by Hood (1992) conducted in five Crown Courts in the West Midlands in 1989 was the first British study comprehensively to study the effect of ethnic origin on type and length of sentence. Data was collected retrospectively from several sources, including Crown Court files and police and probation service files. All male African/Caribbean ($n = 886$), Asian ($n = 536$) and other ethnic minority defendants ($n = 16$) found guilty and sentenced in 1989 were compared with an equivalent random sample of male white defendants ($n = 1443$). A separate analysis was carried out for females of whom 343 were white, 76 were African/Caribbean and 14 were Asian.

The proportion of defendants from each ethnic group who were sentenced to custody varied according to the court and individual judge by whom they were sentenced. Overall, however, 48 per cent of whites, 57 per cent of African/Caribbeans and 40 per cent of Asians received a custodial sentence.

In studying sentencing outcomes, the approach taken by Hood (1992) was to construct a Probability of Custody Score using variables which best predicted the possibility of a custodial sentence. These included: offence seriousness, mode of trial, bail status, plea, number of charges, court orders outstanding, violence in the offence, degree of injury sustained, effect of violence on the victim and their vulnerability, motive for the violence, financial loss incurred, number of previous convictions, whether they had received custody before for the same type of offence, previous breach of a community service order, and being homeless or living in rented accommodation (for women only). An inherent weakness of the study becomes apparent immediately; the analysis takes for granted that these legal factors (for example, seriousness of the offence) are 'racially neutral'. For this reason, Hood's results must be regarded as a conservative estimate of the 'race effect'.

Overall, Hood estimated that only 479 of the 503 African/Caribbean defendants who were sentenced to custody were expected to have received a custodial sentence based on legally relevant factors. Thus, African/Caribbean defendants had a 5 per cent greater probability of being sentenced to custody than their white counterparts even when legally relevant, but not necessarily 'race-neutral' variables were held constant. The mean length of sentence imposed on African/Caribbean and Asian defendants was longer than that received by whites, where the defendant pleaded not guilty. Among those pleading not guilty, once all other factors had been controlled for, Asians, on average, were sentenced to nine months longer and African/Caribbeans three months longer than whites.

The differences between African/Caribbeans and whites appeared to be largely the result of more custodial sentences being imposed on African/Caribbeans for offences within the middle range of seriousness where judges have the most discretion in deciding whether the case warrants a custodial sentence or not. In these types of cases, African/Caribbean defendants (68 per cent) were significantly more likely to be sentenced to custody than whites (60 per cent). It was also found that the unequal treatment of African/Caribbean defendants occurred mainly at Dudley Crown Court (and Warwick and Stafford courts, although the numbers were much smaller), but not at Birmingham Crown Court. At Dudley, it appeared to be the case that judges were less likely to give weight to mitigating factors (such as being young, being on bail, pleading guilty) and to be more likely to impose a custodial sentence where an African/Caribbean defendant was convicted alongside African/Caribbean co-defendants. In addition to court variations, the sentencing practices of individual judges were markedly different. In the analysis Hood found that of 16 judges whose sentencing decisions were examined, three sentenced fewer African/Caribbeans to custody than whites, eight were more 'even-handed' in their decisions, while five imposed custodial sentences on African/Caribbeans to a greater extent than their white counterparts. Once again, it may be that *contextual discrimination* best defines such variation in outcomes.

Hood (1992) also relates his findings to the over-representation of African/Caribbeans in the prison population. In comparing the proportion of African/Caribbean males in the prison population at 24.4 per cent (taking account of sentence to be served) with the 3.8 per cent of the male population served by the courts in the study, Hood estimates that 70 per cent of the over-representation of African/Caribbean males in prison could be explained by the number appearing for sentence. As Hood acknowledges, this does not take account of any discriminatory policing or pre-sentencing factors. According to Hood, 10 per cent of the over-representation was explained by the seriousness of the offence and other legally relevant characteristics. This left 20 per cent which could not be explained by legitimate factors. Hood concludes that 7 per cent of the over-representation of African/Caribbean males in prison was the result of the higher than expected use of custody. The remaining 13 per cent was a consequence of lengthier prison sentences for African/Caribbean males, which was tied to their greater likelihood of pleading not guilty and therefore not receiving the 'sentencing discount' on conviction. This led Hood to suggest that African/Caribbean defendants' greater propensity to plead not guilty (perhaps because of their distrust of the criminal justice system or perhaps because they are, in fact, not guilty) may contribute to indirect discrimination against them, a belief shared by Hudson (1993).

Hood found that African/Caribbean and Asian defendants were less likely than whites to be put on probation. This was partly due to probation officers recommending probation for 26 per cent of whites, but only 16 per cent of African/Caribbeans and 9 per cent of Asians. Instead African/Caribbean defendants more typically received a suspended custodial sentence or a community service order, even where probation was recommended. This was true for African/Caribbeans only in the medium risk category of being imprisoned, suggesting again that where judges have the most discretion in deciding sentence, ethnic minorities fare badly when compared with whites. Generally speaking, it was the case that Asians were more likely to be fined or given a conditional discharge.

Less detailed analyses were conducted with the female sample. Overall, 23 per cent of white female defendants and 29 per cent of African/Caribbean female defendants were sentenced to immediate custody at Birmingham, Dudley and Coventry Crown Courts. Multivariate analysis revealed that legal variables, particularly the seriousness of the offence for which the defendant was convicted, explained the differences in the custody rate of white and African/Caribbean females at Birmingham Crown Court, but, as was the case with males, African/Caribbean females at Dudley Crown Court had higher than expected rates of custody. There were no differences between white and African/Caribbean female defendants in terms of the length of custody imposed. Nor were any differences observed in the pattern of non-custodial sentencing.

Hood's study estimates that there is a 7 per cent greater likelihood of African/Caribbean defendants sentenced at one point in time (in 1989) receiving a custodial sentence when compared with white defendants. If this effect occurred annually, the cumulative impact of the 7 per cent would be rather dramatic. In 1990 another 7 per cent of African/Caribbeans would be unfairly imprisoned, and another 7 per cent in 1991. Of course, this effect is limited by the number of African/Caribbeans convicted and 'available' for sentence. If for the sake of argument it is assumed that all of those people sentenced to custody in 1989 were on average released from custody three years later and subsequently reoffended, we can assume that a large proportion of African/Caribbean offenders released will again appear before the courts for sentencing. This time their criminal history will indicate that their previous highest sentence was a custodial one, which will further increase the likelihood that they will again receive a custodial sentence, and the judge will also probably impose a longer-term. If we assume that the full 7 per cent effect only occurs every three years, this represents an increase of a third in the over-representation of African/Caribbeans in prison, as illustrated in column 3 of the table below. There is no way of knowing whether the 7 per cent has a cumulative effect on an annual basis. Column 4 in the table below illustrates a hypothetical cumulative effect on an annual basis. Within an 11-year period there would be a doubling of the risk of custody for African/Caribbeans.

Table 7.2 Hypothetical cumulative effect of direct racial discrimination in Crown Court sentencing (based on Hood 1992)

	Hood	Three-year estimate	Annual estimate	African/Caribbean males in prison population
Year 0	100	100	100	24.2 (in 1989)
Year 1	107	–	107	
Year 2	–	–	114.5	
Year 3	–	107	122.5	26.1
Year 4	–	–	131.1	
Year 5	–	–	140.2	
Year 6	–	114.5	150.0	27.9
Year 7	–	–	160.5	
Year 8	–	–	171.7	
Year 9	–	122.5	183.7	29.9
Year 10	–	–	196.6	
Year 11	–	–	210.3	
Year 12	–	131.1	225	32.0

The estimates in this hypothetical example are necessarily speculative, but are presented to stimulate further thought on the implications of Hood's findings.

Hood (1992: 190) rejects the conclusions of some commentators, such as McConville and Baldwin (1982), that once ethnic minorities are 'contained' within the court system, they are dealt with in the same way as similarly placed whites, noting that:

> It will not be possible any more to make the claim that all the difference in the treatment of black offenders occur elsewhere in the criminal justice system. At least some of it occurs in the courts, and more often in some localities than others.

Questions still remain about why black defendants are subject to harsher sentencing outcomes than their white and Asian counterparts, but as Hood (1992: 36) acknowledges these may relate to the way judges perceive the seriousness of the offences when committed by African/Caribbeans or the way they react to the appearance and demeanour of defendants in court. He also raises the question as to whether the type and quality of legal representation differs for African/Caribbean defendants so as to affect the sentencing outcome.

Juries

Since we have found some evidence for a 'race' effect on sentencing outcomes, particularly at Crown Courts, it is also important to consider whether the decisions of juries are influenced by the 'race' of the defendant. Very little research has been conducted in the UK to address whether juries act in a racially discriminatory way, although as the CRE (1992: 2) have noted:

> There is no definitive evidence to suggest that an all white jury will necessarily deliver a verdict based on racial discrimination. There is ample evidence, however, to conclude that racial discrimination is a demonstrable fact in other sectors of the public domain and it would be foolhardy to assert that the jury system is somehow immune.

Baldwin and McConville (1979) attempted to examine this issue empirically – albeit indirectly – by studying jury verdicts in around 500 cases tried at Birmingham Crown Court in 1975. By law, the researchers were unable to talk to jurors directly; instead the study involved seeking informed opinions from judges, prosecuting solicitors and the police through questionnaires and interviews. Of 15 convictions defined as doubtful by Baldwin and McConville, eight involved African/Caribbean or Asian defendants, and the majority of these were alleged cases of violence and sexual assault. In contrast, there were only seven of 41 cases that were deemed to be questionable acquittals. Moreover, there was an under-representation of African/Caribbean and Asian jurors in this study. Whether these findings would be produced today – 25 years later – can only be guessed at.

There has also been some discussion of deficiencies in current procedures for jury empanelment, and a call for racially mixed juries by the CRE (1992) and Herbert (1995). Moreover, the results of a Harris Research Centre Opinion Poll conducted in November 1995 would certainly seem to point to a distrust of the jury system by members of African/Caribbean and Asian communities, and, indeed, white people too (see also Gordon 1983). The survey involved face-to-face interviews with 461 white and 488 African/Caribbean and Asian people. Only 22 per cent of African/Caribbeans and Asians interviewed thought that a defendant from an ethnic minority could be tried fairly by an all-white jury, compared with 53 per cent of whites. Indeed, a case was recently taken to the European Court of Human Rights by an African/Caribbean man (*Gregory* v *United Kingdom*) who claimed that the judge in his case failed to ensure a fair hearing when he chose to redirect the jury to focus on the evidence and not the 'race' of the defendant following allegations of jury bias and racial prejudice. The court accepted that his forceful and detailed redirection was sufficient (*Independent*, 5 March 1997).

As a point of principle, the CRE have argued that juries must reflect the multi-racial communities from which they are drawn (see also Dashwood 1972). In the short term this is advocated only when 'race' is a factor of relevance to the trial, but in the longer term as a right for any defendant under any circumstances. A multi-racial jury, consisting of three members of more than one racial group (not strictly matched to the defendant and victim), could be ensured by asking summoned jurors to include an ethnic self-classification, and making selections on this basis. This recommendation was supported by 85 per cent of African/Caribbeans and Asians and two-thirds of whites surveyed by the Harris Research Centre (BBC 1995). Where trials are proposed in areas of low ethnic minority settlement, the CRE recommend that the location of the trial be transferred. It remains to be seen whether multi-racial juries become a feature of British courts; the indication is that this will not be a priority issue in the short term.

Youth justice

The bulk of this chapter has examined prosecution and sentencing in adult courts. Examining the criminal justice processing of juveniles is worthy of separate consideration because of the different rationales of the court systems which prosecute juveniles and adults. A central plank of juvenile justice policy for several decades has been the use of community sentences for juvenile offenders and the use of custody only as a 'last resort', although as Gelsthorpe and Morris (1994) note, there have been times when this has been proved to be more rhetorical than common practice. Indeed, although fewer studies have concentrated on juvenile justice processing, the concerns about an over-representation of ethnic minorities in the imprisoned population also applies to juveniles at both national and local levels (for example, Wilson and Hartley 1989). This is especially important since the imposition of a custodial sentence will have a greater impact on juveniles in their adult years. The methodologies used to study the influence of 'race' on sentencing decisions for juveniles have been similar to those employed in studies of adult defendants, and thus are subject to the same methodological limitations, and typically contrary findings (see Tipler 1989, Walker 1988, Kirk 1996). In addition, these studies are limited by the fact that most have studied only male juvenile defendants or, where they have examined the processing of females, the numbers have been too small for meaningful analyses to be undertaken (see, for example, Kirk 1996).

Finally we come to the work of Mhlanga (1997) which has provided, to date, the most comprehensive study of 'race' and juvenile justice processing. The research set out to examine whether the 'race' of the defendant could predict whether the defendant received a court sentence or was diverted from the formal criminal justice system by way of police diversionary measures. Although a quantitative study, Mhlanga supplements his analyses with participant observation of the local criminal justice system in his role as a social worker. Data were collected on all male defendants aged 10–17 years ($n = 842$ white, $n = 719$ African/Caribbean, $n = 73$ Asian) who were arrested (and lived) in Brent between May 1983 and July 1986. Mhlanga used police records collected from the youth and community section, as well as court records, social services records and information kept at intermediate treatment centres.

Using multivariate analysis, Mhlanga found that there was a greater probability of cases involving young African/Caribbean defendants (aged under 14 years) being acquitted at court due to insufficient evidence, compared to the probabilities of cases being dismissed at court for white and Asian young defendants. Young Asian defendants were more likely to have received police diversionary measures, such as having no further action taken against them at the police station, or being cautioned than being sent to trial, when compared with white and African/Caribbean young people. In the same way that Phillips and Brown (1998) speculated with regard to adults, Mhlanga comments (1997: 83) that this 'implies that the police were much more prepared to prosecute African/Caribbean young persons even on weak evidence and were comparatively more lenient towards white and Asian young persons', even after controlling for all other relevant factors.

This pattern between the ethnic groups was repeated when comparing the imposition of non-custodial sentences at court with the defendant being diverted from the formal criminal justice system by the police, although for the under fourteens, Asians were more likely than African/Caribbean or white children to have been prosecuted at court. Moreover, young African/Caribbean defendants were significantly more likely than their white counterparts to be sentenced to custody and not to have been subject to police diversionary measures. The differences between African/Caribbean and Asian defendants did not reach statistical significance, however. These findings are broadly similar to those reported by Hood (1992) in his study of adults sentenced in the Crown Court. It is also worth noting that Mhlanga, like Hood, found that in addition to the 'race' of the defendant, factors such as the type and number of offences, including those taken into consideration, and the number of arrests or court appearances were of considerable explanatory importance in the decision to impose a custodial sentence.

A limiting feature of Mhlanga's analysis is that it was not possible to compare court outcomes for white, African/Caribbean and Asian defendants. Furthermore, Mhlanga did not have at his disposal data on the remand status of defendants nor the previous highest sentence which juveniles received, which may have altered the findings on differential sentencing for young white, African/Caribbean and Asian defendants. Notwithstanding these limitations, the current knowledge about juvenile justice processing does seem to follow the same pattern as that for adults, where higher custody rates and committals to Crown Court contributes to the over-representation of ethnic minorities in the prison population.

Conclusion

Racially disproportionate outcomes in prosecution and sentencing were outlined in this chapter, produced by processes of direct and indirect discrimination. It may be useful to define this under the umbrella term 'contextual discrimination', since there was evidence of decisions based on 'race' only being made by some judges and in some courts; thus it was context dependent. The presence of indirect discrimination as evident in the high proportion of blacks pleading not guilty and therefore not receiving a sentencing discount assumes that they were guilty of the offences charged. Hood's research in the West Midlands further tied direct and indirect discrimination in the sentencing process to the over-representation of blacks in prison; he argues, however, that the over-representation was mostly explained by the large number of black defendants appearing in court for sentence.

It was not only at the point of sentencing that the research evidence has found discrimination. Hood's research indicated that the bail/remand decision was one which was made with reference to the 'race' of the defendant over and above legally relevant factors, since failing to 'demonstrate community ties' will frequently lead to a remand in custody, a factor which may indirectly discriminate against ethnic minorities. The positive link between the remand in custody decision and a custodial sentence further compounds the situation for ethnic minorities. Moreover, it is somewhat difficult to reconcile the higher acquittal rates and the higher rate of cases withdrawn at court or terminated by the CPS for black defendants with a prosecution process that is free from racial bias. It is fair to say, however, that empirical research in this area has been patchy and it is an area where more systematic and comprehensive research is required. Notwithstanding this, it is clear that sentencing research must also take account of earlier stages in the process, namely with regard to police practices and processing to make sense of final outcomes.

The chapter has also made clear the need for further research on certain aspects of the prosecution process, including – other than that already mentioned – jury practices, legal advice at court and the role of the prosecution team, and to explain why black defendants are more likely to plead not guilty, thus eliminating their chance of receiving a sentencing discount if convicted. In the next chapter we look at the final stage of the criminal justice process: imprisonment and probation.

Chapter 8

Prison and probation

Imprisonment represents the end point of the criminal justice process. Those in prison include both those who have been sentenced and those on remand. It is not possible to consider prison statistics without connecting them with the earlier stages of the criminal justice process, particularly policing, prosecution and sentencing practices, but also, of course, victimisation and offending. Each of these have been considered in their own right in earlier chapters. The criminal justice process taken as a whole, the impact of direct and indirect discrimination and a consideration of alternative explanations of the over-representation of African/Caribbean people in prison will be considered in chapter 10. Our purpose here is to consider the treatment of ethnic minorities once they are in the prison system and also to examine their experiences of probation, one of the more common non-custodial sentencing outcomes.

Ethnic monitoring of the prison population

Even before the results of the first official ethnic monitoring exercise by the Home Office had been published, community organisations had highlighted the over-representation of black people in prison, relative to the general population (Gordon 1983). The Home Office (1982) had also examined the work of its Prison Department and reported an over-representation of ethnic minorities in remand centres and borstals.

Ethnic monitoring of the prison population began in June 1984 to assist with monitoring 'race relations' within prisons. In June 1986, the Home Office presented the first statistics on the ethnic origin of the prison population in England and Wales (Home Office 1986). It showed that in 1985, 8 per cent of the male prison population and 12 per cent of the female prison population were of West Indian, Guyanese or African origin, whereas these groups comprised between 1 and 2 per cent of the general population in England and Wales (EC Labour Force Survey

1984). Asians made up 2.5 per cent of the male prison population and 2 per cent of the female prison population, compared with 3 per cent of the general population. These figures held true for both young offenders (those aged 14–20 years) and adults.

Table 8.1 provides the same breakdown indicating both the 'stocks' (those sentenced) and the 'flows' (those on remand or awaiting sentence of the prison population). In each case the pattern is repeated, with the over-representation being especially marked among the remand population. Longer sentences were also proportionately more common for those from ethnic minorities. For adults, 80 per cent of those sentenced to over 18 months custody were white; 8 per cent were African/Caribbean, 4 per cent were Asian and 3 per cent were Chinese/Arab/Mixed. White prisoners were 90 per cent of those in receipt of custodial sentences of up to 18 months, compared with 6 per cent of African/Caribbeans, 1 per cent both of Asian and Chinese/Arab/Mixed origins. Similarly, of those young offenders sentenced to more than 18 months youth custody, 81 per cent were white, 12 per cent were of African/Caribbean origin, 2 per cent were Asian and 3 per cent were Chinese/Arab/Mixed.

Statistical tests showed that the longer sentences were partially explained by the offence type for which individuals had been convicted, although, of course, this factor may be itself 'racially biased' as a result of 'over-charging' practices by the police (see chapter 6). Comparing like with like, those of West Indian, Guyanese and African origin were more likely to receive longer sentences than their white counterparts for sexual

Table 8.1 Type of prisoner populations on 30 June 1985 by ethnic origin

	Sentenced	Untried	Unsentenced	General population
Males				
White	85	75	81	94
West Indian/Guyanese/African	7	10	9	1
Indian/Pakistani/Bangladeshi	2	3	1	3
Chinese/Arab/Mixed origin	2	2	2	1
Other (or not recorded)	3	10	7	2
Females				
White	81	69	77	93
West Indian/Guyanese/African	12	14	12	2
Indian/Pakistani/Bangladeshi	2	2	4	3
Chinese/Arab/Mixed origin	2	6	3	1
Other (or not recorded)	4	8	4	2

Notes:
1 14–64 for males, 14–54 for females.
2 Collated from Home Office, *Statistical Bulletin* 17/86, tables 2 and 3.
3 Percentages do not always sum to 100 due to rounding.

offences, theft and handling and burglary (but not in the magistrates' court); for drugs offences this was true for Asians. Longer sentence lengths also appeared to explain the finding that ethnic minorities were more likely to be held in closed, rather than open prison establishments. In addition, the court at which the offender was sentenced was also important for understanding sentence lengths. An anomalous finding was that people from ethnic minorities, despite being imprisoned for longer periods of time, were shown to have fewer previous convictions than their white counterparts.

Anticipating the controversy that would result from these data, the Home Office report made this qualification:

> It is important to appreciate the limited explanatory value of these statistics in providing conclusive evidence, both as regards the involvement of particular ethnic groups in crime and in relation to the practices of the courts.
>
> (Home Office 1986: 2)

The report instructs the reader not to assume the predominance of 'race' in explaining these patterns, but also to recognise the importance of the following factors which could explain the figures: police and court practices, the age structure of the ethnic minority population, social class, education, employment status and social deprivation or disadvantage. Despite this, the figures were used by community organisations to lambast the courts for their racism (Walker 1989, Hudson 1989, Gordon 1988).

The Home Office has since included information on the ethnic origin of prisoners in its annual publication *Prison Statistics*. The patterns described earlier have largely remained unchanged, although a change to the ethnic origin classifications (based on the 1991 Census), which were introduced by the prison service in 1992, makes comparison difficult. Moreover, although the pattern of over-representation has remained consistent, there has been an increase in the proportion of African/Caribbeans imprisoned, and this is most marked for females, and probably is related to the younger age structure of the African/Caribbean population. It can be anticipated that Asians may follow the same trend when they are over-represented among those at the peak ages of offending, so we may see a similar percentage increase in their numbers imprisoned in the coming decade (see FitzGerald and Marshall 1996).

Figure 8.1 shows that for males the black prison population has grown steadily as a proportion of the general prison population from 8 per cent in 1985 to 12 per cent in 1999. For the male South Asian and 'Chinese and other ethnic origin' prison populations the increase has been smaller, from 2 per cent in 1985 to 3 per cent in 1999. The ethnic minority male prison population has, broadly, fluctuated with the rises and falls of the white prison population. However, over this 15-year period, the overall increase in the ethnic minority prison population has far outstripped that of the white population. Thus, while the white prison population has increased by 31 per cent, the black population has grown by 101 per cent, the South Asian by 80 per cent, and 'Chinese/other Asian' population has increased 106 per cent.

Figure 8.2 shows that, while the numbers are much smaller, the female prison population has followed a similar pattern to that of the male prison population. In particular there has been a dramatic increase in the number of black prisoners. In the five years between 1985 and 1990, the number of black women nearly doubled from 192 to 369 prisoners, as against a declining white female prison population. The result was that the black population (West Indian, African and Guyanese) of female prisons increased from 12 per cent to 23 per cent, then by one-quarter of the total. Since the early 1990s the female prison population of all ethnic origins has increased sharply and this has been most pronounced for black and 'Chinese/others'. Over the 15-year period for which information is available, the white prison population has increased by 97 per cent, while the black population has increased by 217 per cent (to 609 prisoners) and the Chinese/other has gone up by 188 per cent to (144 prisoners). Against a general trend of increasing imprisonment, the number of South Asian women in prison has remained at a more or less constant low level: while there were 28 South Asian women in prison in 1985, there were still only 34 in 1999, an increase of 21 per cent.

There are a number of possible explanations for these changing patterns of imprisonment. The overall trend of a gradually declining prison population in the late 1980s and a sharp increase thereafter, particularly after 1993, can be explained by changes in policy. Specifically the 1990s saw the introduction of more punitive sentencing policies and a increased tendency among sentencers to use custodial sentences, and to hand down longer custodial sentences.

The sharp increase in the black prison population is, in part, explicable for the same reasons but the fact that the number is increasing at a more rapid rate requires some explanation. It is likely that the younger age structure of ethnic minorities in England and Wales provides part of the answer. This would have had the effect of skewing the proportionality of the prison population, as those entering the risk period for offending behaviour were more likely to be from ethnic minorities. The type of offence for which white and ethnic minorities were convicted would also have contributed to the increase, particularly in relation to drugs offences. Finally, the effects of cumulative disadvantage cannot be ruled out. As we speculated in the last chapter, using the findings from Hood's (1992) study of Crown Court sentencing, the impact of racially discriminatory decisions at sentencing can intensify future criminal justice process outcomes. Thus, some of those black prisoners who were discriminated against by judges in receiving custodial sentences in 1980s would undoubtedly have faced the courts following further offending, but would then have been eligible for another (and longer) custodial term.

196 Prison and probation

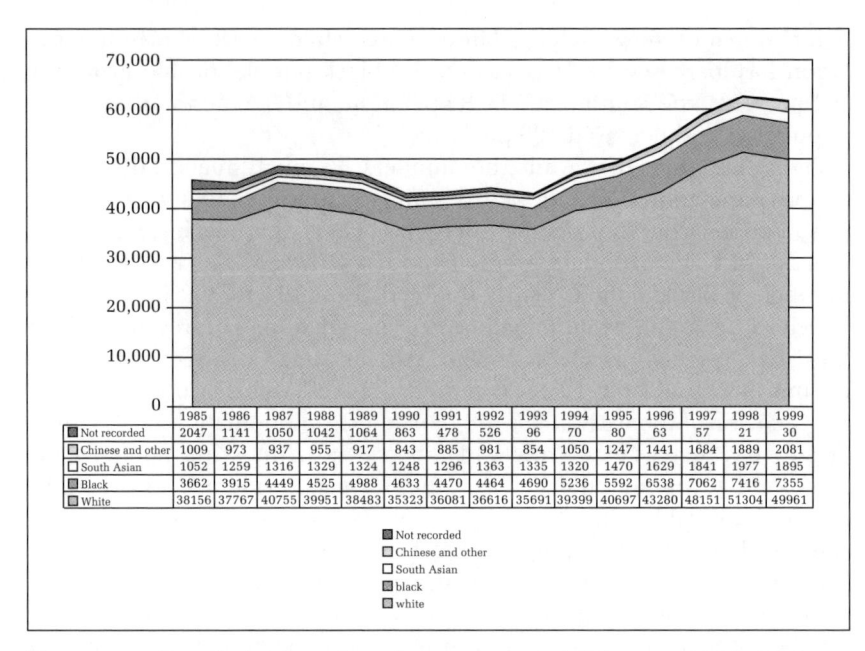

Figure 8.1 Population in prison department establishments 1985–1998 (males)

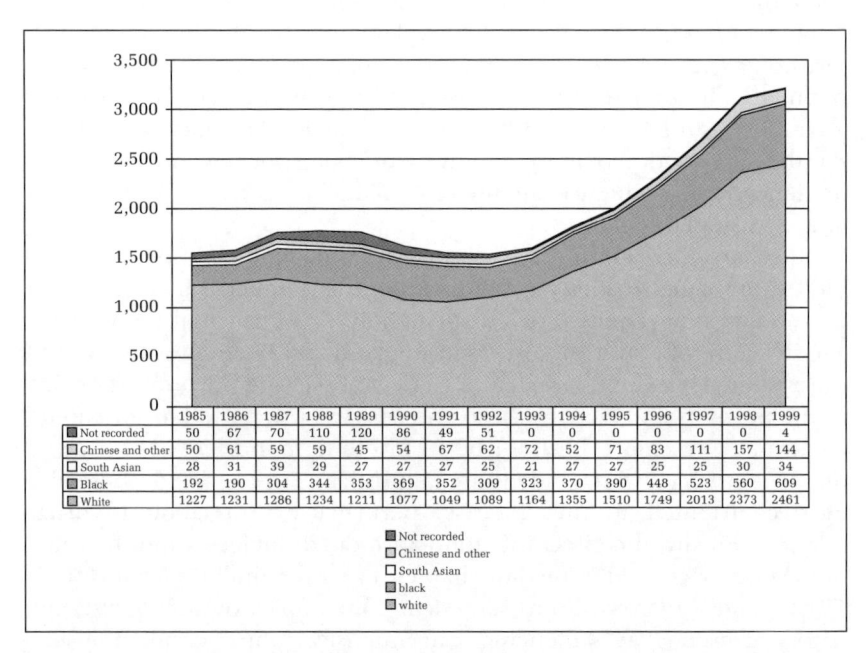

	1985	1986	1987	1988	1989	1990	1991	1992	1993	1994	1995	1996	1997	1998	1999
Not recorded	2047	1141	1050	1042	1064	863	478	526	96	70	80	63	57	21	30
Chinese and other	1009	973	937	955	917	843	885	981	854	1050	1247	1441	1684	1889	2081
South Asian	1052	1259	1316	1329	1324	1248	1296	1363	1335	1320	1470	1629	1841	1977	1895
Black	3662	3915	4449	4525	4988	4633	4470	4464	4690	5236	5592	6538	7062	7416	7355
White	38156	37767	40755	39951	38483	35323	36081	36616	35691	39399	40697	43280	48151	51304	49961

Figure 8.2 Population in prison by ethnic group 1985–1998 (females)

	1985	1986	1987	1988	1989	1990	1991	1992	1993	1994	1995	1996	1997	1998	1999
Not recorded	50	67	70	110	120	86	49	51	0	0	0	0	0	0	4
Chinese and other	50	61	59	59	45	54	67	62	72	52	71	83	111	157	144
South Asian	28	31	39	29	27	27	27	25	21	27	27	25	25	30	34
Black	192	190	304	344	353	369	352	309	323	370	390	448	523	560	609
White	1227	1231	1286	1234	1211	1077	1049	1089	1164	1355	1510	1749	2013	2373	2461

The most recent Home Office statistics show that in 1999, the average number of persons in custody in England and Wales was 64,529, slightly lower than the highest level ever recorded in 1998. On 30 June 1999, there were 12,120 ethnic minorities held in custody in prison service establishments. This amounted to *18 per cent of the male prison population* and *25 per cent of the female population* (Home Office 2000a). Of these, 26 per cent of males and 49 per cent of females were foreign nationals. Among female foreign nationals imprisoned in mid 1999, 77 per cent were incarcerated for drug offences; 70 per cent of these were African/Caribbean.

The list of factors which could legitimately explain the over-representation of African/Caribbeans in the prison population has been expanded to include residence and nationality (see for example Maden, Swinton and Gunn 1992). In order to assess the extent to which ethnic minorities are proportionally represented in prison, the ethnic breakdown of prisoners needs to be compared with their representation in the population of England and Wales, which means excluding those of foreign national status (see table 8.2).

Expressed in terms of incarceration rates, imprisonment per head of population, excluding foreign nationals, the incarceration rate was 1,395 per 100,000 of the population for Caribbeans, 1,399 for other blacks,

Table 8.2 Prison population by ethnic origin and sex (1999)

Ethnic Group	British Nationals, 1999[1]		Resident Population Age 15–64 England and Wales[2]	Incarceration Rates for 1999[3]
	Males	Females	Males and Females	Males and Females
White	86	85	94	184
Black	10	12	2	1,265
Caribbean	6	6	1	1,395
African	1	1	1	713
Other	3	5	<1	1,399
Asian	2	1	3	147
Indian	1	<1	2	93
Pakistani	1	<1	1	260
Bangladeshi	<1	<1	<1	74
Chinese/other	2	2	1	424

Notes:
1 Source: *Statistics on Race and the Criminal Justice System* (Home Office, 2000c).
2 Source: 1991 Census (OPCS, 1993).
3 Source: *Prison Statistics 1999* (Home Office, 2000a).
4 Percentages are rounded to the nearest whole number.

Table 8.3 Proportion of sentenced males (British nationals) in prison by offence type, June 1999

Offence	Whites	Blacks
Violence/sexual	32	28
Robbery	11	26
Burglary	20	13
Drug offences	12	19

Notes:
1 See *Prison Statistics* 1999 (Home Office 2000a) table 6.4.

713 for Africans, compared with 184 per 100,000 for whites. Thus, people of Caribbean and black other origin are nearly eight times more likely to be imprisoned than whites. The incarceration rates indicate over-representation too among Pakistanis (260 per 100,000) and 'other Asians' (914), but an under-representation of Indians (93) and Bangladeshis (74).

Table 8.3 shows the over-representation of black males compared with whites for selected offences, with robbery, burglary and drug offences showing the greatest difference. The proportion imprisoned for drugs offences was even higher for South Asian and Chinese/other males (23 per cent) than for black males (19 per cent) sentenced. For sentenced females, the differences in offence type were starkest for drugs offences even among British nationals: 24 per cent of sentenced white females were imprisoned for drugs offences compared to more than double (52 per cent) of black sentenced females (cf. Maden, Swinton and Gunn 1992). Sentence lengths were longer for ethnic minority prisoners: 50 per cent of adult whites received custodial sentences of over four years, compared with 65 per cent of adult blacks, 57 per cent of South Asians, and 62 per cent of Chinese adults and those of 'other' ethnic origins. This was partially explained by their conviction for drugs offences which attract harsher sentences.

FitzGerald and Marshall (1996) use data from the 1991 National Prison Survey and the 1991 Census to provide socio-demographic contextual information to explain the ethnic disparities among males in the prison population. In 1991, the National Prison Survey interviewed over 4,000 prisoners, based on a random sample of 10 per cent of male and 20 per cent of female inmates. FitzGerald and Marshall suggest that, based on the educational and employment background of African/Caribbeans, it might be expected that they would be over-represented among prisoners, assuming that these socio-economic indicators are related to offending behaviour. While the same would be true of Pakistanis and Bangladeshis, over-representation is offset by their younger age, such that fewer have reached the peak age of offending.

Thus, the picture presented by the statistics is one in which African/

Caribbean people, and to a lesser extent those of Pakistani and 'other Asian' origins, are over-represented among both sentenced and remand populations, while other ethnic minority groups are present in the prison population at a rate comparable with, or lower than, those of the white population. The analysis of trends over the period for which data are available (and can be compared) indicates that the black prison population is growing. Further consideration of these patterns will be explored in the concluding chapter. Here we now consider the experience and needs of ethnic minorities once contained *within* the prison system, beginning first with an historical overview for understanding 'race relations' policies.

The historical and policy context

Paul Gordon's (1983) text, *White Law*, provides a useful background to the treatment and position of ethnic minorities in prison throughout the 1970s and early 1980s. The backdrop to this experience was widespread support for the National Front and extreme racism among prison officers, and the failure of the Home Office to associate this with the frequently brutal experiences of ethnic minority prisoners (Gordon 1983: 117–36). Incidents of brutality and harassment by prison officers were common. Gordon also notes that there was evidence that racist stereotyping was common in prison officers' reports to the parole board. In addition, Gordon highlights the initial tendency of the Home Office to 'play down' confrontations between white and black prisoners. When denial became untenable, the official reaction was to see black prisoners as the problem and to advocate dispersal policies, taking, as Gordon notes, 'the same road as the government in relation to immigration' (ibid.: 120).

Shaw (1990) describes how a series of incidents demonstrating individual and institutional racism in the 1970s and early 1980s provided a further impetus to the development of Home Office prison service policy. Reports of the racist taunting of ethnic minority prisoners by prison officers were made, along with accusations about ethnic minority prisoners being denied favourable prison jobs and being treated more harshly in disciplinary matters. For example, in December 1987, the Court of Appeal in the case of *Alexander* v *Home Office*, ruled in favour of a black inmate who had been discriminated against in being denied a kitchen job position. It was shown that comments in his initial assessment report at Wandsworth prison and a subsequent induction report had led to him being racially discriminated against in his job application, whereby he was treated as a 'racial stereotype' rather than as an individual. The report opined that the prisoner:

> displays the usual traits associated with people of his ethnic background, being arrogant, suspicious of staff, anti-authority, devious and possessing a

very large chip on his shoulder, which he will find very difficult to remove if he carries on the way he is doing.

(CRE 1990: 107)

It also became clear that officers were ill-equipped to respond to the religious and cultural needs of, for example, Asian prisoners. A series of policy documents by the Home Office were produced during 1981 and 1986 to address these inequalities. Indeed, Shaw (1990) argues that they were the most comprehensive of any public organisation in Britain at the time.

Launched in February 1999, the current strategy, Racial Equality for Staff and Prisoners (RESPOND) grew out of a series of focus group meetings of ethnic minority staff working in the prison service. Its key actions for 1999/2000 included a review of complaints procedures, a new investigations strategy, racial harassment training, promotion and selection training, the development of advisory and support groups for ethnic minority staff, exit interviews, a review of recruitment and appraisal systems, and planned outreach recruitment activities.

Racism in prison

The most comprehensive study of 'race relations' in prison to date was commissioned by the Home Office and conducted by Elaine Genders and Elaine Player (1989) in 1985 and 1986. The researchers analysed prison records, conducted interviews with staff and prisoners and observed daily routines in prison. Genders and Player noted that 'race relations' were rarely regarded as a problem by prison officers in two of the prisons where the research was based, largely because of the absence of overt racial conflict and physical confrontations. Indeed, prison staff were highly dismissive of the need for a 'race relations' policy. Notwithstanding this, they reported that rank and file prison officers commonly used racial stereotypes. Black inmates were frequently described as arrogant, lazy, noisy, hostile to authority, with values incompatible with British society, and having 'a chip on their shoulder', because they perceived themselves to be victims of racial persecution. These negative attributes were sometimes presumed to be 'innate' characteristics. Other comments resonated with biological theories of racial inferiority such as an inability to do certain prison jobs and to being unable to undertake further education in prison. In contrast, Asian inmates were perceived as model prisoners being hard-working and polite but also devious and prone to lying (Gordon 1983). Chigwada-Bailey (1997) has drawn attention to the similar way in which African/Caribbean women prisoners are perceived, as troublesome and causing disciplinary problems.

Prison staff interviewed by Genders and Player described the formation of racial groups which they believed provided inmates with a sense of identity and belonging, facilitated shared activities, and increased status and power. Sometimes prison officers felt that this made their job difficult in dealing with disputes, and black inmates, in particular, were regarded as a 'management problem' among 70 per cent, 60 per cent and 40 per cent of prison officers at the three prisons. Staff acknowledged that this meant that black inmates were often treated 'by the book' (that is, formally) more often than their Asian and white counterparts, but prison officers argued that the prisoners were to blame for this situation because of their arrogance and anti-authority attitudes. Not surprisingly, given these views, over half of the uniformed prison officers wanted to limit the numbers of black inmates in any one institution. Asian inmates were cited as the victims of bullying, intimidation and cultural insensitivity.

While prison staff played down the importance of 'race relations' in prison, inmates' perspectives on this issue were more mixed. Asian inmates more commonly reported that there was not a 'race relations' problem in prison. Fifty-two per cent of all racial groups felt that 'race relations' were a problem in prison generally, although two-thirds did not believe there was a problem in their prison. Racial prejudice among inmates existed according to eight out of ten whites, six out of ten African/Caribbeans and three out of ten Asians. It was argued that this largely took the form of avoiding contact rather than overt conflict. Inmates interviewed by Genders and Player were receptive to the provision of special facilities to cater for ethnic minorities, to meet their religious and dietary needs.

In relation to discipline, inmates reported that prison officers were more guarded in the presence of black prisoners, and, to a lesser extent, Asian prisoners. White inmates were more likely than their African/Caribbean counterparts to believe that African/Caribbeans were the target of discrimination by prison officers; African/Caribbeans tended to state that all ethnic minority inmates were victims of racially discriminatory treatment, where it occurred. There was agreement that all racial groups were treated equally by the probation and after-care department.

A question about treatment by prison officers was also asked in the National Prison Survey (1991). There 43 per cent of white prisoners, 46 per cent of black Africans, 44 per cent of Asians, but only 29 per cent of black Caribbeans, 27 per cent of other black prisoners and 28 per cent of those from other ethnic groups said that prison officers treated them well. Black Caribbeans were also more likely to say that they had not been treated well by prison governors.

Genders and Player attempted to examine whether there was any evidence of discrimination in disciplinary procedures by asking inmates to say whether they had been involved in a serious argument or fight, and, if they had, whether prison staff had intervened and taken any action. Twenty per cent of inmates had been involved in a serious confrontation with staff, while 40 per cent had argued or fought with other inmates; whites and African/Caribbeans were proportionately represented, but fewer than expected Asians reported such behaviour. Formal action was taken by prison officers in half the cases involving black and Asian inmates, but in only one-quarter of those where the inmate was white. Fifty per cent of infractions committed by ethnic minority inmates were reported for adjudication, compared with 19 per cent of those reported by whites. This supports the earlier comments by prison officers that they more frequently instigated disciplinary procedures 'by the book' where the inmate was a member of an ethnic minority, a seemingly clear example of direct discrimination. It could also be seen as a further layer of criminalisation against black people in prison.

Genders and Player's analysis of standard classification forms which were completed at intake revealed derogatory comments being made about ethnic minority prisoners (see also Prison Ombudsman 2000: 51). These typically reflected the negative stereotyping related to supposed biological inferiority which was prevalent among prison officers. Among those who had completed vocational training, three-quarters of Asian inmates, two-thirds of white inmates, but only one-half of African/Caribbean inmates were assessed as possessing sufficient work skills. Yet the 1991 National Prison Survey showed that African/Caribbean and Asian prisoners were much more likely than their white counterparts to attend education and training classes (Walmsley, Howard and White 1992). Chigwada-Bailey (1989) reported from a small sample of black female prisoners who felt that they were racially discriminated against when trying to join education classes.

There was no clear indication that accommodation allocations were systematically racially biased in the Genders and Player study, although allocation decisions were sometimes made to disperse African/Caribbean inmates, based on the stereotype of them being noisy or troublesome as a group. The picture was more clear-cut in work assignments. It was apparent that white inmates (71 per cent) much more frequently exercised choice over their prison work than either African/Caribbean (56 per cent) or Asian inmates (31 per cent). An analysis of work allocations at one of the prison establishments found an over-representation of ethnic minorities in the workshops (typically the least favoured jobs), and blacks were significantly more likely to be left unemployed. Another monitoring exercise at the same prison found racial imbalances in a selection of labour allocations. This was further supported in an analysis of job assignments for 386 inmates at another of the prisons. Ethnic minority inmates (14 per cent) were significantly less likely to be employed in the best jobs compared with white inmates (45 per cent). Interviews with 50 work supervisors from the five prison establishments also indicated that ethnic minority inmates were highly under-represented in the most popular jobs. Genders and Player concluded on the basis of these data that 'racial bias lies at the root of the racial imbalance evidenced in labour allocation' (1989: 127).

Such discrimination occurred because work supervisors enjoyed wide discretion to circumvent formal procedures for work allocations by picking their 'own' men or using various means to sack ethnic minority inmates. More generally, prison officers based their decisions on racial stereotypes, while arguing that such decisions were necessary to maintain 'good order and discipline' and to ensure the efficient running of a prison. According to Genders and Player, this was due to the prison department's lack of clarity and precision in defining what prison staff were expected to do under the 'race relations' policy. In addition, inadequacies in implementation of the policy were identified, including failing to attract ethnic minority prison staff, weak strategies in the area of education and training and ineffective monitoring of prison regimes. Finally, Genders and Player pointed to the absence of effective sanctions for unprofessional conduct. They also suggested that prison officers used stereotyping to order their working environments by predicting inmates' behaviour in order to maintain authority at all times. The occupational culture of prison officers promoted internal solidarity and insularity and a 'them and us' outlook, not dissimilar from core police occupational cultures (see also Gordon 1984).

The influence of 'race' and racism in prison was also the focus of research by McDermott (1990). She studied five male prisons which varied in their security categorisation, including an urban local prison, a dispersal prison and an open prison. Two-thirds of the 1,156 prisoners interviewed completed a questionnaire about their prison experiences. For a vast majority of questions the responses of white, black and Asian prisoners did not differ significantly, including those on accommodation, clothing, physical education, facilities, family contact and preparing for release. However, McDermott did find a backlash against the 'race relations' policy, perceptions of racism and unfair treatment by prison staff among black and Asian prisoners, an over-representation of black prisoners and an under-representation of Asian prisoners on disciplinary charges, and ethnic minority prisoners less likely to work in 'trusted' jobs, such as serving in the officers' mess.

Like Genders and Player (1989), McDermott (1990) found that in the higher security prisons, a minority of prison officers (ranging from 8 per cent to 25 per cent) said that they felt vulnerable because of the presence of ethnic minority prisoners. African/Caribbean prisoners particularly were seen to represent a control problem; they were viewed as 'different', 'deviant' and 'foreign'. However, over one-third of the staff reported that they wanted more 'race relations' training. Once again the elements of individual and cultural racism were evident in the responses of inmates and prison officers. Furthermore, as box 8.1 illustrates, some ten years after these early studies of race relations, evidence of racist practices within prisons is still emerging.

Box 8.1 Race relations in prison in the twenty-first century

'Evidence shows that discrimination and harassment exists at Brixton and that systems are not in place to investigate it or eradicate it.'

This was one of the conclusions drawn by the Race Relations Adviser to HM Prison Service Agency following her assessment of race relations at Brixton prison (Clements 2000). Her study uncovered a climate of victimisation, the use of inappropriate language, harassment, abuse and bullying of both ethnic minority staff and prisoners. This was epitomised in the use of the 'Reflections' regime which involved loss of association by prisoners. It was used disproportionately against prisoners from minority ethnic groups, without due process, and without the knowledge of senior managers. The investigation found evidence that senior managers had not prioritised race relations at the prison, that complaints were not fully investigated or actions implemented. The assessment did not find, however, that work and education places were racially biased. Reports of systematic racist abuse and bullying have been made at other prison establishments, including HMP Wormwood Scrubs (HMIP 1999).

Commission for Racial Equality formal investigation

In November 2000, the CRE announced a formal investigation into the HM Prison Service. Its focus will be on racial discrimination and racial harassment in HMP Brixton and Parc prisons and HM Feltham Young Offenders Institution. It has heard representations from the prison service, Racial Equality for Staff and Prisoners (RESPOND) team, and members of the POA following reports of racial discrimination in relation to prisoners and staff.

Racist victimisation

The racist victimisation of prisoners has also been examined in research undertaken by Burnett and Farrell (1994). Interviews were carried out with 220 African/Caribbean inmates, 75 Asian inmates, 78 inmates from other ethnic minorities and 128 white inmates. One hundred and six prison officers were also interviewed, and of these 11 per cent were from ethnic minorities. In addition, discussions were held with prison managers and specialist staff, including race relations liaison officers and board of visitors members.

Burnett and Farrell (1994) found that one in three Asian inmates, one in four African/Caribbean inmates, one in five of inmates of other ethnic origins and one in eight white inmates said that they had been racially abused or attacked by other inmates over a three-month period. The levels of repeat victimisation were high: for African/Caribbean inmates the average number of incidents during the study period was four and for Asian inmates it was five. Black inmates (44 per cent) were more likely than Asian inmates (33 per cent), 'other' ethnic minority inmates (23 per cent) or white inmates to report that they had been victimised by prison staff. Prison officers that were aware of racially motivated incidents in their establishments were less likely than inmates to perceive them as serious, mirroring the experience of ethnic minorities in the general population with regard to the police. The types of inmate-on-inmate incidents reported varied, with assaults, bullying and harassment being less common than incidents of theft. Racist verbal abuse was the most frequently mentioned.

A complaint form was completed, in only 12 per cent of racial incidents were prisoners actively encouraged to make complaints informally and verbally, a finding confirmed by Jackson (1997). Racial incidents were under-reported largely because victims felt that no action would be taken, or the situation in which the incident arose could not be changed, and because of a fear of being seen as a 'trouble-maker'. It was also the case that prison officers and race relations liaison officers did not always consider the need to record racial incidents, instead preferring them to be 'nipped in the bud'. Where an official complaint had been lodged (including those not related to racial incidents), half of the ethnic minority inmates compared with three-quarters of the white inmates believed that their complaint had not been treated fairly.

A number of recent incidents have also questioned the ability of prison officers to protect ethnic minority prisoners from racist harassment and violence. Four black men who spent three months on remand, despite later having charges dropped against them, issued a High Court writ claiming damages for personal injury after being assaulted by a mob of white inmates *(Birmingham Post,* 25 March 1998). In Parc prison in 1998 there was tension and violence between African/Caribbean and racist white prisoners, after racist graffiti was daubed on the walls (*The Times,* 30 May 1998).

Box 8.2

19 year-old Zahid Mubarek was beaten to death by his cellmate on the eve of his release from Feltham Young Offenders' Institution where he was imprisoned for minor property offences. After bludgeoning Zahid to death, Robert Stewart – who was later convicted of murder – scrawled a swastika on the wall of his cell and the words 'just killed me pad mate'. The *Daily Mail* reported that a month before the murder, Stewart had written letters expressing hatred for 'non-whites' and his intention to take 'extreme measures to get shipped out' of Feltham, including "I'll kill me ******* pad mate if I have to … make myself a Ku Klux Klan suit and walk out me pad holding a flaming cross'.[1] This case underlines the twin fallacies that imprisonment protects innocent victims and reforms offenders.

---

[1] Rebecca English, *Daily Mail* (6 November 2000, p. 19)

Parole

Another important means for assessing the treatment of ethnic minorities within the prison system is the use of 'early release' under the Criminal Justice Act 1991, although data with an ethnic breakdown is only available for its predecessor, parole. Early release represents an important stage of the criminal justice process because it is likely to be delayed where inmates have committed disciplinary infractions, and, as we have seen from the previous sections, formal action may be more frequently taken following incidents involving African/Caribbean prisoners compared with whites and Asians.

Parole involves the case review of an individual prisoner to determine whether, after a specified time period, they should be released from prison on licence, or whether they should remain in prison. The use of parole for white and ethnic minority prisoners has not been subject to empirical study and there is limited statistical information. The Home Office (1994a) first presented a statistical bulletin on parole recommendations by ethnic origin in 1990. At this time, the first stage of review lay with the prison via a local review committee, who would consider early release of the prisoner by taking account of the nature of the offence committed, the prisoner's criminal, social and employment history, their behaviour while in prison, medical and home circumstances, employment prospects and the likelihood of the prisoner co-operating with parole supervision (Home Office 1994a). Where the recommendation of the local review committee was not accepted by the Home Secretary (in two-thirds of cases), the cases were referred to the parole board, a panel drawn from the criminal justice professions, academics and lay people.

The Home Office (1994a) studied over 23,000 parole decisions relating to male prisoners made in England and Wales in 1990. The percentage of prisoners who were recommended for parole in 1990 were as follows: white 57 per cent, 'West Indian/Guyanese' 51 per cent, African 35 per cent, Asian 52 per cent, and Chinese/Arab/Mixed 48 per cent. These percentages were lower for all ethnic minority prisoners compared with their white counterparts which appeared to be largely – but not completely – accounted for by the longer sentences being served by ethnic minorities and the time to the 'earliest date of release' specified at the time of sentence. Where rates were 'normalised' to ethnic minorities having the same distribution of offences and time to the earliest date for release, the parole recommendation rate was as follows: whites 60 per cent, 'West Indian/Guyanese' 56 per cent, Africans 61 per cent, Asians 63 per cent, Chinese/Arab/Mixed 55 per cent, still leaving a modicum of difference for West Indian/Guyanese and Chinese/Arab/Mixed prisoners not explained by these two factors (Home Office 1994a).

More recent parole release data provided by the Home Office (2000c) show wider variation between white (40 per cent) and black (43 per cent) prisoners on the one hand, and Asian prisoners (65 per cent) on the other. The same pattern can be seen for those released under the Home Detention Curfew scheme. It is hoped that future research will be able to look more thoroughly at all the factors which influence parole and curfew decision making. This must take account of the outcomes of disciplinary actions which may explain the higher release rates for Asian prisoners.

Foreign nationals

The particular problems facing foreign prisoners as well as their needs within the British system were the focus of research by Cheney (1993). She sought information from all prison race relations liaison officers and medical officers, as well as the embassy/consular offices of 35 countries, and all staff at two prisons with a large foreign prison population. Language and cultural difficulties, isolation from family, few visitors, a lack of understanding of the British criminal justice system and anxiety associated with uncertainty about their fate on return to their home country were all concerns for foreign prisoners, including whites (see also Richards *et al.* 1995a). Other problems included not having others to talk with easily, a lack of entertainment from reading or watching television, being disadvantaged in the prison work environment and lack of other resources, inadequate and unfamiliar diets, and clinical depression. These social and economic deprivations amount to foreign prisoners being in 'a prison within a prison' (Richards *et al.* 1995b: 201). Those being held for offences under the Immigration Act 1971 may suffer these same difficulties, but there is the additional stress associated with the prospect of deportation or delays and indecisions about their immigration status.

According to Cheney (1993), trying to improve the experiences of foreign nationals in prison may be exacerbated by the fact that one in five race relations liaison officers surveyed had no idea how many foreign prisoners they had in their prison. Recommendations made by Cheney included improving the recording of nationality, providing prison notices in foreign languages and using interpreters, increasing facilities and services (such as phone cards for overseas calls), and training prison officers, medical and race relations liaison officers in the special needs and cultures of foreign prisoners.

A recent survey of imprisoned women by Caddle and Crisp (1997) suggests that African/Caribbean women may suffer especially from difficulties associated with separation from their children, since African/Caribbean women (76 per cent) are more likely than their white counterparts (57 per cent) to be mothers. This is particularly acute among women of foreign nationality, the majority of whom had children living with them before their imprisonment (see also Richards *et al.* 1995a).

Immigration detainees and asylum seekers

There is little research on the prison experiences of immigration detainees and asylum seekers. However, recent events suggest that this is an area that requires closer examination. On 20 August 1997 there was a disturbance at the largest of Britain's immigration detention centres, Campsfield House. Following this an unannounced inspection was conducted by HM Chief Inspector of Prisons in October 1997 (Her Majesty's Inspectorate of Prisons, 1998a). The vast majority of detainees held were from Asia or Africa; the largest national groups detained were Indian (21 per cent) and Nigerian (18 per cent). While the average period of detention was 2.5 months, one in ten had been there for more than six months. A group interview with 12 female detainees produced accusations of racism among staff and the use of inappropriate language. The inspection team were also told by a group of male detainees that they had been 'told by staff to go back to their own country if they did not like it here and were told that they would be sent to prison if they did not behave' (Her Majesty's Inspectorate of Prisons 1998a: 35). Despite the inspection team giving the detention centre a largely clean bill of health and identifying several examples of good practice, recommendations were made to clarify the legal status of detention, giving it judicial oversight, and to introduce rules and obligations for both staff and detainees. It was also advised that the Secretary of State should apply time limits to the various stages of the application process (see also Weber and Gelsthorpe 2000).

Brutality and deaths in custody

The deaths of ethnic minorities while in prison custody indicates a pattern of excessive physical restraint, misdiagnosis, disbelieving inmates' claims concerning their health, or the provision of inadequate or inappropriate medical treatment by prison officers and medical staff. As with deaths of African/Caribbeans in police custody (see chapter 6), there is a tendency for prison staff to overreact to disruptive behaviour by African/Caribbean prisoners, whereby the stereotype of 'Big, Black and Dangerous' seems to predominate in determining their response. The deaths of Michael Martin, Joseph Watts and Orville Blackwood are examples of these fatal encounters between African/Caribbean inmates and staff in secure hospital facilities (Prins 1998). Earlier examples are described in the Institute of Race Relations (1991) report, *Deadly Silence*, including the case of Anthony Mahony, who was found semi-naked wandering the streets, arrested for indecent exposure and, despite his own requests for medical attention, was eventually remanded to prison, where he died from viral pneumonia.

In 1991 a jury ruled that Omasase Lumumba had been unlawfully killed while in prison custody. The same verdict was recorded following the death of Alton Manning in March 1998 by contracted prison staff (Prison Reform Trust 1998). In neither case was a prosecution of prison staff brought by the CPS, although in the latter case the CPS are reconsidering papers relating to the case following a judicial review of this decision (Inquest 2000). Yet implicit in the comments of Richard Tilt, then director-general of the prison service, was a denial of the role of racism in deaths in prison custody when, in March 1998, he suggested that black people were more likely than other prisoners to die from positional asphyxia while being restrained than other prisoners because of their genetic disposition to sickle cell anaemia (*Independent*, 28 March 1998, *Hansard*, 22 April 1998: 636, *Independent*, 24 April 1998).

Our attention is also drawn to suicides of African/Caribbeans and other ethnic minorities, which have been aggravated by a lack of concern for their physical and mental health needs and by ignoring previous suicide attempts or, in the case of asylum seekers, because detention is imposed followed by lengthy delays in settling their applications for asylum, and fear of forced repatriation. In January 1997, for example, an inquest recorded a verdict of accidental death aggravated by a lack of care in the case of Peter Austin. He was left hanging by the neck from a light fitting (while held in custody at the magistrates' court for a bail hearing) for over five minutes while private security guards discussed whether he was feigning his death and preparing to attack them. The inquest recognised that the negative stereotyping of Austin as dangerous had contributed to the guards' behaviour, and that his previous suicide attempts and mental health problems had been overlooked (Campaign Against Racism and Fascism 1996).

The probation service

The probation service has a central role in the court process, since probation officers have a responsibility for presenting magistrates with recommendations for sentencing options in individual cases. This takes the form of Pre-Sentence Reports (formerly Social Inquiry Reports) (see chapter 7). In addition to their work in courts and prisons, where convicted defendants are sentenced, either to probation, community service, a combination of the two, or a supervision or curfew order with electronic monitoring, probation officers will be responsible for their supervision in the community. They will also provide many prisoners with a supervision and social work service post-release.

According to Denney (1992), probation policy ignored ethnic minority offenders until the late 1970s. A Home Office circular issued in 1977 requested that probation areas with a significant African, Caribbean or Asian population should appoint a probation officer to develop services for ethnic minorities. The stated opinion at the time was that specialists could mediate any cultural misunderstandings. This position changed following the urban disturbances in the early 1980s, when probation areas began to acknowledge the need to recognise institutional racism and to promote anti-racist probation practice. This coincided with a number of small-scale local studies which monitored different aspects of probation service delivery and identified inequalities in the treatment of ethnic minorities. Recommended solutions in the post-1981 era focused on in-service training to eradicate racism by white probation officers, an increased orientation towards community, and an increase in ethnic minority probation officers. The development of anti-racist policy diminished in the 1990s with little reference to it in the service's three-year plans (Her Majesty's Inspectorate of Probation, 2000).

'Race' and racism in probation practice

Drawing on research with a small sample of probation officers, it has been argued by Green (1989) that the probation service, in practice, denies the racist context in which many black offenders live and the extent to which this contributes to their offending behaviour and personal identity. According to Green, the probation service adopts a 'colour-blind' approach where the organisational response is to treat all offenders in the same way (see also Mavunga 1993). This is largely the result of probation officers being socialised into the service through its institutional ideology, which is white-dominated and where the issue of 'race' has been marginalised. Green's interviews with 13 West Midlands main-grade and senior probation officers revealed a reluctance among staff to learn about racism; instead, officers were interested in learning about the cultural background of their clients. According to Green, the combination of the courts' focus on individual offending rather than its social and economic context, probation officers' emphasis on African/Caribbean family pathology contrasted with a white middle-class 'norm', and their feelings of vulnerability and threats to their professional status raised by black offending behaviour, has led to narrow organisational responses, such as recommending that magistrates and judges impose custodial sentences. It is suggested that probation officers are more willing to recommend custody for black clients, because they have failed to develop a relationship with them and are unable to supervise them in the community.

Denney's (1992) study supported Green's (1989) conclusions and also found that the language used in the reports on black offenders was more often derogatory in nature than was true for reports on white offenders. References to the 'physical presence' of black offenders were common, as were comments about their use of violence. During social work probation practice, officers were reluctant to accept black offenders' concerns about racism and how it had shaped their offending behaviour. Instead, probation officers perceived black offenders to be anti-authoritarian, angry and irresponsible. A probation discourse which was more 'correctional' than 'appreciative' was found in reports concerning black offenders who were seen as 'threatening' and also emphasised that there was less possibility for change among these offenders. White offenders, by contrast, were presented as victims of individual circumstance. However, Denney (1992) notes that there were no differences in the proportion of white and black offenders who were recommended by probation officers for non-custodial sentences. Neither was there any evidence that probation officers provided practical assistance to white offenders more often than to African/Caribbean offenders, or offered differential access to group work for offenders of different racial origins. In contrast, the recent thematic inspection on racial equality raised concerns about differences in the quality of supervision of black offenders, particularly in terms of levels of contact during the later stages of the order (Her Majesty's Inspectorate of Probation 2000).

The probation service responded slowly to allegations that it does little to contextualise the experiences and behaviour of African/Caribbean offenders (Holdaway and Allaker 1990), but there is evidence that local offices are mounting proactive initiatives (see NACRO 1991). Mistry (1993) has detailed her experiences as a probation officer working with young women offenders in the Avon area, adopting both anti-racist and feminist practices to understanding offending behaviour within its socio-economic context and without stereotyping. Similarly, Moss Side Probation Office in Greater Manchester has recognised the importance of exploring critically the role of the police in contributing to offending behaviour and of working collaboratively with ethnic minority community organisations. In one instance, probation officers attached a 'Common Statement' to individual PSRs in mitigation following a drugs operation which outlined socio-economic and political reasons for criminal behaviour, in addition to providing defendants remanded for a PSR with a detailed information sheet explaining their rights in relation to the probation service and the support available to them (Briggs 1995). Crown Court defendants who plead not guilty are also offered a personal interview by probation officers where they are able to voice any concerns they have about policing or questions regarding legal advice. A recent review of separately provided groupwork programmes for black and Asian offenders commissioned by the Home Office has recognised the need for research and development in this area. In particular, there is an acknowledgement that little is known about the needs of ethnic minority probationers, and there is no evidence of 'what works' in reducing reoffending among this group of offenders (Home Office 2001c, see also Lawrence 1996).

Conclusion

The empirical and documentary evidence reviewed in this chapter points to racial disparities in the experience of ethnic minorities in the prison system. A recurrent theme has been the perspective of prison and probation officers who see the management of ethnic minorities as a 'problem'. There is a tendency to see African/Caribbean inmates and probation clients as dangerous, threatening, violent, anti-authority and unable to change. The 'problem' with Asians has been more closely associated with cultural differences that are not assumed to be dangerous – only different and extraordinary. Elements of both direct and indirect racism clearly affect the treatment of ethnic minorities at the end of the criminal justice process. There is evidence of direct racism in prison dispersals in accommodation, in the operation of disciplinary procedures, deaths in custody, and in dealing with racist victimisation. Institutional racism is evident in work assignments where lax rules and more discretion allowed prison staff to recruit inmates according to personal preference which implicitly and directly discriminated against ethnic minorities.

Failing to meet the cultural, educational and dietary needs of African/Caribbean and Asian inmates has also raised concerns about the implementation of the 'race relations' policy in prisons. Similar criticisms have been levelled at probation officers, particularly with regard to defining and accommodating the supervision needs of ethnic minority clients. Of equal concern has been the pathologising of ethnic minority families illustrated by comments in probation reports.

The denial of African/Caribbean and Asian people's experience of racism and exclusion has been another theme in this chapter. Absent is an account of the social, economic and political contexts in which people from ethnic minorities live their lives and sometimes find themselves on 'the wrong side of the law'. This forms a backdrop to the huge over-representation of black people in the prison population. In chapter 10 we consider the influence of 'race' and racism on the criminal justice process taken as a whole and examine future directions for research, policy, politics and practice that might contribute to resolve the problems facing people from ethnic minorities who become enmeshed in the criminal justice and penal systems. Before this we consider the role and experiences of ethnic minority practitioners in the criminal justice professions.

Chapter 9

Practitioners

> A Muslim woman who said she was hounded out of the Metropolitan Police was awarded a record £1 million payout yesterday. (*The Times*, 6 June 2000)
>
> An Asian lawyer who claimed that a culture of racism prevented her from being promoted within the Crown Prosecution Service was awarded £30,000 damages yesterday. (*Daily Telegraph*, 2 February 2000)
>
> The head of the prison service is to apologise to a black worker who was humiliated and abused when he returned to work after winning damages for racial discrimination... Claude Johnson, 43, is set to win damages of up to £100,00 in addition to the £28,000 he won five years ago for injuries to his feelings during three years of discrimination at Brixton prison. (*The Times*, 20 April 2000)
>
> North Wales Probation Committee must pay £3,500 after being found guilty of racial discrimination against the area's only black probation officer. (*Daily Post*, 23 March 1996)

The experiences of people from ethnic minorities in employment in criminal justice agencies – such as the police and prison services – must take account of their experience in employment more generally (see chapters 1 and 2). In particular, until the 1976 Race Relations Act, which made unlawful indirect as well as direct discrimination in employment, there is clear evidence of the 'colour bar', a system of racial segregation which meant that some occupations remained exclusively white, while others attracted a large number of people from ethnic minorities. It is interesting to contrast the employment practices of different uniformed occupations. Some occupations, for example, bus and train driving, ticket inspection, and nursing, provided employment for large numbers of people from ethnic minorities, but others, notably the police, fire service and the armed forces, employed far fewer. There is clear evidence that members of ethnic minorities were directly excluded from these services.

This book has examined, using empirical evidence, the experiences of people from ethnic minority communities as *consumers* of criminal justice services and yet ethnic minorities are also *providers* of criminal justice services. In this, the penultimate chapter, we consider their experience. This is interesting in its own right but also because one strategy that has been suggested as a means to increase ethnic minority communities' 'confidence and trust' in the criminal justice system is to ensure that its officers 'reflect the diversity of the communities they serve'. That means, in most instances, that the police, courts, prison and probation services need to increase the number of ethnic minority practitioners that they employ. This is linked to the idea that officers from ethnic minority communities will treat clients in a more even-handed and sensitive way than white officers. In relation to policing, for example, it is assumed that ethnic minority police officers will not operate with the same working stereotypes as white officers and that understanding and respect for ethnic minority citizens will prevent the kind of oppressive policing that has occurred in contexts where local officers are predominantly, or exclusively, white. It is also argued that the public image of the police will be improved and its credibility increased if the police service reflects the composition of the community it polices. Although these arguments have been advanced most often in the area of policing, they can be extended to all agencies within the criminal justice system. A black prison officer may not operate by stereotyping black prisoner's behaviour as aggressive and worthy of sanction, as they will not share the prejudices held by many white prison officers. Similarly, an Asian probation officer may be best placed to appreciate, and be receptive to, the needs of an Asian client, and so on throughout the criminal justice system. This chapter follows the logical order of chapters 6–8 by reviewing empirical and documentary evidence regarding the position and experience of ethnic minority employees of the criminal justice system as police officers, prosecution and court staff, prison and probation officers. We also look at the experiences of ethnic minority employees of the Home Office, the government department with the largest responsibility for crime prevention, criminal justice and race relations.

Ethnic minority police officers

As people from ethnic minorities struggled to join the police service in the 1970s and 1980s, the treatment they received from their colleagues was often extremely hostile, an attitude which existed towards minority communities in general. Reading today Smith and Gray's (1983) study of 'the Police in Action', it is staggering to recall the language police officers used to speak about black and Asian people. The centrality of racism in the subculture of the police served (and still does in some places) to alienate, marginalise and discriminate against ethnic minority officers. Even the most recent evidence shows that supervisory and senior police officers often fail to discourage and discipline racist comments and actions by police officers (Her Majesty's Inspectorate of Constabulary 1998).

Recruitment

The recruitment of ethnic minority police officers has long been on the agenda of the Home Office and senior police officers, not least because of the Scarman recommendations after urban disorders in the early and mid 1980s (see chapter 1). There has been an increase since 1986 in the proportion of serving police officers who are from ethnic minorities, from 0.7 per cent to 2 per cent of the police service in England and Wales as at 31 March 2000 (Home Office 2000c). This means that they remain considerably under-represented relative to around 7 per cent of the economically active population. According to data collected by Her Majesty's Inspectorate of Constabulary on the 43 forces in England and Wales, around 4 per cent of applications to join the police service were made by ethnic minority individuals during the period 1997/8. Of the applicants, 25 per cent of whites were interviewed compared with 20 per cent of ethnic minority applicants. Similar discrepancies were apparent in the proportion subsequently offered employment and in appointments actually made. Thus, the under-representation of ethnic minorities within the police service is due to both a shortfall in applications and a lower proportion being successful in the recruitment process. A similar picture emerges when it comes to the Accelerated Promotion Scheme for Graduates. In 1998 6 per cent of applications came from ethnic minority graduates, but only one reached the extended interview stage (Her Majesty's Inspectorate of Constabulary 1999, Bland et al., 1999). The Metropolitan Police service response has been to create a Senior Officer Development Programme for minority officers (Her Majesty's Inspectorate of Constabulary 2000).

Practical efforts to encourage local people from ethnic minority backgrounds to join the police service, such as conducting targeted recruitment campaigns with the assistance of community organisations and contacts, running familiarisation and access courses, placement schemes, and providing application forms in minority languages, are all positive ways forward. However, these efforts are hindered by the fact that applicants will carefully consider their likely experiences of racism and discrimination as a minority within a traditional white and male dominated hierarchy (Wilson, Holdaway and Spencer 1984). Indeed, Her Majesty's Inspectorate of Constabulary (1995) reported that existing ethnic minority officers might be unwilling to recommend the police service to potential recruits because of the harassment and difficulties they would face in the job. Clearly, the negative perception that ethnic minorities have of the police has had an impact of the capacity of police forces to recruit ethnic minority police officers. As Holdaway (1996: 143) states, 'race relations' and racialised divisions within the police service itself are inextricably linked with recruitment possibilities:

> Highly publicised individual cases where a black person has received poor treatment at the hands of the police; question marks against police handling of riots; concern about how one will be treated by future police colleagues; and other, related issues will be weighed in the balance when a police career is considered.

Stone and Tuffin's (2000) qualitative study of attitudes of ethnic minorities towards a police service career found a variety of negative factors are associated with joining the police which undermine the more attractive aspects of the job. These included: having to work in a racist environment, isolation, denial of cultural identity, lack of support in threatening situations, concern about the anticipated reactions of friends and family, divided loyalties, sexism, and a perception that promotion prospects would be poor. Views were informed by both personal and vicarious experiences of negative policing and through the media, particularly in the reporting of the Stephen Lawrence Inquiry.

Experiences in the job

Holdaway (1993) found that 26 of 30 African/Caribbean and Asian police officers interviewed in his study reported that racist comments and jokes were routinely part of officers' conversations (see also Holdaway 1996, Holdaway and Barron 1997). Particularly worrying was the finding in a series of seminars organised by the Metropolitan Police service that neither supervisory officers nor senior officers appeared to be concerned with challenging and changing this aspect of the police culture, a finding which also emerged in Her Majesty's Inspectorate of Constabulary (1995) inspection. Indeed, Her Majesty's Inspectorate of Constabulary (1999: 30) revisit to police forces first inspected in 1995 noted that 'there were still too many accounts of distressing behaviour, or, at best, managerial indifference towards ethnic minority staff'. Holdaway reported that the coping strategies the ethnic minority officers used to withstand this behaviour in his study included distinguishing between acceptable and unacceptable racist jokes and tolerating the former, or challenging certain comments. Some officers have brought cases of racial discrimination to industrial tribunals and have received monetary compensation (Holdaway 1996).

It is clear that rank and file 'white' culture permeates all aspects of police work and shapes the experiences of ethnic minority police officers. This helps explain why, despite the fact that black and Asian police officers view themselves as police officers who happen to be from an ethnic minority community, white officers tend to see their ethnic minority colleagues as black or Asian first and their status as officers second. As

Holdaway (1996: 158) observed, this affected working relations, as 'stereotypical thinking and team membership go hand in hand'. Black and Asian officers may be marginalised from work and social networks because they do not accept or collude with negative representations of ethnic minorities, or where, in the case of some Asian officers, religious observance prevents socialisation that revolves around drinking alcohol.

Retention

In light of their experiences on the job, it is not surprising that the 'retention rate' for ethnic minority police officers is lower than for white police officers. Bland *et al.* (1999) revealed that these rates have been steadily decreasing for ethnic minorities, while steadily improving for white officers over the period 1994–8. Rates for resignation and dismissal from the police service were much higher among ethnic minorities than white officers in 1997/8. Holdaway and Barron (1997) have studied the reasons for resignation among a sample of 28 African/Caribbean and Asian former police officers. All had resigned before 1991 and, on average, had been in the police service for 32 months. These respondents' experiences were compared with a group of 18 white resigners. Holdaway and Barron note that the resignation decision was not something that new recruits took lightly; typically, resigners said that they thought about resigning for more than five months. As one of Holdaway and Barron's (1997: 145) interviewees put it: 'Obviously, it doesn't make you feel good at all because you're working with people who you know, who don't really like Asians and blacks.'

The most common specific reasons for black and Asian police officers to resign from the police service was poor management, domestic/personal reasons and the conflict between the occupational culture and the experience of being of African, Caribbean or Asian origin. Thus, racism was one of several reasons cited by the resigners in the study. The frustration with the way supervisory and senior officers dealt with everyday racist banter and aggressive policing of ethnic minorities in the community was also clearly implicated in the resignation decision.

Her Majesty's Inspectorate of Constabulary (1997) have recommended that police forces have mentoring, informal networking and welfare support as part and parcel of their retention policies. Separate ethnic, minority-run professional organisations – such as the Black Police Association (BPA) – which have been set up recently, do provide such support networks. In addition to this supportive role, the BPA provides a forum for ethnic minority officers, and it also has a campaigning and lobbying function. In a recent example, the Black Police Association (1997b) questioned the decision (later reversed) of the National Police Promotion Examination Unit and the Police Promotion Board to exclude ethnic minority police officer assessors and role actors in the police constable-to-sergeants examination. It was argued that using African/Caribbean role actors in the test scenarios presented 'different stimuli' to candidates, which influenced their responses since the test was perceived to be a 'race' or equal opportunities 'issue' rather than a general policing issue. Raising an important question the Black Police Association (1997b: 2) asked:

> the real issue here is with the apparent inability of some candidates to relate to black people without seeing colour as the issue. If this is happening in the controlled environment of an examination, then how might their perception be translated in real operational situations?

The National Black Police Association, established in November 1998, has assisted in the setting up of more than 20 black police associations across the country, representing the views of black police officers and civilians. It is represented on the Home Secretary's Steering Group overseeing the implementation of the recommendations from the Stephen Lawrence Inquiry and has input into national training initiatives.

Promotion

In March 1999 only 14 per cent of ethnic minority officers were to be found in the promoted ranks within the police service compared to 23 per cent of white officers. Seven per cent of white officers were in ranks above sergeant, whereas this was true of only 4 per cent of ethnic minority officers (Home Office 2000c). Comments by ethnic minority police officers reported by Her Majesty's Inspectorate of Constabulary (1995) indicated that repeated threats to their status and the consequent need to constantly establish themselves as police constables meant that seeking promotion was sometimes too large an endeavour or something to be delayed (Her Majesty's Inspectorate of Constabulary 1995, Bland *et al.* 1999). Where promotion is sought, the time to promotion is longer for ethnic minorities. Bland *et al.*'s (1999) career profiling of a matched sample of white and ethnic minority police officers in eight forces showed that the latter take an average of around 12 months longer to be promoted to the sergeant rank (five months longer for Asian officers and 18 months for African/Caribbean officers). It was suggested that this reflected selection bias once officers had passed the sergeant examination that made them eligible for promotion. The time taken by ethnic minorities to reach the rank of inspector was also longer than for their white counterparts (ibid.).

Regarding ethnic minority representation in police specialisms, Her Majesty's Inspectorate of Constabulary data for 1997/8 indicate that the police service had adequate representation of ethnic minority officers as detectives, although this experience tended to come later in an officer's career than was true of white officers. Where under-representation was clearly apparent was in traffic departments where white officers were more than twice as likely to have been posted to a traffic department than their ethnic minority counterparts (Bland *et al.* 1999). This research, using data on career profiles from eight police forces, draws attention to the lower proportion of ethnic minority police officers who have received experience of planning/performance posts and national secondments in 1997/8 compared with white officers.

At the beginning of this chapter, we asked whether the recruitment of ethnic minority police officers in Britain would make a difference to the way in which ethnic minority communities were policed. The indication is that, despite their efforts, ethnic minority police officers in the UK have not been able to impact greatly on the treatment of ethnic minorities as victims and offenders (see Holdaway 1996), since the numbers recruited here have been small.

The US experience suggests that there is a risk that ethnic minority police officers may be 'ghettoised' by being assigned to predominantly minority neighbourhoods (Dulaney 1996, Walker, Spohn and DeLone 1996). However, we have no research evidence to show whether ethnic minority and white officers act in noticeably different ways on the street in these areas. Neither can it be certain that ethnic minority representation in police departments necessarily alters the climate of the department and the way it approaches the policing of minority communities. There is a danger that ethnic minority police officers come to be 'co-opted' into the police culture, which is all-encompassing to the extent that the gulf between 'us and them' is maintained regardless of the 'race' or ethnicity of the police officer (Cashmore 1991). Specifically using ethnic minority officers to police areas of high ethnic minority settlement may disadvantage them if they do not receive the necessary breadth of experience required to be promoted. It can also perpetuate stereotypes that only ethnic minority officers can police ethnic minority communities. As Cashmore (1991: 98) asserts:

> The assumption that black officers may be better attuned to the 'needs' of ghetto residents rested on racist stereotypes. Why should black officers, perhaps unfamiliar with a new territory, be more capable of dealing with routine problems in a sensitive manner than a white officer with several years of practical experience?

The low recruitment rate for ethnic minorities means that this is unlikely to be a major issue for the police service in England and Wales for some time. However, the question of whether British police officers will similarly perpetuate divisions between 'us' and 'them' will be of critical importance in the coming years.

In 1995 Her Majesty's Inspectorate of Constabulary carried out inspections of 13 police forces in England and Wales. These forces varied in size, performance and stage of developing or implementing equal opportunities policies. The position adopted in the report is that fair selection and assessment practices will ensure that individuals perform to their greatest potential, which in turn improves business performance. However, as Her Majesty's Inspectorate of Constabulary (1995) report has noted, there are officers within police forces around the country who are uncertain about the need for an equal opportunities policy. Commitment to such a policy by senior management, they argue, must be unequivocal and highly visible to set the path for junior officers; this is an issue to which we return at the end of this chapter.

Ethnic minorities as prosecution and court staff

The same issues of representation, equality and the absence of discrimination in the treatment of ethnic minorities have been raised in relation to the work of the courts. Faulkner (1988: 24), for example, asks:

> Can a white magistrate be sure that he or she has the same sensitivity and understanding of the situation of a black person as he or she has of the white people among whom he or she has probably spent most of his life?

As was true of policing, ensuring that courts adequately reflect the local population they serve is a laudable aim in and of itself, but it is a jump to assume that swelling the number of ethnic minority practitioners will automatically change sentencing practices.

Important 'actors' of the courts include magistrates, barristers, crown prosecutors, solicitors, justices' clerks, law officers, ushers and also administrative and clerical staff. The most recent figures on the proportion of criminal justice practitioners who are from ethnic minorities are shown in table 9.1 (Home Office 2000c), but beyond this very little is known about the experiences of these professionals in the job, except for those black practitioners, such as court probation officers and lawyers, who have described being stereotyped and mistakenly identified as defendants. What is apparent from the table is that the representation of ethnic minorities in the court professions is roughly proportionate to (and sometimes in excess of) their representation in the wider population, but not their clients. People from ethnic minorities also fare reasonably well in terms of seniority compared with other criminal justice professions. However, an under-representation of ethnic minorities at the most senior levels is to be found in each of the agencies, and this is particularly marked for the judiciary and Queen's Counsel (see also Justices' Clerks' Society 1995).

Two pieces of research have explored the recruitment and selection procedures for ethnic minorities in court professions. King and May's (1985) research on joining the magistracy consisted of a postal survey of Advisory Committees and the Clerks to the Justices, a postal survey of Community Relations Councils, and semi-structured interviews with a selection of court personnel in five areas, particularly those with responsibility for selecting and recruiting magistrates and ethnic minority com-

Table 9.1 Proportion of ethnic minorities represented as practitioners in the courts in 2000

Job	%
Crown Prosecution Service, e.g.	
Level B and below (administrators)	10
Level C (lawyers)	8
Level D and above (administrators and lawyers)	3
Magistrates' court staff, e.g.	
Clerical / administrative / security	5
Court Clerks	6
Justices' Clerks	4
Crown Court staff	
Span 7 and below	5
Span 8 and above	0
Magistracy	
Lay magistrates[1]	5
Stipendiary magistrates	2
Solicitors, e.g.	
Solicitors on the Roll	8
Solicitors in private practice	6
Judiciary, e.g.	
District judges	2
Recorders	3
High Court judges and Lords Justices	0
Barristers in independent practice	9
Queen's Counsel	3

Notes: [1] Excluding the Duchy of Lancaster.
Source: *Statistics on Race and the Criminal Justice System* (Home Office, 2000c).

munity representatives. The assessment by King and May (1985) of the magistrates' selection process did identify direct racist discrimination at work. The consideration of active service in black and ethnic minority community organisations as providing insufficient experience for applicants was an example, while it was demonstrated that it was common to recruit magistrates from mainstream political parties or middle-class organisations. In one area ethnic minority organisations were excluded from the list of local organisations who were approached in the search for candidates.

Moreover, evidence of direct discrimination included the assumption of some selectors that ethnic minority candidates would be more aligned with members from their community at the expense of the pursuit of justice. King and May (1985) also noted that selectors were concerned with the ability of ethnic minority candidates to be accustomed to the 'English way of life', which was not specifically tied to the work of magistrates on the bench. Instances of racial prejudice were observed by individual selectors that involved the negative stereotyping of ethnic minorities, which in turn affected their perceptions of ethnic minorities' ability to do the job of magistrate. These examples probably explained the higher rejection rate (83 per cent) of Asian candidates compared with white candidates (73 per cent) in three of the areas studied by King and May. The perspective of ethnic minority magistrates was typically one in which they saw themselves as ambassadors for ethnic minorities or as interpreters for their culture. Representatives of ethnic minority community organisations focused dissatisfaction with the magistracy on individual instances of discrimination or injustice, rather than on the composition of the magistracy and the issue of selecting black candidates (King and May 1985).

A recent Justices' Clerks' Society (1995) report recommended a local forum to discuss 'race' issues and to monitor racist behaviour and discrimination in magistrates' courts. The society advocates the ethnic monitoring of each bench, and of advisory committees responsible for recruiting lay magistrates. In addition, it is suggested that ethnic minority recruitment may be increased by magistrates visiting local ethnic groups to encourage applications. Training on the cultural and religious practices of local ethnic communities is proposed as essential.[1]

According to King and Israel (1989), the elitism of certain commercial solicitors' firms appears to discourage ethnic minorities from applying for articled clerk positions, and may mean those that do apply are not accepted. Selection processes take no account of differential access to opportunities and may be preoccupied with applicants having the 'right' family background and credentials which will inevitably mean ethnic minority applicants and those from white working-class backgrounds are disadvantaged (ibid., see also Malleson and Banda 2000 in relation to applying for silk and judicial office). More recently, Shiner (1997) in his longitudinal study of law students noted that ethnic minorities had less chance of being accepted on to a legal practice course and in gaining work experience, all of which help, along with family ties, to improve applicants' chances of finding a training contract. Although finding a pupillage and salary differentials did not appear to be influenced by 'race', racial discrimination and harassment were mentioned by 9 per cent of ethnic minority trainee solicitors and 33 per cent of pupil barristers in describing their experiences at work. Salary differentials were, however, a feature for trainee solicitors and perceptions of harassment and discrimination persisted for a small minority of trainee and qualified solicitors (Shiner 1999, Duff *et al.* 2000).

Partly in response to such issues, ethnic-minority-run organisations have emerged to represent African, Caribbean and Asian court practitioners. The longest established is the Society of Black Lawyers, which

---

[1] Judicial Studies Board, Second Annual Report of the Ethnic Minorities Advisory Committee.

was founded in 1973. Its broad remit is to provide legal protection against racism and racial discrimination for black and Asian communities in Britain. This means representing ethnic minority legal practitioners and enhancing their career opportunities and professional needs, encouraging networking, promoting access to legal services by providing community advice in minority communities and highlighting racial discrimination and malpractice in the judicial system. One example of their work is working with the Council of Legal Education to reduce the high failure rate of ethnic minorities in taking the Bar Vocational Course. The African, Caribbean and Asian Lawyers Group has been instrumental in assisting students to enter the legal profession. Their role is to provide professional advice, role models, support classes for final exams (run in association with the Society of Black Lawyers), training, job-search workshops, mini-pupillage schemes, financial advice and social activities to encourage success in the field. In the concluding chapter we consider the training issues associated with the working practices of white staff in relation to ethnic minorities.

Ethnic minority prison officers and staff

As we have described in chapter 8, the prison service has opted for a 'race relations' policy which is concerned with providing clear policy statements on equal opportunities, increasing cultural awareness for dealing with ethnic minority prisoners and staff and increasing the representation of ethnic minorities in the prison service workforce. It is assumed that ethnic minority prison officers will assist the operation of prisons, as they will be more understanding of the behaviour of ethnic minority prisoners and be more responsive to their needs and the specific problems they face. Further, Alfred (1992) suggests that African/Caribbean prisoners may legitimise the authority of ethnic minority prison officers. Conversely, ethnic minority practitioners may be co-opted by their organisational roles that will lessen their impact on the prison life of ethnic minority prisoners.

According to the Home Office (2000c), in March 2000, 3 per cent of prison officers and governors were of ethnic minority origin. The proportion of ethnic minority non-industrial prison service staff was slightly higher at 5 per cent. The representation of ethnic minorities among prison service staff falls below what would be expected, based on the proportion of ethnic minorities in the general population and far below that of the prison population. Of new recruits into the prison service in 1999/2000, 6 per cent were from ethnic minorities. Earlier research by Alfred (1992) reported that ethnic minority staff may be asked questions about 'race' during selection interviews which, if not answered in a satisfactory way, might be used as grounds for rejection, a practice which can also occur in the selection of ethnic minority police officers (Holdaway and Barron 1997). African/Caribbean interviewees reported that they had been asked questions at their interview that sought to find out how they would cope in the job if they were faced with racist comments from prisoners. If this is used as a means of screening ethnic minority candidates it could be deemed discriminatory. Moreover, it is not clear the extent to which anti-racist interviews are conducted which probe whether white prison staff hold racist views.

Little research has been undertaken about the experiences of ethnic minority prison staff in the job, but what little there is indicates that racism is an issue for ethnic minority officers just as research suggests it is for ethnic minority prisoners. Alfred's (1992) research did indicate that African/Caribbean officers faced discrimination, isolation and marginalisation, particularly if they were posted to predominantly white prison establishments where they were separated from family and local community support. McDermott (1990: 223) found this was also true of ethnic minority officers based in the five prisons in the West Midlands that she studied, where they made up only 1 per cent of the staff. One commented, 'I feel so isolated. The blacks think I'm part of the establishment and the whites think I have a chip on my shoulder because I won't laugh at ethnic jokes.' This comment clearly illustrates the contradictions facing ethnic minority prison staff who are working in a 'racialised' context on a daily basis. In addition, the wearing of racist insignia by white staff (now prohibited), feelings of inadequacy and having to prove oneself in the job, and the racist comments directed at prisoners which affected African/Caribbean prison officers as well, were all noted by Alfred (1992) and McDermott (1990). Coping mechanisms included 'being thick-skinned' and 'laughing things off'.

Indeed, despite the ban on prison officers displaying racist insignia, a newspaper reported in 1993 on the display of a cap embossed with a swastika and SS insignia in the reception area of Holme House prison (cf. Gordon 1984). This must, once again, raise concerns about the involvement of racist prison officers in the care and control of ethnic minority prisoners, and their treatment of ethnic minority colleagues. The view of the prison service, according to the director general, communicated from the prison governor, was to treat the incident as 'an in-house joke', thus effectively dismissing the racist nature of the incident (*Independent*, 15 November 1993). Not surprisingly, the courts have seen racial discrimination cases being pursued by ethnic minority prison staff. In one recent case, Claude Johnson, an auxiliary prison officer at Brixton prison, was awarded £28,500 for injury to his feelings and aggravated damages, following the racist remarks and false accusations made against him by his colleagues after his objection to their mistreatment of an African/Caribbean prisoner (*Caribbean Times*, 19 December 1996). He was further compensated when, on his return to work following the case, he experienced further racist abuse (*The Times*, 20 April 2000).

According to the Home Office (1998b), the retention rates in 1997/8 for ethnic minorities (86 per cent) once recruited was slightly lower than for white recruits (91 per cent); the same pattern emerges from the 1999/2000 data (Home Office 2000c). The career progression of ethnic minority prison officers is harder to chart, however, since little information is available on promotions, deployment, transfers or disciplinary hearings (Alfred 1992). Responses from Alfred's interviewees indicated that main grade African/Caribbean prison officers lacked confidence in promotion boards and were more likely to consider increased isolation and marginalisation as a consequence of promotion, rather than the rewards of enhanced status and salary. The training experiences for ethnic minority staff may be off-putting too. Alfred (1992: 31) documented examples of 'race relations' training being led by officers who were inexperienced in the area and who were unable to challenge racist stereotypes and assumptions when they were raised by participants. One interviewee described how they thought:

> It had all 'gone too far' – now white people were at the bottom of the pile. Stories of how people were now being sacked for asking for a black coffee, of how it was illegal to refer to a black binliner, and of how only blacks and lesbians get jobs nowadays circulated in abundance.

Home Office data for 1999/2000 showed almost 5 per cent of promotions were of ethnic minority staff, albeit primarily in junior grades. They made up 10 per cent of successful fast-track promotion candidates (Home Office 2000c).

As has been true in other criminal justice agencies, ethnic minority staff have established support mechanisms in response to their negative experiences in service. The national ethnic minority staff mutual support network for prison officers, RESPECT, was launched in January 2001. Its aims include improving the working environment and career progression of minority ethnic personnel in HM Prison Service Agency, and assisting in the development of new and existing policies which have implications for minority ethnic members of staff.

In contrast to that of the prison service, the representation of ethnic minorities among members of the parole board, at 11 per cent in August 2000, exceeds that in the wider ethnic minority community, although not the ethnic minority prison population. Similarly, as of August 2000, 7 per cent of board of visitor members were ethnic minorities: 4 per cent were African/Caribbean and 3 per cent Asian (Home Office 2000c).

In the final chapter we return to a central issue which contrasts the anticipated benefits of a 'race relations' policy as currently adopted by the Home Office, in comparison with an 'anti-racist policy'. In the latter case, the emphasis is less reformist than transformist in that the focus lies in realigning power relations in prisons. Thus, according to Alfred (1992), in the prison service this would mean taking positive action to ensure that more ethnic minority staff are recruited, particularly into management positions, using disciplinary procedures and improving accountability to deal with racist behaviour by staff and prisoners. This would occur alongside improving cultural awareness and ensuring equal employment opportunities and providing a safe working environment for ethnic minority staff.

Ethnic minority probation officers

According to Home Office (2000c) statistics, as of December 1999, 10 per cent of probation officers were of ethnic minority origin. The total proportion of ethnic minorities as other probation staff was 9 per cent, thus showing that they are proportionately represented if the general population is the baseline, but are under-represented when compared with their clientele. Ethnic minorities made up 6 per cent of those in the senior probation officer grade, but were markedly under-represented in the senior managerial grades, with the first black chief probation officer only recently being appointed (Home Office 2000c).

The climate within which ethnic minority probation officers work was described in the previous chapter, and would suggest that their experience would be little different from that of ethnic minority police and prison officers. Despite little qualitative information being available about the retention of ethnic minority probation officers, claims have been made of an abuse of disciplinary procedures in cases involving ethnic minority officers, which reduces their retention in the probation service (Reardon 1993). Indeed, figures for 1997–9 indicated higher losses of ethnic minority staff compared with their white counterparts (see Home Office 2000b). Similarly, just as has been the case in the police and prison services, ethnic minority probation officers have won claims for damages resulting from racial discrimination.

Marginalisation, particularly among managers, has also been an issue, as has 'work overload', where ethnic minority officers are expected to 'advise' on all 'race' issues (see Mavunga 1993, Reardon 1993, Francis-Spence 1995). The recent Her Majesty's Inspectorate of Probation (2000) thematic inspection noted the isolation that some minority ethnic staff felt, particularly those located in predominantly white areas. It also referred to staff's concern about managers failing to challenge unacceptable behaviour. Being mistaken for criminal defendants is not a rare occurrence for ethnic minority probation officers (Mavunga 1993).

Dominelli *et al.* (1995) have drawn our attention to the difficulties that African/Caribbean probation officers face, despite the introduction of equal opportunities policies within the probation service. It has been suggested that new African/Caribbean entrants to the probation service may be subjected to tests of their credibility which do not occur for white entrants. The same may also be true for more senior officers (see Mavunga, 1993). Dominelli *et al.* advocate the inclusion of ethnic minority workers' support networks within the rubric of equal opportunities policies. A further difficulty facing African/Caribbean workers is the backlash against equal opportunity policies, which are interpreted as being a form of favouritism, once again similar to the viewpoint of prison officers.

The Association of Black Probation Officers was formally established in 1984 (Dominelli *et al.* 1995). One of its major tasks is providing a support network for members. Ensuring the representation of African/Caribbean perspectives on professional issues, promoting antiracist/discriminatory practices in the probation service and the criminal justice system and supporting the monitoring and evaluation of services to African/Caribbean clients, are also key objectives of the organisation (ABPO 1995). Other proposals have included a surgery in Brixton, which will provide information and support, as well as black history classes and rehabilitative initiatives for ex-offenders (*Weekly Journal*, 6–12 November 1996). The National Association of Asian Probation Staff, formed in 1987, was established in response to what was felt to be a misrepresentation of Asian probation staff as 'black'. Its recent work has included a conference addressing issues related to working with Asian offenders (NAAPS 1997). Both organisations assist staff with promotion preparation and mentoring support, complemented by probation service local support groups where they exist (Her Majesty's Inspectorate of Probation 2000).

Chigwada-Bailey's (1997) interviews with black women in prison did not indicate an automatic preference for black probation officer support. At least half of the women were concerned with the quality of the response they received from probation officers, regardless of their 'race', although for some of the women interviewed, a preference was stated for same-'race' probation officers 'as she knows where I am coming from'. It was recognised that black probation officers might still not be able to represent black women if they act 'white-minded', as 'coconuts' (Chigwada-Bailey 1997: 59).

Ethnic minorities employed in the Home Office

The empirical picture regarding the position of ethnic minorities in the criminal justice professions is one of under-representation at senior levels, and typically negative experiences in the job. This experience is mirrored for employees working in the government department that has responsibility for criminal justice and race relation policies. Although in August 2000, almost 15 per cent of staff employed in the Home Office were of ethnic minority origin (5.3 per cent were black, 8.4 per cent were Asian and 1.1 per cent were of other ethnic origins), this was below the proportion of ethnic minorities living in London (where a majority of positions are based), and they were most typically employed in the most junior grades of the civil service as administrative officers or administrative assistants (Home Office 2000c).

Ethnic minorities made up only 2 per cent of those at senior management (Grade 7 or above) level, leaving the upper echelons of the senior Civil Service almost exclusively white (Home Office 2000c). A study commissioned by the Cabinet Office to examine under-representation of ethnic minorities (and women and those with disabilities) identified a deeply embedded white, middle-class male culture as still being at the heart of the senior Civil Service (Schneider Ross 1999). There was a strongly held perception that promotions were not entirely based on merit and that networking and patronage were influential in advancing in the senior Civil Service.

Moreover, even though the Home Office Staff Survey of 2,072 employees conducted in 1999 showed that although there was widespread agreement that the Home Office was committed to being an equal opportunities employer, 33 per cent of black employees and 30 per cent of Asian staff reported experiences of racial discrimination. Around one in five black and Asian Home Office staff had experienced racist harassment at work, and about 10 per cent said that they had been the victims of workplace bullying. Overall, a third of black and Asian staff reported encountering either racial discrimination, harassment or bullying in the previous 12 months (BMRB 1999).

Following the example of other ethnic minority-run support organisations set up in the criminal justice professions, in November 1999 the Home Office Ethnic Minority Network was launched with the support and funding of the Home Office Management Board. Its aim is to improve the working environment and career progression of ethnic minority staff in the Home Office, providing a support network for all ethnic minority staff, fostering better relations between management and staff and ensuring equality of opportunity in new and existing policies.

Equal opportunities in criminal justice agencies

The development of equal opportunity and anti-racist policies began in earnest in the late 1970s and early 1980s within police, prison and other services (Brown 1997). The Crown Prosecution Service, the Home Office and the Law Society now profess to being 'equal opportunities employers'. Recently, the Judicial Studies Board and the Criminal Justice Consultative Council have declared an intention to provide better opportunities for ethnic minority staff within the police and other criminal justice agencies (Strategic Plan 1999–2001, Criminal Justice Consultative Council 2000).

There have, however, been indications of a resistance to these policies among some senior managers, and, more importantly perhaps, among the rank and file. The inherent value of these policies seems to be contested. Within the police service, some police officers (of all ranks) do not see the need for equal opportunities policies or procedures for monitoring implementation (see, for example, FitzGerald and Sibbitt 1997). Officers who support these policies are often marginalised within police forces. It is also evident that equal opportunities policies are seen by some officers – in police, prison and probation services – as favouritism towards individuals from ethnic minorities in recruitment and promotion, which is, in turn, used as an explanation for resentment against ethnic minorities (Holdaway and Barron 1997, Alfred 1992, Dominelli *et al.*, 1995).

In the policing context, Brown (1997) has argued that equal opportunities policies offer the potential for improving the skills of all members of the workforce and getting officers to interact better with local communities, for reducing police misconduct and changing operational policing and reordering priorities to deal with community safety and crime issues. Existing policies tend to focus on the cultural needs of ethnic minorities and monitoring procedures. As Gordon (1993: 91) notes:

> The dominant response in recent years to the interaction of race and the criminal justice systems has mirrored that adopted by many other professions in Britain. This is an approach which is best described as 'multicultural' in which the 'answer' is seen to lie in greater 'sensitivity' towards black people, greater understanding of their cultures and lifestyles, and so on – usually to be achieved through multifarious forms of 'training' combined with 'equal opportunity' policies and the recruitment of more black personnel, whether as lawyers, probation officers, magistrates or whatever. Such an approach ignores the central question of racism, the institutional practices of a society based on unequal social, economic and power relations.

Linking equality of service with equality of opportunity

Even if the numbers of ethnic minority employees are increased very dramatically, it will remain important to consider the working practices of white staff who will inevitably form the overwhelming majority, comprising, as they do, 94 per cent of the working population. The literature on the criminal justice professions highlights the importance of the relationship between the equality of opportunity for employees *within* a service and the quality of service that it provides to the public. The Commission for Racial Equality, for example, argues that producing a police service which more closely reflects the population it serves is important not only as a goal in itself but also as a means to the end of improving service provision. That is, it increases the chances that services provided will be appropriate, relevant and accessible to all members of the community. As Brown (1997) points out, including groups previously excluded can have the effect of transforming the organisation. Brown argues that just by 'being there', women inevitably bring new and different perspectives and become catalysts for change within the organisation. Similarly, the presence of black officers affects some features of the organisational culture. It seems clear, for example, that the increasing presence of black and

Asian officers within the organisation has impacted on the willingness of all to use racist 'banter' and other more overt forms of racial prejudice and discrimination within the service (Holdaway 1996, Torkington and Protaxia 1991).

Furthermore, the actual positions that minority workers hold is crucial to maximising their contribution to the change process. To have any real effect on service provision, they must be able to contribute to decision making. As Bayne-Smith and McBarnette (1996) comment in the context of health care provision, people from ethnic minorities must be included in policy-making positions if quality of service is to be improved. Harrison (1995) makes a similar point in relation to housing, suggesting that minority employees must be empowered to contribute to decisions about prioritisation. It should not be thought, however, that in service-delivery terms representation of ethnic minority groups in the higher ranks of the service should be seen as a goal in itself. The present autocratic management style of the police, in Brown's (1997) view, is not conducive to eradicating discriminatory practice even with minorities as key players in the process. She argues that a 'feminising' influence is the key to changing the culture of policing in such a way that the representation of all groups can be enhanced. This would involve shaping a new image of policing to one which does not just accommodate women and ethnic minority officers, but which makes them a 'visible feature of the policing landscape' (Berry 1996 cited by Brown 1997).

Testing and selection

One strategy proposed to counter the under-representation of minorities in the police service and of other institutions has been to evaluate selection and testing procedures for cultural bias (the Rotterdam Charter 1996). This has already begun to be realised, with the police service dispensing of the minimum height requirement, which placed Asian people, in particular, at a disadvantage at the stage of recruitment. It seems that this must be extended further to modify recruitment practices to attract more minority groups, including women and non-visible sexual minorities (Chan 1997). This would not mean lowering standards, but *changing standards*. For instance, recruitment or promotion could emphasise social rather than physical skills. Such skills as the ability to interpret and translate should be criteria for selection – a skill that should be appropriately recognised and rewarded as a valuable asset (Bagilhole 1997).

Meeting recruitment targets

In 1998, the Home Secretary published local or national targets for the increased recruitment, retention, career progression and senior level representation of ethnic minority operational and non-operational staff in the Home Office, police, prison and probation services (Home Office 1999c). Proponents of targets argue that such a strategy can be effective if it is operated in a regulatory framework that monitors representation within a timetable. Although representation of ethnic minorities, women and other minorities within these services have increased steadily over the past three decades (the first three 'visible minority police officers' were appointed in 1966), there is still a long way to go. Indeed, the first progress report on meeting these ten-year employment targets revealed a mixed picture. On recruitment, good progress towards employment targets had been reached in the Home Office and probation service. On the other hand, some problems were evident in recruiting ethnic minorities to meet the targets set in the police and prison services. The evidence on retention and promotion rates varied across the Home Office and its service areas, while levels of senior representation still remained low in most (Home Office 2000b).

Positive or affirmative action aims to achieve equality of representation over a given time. It has a symbolic value which demonstrates that society regards discrimination as a serious issue. It also enables different communities to put forward talented individuals who may act as role models for others. Indeed, the Rotterdam Charter (1996) argues that where under-representation is apparent, affirmative action programmes should be in place. In order to avoid a backlash, the charter suggests that public statements are required to explain why such action is necessary and that such action is not 'favouritism' but stems from a requirement that the service should reflect the community they serve. There is a further objection which must be addressed that there is a danger of disadvantaging relatively underprivileged members of advantaged groups (working-class white women for example) and that the real targets are missed by benefiting only relatively privileged members of disadvantaged groups (middle-class black men, for example).

Research shows that a higher success rate for complainants, greater understanding and sympathy for those alleging discrimination, and more effective procedures and remedies will enhance the credibility of the law in the eyes of ethnic minorities both within and outside of the force (the Rotterdam Charter 1996). Indeed, it is unchallenged racist 'banter' within the organisation that has turned many officers away (Brown 1997, Holdaway 1991, Stone and Tuffin 2000). There needs to be, therefore, positive stances towards policies to deal with discrimination to confront cultural and behavioural issues (Her Majesty's Chief Inspectorate of Constabulary 1997) – through legal remedies, for example.

Conclusion

The empirical evidence shows that direct and indirect discrimination are at work *inside* the criminal justice professions, and that ethnic minority practitioners have similar experiences to those of ethnic minorities who come into contact with the criminal justice system as suspects, defendants and inmates. Reflecting on these findings and considering ways to remedy this situation is one of the key tasks in the next, concluding chapter.

Chapter 10

Conclusion

This book has explored the ways that racism influences the English criminal justice process and shapes patterns of crime and victimisation. We were not guided in this task by a pre-existing over-arching theoretical framework. Instead we have presented the patchy and sometimes contradictory findings from criminological research and documentation, alongside a schematic analysis of theories of racism, ethnicity, crime and justice. The aim of this chapter is to look at the linkages between patterns of crime and criminal justice practice and the effects on each of discrimination and disadvantage in broader social and economic spheres. After that we explore the implications for the wider political and policy debates centred on 'zero' tolerance', anti-racism and the protection of fundamental human rights.

Ethnicity and criminal justice

Criminal justice agencies – the police, prisons and probation service – do not work together as a seamless 'system', but neither do they work in isolation. Officers increasingly work in collaboration with one another and share information about suspect populations.

Decisions taken at one point in the system often affect what occurs at another. Because the capacity of the system is limited, at each stage there is extensive 'attrition' or 'diversion' with fewer and fewer cases making it from one stage to the next. Individual offenders are, in effect, diverted or 'filtered out' of the process between the commission of a deviant act, its discovery by the victim, reporting to the police, then during prosecution, conviction, at the point of sentence and imprisonment. In chapter 4, we noted that an offender will be convicted in only 2 per cent of all offences that are committed, while only three out of every 1,000 offences results in imprisonment. Following the approach of studies conducted in the USA (Blumstein 1982, 1993, Langan 1985) and in the UK (Smith 1997a and

234 Conclusion

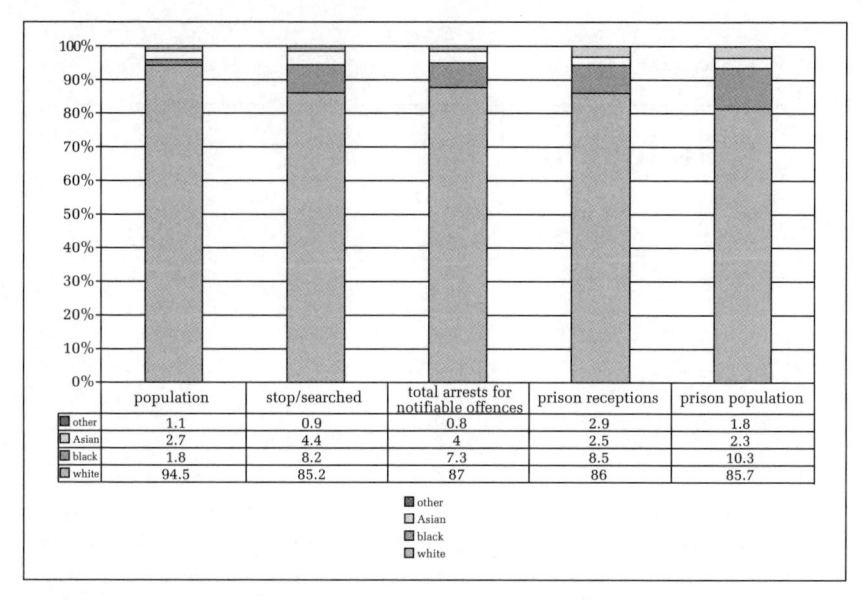

	population	stop/searched	total arrests for notifiable offences	prison receptions	prison population
other	1.1	0.9	0.8	2.9	1.8
Asian	2.7	4.4	4	2.5	2.3
black	1.8	8.2	7.3	8.5	10.3
white	94.5	85.2	87	86	85.7

Figure 10.1 Representation of ethnic groups at different stages of the criminal process in 1999 (England and Wales)
Source: Home Office, (2000c)

b), it is possible to compare criminal justice statistics – from undetected offences to imprisoned offenders – to discover whether this attrition is consistent for all suspected offenders, regardless of ethnic origin. This analysis must be approached cautiously because it incorporates the accumulated conceptual, methodological and empirical problems associated with each individual source of data.

Figure 10.1 compares the population as a whole with the proportion stopped and searched, arrested, sentenced to custody and incarcerated based on statistics published by the Home Office (2000c). This shows that the proportion of 'white' people in prison is smaller than those sentenced to custody, which is slightly less than those arrested by the police, suggesting a greater likelihood for white offenders to be diverted from court and custody. Conversely, for 'black' and 'other' ethnic groups, the likelihood of being 'filtered in' is greater with each step after arrest with resulting very high incarceration rates. The pattern for Asians is more complex and also conflates Indian, Pakistani and Bangladeshi populations who have very different experiences of crime and criminal justice. As we argued in chapter 4, these statistics are unhelpful in estimating the extent of crime among the different communities. Further questions concern the impact of legal factors (such as offence type and seriousness) and non-legal factors (such as housing and employment) which differ widely among various ethnic groups. Nonetheless, these data add weight to the claim that the criminal justice process works cumulatively to the disadvantage of ethnic minority groups.

Drugs enforcement

Based upon self-report data collected in the 1996 British Crime Survey about 6.3 million people in England and Wales have tried cannabis (the most commonly used drug), 2.55 million in the previous year (Ramsay and Percy 1997). In 1996, the reference year for Ramsay and Percy's study, the Home Office reported that there were about 73,000 convictions for cannabis offences (65,000 for simple possession, Corkery 2000), which accounts for less than 3 per cent of cannabis users. Only a very small minority of those people who are convicted and sentenced by the courts for drug offences, particularly possession and small trades in cannabis, receive a custodial sentence. Clearly there exists huge scope for individual discretion to affect who is, and who is not, diverted out of the process between the 'criminal act', conviction and imprisonment. The question then arises, to what extent does ethnicity impact on the chances of being 'filtered out' of the criminal justice process? Figure 10.2 compares drug users in the general population (as recorded by the British Crime Survey), those who are stopped and searched on suspicion of possessing drugs and subsequently arrested (as recorded by the police) and those who are imprisoned (as recorded by the prison service).

Self-report studies (described in detail in chapter 4) suggest that the overwhelming majority of UK drug users are white, not only because they comprise 94 per cent of the general population, but also because the extent of drug use is somewhat higher than that among ethnic minority communities. In the most recent British Crime Survey, 23 per cent of

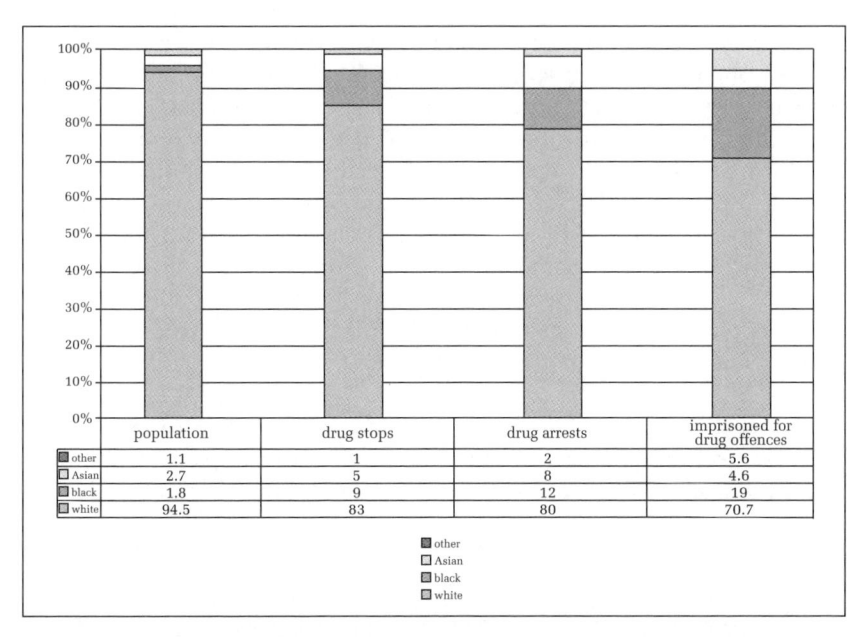

	population	drug stops	drug arrests	imprisoned for drug offences
other	1.1	1	2	5.6
Asian	2.7	5	8	4.6
black	1.8	9	12	19
white	94.5	83	80	70.8

Figure 10.2 Drug enforcement by ethnic origin, England and Wales 1997

whites, 18 per cent of blacks, 10 per cent of Indians and 8 per cent of Pakistanis and Bangladeshis said they had never used cannabis (Ramsay and Spiller 1997, see table chapter 4). The evidence from a range of sources summarised by the Institute for the Study of Drug Dependency suggests that 'the most likely drug user is a young white male in AB or C1 socio-economic groups' (ISDD 1997: 5). By contrast, stop and search figures show that a black person is much more likely than their white counterpart to be stopped by the police on suspicion of possessing drugs (Home Office 2000c: 12). It is also clear that, in the vast majority of cases, this suspicion turns out to be unfounded. For every 17 black people stopped by the Metropolitan police in 1997 suspected of being in possession of drugs, only one was arrested, compared with one in 11 white people (Metropolitan Police 1998). Even though people from 'black' and 'other' ethnic minorities are less likely to be found in possession of contraband than their white counterparts, this does not prevent 'proactive' drugs policing from increasing their likelihood of being drawn into the criminal justice system for the possession of drugs. The scale of the disproportionate stop and search of black people means that even though the stops usually prove to be fruitless, a greater proportion of black drug users will be arrested than their white counterparts.

It might be argued that only a small proportion of drug offenders are sent to prison, so drug enforcement is unlikely to impact significantly on the prison population. However, around 120,000 people are cautioned or convicted for drugs offences each year, 7,000 of whom are sentenced to immediate custody. Moreover, in 1998, drug offenders made up 14 per cent of male prisoners and 34 per cent of female prisoners (Home Office 1999b). Among black prisoners, one in six of the men and fully one-half of the women are under sentence for drug offences.[1] Home Office data show that while at least 95 per cent of drug users in England and Wales are white, this compares with around 70 per cent of the people imprisoned for drugs offences each year. While the 'white' population seems overall to benefit most from diversion, the black population appears to lose out most. That is, while the black population makes up about 2 per cent of the general population (and probably also of drug users nationally), it makes up nearly 20 per cent of the prison population serving a sentence for a drugs offence. A similar picture is true for 'other' ethnic groups while the pattern for Asians is more complex (Home Office 2000c).

The most obvious problem with these data is that not all 'drug offences' are alike and there is insufficient detailed data to compare involvement in different kinds of drugs or to contrast the treatment of drug dealers

---

[1] These figures are for British nationals only. Among black people who are non-British nationals, 38 per cent of males and 86 per cent of females are serving sentences for drug offences (Prison Statistics, table 6.4)

with drug users (Kalunta-Crumpton 1999). Nonetheless, the statistics illuminate a pattern that requires explanation and this is our next task.

In the next sections, we draw on the analysis of the criminal justice process set out in the middle chapters of this book to build an explanation of what appears – prima facie – to be racial discrimination in the process of criminalisation.

Reporting by the public

The first step in the criminal justice process is when an offence is brought to the attention of the police. In the case of drugs and other 'victimless' offences, this might be the result of police targeting but in the majority of cases it will be result of a victim or witness informing the police. It is clear from the British Crime Survey that only a minority of offences are reported to the police – for example, only about one in five robberies are reported – and this process is uneven depending on the ethnic origin of victims and suspects. People from ethnic minority communities may under-report offences committed against them because they distrust the police, or feel that they will not be believed, taken seriously or treated fairly. There is also some evidence that white victims are more likely to report incidents involving ethnic minority suspects, especially where there is little or no injury involved (FitzGerald and Hale 1996: 33, Shah and Pease 1992). The effects of stereotyping and prejudice may also lead white victims sometimes to say that offences committed against them have been committed by black people, even when they are not sure who was involved (McConville and Shepherd 1992, Bowling 1999a, see chapter 4).

Selective police enforcement

Criminal justice statistics indicate that the areas with the greatest concentration of communities of ethnic minority origin are also those that have the greatest deployment of police officers and are the subject of 'enforcer-style' policing (see chapter 6). Both police and survey data indicate that black people, and, to a lesser extent, people of other ethnic minority origins have a much greater likelihood of being stopped by a police officer and questioned in the street (Skogan 1994, Home Office 2000c). Once stopped, people from ethnic minority communities are more likely than their white counterparts to have their clothing, bags or vehicles searched and are also much more likely to be stopped and searched repeatedly (Skogan 1994). How are these findings to be explained?

'Proactive policing' – enforcement activity initiated by the police – has greater autonomy and involves much more extensive individual discretion than 'reactive policing', where an officer responds to a call from the public. 'Proactivity' can take the form of 'stop and search', 'on-street interrogation' and clothing searches, as well as more sustained and strategic practices, such as 'intelligence-led policing', and 'problem-oriented policing'. The use and abuse of police 'stop and search' powers contributes to the disproportionate flow of people from ethnic minorities into the criminal justice process because it is frequently directed specifically at these groups (see chapter 6). The tactic takes a wide variety of forms and is conducted under a range of powers. Under PACE codes of practice, the decision to stop and search is not justifiable on the basis of criminal justice statistics on 'offending rates' or on a person's 'criminal history', but only on the basis of 'reasonable suspicion'. However, it is clear that in many cases no grounds for suspicion exist and there is widespread and arbitrary use of the power. The wide use of discretion, low supervision, accountability and visibility, are precisely the contextual conditions that enable discrimination. The pattern of selective enforcement is consistent with cultural stereotyping and the 'heightened suspicion' of black people in general noted in the 1980s by Holdaway (1983), Smith and Gray (1985), Graef (1989), Reiner (1991) and more recently by FitzGerald and Sibbitt (1997) and Bowling (1999b). In the 1980s, stereotypes were freely expressed. For example, Smith and Gray's interviewees commented that they stopped black people because 'nine times out of ten they would have drugs' (Smith and Gray 1983: 129). This is a clear example of where a stereotype (black people are drug users) forms a component of a prejudiced way of thinking (this black person is likely to possess drugs) which implies a course of action (this black person should be stopped and searched).

The use of the conduct of 'PACE searches' as a performance indicator (i.e. the more the better) exemplifies the problem of institutional racism. In areas of high ethnic minority concentration, and indeed in relatively poor, almost exclusively 'white' parts of Northern England, such as Hartlepool and Middlesbrough, stop-search practices were promoted enthusiastically as a means of demonstrating effective job performance (Dennis 1997, Bowling 1999c). While it may not be the intention of Home Office ministers and police managers to escalate the disproportionate use of coercive power against black people, this has, in fact, been its effect. Disproportionate stop and search activity makes it more likely that wrongdoing among black people comes to the attention of the police than wrongdoing among other ethnic groups. Enforcement activity of this kind is *experienced* as police harassment, which is a problem in itself, but also leads to distrust and fear of the police and the criminal justice system more generally. This distrust sets the context for police–public encounters and hostility on the part of a person suspected by the police where any 'challenging demeanour' may increase the likelihood of being arrested. The evidence is clear that the police tend to act formally if a person stopped 'fails the attitude test'. Proactive policing contributes to the criminalisation of ethnic minorities, and also to damaging the confidence and trust of these same communities. In giving evidence to the

Stephen Lawrence Inquiry, Sir Paul Condon acknowledged the 'unfair use' of 'arbitrary powers' and that current senior officers are aware that the powers are being used unlawfully. Monitoring and supervision of the use of these proactive powers is a necessity. The Lawrence Inquiry recommended that police officers should be held more fully to account for the use of stop and search powers. This is to entail recording the reason for the stop, the outcome and the self-defined ethnicity of the person stopped. These records are to be monitored and analysed by the police service and the police authorities and to be published (Macpherson 1999, recommendations 61–3). The question is whether these changes will result, in the long term, in a more acceptable and equitable use of stop and search powers. If not, arguments for the outright abolition of the power will become increasingly persuasive (Institute of Race Relations, 1987, Bowling 1999c, Bridges 2000: 317–19, Herbert 2001).

Pre-trial decisions: arrest, prosecution, remand and mode of trial

Black people are disproportionately likely to be arrested by the police for a wide range of offences in comparison to both their 'white' and Asian counterparts (see chapter 6). Once in police detention they are less likely to be cautioned or to have no further action taken against them, and are consequently more likely to be formally proceeded against by the police. In the case of juveniles, black suspects are less likely to be referred to a multi-agency panel which is an important mechanism for diverting individuals from prosecution. In some instances these outcomes appear to be the result of direct discrimination by police officers who deliberately 'overcharge' black suspects. In another example of indirect discrimination, black arrestees, who are more likely than their white counterparts to deny the offence for which they have been arrested, are unable to take advantage of the less severe outcomes of the arrest process and face a greater chance of facing formal action.

Defendants of African, Caribbean and Asian origin are more likely to have their cases terminated by the Crown Prosecution Service either because the evidence presented by the police is weak or because the public interest was against prosecution (if the allegation was trivial, for example) (Phillips and Brown 1998, Mhlanga 1999 see chapter 7 above). Although black and Asian lawyers have complained of racism within the legal profession (and it would be surprising if there were none) the role of the CPS does appear to be anomalous in that its decisions tend to favour ethnic minority defendants. This might be explained by the fact that CPS decision making is largely recorded, subject to detailed guidance for prosecution and taken mainly on the neutral criteria set out in the Code for Crown Prosecutors. It is noteworthy that Phillips and Brown (1998) found that in about 40 per cent of cases, prosecutors had no information about the arrestee's ethnic origin. Prosecution is a point in the criminal justice process where levels of discretion are at their lowest and where subjective factors play the least prominent role. It is also the case that the ethnic diversity of the CPS is much greater than the police service and many other criminal justice agencies.

One of the clearest examples of indirect discrimination is the effect of remand status on subsequent sentencing decisions (see chapter 7). Empirical research studies show that black people are significantly more likely to be remanded in custody before and during their trial. This is very important because studies of prosecution and sentencing show that there is an increased likelihood that a defendant who has been remanded in custody during the court process will be sentenced to custody if they are subsequently convicted. Being 'of no fixed abode' is one of the most common criteria for refusing bail; homelessness or unstable housing conditions disproportionately affects ethnic minorities who are, as a result, more frequently remanded in custody. Defendants who are remanded in custody have fewer opportunities to prepare their defence and to appear clean and well dressed in court, with the effect that, on conviction, they stand a greater chance of being sentenced to custody. Thus, the apparently neutral legal factor, related to the likelihood of court appearance, is loaded against ethnic minorities (see chapter 7).

A similar indirect effect occurs in relation to election for Crown Court trial and not guilty pleas, options which are taken more commonly by black defendants who appear to be more hopeful of a fair trial by jury rather than magistrate. Black defendants also lose out on discounts for guilty pleas when they plead 'not guilty' either because they are genuinely innocent, believe themselves to be innocent or simply feel unable to trust the system. However, election for Crown Court and entering a 'not guilty' plea both increase the likelihood of the most serious sentence being imposed in the event of a conviction. Each of these practices cumulatively disadvantages ethnic minority defendants, especially those of African/Caribbean origin (see chapter 7).

Sentencing and imprisonment

The empirical research evidence indicates that, on conviction, black people are more likely to be sentenced to custody, even once all other legally relevant factors have been considered (chapter 7). When imprisoned, sentences are longer for both blacks and Asians than whites. Hood's (1992) study of sentencing research in the West Midlands found that in the region's Crown Courts in one year, black defendants had a 5 per cent greater probability of having a custodial sentence imposed than white defendants once legally relevant factors were accounted for. This is conclusive evidence of direct discrimination and an important contributory factor in explaining black over-representation in prison in addition to the indirect effects explained above.

Compared with white people, those of African and Caribbean origin have significantly higher rates of imprisonment (chapter 8). Among people of Asian origin, Pakistani, Chinese and 'other Asian' people have rather higher per capita rates of imprisonment than whites, but those of Indian and Bangladeshi origin have lower rates. Prison Statistics, collected and analysed by the Home Office, suggest that around one and one-quarter per cent of the black population in England and Wales is in prison, about eight times that of the white population. The figures for other ethnic minority groups lie mostly between these two poles, the exception being the Indian population that has rates rather lower than whites. We do not, at present, know the per capita rate of black imprisonment among particular age groups, or the 'lifetime imprisonment' rate. Obviously, the disproportionate rate at which African/Caribbean and other ethnic minority communities are processed by the criminal justice system means that many more people from these communities have criminal records than their white counterparts.

Once in prison, people from ethnic minority communities are likely to be discriminated against, suffering racist abuse and a lower likelihood of early release (see chapter 8). Stereotyping of black people as 'violent' and 'dangerous' legitimises brutality against them, and allows their mental and physical health needs to be overlooked when in the care of police and prison services. Similarly, prison officers' desire to 'disperse' black prisoners because of 'control' and 'management difficulties' resonates with stereotypes and the 'numbers game' in the immigration debate. The 'textbook management' of disciplinary infractions and misbehaviour by African/Caribbean prisoners is another instance of the 'abuse of discretion' that has the effect of black people being treated more harshly through the imposition of sanctions under prison disciplinary codes. On release, African/Caribbeans are faced with discrimination in finding a job because of being both ex-offenders and members of an ethnic minority community. If this leads them back into offending and the criminal justice process, a previous custodial sentence will increase the chances that on conviction they will be imprisoned again.

Cumulative discrimination

The empirical evidence demonstrates the existence of both direct and indirect discrimination in the criminal justice process. This appears to have a cumulative effect on people of African and Caribbean origin but does this fully explain the over-representation of these groups in the prison population? According to David Smith (1997), this would require that black people be most over-represented in prison for offences which relied on proactive detection and investigation techniques, that is, those where the police have the greatest latitude to exercise discretion. Here, we agree with Smith (1997a: 133) who notes, 'black people end up in prison because of selective reporting of offences and discretionary law enforcement' and comments that this is particularly true for drug offences as we have illustrated. However, Smith goes on to argue that, for the effect of cumulative disadvantage to explain the over-representation of black people in prison, there would need to be an increase in the proportion arrested by the police, and then at every other stage of the criminal justice process.[2] On this basis, Smith concludes that an increase consistent with the cumulative effects theory cannot be demonstrated.

We think that there are some weaknesses in Smith's analysis that make his position untenable. His analysis ignores the limitations of UK research data to prove or disprove this thesis. This question cannot fully be addressed without more robust self-report offending data and until national data are available for different types of offences at each stage of the criminal process, including: stop and search; arrest; the decision to charge, caution or take no further action; case review by the CPS; trial and sentencing. Smith's analysis of the impact of discriminatory practices on black over-representation in prison is largely based on direct discrimination. Consequently it fails to take account of institutional racism, and the impact that disadvantage in other spheres (such as housing, education and employment) has on criminal justice practices. In our view it is not necessary for there to be discrimination *at each and every stage* in the process in order for the over-representation of black people in prison to be the result of cumulative discrimination. If a larger number of black people are brought into the process through proactive policing, and then there is discrimination again at the remand and sentencing stages, does it really matter if there are countervailing tendencies at other points in the system? If the CPS, by terminating cases where there is insufficient evidence, acts as a 'brake' on the tendency of the police to over-charge black suspects, this qualifies, rather than refutes, the cumulative effects thesis.

There is also an important historical dimension that has to be incorporated into any analysis of the effects of 'cumulative disadvantage'. Few police officers, government officials and others would deny that the overtly racist law enforcement and criminal justice practice in the 1970s and 1980s led to the criminalisation of the English black population. Many people who worked in the system at that time and are now in senior positions admit freely either that they themselves played out their prejudices in discriminating against members of the ethnic minority public, or that they witnessed it and did nothing. The Crown Prosecution Service has only been in existence since 1986, prior to which the police prepared cases for prosecution. People coming into contact with the criminal jus-

---

[2] US research has typically found that around 20 per cent of the over-representation of African Americans in prison could not be explained by their disproportionate rate of arrest (or from victimisation survey reports); this rose to around 50 per cent for drugs offences (Blumstein 1982, 1993, Langan 1985).

tice system before then will not have had the advantage of case review prior to prosecution with the result that many more cases with weak evidence or trivial charges would have been prosecuted. There was, during the Lawrence Inquiry, an attempt to 'draw a line over the past', to say 'that was then, this is now' (McLaughlin and Murji 1999). Sadly, the processes set in train in the 1970s have had material consequences for the present time and these will continue to be felt long into the future. The result of this process of criminalisation is that a disproportionate number of the black population have criminal records. They are therefore more likely to fall under suspicion when driving as vehicle records and criminal records are linked. The implication of this is that any appeal to a more 'intelligence-led' approach to policing and criminal justice practice will simply entrench existing patterns of discrimination and the spiralling process of deviancy amplification.

Future research in this area will need to approach the question of criminal justice processing with a more nuanced and sophisticated analysis than the 'single-point' approach adopted at the moment. Greater attention will need to be paid to how decisions taken at one point in time impact on later decisions, and on the cyclical nature of criminal justice processing and its interaction with the conditions of life outside prison. Answers to these questions will become more accessible as the amount and quality of data produced by criminal justice agencies increases. However, the statistical data will only take us so far and we need much more qualitative data to understand criminal justice decision-making processes that will enable us to make further progress towards a contextual theory of discrimination.

Ethnicity and crime

Having assessed the evidence of discrimination in the criminal justice process, we now return to the question of ethnic differences in involvement in crime. Some British criminologists have argued that this question is unanswerable due to methodological and conceptual problems inherent in defining and measuring crime. Others have argued that the extent of disproportionate imprisonment is too great to be explained through reference to discrimination in the criminal justice process, so must, therefore, indicate a 'real' disproportionate involvement in crime (see chapter 4). In this section, we draw our own conclusions on this question.

As we have demonstrated earlier in this chapter, by the end of the criminal justice process there is undeniably a disproportionate number of people from ethnic minority communities who have been stopped 'under suspicion' by the police, arrested and imprisoned. This is particularly true of people of African and Caribbean origin, but it also applies to those of Pakistani, 'other Asian' and 'other' ethnic minority communities. The criminal records are relatively robust, but they only tell us about who gets caught and processed, and comprise, therefore, only an account of state intervention in deviance, rather than a measure of deviance itself. Surveys, by contrast, provide a much better account of offending and victimisation as experienced by members of the general public, but have their own methodological weaknesses (see chapter 4).

Victimisation surveys conducted in England and Wales have consistently found that people from ethnic minorities are significantly more likely than white people to be victims of household burglary, robbery and thefts from the person. It seems probable that many (but by no means all) instances of personal crime are intra-ethnic (that is, victim and offender from the same ethnic group) and this is particularly true for personal crimes, such as homicide and domestic violence. Ethnic minority communities are also at much greater risk of being targeted specifically for racist victimisation.

Self-reported offending studies have also shown consistently that rates of involvement in offending are similar among young people from white and African/Caribbean communities and significantly lower among Indian, Pakistani and Bangladeshi communities (see chapter 4). Self-reported drug use data from five Home Office studies in the 1990s all found that rates of drug use are highest among white communities (particularly among middle-class whites), followed closely by African/Caribbean communities and are lowest among Asian communities. Of course, self-report studies are only as reliable as the honesty of the people who agree to be interviewed. This means that the method is open to the charge that willingness to admit deviance is lower among minority communities.

Quantitative criminal justice data on offending are inconclusive on the extent and nature of offending when compared among different ethnic groups: self-report data point in one direction and arrest data point in the other. Commentators are therefore left with a choice between contradictory and questionable statistics or merely to speculate about differences in offending based on their theoretical starting point. There is one exception to this general point: homicide. While homicide shares some of the problems with other recorded crime statistics, they are significantly more robust than those relating to other forms of crime. The data recorded by the police indicate that a disproportionate number of homicides involve people from ethnic minorities as both victims and suspects. In the 2,003 cases recorded as homicide between 1997 and 2000, about 10 per cent of both victims and suspected offenders were black, 6 per cent were Asian and 3 per cent were of 'other' ethnic origin (Home Office 2000c: 16–17). The qualitative studies that might shed light on patterns of crime among different ethnic groups are thin on the ground. Overall, we lack a convincing description of the extent and nature of offending within minority communities because of equivocal statistical data, a dearth of empirical research.

If the research and statistical evidence on patterns of offending among ethnic minority communities is inconclusive, what justification is there for attempting to develop specific explanations of crime among 'black', 'Asian' or 'white' communities? Does such a task amount to Michael Keith and Karim Murji's accusation of "taking 'black criminality' as given" and then 'apologising for it' using criminological theory. Does it risk contributing to the creation of false pathologies which might then serve to 'naturalise' and reify images of black people as criminal? Does it risk 'collusion and treachery-by-default' (Alexander 2000b) and act as a 'let-off' for police and prison managers who might point to criminal justice statistics to justify disproportionate stop/search and imprisonment rates?

We know that people from ethnic minority groups, and black people in particular, are more likely to be arrested and imprisoned than their white counterparts and, in our view, the issue of *criminalisation* – literally being 'turned into a criminal' by being arrested and imprisoned – has relevance for theorising involvement in crime. The research evidence shows that, irrespective of prior involvement in crime, the experience of being arrested, prosecuted and imprisoned has negative consequences for life chances in the future, including the chance of becoming involved in further criminal offences.

Serious crimes such as robbery and homicide have generated significant concern within ethnic minority communities.[3] While we agree with those who argue that the evidence remains questionable, we think that suggesting lines of enquiry for further research and speculating about why a particular crime pattern might be emerging seems like a responsible first step. We have reached the conclusion that the dangers in ignoring the question of offending among ethnic minority communities is greater than those inherent in confronting them. Despite their obvious and well-known limitations, arrest and imprisonment statistics are taken by some as synonymous with offending rates and, on this basis, some authors have embarked upon speculative lines of theorising about the nature of 'black criminality'. Some of these theories have been based on neo-Lombrosian and neo-classical approaches that have alarming ethical, political and policy implications. Into the vacuum left by the absence of theoretically robust, methodologically rigorous and properly considered research studies of offending within minority communities has flowed, on one hand, ill-thought-out versions of deterrence and incapacitation theories and, on the other, neo-positivism based on psychobiology and the new genetics. Both of these developments have the potential to lead to policies that are likely to entrench criminalisation and cause unfair restrictions on liberty. We think it is our responsibility to grasp this most thorny issue and set out what we think are helpful avenues for future research.

---

[3] 'Act now before it is too late: Stark warning as black kids account for more than half of London street muggings', *Voice*, 4 October 2000, p. 2; 'Crime Figure Black Londoners can't ignore', Hugh Muir, *Evening Standard*, 27 October 2000.

The structural context of offending within minority communities

Our starting point is the structural context of life within ethnic minority communities. As we have indicated throughout this text, 'race' and ethnicity are not ahistorical essences, but socially constructed categories upon which iniquitous social structures are based. Acting as though these 'racial' categories are 'real', immigration officials, employers, estate agents, housing officers, teachers and other public officials have used such categories implicitly or explicitly in the management of competition for scarce resources (such as jobs and homes). The consequence of these patterned but dynamic social practices is a set of social and economic conditions that lead to some, but not all, ethnic minority groups (including some 'whites') becoming marginalised and socially excluded.

In chapter 2, we illustrated the impact of this process on the social and economic positions of ethnic minority communities based on social policy research and statistics. This literature shows that, in general, people from ethnic minority communities are concentrated into the cities and into the most disadvantaged boroughs and neighbourhoods. Their housing conditions are markedly worse than their white counterparts and they are much more likely to lack basic amenities, to be overcrowded and in poor repair. Black and Asian people are more likely to be unemployed or casually employed and concentrated into occupations of low status and low income. Levels of absolute poverty and destitution are significantly higher among ethnic minority communities, particularly those of African/Caribbean, Pakistani and Bangladeshi origin. Linked to these broader processes of economic exclusion and concentrations of poverty, it is also clear that the schools that children from ethnic minority communities attend offer a poorer quality of education, have fewer financial, human and other resources, achieve poorer examination results and have higher rates of truancy and exclusions. These processes of social exclusion are mutually reinforcing: poverty, poor housing, poor schools, educational failure, exclusion from the mainstream of the jobs market are all interrelated.

In the English context, racist ideas have contributed to creating material conditions in which some, but not all, ethnic minority groups, are *de facto* excluded from specific areas of residential space, sectors of the housing market, sectors of the economy and labour market. Moreover, aggregate statistics conceal micro-level variations in socio-economic conditions and the meaning of these statistics in terms of how they are experienced in everyday life. Disproportionate imprisonment compounds and concentrates poverty among those who are already most likely to be socially excluded, and in particular people of African/Caribbean origin.

Social exclusion and criminalisation

Criminological research shows that victimisation clusters in conditions of social exclusion, such as high unemployment, high housing density, crumbling infrastructure and poor schools (chapter 3). On the basis of the social and economic position of ethnic minority communities, structural theories of crime – including those based on such concepts as anomie, strain, social disorganisation, absolute and relative deprivation – would all posit that people from ethnic minority communities are disproportionately likely to be found in criminogenic contexts and that the extent of crime and deviance would be greater than among communities who are not socially excluded.

The material conditions that provide the context for the commission of certain specific forms of deviance also mean that many offences occur in specific contexts, such as in urban settings or in public places, with greater visibility and liability to surveillance and police intervention. The conclusion that monitoring, surveillance and other information-gathering processes impact on African and Caribbean minority communities irrespective of their involvement in crime is underlined by the fact that the power to stop and search under the 1989 Prevention of Terrorism Act was used extensively against black and Asian people in the 1990s even though the target of the Act was the Provisional IRA. The impact of contact with the criminal justice system continues the process of social exclusion. It is clear that a significant proportion of African/Caribbean people will have acquired criminal records including intelligence files, stop and search and arrest histories, criminal convictions and prison records. In England and Wales as a whole, one in three males born in 1953 will have acquired a criminal record by the time they are 40 years old and 7 per cent will have served a prison sentence (Prime *et al.* 2001), figures which will be much higher for people of African/Caribbean origin and other excluded groups. Criminalisation and prisonisation have predictable effects, such as exclusion from the job market, inability to maintain rented property, to secure a mortgage and support families. Prison splits families, exerts greater stress on the partner, children and others who are left behind when a mother, father or partner is behind bars. Criminalisation is the fulcrum of racialised social exclusion; it is where the metaphor of social exclusion is transformed into an explicit, formal social practice and into the personal experience of being literally excluded from society through imprisonment and all that flows from that.

Deviant behaviour among socially and economically marginalised people is much more likely to be labelled as criminal, to result in formal sanctions by the state and lead offenders to be propelled through the criminal justice process towards imprisonment. Processes of social and economic marginalisation and involvement in deviant behaviour among minority groups are compounded by policing, overcharging on arrest and disproportionately harsh sentencing and prison discipline. Criminal justice agencies openly, tacitly or indirectly use 'ethnicity' as a basis for intrusive, coercive decisions that lead ultimately to amplification and entrenchment of patterns of crime.

Contemporary neo-classical theory inspires 'zero tolerance' policing (to increase the certainty of punishment), reducing delays in the criminal justice process (to make punishment swifter), increasing sentence lengths (to sharpen the deterrent effect) and larger prison populations (to extend incapacitation). The consequences of such an approach are not only questionable in terms of their capacity to reduce crime, but have some 'unintended' or, at least, 'unwanted' consequences, including spiralling costs of criminal justice processing and 'warehousing' huge numbers of prisoners. The damaging effects of the prison experience, dislocation and pauperisation of families have been known since the birth of the prison. Moreover, where criminal justice processes are felt to be unfair, the institutions of the police and magistracy, and 'the law' itself, are less likely to be seen as legitimate. If the coercive state is seen as illegitimate, this reduces willingness to conform to the law (Tyler 1990).

High arrest and imprisonment rates are, in a final hegemonic twist, used to support the ideologies of 'race and crime'. The widespread belief that 'immigrants increase crime rates' noted in chapter 2 is given legitimacy by official statistics and an actual higher incarcerated population of people from ethnic minority communities (Pearson 1983). The extent of criminalisation is taken not as the outcome of a specific set of ideological and material processes, but as an index of *criminality*. This essence – a flaw in the rational mind, perhaps, or a strip of genetic code – is reified, pushed out of history into the realm of natural and inevitable events.

A structural analysis of culture?

Structural theories can be caricatured as economic determinism that seems to imply that poor people and the unemployed are propelled towards crime. They cannot account for the fact that most poor people do not offend and that some economically marginalised communities have greater arrest and imprisonment rates than others. For example, an analysis based on economic activity, unemployment and exclusion from the labour market cannot, by itself at least, explain why there are hardly any women of Pakistani or Bangladeshi origin in British prisons in comparison with African/Caribbean women who make up a significant proportion of the female prison population (Chigwada-Bailey 1997: 14).

Observing the limitations of a structural account in explaining deviance within minority communities, some critics have turned to cultural analyses for help. The problem here is that many cultural theories are based on stereotypes of African, Caribbean and Asian communities, falsely portraying them as having pathological family functioning and as being inherently deviant. Such theories are ultimately detached from the economic and social contexts within which cultures are formed. Some cultural theories – such as that at the centre of Murray's (1990) underclass theory – use the shape and character of minority families and communities as a way of explaining their structural position. Using notions like 'the culture of poverty', such theories become a way of blaming the victims of discrimination for the conditions in which they find themselves. A way through these debates may be a structural analysis of culture that seeks to unearth the *effects* of severe economic exclusion on self-image, aspirations and behaviour (see chapter 3, pages 71–4).

The poverty of positivism

Neither 'race' nor 'crime' are ahistorical essences, but are social practices that occur in a structural context. We, therefore, reject individual positivism based on genetics, endocrinology, physique or intelligence and can see no greater relevance for biological analyses of crime and deviance than for analyses of police discrimination, corruption and abuse of power. Biologistic discourse does play a part in the social, economic and cultural processes of racialisation and criminalisation in that it serves to fix race and criminality in the body of the actor, rendering such facts as overrepresentation in prison as 'natural', outside of history and, in some accounts, beyond the scope of social and criminal justice policy interventions. There is a risk with any criminological analysis that the subjects of research are portrayed as the passive victims of circumstances, lacking the ability or will to do anything to change the conditions of their lives. Neo-positivism does this by suggesting that the causes of crime are fixed in the criminal's mind or body while neo-classicism implies that individual choices are determined, like Pavlov's dog, by the state's manipulation of rewards and punishments. The basic position of a contextual analysis is that, while individuals make choices, they do so in structural circumstances that are not of their own making.

More than 20 years ago Stuart Hall and his colleagues rejected a romantic portrayal of crime within minority communities, characterising robbery in public places as a 'desperate and illegal solution to the survival problems which confront the community' (Hall *et al.* 1978: 358). This reflects the position of black activists within the community. The editorials of *Race Today*, for example, were 'uncompromisingly against mugging' and argued that getting money by force or stealth was counter-productive politically and disabled and degraded those who perpetrate it (Hall *et al.* 1978: 396):

> A certain glamour may temporarily attach itself to the life of petty crime; but accounts of those who have to survive in this way for long, or those now languishing in detention centres, or in prison, clearly show that there is nothing remotely romantic about it. It is a precarious, haphazard and

> desperate existence, always on the edge of a violence which brutalises all those who engage in it, for whatever motives.
>
> (ibid.: 360).

There have, since this time, been many members of black and other ethnic minority communities who have engaged in practical and political work to address offending and criminalisation especially among young men. This has involved joining the criminal justice professions, such as the police force, probation and social work, as well as working with young people on the streets and in youth clubs. It has also involved such public figures as Ian Wright who supported a campaign to prevent gun crime in Lambeth.[4] We think that this work requires much greater support both politically and financially. There has been an emergent debate within minority communities on the issues of 'black-on-black' crimes of all kinds, and there is certainly a need to engage further especially on the issues of domestic violence and robbery. Recent moves by newspapers, such as the *Voice*, and black activists to stimulate debates within minority communities to develop ways to reduce the extent to which their young people drift towards criminalisation are an important catalyst. However, it is vital that these debates are set properly within the context of the clear evidence of racism and exclusion within and without the criminal justice process.

Racist victimisation

In recent years, racist violence has moved to the centre of debates about 'race and crime'. In addition to disproportionate victimisation arising from the social and economic conditions within which ethnic minority communities live, they face widespread racist violence, targeted at them specifically. Historical research (for example, Panayi 1996) and contemporary qualitative and quantitative, evidence points to racist harassment and attacks being common and having a significant impact on the lives of ethnic minority communities (see Virdee 1995, Bowling 1999a, Chahal and Julienne 1999). Research on the perpetrators of racist harassment shows very clearly the ways in which popular and political forms of racism provide a direction for violence and targets for violence (Sibbitt 1997, Webster 2001, Ray *et al.* 2000). Racist violence provides an example of the impact of direct, individual racism. Frequently, members of extreme racist organisations or their sympathisers have set out specifically to maim or kill people from ethnic minorities. Among the many examples that

---

[4] 'How we'll take the guns out of Brixton', *Evening Standard*, 27 October 1997 reported that Ian Wright (then England and Arsenal footballer) joined Home Secretary Jack Straw to launch a guns amnesty in Brixton. Wright was reported as saying, 'I have heard that some people think that it's cool or fashionable to possess a gun. But I have a message for them – it's not cool, it's not fashionable, in fact I think it is downright stupid. Guns have only one purpose; that is to kill.'

could be cited of overt racist violence in recent British history, David Copeland's nail-bombing campaign in April 1999 stands out as among the most horrific (see chapter 5, box 5.1).

Racist violence is sometimes portrayed as the inexplicable madness of individuals, 'mindless' or even, simply, 'politically motivated'. However, it is a much broader phenomenon that includes violence perpetrated by individuals and groups of young men whose supremacist and exclusionary values are shared among a much broader section of the English population (see Sibbitt 1997, Ray *et al.* 2000, Webster 2001). Research on prejudice and racism among 'ordinary' white people in England suggests that many share the beliefs of the perpetrators of racial harassment. For example, many believe that people from ethnic minorities should be discouraged from moving into 'their' neighbourhood (for example, Husbands 1983, Hesse *et al.* 1992), even if they do not agree with the means (that is, violence) which is used to achieve this (for example, Sibbitt 1997, Foster 1998).

Explaining racist violence may require an analysis of the motivations of racist individuals, but these must be set in the context of a culture which defines people as problematic, threatening and (simultaneously) vulnerable on the basis of their race or ethnic origin (Bowling 1999a). Taking a still broader view, racist culture does not exist in a vacuum but is formed, transformed and reformed in a specific historical, geographical, social and political context. Racism occurs in the context of the racialisation and politicisation of competition for scare resources. Where class relations determine the way in which goods (as well as 'bads') and services are distributed, 'race' divides people who would otherwise find themselves in more or less the same material conditions. In short, the over-victimisation of ethnic minority communities through violent racism in particular is the result of individual action, cultural racism and the indirect impact of structural forces.

Under-protection

The disproportionate risk of victimisation experienced by minority communities – whether this is inter- or intra-ethnic – is compounded by under-protection by the police and authorities. Survey evidence suggests that people from ethnic minorities more frequently report that police are not interested in their case, are unsympathetic, do not do enough, make mistakes and handle their cases badly (Skogan 1990, 1994, Bowling 1999a, Spencer and Hough 2000). These survey results pointing to 'under-protection' by the police are echoed in accounts from individuals, community organisations and law centres (Institute of Race Relations 2001). Part of the explanation for these more common complaints from ethnic minorities is that they live in places where victimisation is greater, demands are higher and resources to respond are scarcer. As we have argued, however, the social and economic position of ethnic minority communities is not an historical accident, but the results of a social process of marginalisation, exclusion and discrimination (see chapters 1 and 2).

Until recently, the police and public authorities typically downplayed or ignored racist violence and, more generally, have taken insufficient account of the disproportionate victimisation of minority communities. This may partly explain the survey evidence indicating that levels of satisfaction with the police response to racist incidents are lower than for 'ordinary crime' experienced by ethnic minority communities. This failure in the police response to violent racism is partly the result of inaction on the part of individual police officers who more closely identify with the offending, rather than the victimised, communities (Bowling 1999a). However, it would be wrong to see this simply as the response of 'bad apples' within the police service if only because racist views are widely shared among many members of the police organisation and elsewhere in the criminal justice system (Cathcart 1999, Keith 1993). Additionally, the police organisation does not respond well to systematic, repeated victimisation. Since many incidents of racial harassment consist of repeated, legally 'non-serious' offences, it may be that the failure of the organisational response cannot be seen only as a consequence of individual and cultural racism, but institutional discrimination and the failure of routine organisational practice (Bowling 1999a).

Although research studies conducted in the late 1970s and early 1980s indicated that many police officers expressed strong sympathy with extreme racist political movements, no recent studies have found anything like the blatant racist talk uncovered by researchers such as Smith and Gray (1983), Holdaway (1983) and others. However, many studies of policing in the late 1980s and 1990s found racist language, assumptions and stereotypes were commonplace and used casually and overtly (see Graef 1989, Reiner 1991, Bowling 1999a, Her Majesty's Inspectorate of Constabulary 1997). There is certainly evidence of widespread racist assumptions, prejudice and stereotyping in the culture of the organisation. As Bowling (1999a) documents, many police officers are not only *not opposed* to racism, but actually share the values of the people targeting violence at ethnic minority communities. These racist attitudes and prejudices are clearly reflected in the behaviour towards black and Asian victims, witnesses, suspects, employees and the general public. Compounding the effects of individual and cultural racism, is the *institutional racism* that is built into the policies and practices of the organisations and which leads to systemic discrimination against people from ethnic minorities irrespective of the intent of individuals (see chapter 2, pages 40–42). The ultimate consequence of individual, cultural and institutional racism is a failure to deliver either a *quality service* or *equality* of protection.

The question of equal protection obviously extends to the proper treatment of victims of racially aggravated crimes, but it must also be concerned with adequate responses to offending *within* minority communities. The research findings set out in this book pose a dilemma for reformers concerned to ensure the safety of ethnic minority communities and protection from the abuse of police powers. The call for crackdowns – whether these are directed against robbery or racist violence – inevitably risks further criminalising the very communities who are seeking greater public protection. There is an absence of research on good practice in reducing offending and reoffending specifically within ethnic minority communities. Until now, the emphasis has largely been on the use of coercive policing and the criminal justice process and generic offender behaviour programmes. There is now a pressing need for new thinking in this area.

New Labour, racism, crime and justice

If one 'soundbite' from the 1997 election campaign will be remembered by criminology, it will be 'tough on crime, tough on the causes of crime'. This phrase, hardened by 'zero tolerance' rhetoric, accompanied a raft of punitive criminal justice policies in the 1990s. In opposition, New Labour had abstained on the 1994 Criminal Justice and Public Order Act which permitted courts to draw inferences from the refusal to answer a question put to the accused by the police (thereby limiting the right to silence) and curtailed freedom of movement and assembly in an attempt to control the ravers, protestors and other 'folk devils' of the early 1990s. The Labour opposition also abstained on the 1997 Crime Sentences Act (the 'two strikes' law) which created mandatory minimum sentences for a third serious, violent or drug supply offence. Labour government ministers have made clear that punishment and crime reduction are the heart of its thinking on social policy, and that being 'tough on crime' means imprisoning more people, including more young people and women.

Tough on crime?

The Crime and Disorder Act 1998 was the centrepiece of the New Labour government's thinking on zero tolerance (Fionda 1999, Bowling 1999c: 533). While the draconian Anti-Social Behaviour Orders – the legal solution to the 'neighbours from hell' – were the focus of much debate, as were child curfews and parenting orders, many of these provisions have not been used extensively. However, the Act abolished the police juvenile caution in favour of a 'reprimand' and a 'final warning' (a sort of two strikes for children) and this may lead to a significant increase in the number of juveniles charged by the police, and therefore to more prosecutions and court hearings. If this is a form of 'narrowing the mesh' in the nets of social control, the new Referral Order introduced by the

Youth Justice and Criminal Evidence Act 1999 is predicted to have the effect of creating new nets (Ball 2000). It seems likely that the abolition of the right to elect for jury trial in 'either-way cases' – proposed in the Mode of Trial Bill – would have a discriminatory effect on black suspects. This would, according to Lee Bridges, further undermine the ability of black people to defend themselves through the criminal courts and to resist racist 'over-charging' at the police station (2000: 321).

It seems to us that these laws entrench the drift to a 'law and order' society identified by Stuart Hall in the late 1970s (Hall 1980). In each of the last years of the 1990s, the police in England and Wales stopped and searched around one million people; nine times the number in 1986. Even with the drop to 800,000 searches in 1999/2000, this still represents an extraordinary use of police coercive powers. Unprecedented numbers of people were processed through the criminal justice system including 112,000 people cautioned or convicted for drug possession (five times the number in 1985) (Corkery 2000). The prison population, hovering at around 65,000, is the largest this century, and predicted to reach between 72,000 and 79,000 by 2007 (Elkins, Gray and Rogers 2001).

If 'tough on crime' means increasing police powers and the severity of criminal justice sanctions, what does it mean to be tough on the 'causes of crime'? As we illustrated in chapter 3, the range of theories that have been attempted to explain those causes is extremely wide. Indeed one prominent school of 'popular' criminological thought declares: 'the root cause of crime is the criminal' (Bratton 1997). This position sees offending as the result of insufficient discipline at home, school and on the streets. Current policies intended to tackle causes include neo-classical approaches such as the use of surveillance and other 'situational measures'. Advocates of situational crime prevention are not interested in the 'causes' of crime, nor do they believe they can do anything about them; instead they focus on the crime event and on reducing opportunities for crime commission. From this flows a range of 'community policing' strategies, such as problem-oriented and 'targeted' policing, social approaches targeting 'problem families' and mentoring schemes for 'at risk' individuals. The government has committed a total of around £400m over three years for crime prevention pilot projects, though this amounts to only about 3 per cent of the total crime budget (Home Office 1999d).

The tension between crime reduction (or 'crime control') and justice (or 'due process') is complicated by a range of other currents moving through contemporary criminal justice policy-making discourses. For example, there is an increasing call for 'public voice and participation' and to open up the institutions of criminal justice to greater outside scrutiny. Linked to this development is the much more significant growth of 'managerialism', the idea that problems within organisations – whether public or private – can be solved through 'better management' and the introduction of performance management and information technology. Many criminal justice organisations are identifying goals, setting targets, completing forms and examining the rises and falls in 'key performance indicators'. Central to contemporary criminal justice policy-making is a focus on 'outcomes'. An 'outcome-based' approach holds that the criteria to measure the effectiveness of the criminal justice system should not be the *intention* or *desire* to achieve community safety or justice, or even the visible activity put into these tasks. Rather, what is actually achieved, or the *outcomes of practice,* should be the criteria on which success should be judged. The key principles, drawing on the aims and objectives set out by the Home Office, suggest that the criminal justice system should aim to ensure:

- **Safety** and personal security of individuals and the protection of their homes and possessions;
- **Justice** through effective and efficient investigation, prosecution, trial and sentencing, and support for victims;
- **Liberty** and freedom from unnecessary intrusion into private life, restriction of freedom of movement and association;
- **Protection from discrimination** on race, sex or any other improper ground;
- **Tolerance of difference** in a society where the rights and responsibilities of both majority and minority communities can be assured.

To what extent are 'safety', 'justice' and 'liberty' fairly distributed and free from discrimination and intolerance? Throughout this text we have identified *racially disproportionate outcomes.* These outcomes, as we argued in chapter 2, present a *prima facie* case that direct or indirect discrimination have shaped the experiences of different ethnic groups. The research and statistical evidence shows that safety, justice and liberty are not equally distributed through British society. People from ethnic minority communities (and other marginalised groups) are at greater risk of both criminalisation and victimisation than their white counterparts. They are less likely to feel protected by the police and this reflects a policing perspective which has tended to ignore or downplay the fears of minority communities. As a consequence, British black and Asian people feel angry, unsafe and insecure. The 'double whammy' faced by these communities is that they are widely seen by the police and prison services as problematic, suspicious and, sometimes, simply criminal. This perception has, for 30 years, justified a style of policing, institutionalised in the 1970s and 1980s, which determines the conditions under which many black people enter the criminal justice system, as a result of proactive (and frequently conflictual) policing which, in turn, launches them on a different trajectory through the system.

The implementation of an exceptionally fierce crime control policy – including elements of 'zero tolerance' and 'two strikes and you're out' borrowed from the USA – increases the concentration of policing activity and the number of people against whom formal action is being taken.

Measures to increase the speed of criminal justice processing are likely further to increase the flow of people *through* the justice system and *into* the prison system. The result is a prison population which is not only increasing, but within which the ethnic minority population is growing most strongly. While the number of white people in prison has risen by 39 per cent since 1985, the prison population increased by 80 per cent among Asians and nearly 100 per cent among blacks.

Tough on justice?

There is little doubt that New Labour are 'tough on crime', but are they 'tough on justice'? One of the first indications that Labour were concerned about the quality of justice was the introduction of the Human Rights Act 1998 (which incorporates the European Convention on Human Rights into English law), implemented on 1 October 2000. This Act sets expectations for law enforcement and criminal justice agencies in the areas such as freedom of movement and association, freedom from detention, and freedom from discrimination. The basic principle in human rights jurisprudence is that the state has the power to intrude into the rights of the individual only to the extent that this is within certain clear limits. For example, the power used (such as the use of force to conduct a search) must have a basis in law (the principle of *legality*), be proportionate to any risk or threat (*proportionality*), must rest with the individual for a specific threat (*finality*) and be the least coercive or intrusive response (*subsidiarty*) (Justice 1999). The Human Rights Act seems to offer the potential to protect fundamental rights and freedoms and to create a culture of openness and accountability. However, the Act has to be interpreted by judges in reaching an opinion on specific cases brought by individuals. The impact of the Human Rights Act has yet to be seen.

Tough on racism?

The inquiry into the murder of Stephen Lawrence, hailed as a 'landmark in race relations', was initiated within a few months of the election of New Labour (see chapter 1, pages 414–17). The inquiry revealed a lack of competence and professionalism in routine investigative practice but also showed that these issues of competence were tied up with the issues of discrimination and accountability. The debates about racism changed in character during the Lawrence Inquiry, prior to which the dominant view was based firmly on the 'bad apple theory'. During the Lawrence Inquiry, Sir Paul Condon, Commissioner of the Metropolitan Police, stuck to the Scarman position that, while there were racist individuals within the organisation, the police did not discriminate 'knowingly as a matter of policy'. However, written and oral evidence submitted to 'part II' of the Lawrence

Inquiry, which dealt with the 'matters arising' from the murder of Stephen Lawrence, suggested that, irrespective of formal policy, the police were routinely discriminating against people from ethnic minorities. There was evidence of discrimination in routine policies, in the demographic composition and culture of the police service, stop and search, complaints against the police, and the lack of openness, transparency and accountability in policy. In particular, the written submissions by the Black Police Association (1998), the 1990 Trust (1998) and Commission for Racial Equality (1998), among others, provided evidence that the Metropolitan Police service had racist cultural norms and values which encouraged stereotyping and discrimination against people from minority communities. This evidence, as Cathcart (1999) was to put it, signalled 'the end of the bad apple theory'. Although the Metropolitan Police Commissioner maintained throughout the inquiry that the term 'institutional racism' would leave the public thinking that every police officer was racist, he did eventually accept the inquiry's definition of institutional racism, and committed the organisation to becoming 'actively anti-racist' (Metropolitan Police 1998).

The question of accountability in the Metropolitan Police had been recognised as deficient for many years, on the grounds that it had only ever had oversight from the Home Office and was, therefore, accountable only to a minister of Her Majesty's Government rather than the people of London. The Labour party had a long-standing commitment to creating a police authority for London and Jack Straw himself had brought private members bills to parliament unsuccessfully in the 1980s. The Greater London Authority came into existence in May 2000 and with it the Metropolitan Police Authority which started work in July of that year. The Lawrence Inquiry recommendation also acted as a catalyst in the process towards a fully independent police complaints authority, proposals for which are expected in a new Police Bill in autumn 2001.

Arguably the most important 'post-Lawrence' development in anti-discrimination law is the form of the Race Relations (Amendment) Act 2000, the first new legislation in this field of law since the 1976 Race Relations Act a quarter of a century earlier. The main purpose of this legislation is to bring public authorities such as the police, prisons and immigration service into the ambit of UK anti-discrimination law. This is a step forward because it establishes for the first time that it is unlawful for the police or other authorities to provide demonstrably inferior treatment to people on the basis of their ethnic origin. This includes 'service provision' – for example, interviewing crime victims or witnesses or providing a response to emergency calls – and also the use of coercive powers, such as suspect interviews, searches and arrests. This legislation, used in conjunction with the Human Rights Act, might provide the basis for civil actions to ensure compliance. Again, this will involve individual complainants bringing cases against the authorities and it will be up to the judges to decide firstly what constitutes unequal treatment and also whether such inequality can be justified.

It seems that the enthusiasm for these proposals within the Labour government is not as strong as for tough talk on crime. The first draft of the Race Relations (Amendment) Bill, for example, excluded indirect discrimination as defined by the 1976 Act. Had indirect discrimination been excluded it is doubtful that much protection would be gained from institutional racism. Critics pointed out that the Lawrence Inquiry recommended that the 'full force' of anti-discrimination legislation should be applied to the police and urged the government to reconsider. The government backed down only at the last minute after the threat of a Lords rebellion. It is also the case that some of the most sensitive decisions remain exempt from the Act, such as some aspects of the work of the immigration service where there is clear evidence of discrimination in the application of decisions to refuse entry, and to detain (Hugo Young, *Guardian*, 8 May 2001).

Backlash

Not everyone welcomed the Macpherson Report. While dissent was muted at the time of publication, an increasingly vocal opposition mounted in the months that followed. Even before the report was published, right-wing newspapers questioned the conduct of the inquiry, the strength of the evidence that it adduced and the validity of its conclusions. This position was given some intellectual support by the right-wing think-tank, the Institute for the Study of Civil Society. In their *Racist Murder and Pressure Group Politics*, Dennis, Erdos and Al-Shahi (2000) accused the Lawrence Inquiry of making claims not based on evidence, putting people on trial for thought crimes, of incompetence in its own proceedings and undermining public security.

This articulate backlash has also claimed that the Lawrence Inquiry has had a 'disastrous effect' on the fight against crime by lowering police morale and affecting police officers who were now afraid to detain suspected offenders.[5] This, it is argued, has resulted in a decline in willingness to stop and search black people, which is, in turn, responsible for an increase in violent crime, and especially 'street crime' and 'violence'. In a speech to the Centre for Policy Studies, William Hague, then leader of the Conservative party, claimed that 'the Macpherson Report has been used to brand every officer and every branch of the force as racist, has contributed directly to a collapse of police morale and recruitment, and has led to a crisis in our streets'.[6] It is difficult to assess what impact these debates have on the rank and file police officers required to deliver a service to the community. However, it seems unlikely to do anything to

---

[5] Crime Soars After Lawrence Report, David Bamber, *Sunday Telegraph*, Aug 8, 1999, p1., editorial 'The cost of Macpherson', p 28.
[6] Conservative party news release, Thursday 14 December 2000.

encourage police officers to respond positively to a process that was set in train by an inquiry characterised at the time as being akin to Stalinist show trials and Mao's cultural revolution.[7]

The claim that the Lawrence Inquiry had a bad effect on police morale is certainly supported by public statements made by the police unions and individual police officers. However, this seems a predictable consequence of the repeated exposure of incompetence within the police service. While stop and search did decline after the Lawrence Inquiry report, it was actually a relatively modest reduction, after more than a decade of sharply escalating use of the power (see chapter 6).[8] Moreover, the reduction of stop and search seems to have been *intended* by senior police officers, who had accepted that the power was being used unfairly, often without 'reasonable suspicion' (and therefore unlawfully), and was costly, ineffective and damaging to confidence in the police. It is interesting to note that the 'post-Lawrence' decline in the use of stop and search was greater for the white population than for communities of ethnic minority origin. The claim that the decrease in stop and search had an effect on crime is not supported by the evidence (Miller *et al.* 2000). The rise in crime has been attributed to changes in the Home Office counting rules, which came into effect over the same period, and encouragement to report incidents to the police (Bowling 1999c).

Malign neglect

The present situation for people from ethnic minority communities in Britain parallels that in the USA, described in detail in Michael Tonry's (1995) *Malign Neglect*. Tonry argues that the US 'War on Drugs' had an extremely damaging effect on the nation's inner-city ethnic minority residents. This effect, he argues, was clearly foreseeable by policy makers who should be held 'morally accountable for the havoc they have wrought among disadvantaged members of minority groups' (1995: 104). Despite indications that drug use was in decline before the 'war' was mounted and that drug use was lower among African Americans than their white counterparts, drug trafficking was portrayed in the media as a phenomenon of the inner city. 'Supply-reduction' approaches increased levels of law enforcement by the police in minority communities and led to harsher sentencing and the exclusion of education and drug treatment programmes. The result was a doubling of the prison population after

---

[7] *Police: The Voice of the Service*, March 1999, editorial
[8] Fluctuations in stop and search figures are difficult to interpret. Increasingly stringent requirements to record the stop and search increased compliance with requirements. Official recordings of the use of the powers under-represents its actual use: most stop/searches go unrecorded because they are conducted 'by consent' of the suspected person.

1980 and a sharp increase in the disproportionality of imprisonment among ethnic minority communities.

As a policy response to this overwhelming evidence, Tonry (1995) proposes that sentencing policy be reconstructed to produce the *least punitive and restrictive punishment* in each case. Alongside this he advocates a rehabilitative approach for prisoners, which enhances their life chances by investing in human capital, emphasising drug treatment and educational programmes. More controversially, Tonry suggests that judges should engage in informal mitigation so that sentences reflect the circumstances of individual offenders. In essence, he is arguing for a return to a sentencing policy which focuses on the defendant rather than the offence, but which is strictly proportionate so as to avoid the imposition of disproportionately lengthy sentences for poor and minority offenders based on class and 'race' bias by judges. This is in recognition of the 'illusion of like-situated offenders' whereby sentencing policy guides judges according to the characteristics of the offence and the offender's criminal history. Tonry instead argues that 'just desserts in an unjust world' are reprehensible. He is not suggesting positive discrimination for minorities, but connects the impact of social disadvantage with criminal offending for all offenders regardless of their 'race', linking the problem of racial disparities in the criminal justice system with socio-economic class differences. Von Hirsch and Roberts (1997) suggest, a 'social adversity mitigation' policy would require tight controls to prevent ethnic minority offenders having their employment and social status held against them when judges decide sentences.

Smith (1994, 1997a) has addressed the issue of policies that indirectly discriminate against ethnic minorities and what he sees as the limits of equal treatment within English criminal justice. He suggests that where there is no violation of a fundamental principle, criminal justice policies should be changed where they are shown to disadvantage a particular ethnic group. The example given is the use of family circumstances to determine the defendant's remand/bail status which, as we have seen, disproportionately affects black people, who, having been remanded in custody, are, in turn, more likely to be imprisoned if convicted. Von Hirsch and Roberts (1997) have considered convictions for small trades in cannabis and sentencing discounts for guilty pleas, both of which lead to the disproportionate imprisonment of black people. They conclude that 'there should be an explicit aim of seeking to alleviate gross racial imbalances in the criminal justice system'.

In an outcomes-led world, where equality of treatment is the stated goal of government, it is an indictment of the English criminal justice system that fairness and justice are so unevenly distributed. We are of the view that present trends in criminal justice practices will increasingly marginalise, criminalise and socially exclude ethnic minority communities in England, especially those of African/Caribbean origin. These trends, which are exacerbated by direct and indirect discrimination in policing and the criminal justice process, are now visible. If the results of this 'malign neglect' turn out to be as we suggest, no politician or policy maker will be able to claim that the racially disproportionate results were 'unwitting'. Rather, discriminatory law enforcement and criminal justice will result 'knowingly, as a matter of policy'.

Guide to further reading

Introduction

The literature on racism, crime and justice in Britain has been growing steadily since the pioneering studies of the 1970s. One of the earliest overviews of the field is Paul Gordon's (1983) short but critical *White Law: Racism in the Police, Courts and Prisons*, which itself owes a lot to the Institute of Race Relations (1979) contribution to the Royal Commission in that year. The most recent summary of the empirical data is David Smith's (1997b) contribution to *The Oxford Handbook of Criminology*, a version of which also appears in Michael Tonry's (1997) *Ethnicity, Crime and Immigration*. For a statistical overview, consult the most up-to-date version of the 'section '95 paper', for example, Home Office (2000c) *Statistics on Race and the Criminal Justice System 2000: A Home Office Publication Under section 95 of the Criminal Justice Act 1991*. Readers wishing to gain an overview of the research in this field should consult one of the two edited collections focusing on the situation in the UK – Dee Cook and Barbara Hudson's (1993) *Racism and Criminology* or Loraine Gelsthorpe's (1993) *Minority Ethnic Groups in the Criminal Justice System* – or one of the two with a more international perspective: Ineke Marshall's (1997) *Minorities, Migrants, and Crime: Diversity and Similarity Across Europe and the United States* or Michael Tonry's (1997) *Ethnicity, Crime and Immigration*.

As one might expect, research in the USA is far more extensive than in the UK. The two classic opposing texts in the USA are William Willbanks's *The Myth of a Racist Criminal Justice System* (1987) and Coramae Richey Mann's (1993) *Unequal Justice: A Question of Colour*, both of which are helpfully summarised in MacLean and Milovanovic's *Racism, Empiricism and Criminal Justice* (1990). The most up-to-date survey, from which we have borrowed an idea or two, is Sam Walker *et al.*'s (2000) *The Color of Justice: Race, Ethnicity, and Crime in America* (2nd editon).

Chapter 1 History

There is now an extensive literature documenting the experiences of people of colour in Britain, among which Peter Fryer's (1984) *Staying Power: The History of Black People in Britain* still stands out as the most comprehensive and thought provoking. Sivanadan's (1982) *A Different Hunger* is an influential critical text on the development of black communities in Britain. Miles and Phizacklea's *White Man's Country* provides an early critical account of the development of the social construction of 'race' in Britain. An accessible and somewhat more up-to-date reading of the history of 'race relations' in Britain can be found in Dilip Hiro's *Black British White British*. Biographical accounts of recent black British experiences are presented in Harris and White's (1999) *Changing Britannia*. Among the edited collections that shed light on black and Asian British history is James and Harris's (1993) *Inside Babylon*.

Chapter 2 Concepts

Readers wishing to read further about the concepts of ethnicity, 'race', racism and discrimination and the wide range of theories that have been proposed to explain these social phenomena will find a bewildering array of monographs and texts. A starting point for readers new to the field are the textbooks in this area including John Solomos's (1993) *Race and Racism in Contemporary Britain*, David Mason's (1995) *Race and Ethnicity in Modern Britain*. Milton Kleg's (1993) *Hate Prejudice and Racism*, John Solomos and Les Back's (1996) *Racism and Society,* Mairtin Mac an Ghaill's (1999) *Contemporary Racisms and Ethnicities*. Reflecting the growth in the interest in this area and the sheer extent and diversity of theorising, there are several recent readers including Les Back and John Solomos's (2000) *Theories of race and racism: A reader*. Those interested in research and statistics describing the position of ethnic minority communities should consult Modood, *et al.*'s (1997) report on the fourth PSI survey *Ethnic Minorities in Britain: Diversity and Disadvantage* or The Runnymede Trust's (2000) report on the *Future of Multi-Ethnic Britain*. Many of the sources cited here or in the text deal with the issues of anti-discriminatory practice, but for more specialised resources, readers are referred to Sebastian Poulter's (1998) *Ethnicity, Law and Human Rights* and Alistair Bonnet's (2000) *Anti-Racism*. Ellis Cashmore's (1996) *Dictionary of Race and Ethnic Relations,* now in its fourth edition, is a handy companion to the literature.

Chapter 3 Criminological theory

There is no single source that covers racism, ethnicity and criminological theory, though the chapters by Robert Reiner and others in Gelsthorpe's

(1993) *Minority Ethnic Groups in the Criminal Justice System* or John Pitts's 'Thereotyping: Anti-Racism, Criminology and Black Young People', in Cook and Hudson's (1993) *Racism and Criminology* offer a starting point. Readers unfamiliar with criminological theory are advised to start with the theoretical chapters in Maguire *et al.*'s (1997) *The Oxford Handbook of Criminology* or one of the many criminology textbooks (for example, Bierne and Messerschmidt's (1995) *Criminology*, Vold, Bernard and Snipes's (1998) *Theoretical Criminology* or Muncie and MacLaughlin's (1998) *Criminological Perspectives*. These texts cover the various theoretical perspectives described schematically in this book, but the reader will have to work hard to apply these theories to contemporary society. At present those who are interested in theories of crime within minority communities or on the relationships between racism, ethnicity and crime will have to read across 'generic' criminological theory to identify the places where theories shed any light on the matter. There is very little work that attempts to provided an analysis of gender, race and crime, an exception being Marcia Rice's black feminist critique in Loraine Gelsthorpe and Alison Morris's (1990) *Feminist Perspectives in Criminology*. Two recent US textbooks that contain pointers for a minority perspective in this field are Anne Sulton's (1996) edited collection *African-American Perspectives on Crime Causation, Criminal Justice Administration and Crime Prevention* and Helen Taylor Greene and Shaun Gabbidon's (2000) *African American Criminological Thought*.

Chapter 4 Offending and victimisation

As with criminological theory, studies relating specifically to the relationship between racism, ethnicity and offending are thin on the ground, though patterns of crime among different ethnic groups are touched on in many studies. An obvious starting point in this area is to look at officially recorded data such as arrest and prison statistics and records of victims and suspects in homicide offences published in the Home Office (2000c) 'Section 95' report *Race and the Criminal Justice System*. Since the late 1980s, surveys have shed some light on patterns of victimisation and offending and readers should consult the most recent British Crime Survey reports and the results of Home Office self-report studies such as Graham and Bowling's (1995) *Young People and Crime*, Flood Page *et al.*'s (2000) and Ramsay and Partridge's self-report drug use studies. Readers interested in the social construction of ethnicity and criminality should consult Stuart Hall *et al.*'s (1978) *Policing the Crisis*, Geoffrey Pearson's (1983) *Hooligan*, Paul Gilroy's (1987a) *There Ain't No Black in the Union Jack*, Solomos's 'Constructions of Black Criminality' in Cook and Hudson *Racism and Criminology*, Webster's (1997) 'The Construction of British "Asian" Criminality', in the *International Journal of the Sociology of Law*, Ali Wardak's (2000) *Social Control and Deviance* and Claire Alexander's

(2000a) *The Asian Gang*. An empiricist account of 'ethnic origins and crime' can be found in David Smith's (1997b) chapter in *The Oxford Handbook of Criminology*.

Chapter 5 Racist violence

There is now an extensive literature looking specifically at racist violence. For an historical perspective, Panikos Panayi's (1996) *Racial Violence in Britain* is an excellent starting point. Ben Bowling's (1999a) *Violent Racism* is an empirical study of racist violence in East London and also provides an exhaustive overview of the literature in the field and the preface to the revised edition places this work in the context of the Lawrence Inquiry. Recent empirical research studies include Satnam Virdee's (1995) *Racial Violence and Harassment*, Rae Sibbitt's (1997) *The Perpetrators of Racial Harassment and Racial Violence*, Kusminder Chahal and Louise Julienne's (1999) *We Can't All be White! Racist Victimisation in the UK*. Readable journalistic accounts include David Rose's (1996), *In the Name of the Law: The Collapse of Criminal Justice* (especially chapter 2), Bill Bufford's (1991) *Among the Thugs* and Brian Cathcart's (1999) *The Case of Stephen Lawrence*. The first state response to this issue was the 1981 Home Office Report on *Racial Attacks*, since when there have been numerous House of Commons reports in this area and, most recently, *The Stephen Lawrence Inquiry* (Macpherson 1999) which changed the terms of debate in this field. The new 'racially aggravated offences' created by the 1998 Crime and Disorder Act are the subject of a critical review by Maleiha Malik (1999) in the *Modern Law Review*. A critical appraisal of post-Lawrence developments can be found in a recent report by the Institute of Race Relations (2001). For a broader international perspective readers are referred to Mark Hamm's (1993) *Hate Crime: International Perspectives on Causes and Control*, Tore Bjørgo and Rob Witte's (1993) *Racist Violence in Europe* and Jeffrey Kaplan and Tore Bjørgo's (1998) *Nation and Race*.

Chapter 6 Policing

The research specifically on policing and ethnic minority communities and on 'race' and racism within the police service is very extensive, but there are few texts that adequately pull this material together. Simon Holdaway's (1996) *The Racialisation of British Policing* covers many of the key areas while Cashmore and McLaughlin's (1991) edited collection, *Out of Order?: Policing Black People*, reports on work covering the period until the end of the 1980s. Empirical studies of racism in policing in the 1980s include Simon Holdaway (1983) *Inside the British Police*, David Smith and Jeremy Gray's (1985) *Police and People in London*, while narrative and documentary accounts during that period include Institute of Race

Relations (1987) *Policing Against Black People* and (1991) *Deadly Silence: Black Deaths in Custody*, Darcus Howe's (1988) *From Bobby to Babylon*, Christine Dunhill's (1989) *The Boys in Blue: Women's Challenge to the Police*, Martin Kettle and Lucy Hodges (1982) *Uprising*, and, of course, the *Scarman Report* (1981).

The starting point for any theoretical study of racism in British policing, from a critical perspective at least, is Stuart Hall *et al.*'s (1978) *Policing the Crisis* and there are number other theoretically informed studies including Paul Gilroy's (1987a) *There Ain't No Black in the Union Jack*, Benyon and Solomos's (1987) *The Roots of Urban Unrest*, Solomos's (1988), *Black Youth, Racism and the State* and Michael Keith's (1993) *Race, Riots and Policing*, Mike McConville and Dan Shepherd's (1992) *Watching Police Watching Communities*, and Janet Chan's (1997) account of 'race' and policing in New South Wales, *Changing Police Culture*. There is an extensive literature on black police in the USA, the best of which is Dulaney's (1996) readable and fastidiously researched *Black Police in America*.

The Home Office has conducted much of the empirical work in this area, from Stevens and Willis's (1979) study of *Race, Crime and Arrests*, to more recent studies emerging from the British Crime Survey. Work by Wes Skogan (1990, 1994), Tom Bucke (1995, 1997) and others on *Policing and the Public* have looked at attitudes towards the police based on both police- and public-initiated encouters. FitzGerald and Sibbitt's (1997) consideration of the advent of ethnic monitoring in the police service is helpful in outlining different police perspectives on policing in ethnic minority communities. Phillips and Brown's (1998) quantitative study, *Entry into the Criminal Justice System: A Survey of Police Arrests and Their Outcomes* examined aspects of police decision making and suspect behaviour, and followed a sample of charged suspects through to the prosecution process. The Home Office research programme on stop and search (carried out by Bland, Miller, Quinton and others (2000)), instituted in the wake of the Stephen Lawrence Inquiry, is particularly informative, and provides an important insight into police practices in the 1990s. Statistical data on policing practices, such as stop/search, deaths in police custody, arrests and cautioning, are published in the Home Office section 95 publication, *Statistics on Race and the Criminal Justice System* (2000c). There have been three reports published by Her Majesty's Inspectorate of Constabulary (1997, 1998, 2000) all with the dubiously punning title *Winning the Race* and several recent studies conducted by the Commission for Racial Equality including the (1996) *Race and Equal Opportunities in the Police Service*.

No review of contemporary discussion of racism in British policing would be complete without reference to the (1999) *Stephen Lawrence Inquiry* report and such commentaries upon it such as Brian Cathcart's (1999) *The Case of Stephen Lawrence* or Norman Dennis *et al.*'s (2000) *Racist murder and pressure group politics*.

Chapter 7 Prosecution and sentencing

Roger Hood's (1992) landmark study *Race and Sentencing*, stands out in this area, not least because it was the first to undertake multivariate analysis of the influence of legal and extra-legal factors in Crown Court sentencing. For empirical studies on prosecutorial decision making, readers should see Coretta Phillips and David Brown's (1998) *Entry into the Criminal Justice System: A Survey of Police Arrests and Their Outcomes* and Gordon Barclay and Bonny Mhlanga's (2000) *Ethnic Differences In Decisions on Young Defendants Dealt With by the Crown Prosecution Service*. Readers are also referred to Anita Kalunta-Crumpton's (1999) *Race and Drug Trials*. In the juvenile justice arena Bonny Mhlanga's (1997) book *The Colour of English Justice: A Multivariate Analysis* is the most comprehensive.

Chapter 8 Prison and probation

For an historical and political perspective on the experiences of ethnic minorities in the prison system, Paul Gordon's (1984) *White Law* is recommended, while Shaw's (1990) paper in *New Community*, 16, 4, 533–50 covers much of the early policy context on race relations. There is no one recent overview of the position of ethnic minorities in the prison system, though Elaine Genders and Elaine Player's (1989) study of *Race Relations in Prison* remains the most comprehensive, though now dated, study on the impact of racism. Basic information on ethnicity and imprisonment can be found in the Home Office's annual *Prison Statistics* (2000a) and from the annual report Home Office (2000c) report, *Statistics on Race and the Criminal Justice System*. Most other research in this area tends to be found in journals and edited collections where 'race' and ethnicity are taken to be part of a wider agenda about imprisonment more generally. Marian FitzGerald and Peter Marshall's (1996) chapter on 'Ethnic Minorities in British Prisons' (in Matthews and P. Francis, edited collection *Prisons 2000*) provides an overview of empirical work in the field and raises some theoretical concerns. Some comparisons between the UK and US can be found in Michael Tonry's (1994) article on 'Racial Disproportion in US Prisons', *British Journal of Criminology*, 34, 97–115. The Institute of Race Relations (1991) study *Deadly Silence: Black Deaths in Custody* includes a discussion of deaths in prison custody.

Studies of probation practice include Holdaway and Allaker's (1990) *Race Issues in the Probation Service: A Review of Policy*. Wakefield: Association of Chief Officers of Probation. Denney's (1992) study is insightful in its critique of probation policy, particularly in its failure to contextualise offending by ethnic minorities. The recent thematic inspection, *Towards Race Equality*, carried out by Her Majesty's Inspectorate of Probation (2000) provides some useful background on the development of policy in the service and recent information on probation practices.

Chapter 9 Practitioners

Statistical information on the levels of ethnic minority representation across the criminal justice system are usefully contained in the Home Office's (2000c) section 95 publication *Statistics on Race and the Criminal Justice System*. A review of progress on meeting the employment targets on recruitment, retention, promotion and seniority for the Home Office and its service areas can be found in the Home Office (2000b) report *Race Equality – the Home Secretary's Employment Targets: First Annual Report on Progress*.

Otherwise research in this area comes from two sources: individual research studies on the experiences of ethnic minority practitioners in particular criminal justice agencies, such as the police; and from reports of Her Majesty's Inspectors. As regards the former, the empirical literature is most extensive for policing, for example Holdaway (1996) *The Racialisation of British Policing*, Holdaway and Barron's (1997) *Resigners? The Experience of Black and Asian Police Officers* and Bland *et al.*'s (1999) *Career Progression of Ethnic Minority Police Officers*. Shiner's (1997) longitudinal study of law students, Alfred's (1992) *Black Workers in the Prison Service*, and Francis-Spence's (1995) 'Justice: Do They Mean for Us? Black Probation Officers and Black Clients in the Probation Service', in D. Ward and M. Lacey (eds), *Probation: Working for Justice*, are suggested for further reading on the experiences of ethnic minorities in the other criminal justice agencies.

There is now an extensive literature published by the various inspectorates such as Her Majesty's Inspectorate of Constabulary (1995) *Developing Diversity in the Police Service*, (1997) *Winning the Race: Policing Plural Communities*, (1999) *Winning the Race Revisited: Policing Plural Communities*, (2000) *Winning Consent: a Review of Murder Investigation and Community and Race Relations in the Metropolitan Police Service*, and Her Majesty's Inspectorate of Probation (2000) *Towards Race Equality*. Details about ethnic minority professional associations, including the Black Police Association, the Society of Black Lawyers, the African, Caribbean and Asian Lawyers Group, and the Association of Black Probation Officers, can be found by searching the 1990 Trust website *www.blink.org.uk*.

Chapter 10 Conclusion

Thinking about the future of racism, crime and justice is by definition speculative. We identify positive developments such as the implementation of the Stephen Lawrence Inquiry recommendations, the introduction of the 1998 Human Rights Act and the 2000 Race Relations (Amendment) Act, the impact of which is too early to judge. We are drawn, however, to signs that New Labour are seeking to emulate the fierce crime control measures that have had such a devastating impact on African American communities in the USA. We direct the reader to Michael Tonry's (1995) *Malign Neglect: Race, Crime, and Punishment in America*, Jerome Miller's (1996) *Search and Destroy*, Kathryn Russell's (1998) *The Color of Crime* and David Garland's (2001) *The Culture of Control.*

Bibliography

1990 Trust (1998) *Submission to part II of the Stephen Lawrence Inquiry*. London: 1990 Trust.

ABPO (1995) 'The Association of Black Probation Officers', Leaflet.

Agozino, B. (1997) *Black Women and the Criminal Justice System: Towards the Decolonisation of Victimisation*. Aldershot: Ashgate.

Albrecht, H-J. (1997) 'Ethnic Minorities Crime and Criminal Justice in Germany', in Tonry (ed.), *Ethnicity, Crime and Immigration*, Crime and Justice, 21. London: University of Chicago Press.

Alexander, C. (2000a) *The Asian Gang: Ethnicity, Identity, Masculinity*. Oxford: Berg.

Alexander, C. (2000b) '(Dis)Entangling the "Asian Gang": Ethnicity, Identity and Masculinity', in B. Hesse (ed.), *Un/settled Multiculturalisms*. London: Zed Books.

Alfred, R. (1992) *Black Workers in the Prison Service*. London: Prison Reform Trust.

All Faiths for One Race (1978) *Talking Blues*. London: AFFOR.

Allport, G.W. (1954) *The Nature of Prejudice*. Reading, MA: Addison-Wesley.

Anthias, F. (1992) 'Connecting "Race" and Ethnic Phenomena', *Sociology*, 26, 3, 421–38.

Anthias, F. and Yuval-Davis, N. (1992) *Racialized Boundaries*. London: Routledge.

Asafu-Adjaye, J. (1996) 'A Force to be Reckoned With', *Weekly Journal*, 6–12 November.

Atkinson, G (1993) 'Germany: Nationalism, Nazism and Violence', in T. Bjørgo and R. Witte (eds), *Racist Violence In Europe*. London: Macmillan.

Audit Commission (1999) *Missing Out: LEA Management of School Attendance and Exclusion*. Abingdon: Audit Commission Publications.

Audit Commission (date)

Aye Maung, N. (1995) *Young People, Victimisation and the Police: British Crime Survey Findings on the Experiences and Attitudes of 12–15 Year Olds*, Home Office Research Study 140. London: Home Office.

Aye Maung, N. and Mirrlees-Black, C. (1994) *Racially Motivated Crime: A British Crime Survey Analysis*, Home Office Research and Planning Unit Paper 82. London: Home Office.

Back, L. (1996) *New Ethnicities and Urban Culture*. London: University College Press.

Back, L., Keith, M. and Solomos, J. (1998) 'Racism on the Internet: Mapping Neo-Fascist Subcultures in Cyberspace', in J. Kaplan and T. Bjørgo, *Nation and Race*. New York: New York University Press.

Back, L. and Solomos, J. (2000) *Theories of Race and Racism: A Reader*. London and New York: Routledge.

Bagilhole, B. (1997) *Equal Opportunities and Social Policy*. London: Longman.

Baldwin, J. and McConville, M. (1979) *Jury Trials*. Oxford: Clarendon Press.

Ball, C. (2000) 'The Youth Justice and Criminal Evidence Act 1999', *Criminal Law Review*, pp 211–22.

Banton, M. (1967) *Race Relations*. London: Tavistock.

Banton, M. (1988) *Racial Consciousness*. London: Longman.

Banton, M. (1994) *Discrimination*. Milton Keynes: Open University Press.

Banton, M. (1996) *International Action Against Racial Discrimination*. Oxford: Clarendon Press.

Barclay, G.C. (1995) *The Criminal Justice System in England and Wales*, Digest 3. London: Home Office.

Barclay, G. and Mhlanga, B. (2000) 'Ethnic Differences in Decisions on Young Defendants Dealt With by the Crown Prosecution Service', Home Office Section 95, Findings 1. London: Home Office.

Barker, M. (1981) *The New Racism*. London: Junction.

Barker, M. *et al.* (1993) 'The Prevention of Street Robbery'. Police Research Group Crime Prevention Unit Paper 44. London: Home Office.

Bayne-Smith, M. and McBarnette, L. (1996) 'Redefining Health in the Twenty-First Century', in M. Bayne-Smith *Race, Gender and Health*. Thousand Oaks, CA, London and New Delhi: Sage.

BBC (1995) 'Juries Suspected of Race Bias, According to Harris Poll', BBC News Release, 28 November.

Beck, E.M. and Tolnay, S.E. (1995) 'Violence toward African Americans in the Era of the White Lynch Mob', in D. Hawkins (ed.), *Ethnicity, Race and Crime: Perspectives across Time and Place*. Albany: State University of New York Press.

Becker, H.S. (1963) *Outsiders: Studies in the Sociology of Deviance*. London: Free Press of Glencoe.

Becker, H.S. (1967) 'Whose Side Are We On?', *Social Problems*, 14, 3, 239–47.

Bennetto, J. (1998) 'Prison Officers Accused of Brutality and Racial Abuse Assaults on Inmates', *Independent*, 19 March.

Benyon, J. (ed.), (1984) *Scarman and After*. Oxford: Pergamon.

Benyon, J. and Solomos, J. (eds), (1987) *The Roots of Urban Unrest*. Oxford: Pergamon.

Berthoud, R. (1997) 'Income and Standards of Living' in T. Modood and R. Berthoud, *Ethnic Minorities in Britain*. London: Policy Studies Institute.

Berthoud, R. and Beishan, S. (1997) 'People, Families and Households', in R. Berthoud and T. Modood, *Ethnic Minorities in Britain*. London: Policy Study Institute.

Bethnal Green and Stepney Trades Council (1978) *Blood on the Streets*. London: Bethnal Green and Stepney Trades Council.

Bierne, P. and Messerschmidt, J. (1995) *Criminology* (2nd edn). Fort Worth: Harcourt Brace College Publishers.

Birmingham Post (1968) 'Speech that has raised a storm', 22 April.

Bittner, E. (1970) *The Functions of the Police in Modern Society: A Review of Background Factors, Current Practices and Possible Role Models*. Chevy Chase, MD: National Institution of Mental Health.

Bjørgo, T. (1993) 'Terrorist Violence Against Immigrants and Refugees in Scandinavia: Patterns and Motives', in. T. Bjørgo and R. Witte (eds), *Racist Violence in Europe*. London: Macmillan.

Bjørgo T. and Kaplan, J. (eds) (1998), *Nation and Race: The Developing Euro-American Racist Subculture*. Boston, MA: Northeastern University Press.

Bjørgo, T. and Witte, R. (eds) (1993), *Racist Violence in Europe*. London: Macmillan.

Black Justice Project (1995) *Black Justice Project: Annual Report April 1994–March 1995*. Sheffield: Black Justice Project.

Black Police Association (1997a) *Annual Report 1996–97*. London.

Black Police Association (1997b) 'Black Police Officers to be Excluded From National Police Promotions Exam', *Headliner*, 1, 1, 1–4. London.

Black Police Association (1998) *Submission to part II of the Stephen Lawrence Inquiry*. London: BPA.

Bland, N. and Miller, J. (2000) *Police Stops, Decision-Making and Practice Police*, Home Office Police Research Series Paper 130. London: Home Office.

Bland, N., Miller, J. and Quinton, P. (2000) *Upping the PACE? An Evaluation of the Recommendations of the Stephen Lawrence Inquiry on Stops and Searches*, Home Office Police Research Series Paper 128. London: Home Office.

Bland, N., Mundy, G., Russell, J. and Tuffin, R. (1999) *Career Progression of Ethnic Minority Police Officers*. Home Office Police Research Series Paper 107, London: Research, Development and Statistics Directorate. London: Home Office.

Blom-Cooper, L. and Drabble, R. (1982) 'Police Perception of Crime: Brixton and the Operational Response', *British Journal of Criminology*, 22, 184–7.

Blumenbach, J.F. (1865) *The Anthropological Treatises of Friederich Blumenbach*, trans and ed. by Thomas Bendyshe. London: Anthropological Society.

Blumstein, A. (1982) 'On the Racial Disproportionality of United States' Prison Populations', *Journal of Criminal Law and Criminology*, 73, 1259–81.

Blumstein, A. (1993) 'Racial Disproportionality of US Prison Populations Revisited', *University of Colorado Law Review*, 64, 743–60.

Bonnett, A. (1995) *Radicalism, Anti-racism and Representation*. London: Routledge.

Bonnett, A. (2000) *Anti-racism*. London: Routledge.

Bottomley, A.K. and Coleman, C.A.C. (1981) *Understanding Crime Rates: Police and Public Roles in the Production of Official Statistics*. Farnborough, Hants: Gower.

Bottomley, A.K. and Pease, K. (1986) *Crime and Punishment: Interpreting the Data*. Milton Keynes: Open University Press.

Bottoms, A.E. and Wiles, P. (1994) 'Crime and Insecurity in the City', Paper to be presented at the International Society of Criminology International Course on 'Changes in Society, crime and criminal justice in Europe', Leuven, Belgium, May 1994. Cambridge: Cambridge Institute of Criminology.

Bourgois, P.I. (1995) *In Search of Respect: Selling Crack in El Barrio*. Cambridge: Cambridge University Press.

Bourne, J., Bridges, L. and Searle, C. (1997) *Outcast England: How Schools Exclude Black Children*. London: Institute for Race Relations.

Bourne, J., Searle, C. and Bridges, L. (1994) *Outcast England*. London: Institute of Race Relations.

Bowling, B. (1990) 'Conceptual and Methodological Problems in Measuring "Race" Differences in Delinquency: A Reply to Marianne Junger', *British Journal of Criminology*, 30, 483–92.

Bowling, B. (1991) 'Ethnic Minority Elderly People: Helping the Community to Care', *New Community*, 17, 4, July, 645–54.

Bowling, B. (1993a), 'Racial Harassment and the Process of Victimization: Conceptual and Methodological Implications for the Local Crime Survey', *British Journal of Criminology*, 33, 1, 231–50.

Bowling, B. (1993b) 'Racial Harassment in East London', in M.S. Hamm (ed.), *Hate Crime: International Perspectives on Causes and Control*. Cincinnati, OH: Academy of Criminal Justice Sciences/Anderson Publications.

Bowling, B. (1996a) 'Violent racism in Britain 1958–1981' in P. Panayi (ed.), *Racial Violence in Britain* (2nd edn). London: Leicester University Press/ Pinter.

Bowling, B. (1996b) 'Cracking Down on Crime in New York City', *Criminal Justice Matters*, No. 25, Autumn.

Bowling, B. (1998) 'Violent Racism: Submission to the Stephen Lawrence Inquiry', Cambridge: Cambridge Institute of Criminology.

Bowling, B. (1999a) *Violent Racism: Victimisation, Policing and Social Context* (Revised edn). Oxford: Oxford University Press.

Bowling, B. (1999b) 'The Rise and Fall of New York Murder: Zero Tolerance or Crack's Decline?', *British Journal of Criminology*, 39, 4, Autumn, 531–54.

Bowling, B. (1999c) '*Arresting the Abuse of Police Power: Review of the Met's Report on Stop and Search*. "Diversity on Line",' December 1999.

Bowling, B. (2001) 'Racist offenders: punishment, justice and community safety', *Criminal Justice Matters*, No. 43, Spring 30–31.

Bowling, B., Graham, J. and Ross, A. (1994) 'Self-reported offending among young people in England and Wales', in J. Junger-Tas, J.G. Terlouw and M. Klein, *Delinquent Behaviour Among Young People in the Western World*. Amsterdam: Kugler.

Bowling, B. and Campbell, C. (1999) 'Towards an Anti-Racist Policing Strategy for the Metropolitan Police Service', London: Metropolitan Police.

Bowling, B., Malik, M. and Wintemute, R. (2000) 'Comment on Proposed Legislative Measures and Action Plan', Based on Article 13 of the EC (Implementing the Principle of Equal Treatment between Persons Irrespective of Racial or Ethnic Origin), Submission to the House of Lords European Union Committee, Sub-committee F (social affairs, education and home affairs), London: House of Lords.

274 Bibliography

Bowling, B. and Saulsbury, W.E. (1993) 'A Local Response to Racial Harassment', in T. Bjørgo and R. Witte (eds), *Racist Violence in Europe*. London: Macmillan.

Box, S. (1981) *Deviance, Reality and Society* (2nd edn). London: Holt, Rinehart & Winston.

Box, S. (1987) *Recession, Crime and Punishment*. Basingstoke: Macmillan.

Bradford Commission Report (1996) *The Bradford Commission Report: The Report of an Inquiry into the Wider Implications of Public Disorders in Bradford which Occurred on 9, 10 and 11 June 1995*, Bradford Congress. London: Home Office.

Bratton, W. (1997) 'Crime is Down in New York: Blame the Police', in N. Dennis (ed.), *Zero Tolerance: Policing a Free Society*. London: Institute of Economic Affairs.

Brennan, P.A., Mednick, S.A. and Yolavka, J. (1995) 'Biomedical Factors in Crime', in J.Q. Wilson and J. Petersilia (eds), *Crime*. San Francisco, CA: ICS Press.

Bridges, L. (2000) 'The Lawrence Inquiry – Incompetence, Corruption and Institutional Racism', *Journal of Law and Society*, 26, 3, September, 289–322.

Bridges, D. and McLaughlin, T.H. (eds) (1994) *Education in the Market Place*. London and Washington, DC: Falmer Press.

Bridges, L. (1982) 'Racial Attacks', *Legal Action Group Bulletin*, January.

Briggs, C. (1995) 'Policing Moss Side: a Probation Response', *Probation Journal*, 42, 2, June, 66–6.

Britton, J. (1997) *An Evaluation of the Sheffield Black Justice Project*, Sheffield Department of Sociological Studies: Sheffield University.

Britton, N.J. (2000) 'Race and Policing: A Study of Police Custody', *British Journal of Criminology*, 40, 639–58.

BMRB (1999) *Social Research Report: Home Office Staff Survey*, London: BMRB.

Broadwater Farm Inquiry (1985) *Report of the Independent Inquiry into Disturbances of October 1985 at the Broadwater Farm Estate, Tottenham*, Chaired by Lord Gifford QC. London: Karia Press.

Brown, B. (1990) 'Reassessing the critique of biologism', in L. Gelsthorpe and A. Morris (eds), *Feminist Perspectives in Criminology*. Milton Keynes: Open University Press.

Brown, C. (1984) *Black and White Britain: The Third PSI Survey*. London: Heinemann.

Brown, D. (1997) *PACE Ten Years On: A Review of the Research*, Home Office Research Study 155, Home Office Research and Statistics Directorate. London: Home Office.

Brown, J. (1984) *Policing and Social Policy: The Cranfield-Wolfson Colloquium on Multi-Ethnic Areas in Europe*. London: Police Review Publishing Company.

Brown, J. (1997) 'Equal Opportunities and the Police in England and Wales: Past, Present and Future Possibilities', in P. Francis, P. Davies and V. Jupp (eds), *Policing Futures: The Police, Law Enforcement and the 21st Century*. Basingstoke: Macmillan.

Brown, I. and Hullin, R. (1992) 'A Study of Sentencing in the Leeds Magistrates' Courts', *British Journal of Criminology*, 32, 1, 41–53.

Brown, I. and Hullin, R. (1993) 'Contested Bail Applications: The Treatment of Ethnic Minority and White Offenders', *Criminal Law Review*, 93, 160, 107–13.

Browne, D. (1997) *Black People and 'Sectioning': The Black Experience of Detention under the Civil Sections of the Mental Health Act.* London: Little Rock.

Browne, D. (1990) *Black People, Mental Health and the Courts.* London: NACRO.

Bucke, T. (1995) *Policing and the Public: Findings from the 1994 British Crime Survey*, Research Findings No. 28, Home Office Research and Statistics Department. London: Home Office.

Bucke, T. (1997) *Ethnicity and Contacts with the Police: Latest Findings from the British Crime Survey*, Home Office Research Findings 59. London: Home Office.

Bucke, T. and Brown, D. (1997) *In Police Custody: Police Powers and Suspects' Rights Under the Revised PACE Codes of Practice*, Home Office Research Study 174. London: Home Office.

Bufford, B. (1991) *Among the Thugs.* London: Mandarin.

Burleigh, M. (1994) *Death and Deliverance: 'Euthanasia' in Germany c.1900–1945.* Cambridge: Cambridge University Press.

Burleigh, M. and Wipperman,W. (1991) *The Racial State: Germany 1933–1945.* Cambridge: Cambridge University Press.

Burnett, R. and Farrell, G. (1994) *Reported and Unreported Racial Incidents in Prisons*, Occasional Paper No. 14. Oxford: University of Oxford Centre for Criminological Research.

Burney, E. (1990) *Putting Street Crime in Its Place: A Report to the Community/Police Consultative Group for Lambeth*, London: Centre for Inner City Studies, Department of Social Science and Administration, Goldsmiths' College.

Burrell, I. (1998) 'Jails Chief Urged to Quit Over Race Claim', *Independent*, 24 April.

Burrows, J.N., Henderson, P.F. and Morgan, P.M. (1995) *Improving Bail Decisions: The Bail Process Project, Phase 1.* London: Home Office.

Burrows, J.N, Henderson, P.F and Morgan, P.M. (1994) *Improving Bail Decisions: The Bail Process Project, Phase I.* Home Office Research and Planning Unit Paper 90. London: Home Office.

Butler, G. (1999) *Inquiry into Crown Prosecution Service Decision-Making in Relation to Deaths in Custody and Related Matters*, August 1999. http://www.official-documents.co.uk/document/cps/custody/contents.htm

Butler, J. (1997) *Excitable Speech: A Politics of the Performative.* London and New York: Routledge.

Caddle, D. and Crisp, D. (1997) *Imprisoned Women and Mothers*, Home Office Research Study 162. London: Home Office.

Cain, M. (1973) *Society and the Policeman's Role.* London: Routledge.

Cain, M. (1986) 'Realism, Feminism, Methodology, and Law', *International Journal of the Sociology of Law*, 14, 255–67.

Cain, M. and Sadigh, S. (1982) 'Racism, the Police and Community Policing: A comment on the Scarman Report', *Journal of Law and Society*, 9, 1, pages.

Campaign Against Racism and Fascism (1981) *Southall: The Birth of a Black Community*, London Institute of Race Relations and Southall Rights.

Campaign Against Racism and Fascism (1996).

Campaign Against Racism and Fascism (1997) No. 39, August/September.

Campbell, A. I. (1998) *Racism on the Internet: Towards a "Virtual" Ethnography*, Unpublished M.Phil thesis. Cambridge: Cambridge Institute of Criminology.

Campbell, B. (1993) *Goliath: Britain's Dangerous Places*. London: Methuen.

Cao, L., Adams, A. and Jensen, V. (1997) 'A Test of the Black Subculture of Violence Thesis: A Research Note', *Criminology*, 35, 2,

Caribbean Times (1996) 'Record Damages to Racially Abused Prison Officer', 19 December.

Carmichael, S. and Hamilton, C. (1968) *Black Power: The Politics of Liberation*. Harmondsworth: Penguin.

Carter, B., Harris, C. and Joshi, S. (1993) 'The 1951–55 Conservative Government and the Racialisation of Black Immigration', in W. James and C. Harris (eds), *Inside Babylon*. London: Verso.

Cashmore, E. (1991) 'Black Cops Inc.', in E. Cashmore and E. Mclaughlin (eds) (1991) *Out of Order?: Policing Black People*. London: Routledge.

Cashmore, E. (1996) *Dictionary of Race and Ethnic Relations* (4th edn). London: Routledge.

Cashmore, E. and McLaughlin, E. (1991) *Out of Order?: Policing Black People*. London: Routledge.

Cathcart, B. (1999) *The Case of Stephen Lawrence*. London: Viking.

Cavadino, M. and Dignan, J. (1992) *The Penal System: An Introduction*. London: Sage.

Cavalli-Sforza, L.L., Menozzi, P. and Piazza, A. (1994) *The History and Geography of Human Genes*. Princeton, NJ and Chichester: Princeton University Press.

CCSC (1982) *The Empire Strikes Back: Race and Racism in 70s Britain*. London: Hutchinson in association with the Centre for Contemporary Cultural Studies.

Chahal, K., and Julienne, L. (1999) *'We Can't All be White!': Racist Victimisation in the UK*. York: York Publishing Services.

Chambliss, W.J. and Nagasawa, R.H. (1969) 'On the Validity of Official Statistics – A Comparison of White, Black and Japanese High School Boys', *Journal of Research in Crime and Delinquency*, 6, 71–7.

Chan, J. (1997) *Changing Police Culture: Policing in a Multicultural Society*. Cambridge: Cambridge University Press.

Cheney, D. (1993) *Into the Dark Tunnel: Foreign Prisoners in the British Prison System*. London: Prison Reform Trust.

Chigwada-Bailey, R. (1989) 'Black Women's Unequal Experiences of Prison Education', *Gender and Education*, 1, 2, 199–201.

Chigwada-Bailey, R. (1997) *Black Women's Experiences of Criminal Justice: Discourse on Disadvantage*. Winchester: Waterside Press.

Choong, S. (1998) *Policing as Social Discipline*. Oxford: Oxford University Press.

Clements, J. (2000) 'Assessment of Race Relations at HMP Brixton', http://www.hmprisonservice.gov.uk/filestore/202_206.pdf

Cloward, R.A. and Ohlin, L.E. (1961) *Delinquency and Opportunity: A Theory of Delinquent Gangs.* London: Routledge & Kegan Paul.

Cohen, A. (1955) *Delinquent Boys: The Culture of the Gang.* New York: The Free Press.

Cohen, P. (1997) *Rethinking the Youth Question: Education, Labour and Cultural Studies.* Basingstoke: Macmillan.

Cohen, P. (1999) *New Ethnicities, Old Racisms.* London: Zed.

Cohen, S. (1972) *Folk Devils and Moral Panics: The Creation of Mods and Rockers.* London: MacGibbon & Kee.

Coleman, A. and Gorman, L. (1982) 'Conservatism, Dogmatism and Authoritarianism in British Police Officers', *Sociology*, February.

Coleman, C. and Moynihan, J. (1996) *Understanding Crime Data: Haunted by the Dark Figure.* Milton Keynes: Open University Press.

Collinson, M. (1996) 'In Search of the High Life: Drugs, Crime, Masculinity and Consumption', *British Journal of Criminology*, 36, 3, 428–44.

Commission of the European Communities (1999) Communication from the Commission No. 564, 25 November 1999. Brussels.

Commission for Racial Equality (1979) *Brick Lane and Beyond: An Inquiry into Racial Strife and Violence in Tower Hamlets*, London: Commission for Racial Equality.

Commission for Racial Equality (1989 *Racial Justice in Magistrates' Courts: The Case for Training.* London.

Commission for Racial Equality (1990a) *Bail Hostels and Racial Equality.* London.

Commission for Racial Equality (1990b) *Sorry, It's Gone: Testing for Racial Discrimination in the Private Rented Housing Sector.* London.

Commission for Racial Equality (1991) *Second Review of the Race Relations Act 1976: Consultative Paper.* London.

Commission for Racial Equality (1991b) *The Point of Order: A Study of Consultative Arrangements under Section 106 of the Police and Criminal Evidence Act*, London.

Commission for Racial Equality (1992) *Cautions v. Prosecutions: Ethnic Monitoring of Juveniles by Seven Police Forces.* London.

Commission for Racial Equality (1995) *Further Education and Equality: A Manager's Manual.* London.

Commission for Racial Equality (1997) *Exclusion from School and Racial Equality: Research Report.* London.

Commission for Racial Equality (1998) *Submission to Part II of the Lawrence Inquiry.* London.

Commission for Racial Equality (1999) *Royal Commission on Criminal Justice: CRE Supplementary Evidence: Racially Mixed Juries.* London.

Cook, D. and Hudson, B. (1993) *Racism and Criminology.* London: Sage.

Corkery, J. (2000) *Drug Seizure and Offender Statistics,* United Kingdom, 1998, Home Office Statistical Bulletin 31/00, 16 February. London: Home Office.

Cornish, D.A. and Clarke, R.V. (1986) *The Reasoning Criminal: Rational Choice Perspectives on Offending.* New York: Springer.

Corsellis, A. (1995) *Non-English Speakers and the English Legal System*, Cropwood Occasional Paper No. 20. Cambridge: Cambridge Institute of Criminology.

Cotton, J. and Povey, K. (1997) *Police Complaints and Deaths in Police Custody in England and Wales*, Home Office Statistical Bulletin 21/97. London: Home Office.

Crandon, L. (1997) 'Multi-Cultural Revolution', *Police Review*, 105, 5447, 22–3.

Crawford, A. (1999) *Crime Prevention and Community Safety*. London: Longman.

Crawford., Jones, T., Woodhouse, T. and Young, J. (1990) *The Second Islington Crime Survey*. Middlesex: Middlesex Polytechnic Centre for Criminology.

Crenshaw, R., Delvin, B. and Williamson, T. (1998) *Human Rights and Policing: Standards for Good Behaviour and a Strategy for Change*. London: Kluwer.

Criminal Justice Consultative Council Race Sub-group (2000) *Race and the Criminal Justice System: Joining Up to Promote Equality and Encourage Diversity*.

Crisp, D. and Moxon, D. (1994) *Case screening by the Crown Prosecution: How and Why Cases are Terminated*, Home Office Research Study 137. London: Home Office.

Cross, M. and Smith, D.I. (1987) *Black Youth Futures: Ethnic Minorities and the Youth Training Scheme*. Leicester: National Youth Bureau.

Crow, I. and Cove, J. (1984) 'Ethnic Minorities in the Courts', *Criminal Law Review* (July), 413–17.

Crown Prosecution Service (1994) *The Code for Crown Prosecutors*. London: CPS.

Curtis, L. (1974) *Criminal Violence: National Patterns and Behavior*. Lexington, MA: D.C. Heath & Co.

Daniel, W.W. (1968) *Racial Discrimination in England*. Harmondsworth: Penguin.

Darwin, C. (1859) *On the Origin of Species* (The Origin of species by means of natural selection, or, The Preservation of favoured races in the struggle for life). The Works of Charles Darwin, vol. 15. London: John Murray.

Dashwood, A. (1972) 'Juries in a Multi-Racial Society', *Criminal Law Review* (February), 85–94.

Demuth, C. (1978) *'Sus' a Report on the Vagrancy Act 1824*. London: Runnymede Trust.

Denney, D. (1992) *Racism and Anti-Racism in Probation*. London: Routledge.

Dennis, N. (ed.) (1997) *Zero Tolerance: Policing a Free Society* (2nd edn). London: IEA Health and Welfare Unit.

Dennis, N., Erdos, G. and Al-Shahi, A. (2000) *Racist Murder and Pressure Group Politics: The Macpherson Report and the Police*. London: Institute for the Study of Civil Society.

Department for Education and Employment (2000) *Statistics of Education: Permanent Exclusions from Maintained Schools in England*. Bulletin Issue No. 10/00. London.

Desai, P. (1998) *Spaces of Identity, Cultures of Conflict: The Development of New British Asian Identities*, Ph.D dissertation, Goldsmiths' College, University of London.

Dilulio, J. (1987) *Governing Prisons: A Comparative Study of Correctional Management*. New York: Free Press.

Dixon, D., Coleman, C. and Bottomley, K. (1990) 'Consent and the Legal Regulation of Policing', *Journal of Law and Society*, 17, 3, 345–59.

Dominelli, L., Jeffers, L., Jones, G., Sibanda, S. and Williams, B. (1995) *Anti-Racist Probation Practice*. Aldershot: Arena.

Dowds, L. and Young, K. (1996) 'National Identity', in R. Jowell *et al.*, (eds), *British Social Attitudes: The 13th Report*. Dartmouth: Dartmouth Publishing Company.

Downes, D.M. (1966) *The Delinquent Solution: A Study in Subcultural Theory*. London: Routledge & Kegan Paul.

Drury, B. (1992) 'Education', The Education Reform Act 1988 and Racial Equality Centre for Research in Ethnic Relations.

Dubois, W.E.B. (1901) *The Souls of Black Folk*. Harmondsworth: Penguin.

Duff, E., Shiner, M., Boon, A. and Whyte, A. (2000) 'Entry into the Legal Professions: The Law Student Cohort Study Year 6', Law Society Research and Policy Planning Unit No. 39. London: Law Society.

Dulaney, M.W. (1996) *Black Police in America*. Bloomington: Indiana University Press.

Dyer, C. (1997) 'Judge Given Rebuke for Race Remark', *Guardian*, 27 March.

Dyer, R. (1988) 'White', *Screen*, 29, 4, 44–5.

Economic and Social Research Council (1998) 'VRP: Violence Research Programme Economic and Social Research Council', Swindon.

Ekblom, P. and Simon, F. (1988) *Crime and Harassment in Asian-Run Small Shops: The Scope for Prevention*, Home Office Crime Prevention Unit Paper 15. London: Home Office.

Ekwe-Ekwe, H. and Nzegwu, F. (1995) *African and Asian Peoples and Bail Hostel Services: a Case Study of Berkshire*. Reading: International Institute for Black Research.

Elkins, M., Gray, C. and Rogers, K. (2001) 'Prison Population Brief', Home Office Research Development Statistics. London: Home Office.

Elliott, D.S. (1982) 'Review essays on Measuring Delinquency', *Criminology*, 20, 527–37.

Engels, F. (1845) *Der Lage der arbeitenden Klassen in England* ('The condition of the working class in England'). Transl. and ed. by W.O. Henderson and W.H. Chaloner 1958. Oxford: Blackwell.

Etzioni, A. (1995) *The Spirit of Community: Rights, Responsibilities, and the Communitarian Agenda*. London: Fontana.

Evans, R. and Wilkinson, C. (1990) 'Variations in Police Cautioning Policy and Practice in England and Wales', *Howard Journal of Criminal Justice*, 29, 155–76.

Eze, E. (1997) *Race and The Enlightenment: A Reader*. Oxford: Blackwell.

Fanon, F. (1967) *Peau noire, masques blancs* ('Black skin, white masks'). Translated by Charles Lam Markmann. New York, NY: Grove Weidenfeld.

Farall, S. and Bowling, B. (1999) 'Structuration, Human Development and Desistance from Crime', *British Journal of Criminology*, 39, 2, Spring, 252–67.

Farrington, D. (1997) 'Human Development and Criminal Careers', in

M. Maguire, R. Morgan and R. Reiner (eds), *The Oxford Handbook of Criminology*, Oxford: Oxford University Press.

Farrington, D.P. and Bennett, T. (1981) 'Police Cautioning of Juveniles in London', *British Journal of Criminology*, 21, 2, 123–35.

Faulkner, D.E.R. (1988) 'Magistrates' Courts and Race Issues', *Magistrate*, 44, 2, 24–5.

Feagin, J.R. and Sikes, M.P. (1994) *Living with Racism: The Black Middle-Class Experience*. Boston, MA.: Beacon Press.

Fekete, L. (1991) 'The Far Right in Europe: A Guide', *Race and Class*, 32, 3, January–March, 127–49.

Ferri, E. (1895) *Criminal Sociology*. London: Fisher Unwin.

Field, S. (1990) *Trends in Crime and Their Interpretation: A Study of Recorded Crime in Post-War England and Wales*, Home Office Study 119. London: Home Office.

Fielding, N. (1995) *Community Policing*. Oxford: Clarendon.

Fionda, J. (1999) 'New Labour, Old Hat: Youth Justice and the Crime and Disorder Act 1998', *Criminal Law Review*, 36–47.

FitzGerald, M. (1993a) 'Racial Discrimination in the Criminal Justice System', Research Bulletin No. 34, Home Office Research and Statistics Department. London: Home Office.

FitzGerald, M. (1993b) *Ethnic Minorities in the Criminal Justice System*, Research Study 20, Royal Commission on Criminal Justice. London: Home Office.

FitzGerald, M. (1997) 'Minorities, Crime, and Criminial Justice in Britain', in I.H. Marshall (ed.), *Minorities, Migrants, and Crime: Diversity and Similarity Across Europe and the United States*. Thousand Oaks, CA: Sage.

FitzGerald, M. (1999) *Searches in London under Section 1 of the Police and Criminal Evidence Act*, London: Metropolitan Police.

FitzGerald, M. and Hale, C. (1996) *Ethnic Minorities: Victimisation and Racial Harassment: Findings from the 1988 and 1992 British Crime Surveys*, Home Office Research Study 154. London: Home Office.

FitzGerald, M. and Marshall, P. (1996) 'Ethnic Minorities in British Prisons: Some Research Implications', in R. Matthews and P. Francis (eds), *Prisons 2000: An International Perspective on the Current State and Future of Imprisonment*. London: Macmillan.

FitzGerald, M. and Sibbitt, R. (1997) *Ethnic Monitoring in Police Forces: A Beginning*, Home Office Research Study 173, Home Office Research and Statistics Directorate. London: Home Office.

Fitzpatrick, B., Hegarty, A. and Maxwell, P. (1995) 'A Comparative Review of Fair Employment and Equal Opportunity Law', in D. Magill and S. Rose (eds), *Fair Employment Law in Northern Ireland: Debates and Issues*. Belfast: SACHR.

Flood Page, C., Campbell, S., Harrington, V. and Miller, J. (2000) *Youth Crime: Findings from the 1998/99 Youth Lifestyle Survey*, Home Office Research Study 209. London: Home Office.

Ford, R. (1998) 'High-Tech Jail Finds the Key', *The Times*, 30 May.

Foster, J. (1989) 'Two Stations: An Ethnographic Study of Policing in the Inner City', in D. Downes (ed.), *Crime in the City*. London: Macmillan.

Foster, J. (1990) *Villains: Crime and Community in the Inner City*. London: Routledge.

Foster, J. (1998) *Docklands: Urban Change and Conflict in a Community in Transition*. London: UCL Press.

Foucault, M. (1977) *Discipline and Punish: The Birth of the Prison*. London: Allen Lane.

Foundation 2000 (1995) *Bradford Riots*

Francis-Spence, M. (1995) 'Justice: Do They Mean for Us? Black Probation Officers and Black Clients in the Probation Service', in D. Ward and M. Lacey (eds), *Probation: Working for Justice*. London: Whiting & Birch.

Frazier, C.E. and Bishop, D.M. (1995) 'Reflections on Race Effects in Juvenile Justice', in K. Kempf Leonard, C.E. Pope and W.H. Feyerherm (eds), *Minorities in Juvenile Justice*. Thousand Oaks, CA: Sage.

Fryer, P. (1984) *Staying Power: The History of Black People in Britain*. London: Pluto.

Galton, Sir. F. (1869) *Hereditary Genius: An Inquiry into Its Laws and Consequences* (1st edn). London: Macmillan.

Garland, D. (2001) *The Culture of Control*. Oxford: Oxford University Press.

Gates, H.L. Jr (1986) *'Race', Writing and Difference*. Chicago: University of Chicago Press.

Gelsthorpe, L. (1992) 'Social Inquiry Reports: Race and Gender Considerations', *Research Bulletin 52*, Home Office Research and Statistics Department. London: Home Office.

Gelsthorpe, L. (ed.) (1993) *Minority Ethnic Groups in the Criminal Justice System*, Papers Presented to 21st Cropwood Roundtable Conference 1992. Cambridge: Cambridge Institute of Criminology.

Gelsthorpe, L. and Morris, A. (1990) *Feminist Perspectives in Criminology*. Milton Keynes: Open University Press.

Gelsthorpe, L. and Morris A. (1994) 'Juvenile Justice 1945–1992', in M. Maguire, R. Morgan and R. Reiner (eds), *The Oxford Handbook of Criminology*. Oxford: Oxford Universtiy Press.

Genders, E. and Player, E. (1989) *Race Relations in Prison*. Oxford: Clarendon Press.

Genn, H. (1988), 'Multiple Victimisation', in M. Maguire and J. Pointing (eds), *Victims of Crime: A New Deal?* Milton Keynes: Open University Press.

Gilroy, P. (1982) 'Police and Thieves', in *CCCS The Empire Strikes Back*. London: Hutchinson.

Gilroy, P. (1987a) *There Ain't No Black in the Union Jack*. London: Hutchinson.

Gilroy, P. (1987b) 'The Myth of Black Criminality', in P. Scraton (ed.), *Law, Order and the Authoritarian State*. Milton Keynes: Open University Press.

Gilroy, P. (1993) *Small Acts: Thoughts on the Politics of Black Cultures*. London and New York: Serpent's Tail.

Gilroy, P. (2000) *Between Camps: Race, Identity and Nationalism at the End of the Colour Line*. London: Allen Lane, The Penguin Press.

Gilroy, P. and Sim, J. (1987) 'Law, Order and the State of the Left', in

P. Scraton (ed.), *Law, Order and the Authoritarian State*. Milton Keynes: Open University Press.

Glaser, B. and Strauss, A. (1967) *The Discovery of Grounded Theory: Strategies for Qualitative Research*. Chicago, IL: Aldine.

Gobineau, A. de. (1853) *The Inequality of Human Races* (translation 1915). New York: Howard Fertig.

Goldberg, D.T. (1993) *Racist Culture*. Oxford: Blackwell.

Goldhagen, D. J. (1996) *Hitler's Willing Executioners: Ordinary Germans and the Holocaust*. London: Little Brown.

Goldsmith, A. (1991) *Complaints Against the Police: The Trend to External Review*. Oxford: Clarendon.

Gordon, P. (1983) *White Law: Racism in the Police, Courts and Prisons*. London: Pluto.

Gordon, P. (1987) 'Community Policing: Towards the Local Police State', in P. Scraton (ed.), *Law, Order and the Authoritarian State*.

Gordon, P. (1988) Black People and the Criminal Law: Rhetoric and Reality, *International Journal of the Sociology of Law*, 16, 295–313.

Gordon, P. (1990) *Racial Violence and Harassment* (2nd edn). London: Runneymede Trust.

Gordon, P. (1993) 'The Police and Racist Violence in Britain'. In T. Bjorgo and R. Witte (eds.) *Racist Violence in Europe*. London: Macmillan.

Gordon, P. and Rosenberg, D. (1989) *Daily Racism: The Press and Black People in Britain*. London: Runneymede Trust.

Goring, C.B. (1913) *The English Convict: A Statistical Study*. London: Home Office.

Gottfredson, M.R. and Hirschi, T. (1990) *A General Theory of Crime*. Stanford, CA: Stanford University Press.

Graef, R. (1989) *Talking Blues: The Police in Their Own Words*. London: Collins Harvill.

Graham, J. and Bowling, B. (1995) *Young People and Crime*, Home Office Research Study 145. London: Home Office.

Green, R. (1989) 'Probation and the Black Offender', *New Community*, 16, 1, 81–91.

Greene, H. and Gabbidon, S.L. (2000) *African American Criminological Thought*. Albany NY: State University of New York Press.

Grimshaw, R. and Jefferson, R. (1987) *Interpreting Policework*. London: Allen & Unwin.

Gurdip Kaur Campaign, 'Fighting for Justice', in C. Dunhill, *The Boys in Blue*. London: Virago.

Gutzmore, C (1983) 'Capital, 'black youth' and crime' *Race and Class*, 25, 2, 13–21.

Guze, S. B. (1976) *Criminality and Psychiatric Disorders*. New York: Oxford University Press.

Hales, J. and Stratford, N. (1996) '1996 British Crime Survey (England and Wales)', Technical Report. London: Social and Community Planning Research.

Halevy, T. (1995) 'Racial Discrimination in Sentencing? A Study with Dubious Conclusions', *Criminal Law Review*, 267–71.

Hall, S. (1980) *Drifting in to Law and Order Society*. London: Cobden Trust.

Hall, S. (1988) 'New Ethnicities', in K. Mercer (ed.), *Black Film/British Cinema*. London: Institute of Contemporary Arts.

Hall, S., Critcher, C., Jefferson, T., Clarke, J. and Roberts, B. (1978) *Policing the Crisis: Mugging, the State and Law and Order*. London: Macmillan.

Hall, S., Lewis, G. and McLaughlin, E. (1998) *The Report on Racial Stereotyping* (prepared for Deighton Guedalla, solicitors for Duwayne Brooks, June 1998). Milton Keynes: Open University.

Hamm, M.S. (1993) *American Skinheads: The Criminology and Control of Hate Crime*. Westport, CO: Praeger.

Hamm, M.S. (ed.) (1994), *Hate Crime: International Perspectives on Causes and Control*. Cincinnati, OH: Academy of Criminal Justice Sciences/Anderson Publications.

Haney-Lopez, I. (1996) *White by Law: The Legal Construction of Race*. New York: New York University Press.

Hansard (1987) 'Written Answers', 30 October. London: Home Office.

Hansard (1996) 'House of Commons Official Report', Parliamentary Debates, Commons 1995–1996 Volume 274. London: Home Office.

Hansard (1998) 'Positional Asphyxia'. 22 April 1998: Column 636. London: Home Office.

Harding, L. (1998) '£200,000 for Police Fit-up', *Guardian*, 20 January.

Harris, C. (1988) 'Images of Blacks in Britain: 1930–60', in S. Allen and M. Macey (eds), *Race and Social Policy*. London: Economic and Social Research Council.

Harrison, M. (1995) *Housing, 'Race', Social Policy and Empowerment*. Aldershot: Avebury.

Hedderman, C. and Moxon, D. (1992) *Magistrates' Court or Crown Court?: Mode of Trial Decisions and Sentencing*, Home Office Research Study 125. London: Home Office.

Herbert, D. P. (1995) 'Racism, Impartiality and Juries', *New Law Journal*, 1138–40.

Her Majesty's Inspectorate of Constabulary (1995) *Developing Diversity in the Police Service. Equal Opportunities Thematic Inspection Report 1995*. London: Home Office.

Her Majesty's Inspectorate of Constabulary (1997) *Winning the Race: Policing Plural Communities*, HMIC Thematic Inspection Report on Police Community and Race Relations 1996/7. London: Home Office.

Her Majesty's Inspectorate of Constabulary (1999) *Winning the Race Revisited: Policing Plural Communities. A Follow-up to the Thematic Inspection Report on Police Community and Race Relations 1998/9*. London: Home Office.

Her Majesty's Inspectorate of Constabulary (2000) *Policing London. Winning Consent: A Review of Murder Investigation and Community and Race Relations Issues in the Metropolitan Police Service*. London: Home Office.

Her Majesty's Inspectorate of Constabulary (2000) *Winning the Race: Embracing Diversity. Consolidation Inspection of Police Community and Race Relations 2000*. London: Home Office.

284 Bibliography

Her Majesty's Inspectorate of Constabulary (2001) *Winning the Race III: Embracing Diversity*. London: Home Office.

Her Majesty's Inspectorate of Prisons (1998a) *Campsfield House Detention Centre, Report of an Unannounced Short Inspection 13–15 October 1997*. London: Home Office.

Her Majesty's Inspectorate of Prisons (1998b) *Tinsley House Immigration Detention Centre, Gatwick Airport, Report of a Full Inspection 4–7 August 1997*. London: Home Office.

Her Majesty's Inspectorate of Prisons (1999) *Report of an Unannounced Inspection of HM Prison Wormwood Scrubs*, London: Home Office.

Her Majesty's Inspectorate of Probation (2000) *Towards Race Equality. Thematic Inspection*, London: Home Office.

Herbert, P. (2001) *Metropolitan Police Stop and Search*, Unpublished Discussion Paper.

Hercules, T. (1999) *Labelled a Black Villain*. London: Fourth Estate.

Herrnstein, R.J. (1995) 'Criminogenic Traits', in J.Q. Wilson and J. Petersilia, (eds) *Crime*, San Fransico, CA: ICS Press.

Herrnstein, R.J. and Murray, C. (1994) *The Bell Curve: Intelligence and Class Structure in American Life*. New York and London: Free Press.

Hesse, B., Rai, D.K., Bennett, C. and McGilchrist, P. (1992) *Beneath the Surface: Racial Harassment*. Aldershot: Avebury.

Hindelang, M., Hirschi, T. and Weis, J. (1981) *Measuring Delinquency*. Beverly Hills: Sage.

Hiro, D. (1992) *Black British White British: A History of Race Relations in Britain*. London: Paladin.

Hirschi, T. and Hindelang, M. (1997) 'Intelligence and Delinquency: A Revisionist Review', *American Sociological Review*, 42, 571–87.

Hobbs, D. (1988) *Doing the Business*. Oxford: Open University Press.

Holdaway, S. (1983) *Inside the British Police*. Oxford: Blackwell.

Holdaway, S. (1991) *Recruiting a Multi-Ethnic Police Force*. London: Home Office.

Holdaway, S. (1993) *The Resignation of Black and Asian Officers from the Police Service*. London: Home Office.

Holdaway, S. (1996) *The Racialisation of British Policing*. London: Macmillan.

Holdaway, S. (1997) 'Some Recent Approaches to the Study of Race in Criminological Research: Race as Social Process', *British Journal of Criminology*, 37, 3, 383–400.

Holdaway, S. and Allaker, J. (1990) *Race Issues in the Probation Service: A Review of Policy*. Wakefield: Association of Chief Officers of Probation.

Holdaway, S. and Barron, A. (1997) *Resigners? The Experience of Black and Asian Police Officers*. London: Macmillan.

Holmes, C. (1988) *John Bull's Island: Immigration and British Society, 1871–1971*. London: Macmillan.

Home Office (1981) *Racial Attacks*. London: Home Office.

Home Office (1982) *Report on the Work of the Prison Department 1981*, Cmnd 8543. London: Home Office.

Home Office (1983) *Crime Statistics for the Metropolitan Police District Analysed by Ethnic Group*, Home Office Statistical Bulletin Issue 22/83. London: Home Office.

Home Office (1984) *Police and Criminal Evidence Act 1984 (s. 66) Code of Practice (A) on Stop and Search*, London: Home Office.

Home Office (1986) *The Ethnic Origins of Prisoners: the Prison Population on 30 June 1985 and Persons Received, July 1984–March 1985*, Home Office Statistical Bulletin Issue 17/86. London: Home Office.

Home Office (1989a) *Crime Statistics for the Metropolitan Police District by Ethnic Group, 1987: Victims, Suspects and Those Arrested*, Home Office Statistical Bulletin Issue 5/89. London: Home Office.

Home Office (1989b) *The Ethnic Group of Those Proceeded Against or Sentenced by the Courts in the Metropolitan District in 1984 and 1985*, Home Office Statistical Bulletin 6/89. London: Home Office.

Home Office (1992) *Race and the Criminal Justice System 1992*, A Home Office Publication under Section 95 of the Criminal Justice Act 1991. London: Home Office.

Home Office (1994a) *Parole Recommendations and Ethnic Origin: England and Wales 1990*, Home Office Statistical Bulletin Issue 2/94, Home Office Research and Statistics Department. London: Home Office.

Home Office (1994b) *Race and the Criminal Justice System 1994*, A Home Office Publication under Section 95 of the Criminal Justice Act 1991. London: Home Office.

Home Office (1994c) *The Ethnic Origins of Prisoners*, Home Office Statistical Bulletin Issue 21/94, Home Office Research and Statistics Department. London: Home Office.

Home Office (1995) *Digest 3: Information on the Criminal Justice System in England and Wales.* London: Home Office.

Home Office (1996a) *Race and the Criminal Justice System 1995*, A Home Office Publication under Section 95 of the Criminal Justice Act 1991. London: Home Office.

Home Office (1996b), *Taking Steps: Multi-Agency Responses to Racial Attacks and Harassment*, The Third Report of the Inter Departmental Racial Attacks Group. London: Home Office.

Home Office (1996c) *Probation Statistics 1995*. London: Home Office.

Home Office (1997a) *Race and the Criminal Justice System*, A Home Office Publication under Section 95 of the Criminal Justice Act 1991. London: Home Office.

Home Office (1997b) *Prison Statistics England and Wales 1996*, Cm 3732. London: Home Office.

Home Office (1997c) *Police and Criminal Evidence Act 1984 (s. 66) Code of Practice (A) on Stop and Search.* London: Home Office.

Home Office (1998a) *Prison Statistics England and Wales 1997.* Cm 4017 London: Home Office.

Home Office (1998b) *Statistics on Race and the Criminal Justice System 1998*, A Home Office publication under Section 95 of the Criminal Justice Act 1991. London: Home Office.

Home Office (1999a) *Action Plan. Response to the Stephen Lawrence Inquiry*. London: Home Office.

Home Office (1999b) *Prison Statistics England and Wales 1998*. London: Home Office.

Home Office (1999c) *Race Equality – the Home Secretary's Employment Targets: Staff Targets for the Home Office, the Prison, the Police, the Fire and the Probation Services*, A Home Office Publication under Section 95 of the Criminal Justice Act 1991. London: Home Office.

Home Office (1999d) *Digest of Criminal Justice Statistics*, Digest 4. London: Home Office.

Home Office (1999e) *Statistics on Race and the Criminal Justice System 1999*, A Home Office Publication under Section 95 of the Criminal Justice Act 1991. London Home Office.

Home Office (1999f) *The Stephen Lawrence Inquiry: The Home Secretary's Action Plan*, March. London: Home Office.

Home Office (2000a) *Prison Statistics England and Wales 1999*, Cm 4805. London: Home Office.

Home Office (2000b) *Race Equality – the Home Secretary's Employment Targets: First Annual Report on Progress. Staff Targets for the Home Office, the Prison, the Police, the Fire and the Probation Services*. London: Home Office.

Home Office (2000c) *Statistics on Race and the Criminal Justice System 2000*, A Home Office publication under section 95 of the Criminal Justice Act 1991. London: Home Office.

Home Office (2001a) *Stephen Lawrence Inquiry Home Secretary's 2nd Annual Report on Progress*. London: Home Office.

Home Office (2001b) *Race Relations (Amendment) Act 2000: New Laws for a Successful Multi-Racial Britain. Proposals for Implementation*. Home Office.

Home Office (2001c) 'What Works', Diversity Issues, Probation Circular 14/01. London: Home Office.

Hood, R. (1992) *Race and Sentencing*. Oxford: Clarendon Press.

Hope, T. and Foster, J. (1993) *Housing, Community, and Crime: The Impact of the Priority Estates Project*, Home Office Research Study 131. London: Home Office.

House of Commons (1972) 'Select Committee on Race Relations and Immigration Session 1971–2', Police/Immigration Relations, 1, 471.

House of Commons (1976) 'Select Committee on Race Relations and Immigration Session 1975–6', The West Indian Community.

House of Commons (1994) *Racial Attacks and Harassment*, Home Affairs Committee, Third Report. London: Home Office.

House of Commons Home Affairs Committee (1982) *Racial Attacks*, Second Report of the Home Affairs Committee, Session 1981–2, HC 106. London: Home Office.

Howe, D. (1988) *From Bobby to Babylon: Blacks and the British Police*. London: Race Today Publications.

Hudson, B. (1989) 'Discrimination and Disparity: The Influence of Race on Sentencing', *New Community*, 16, 1, 23–34.

Hudson, B. (1993) *Penal Policy and Social Justice*. Basingstoke: Macmillan.

Hughes, G. (1996) 'Black Officer Wins Race Case', *Daily Post*, 23 March.

Human Rights Watch (1997) *Racist Violence in the United Kingdom*. London: Human Rights Watch Helsinki.

Hunte, J. (1966) *Nigger Hunting in England?*. London: West Indian Standing Conference.

Husbands, C. (1982) 'East End Racism 1900–1980: Geographical Continuities in Vigilantist and Extreme Right-Wing Political Behaviour', *London Journal*, 8, 1.

Husbands, C. (1983) *Racial Exclusionism and the City: The Urban Support for the National Front*. London: Allen & Unwin.

Inquest (Mick Ryan) (1996) *Lobbying from Below: INQUEST in Defence of Civil Liberties*. London: UCL Press.

Institute for the Study of Drug Dependence (ISDD) (1997) *Drug Misuse in Britain 1996*. London: ISDD.

Institute of Race Relations (1979) *'Police Against Black People': Evidence Submitted to the Royal Commission on Criminal Procedure*. London: Institute of Race Relations.

Institute of Race Relations (1987) *Policing Against Black People*. London: Institute of Race Relations.

Institute of Race Relations (1991) *Deadly Silence: Black Deaths in Custody*. London: Institute of Race Relations.

Institute of Race Relations (2001) 'Counting the Cost: Racial Violence since Macpherson'. London: IRR/London Borough Grants.

Jackson, J. (1997) *Race Equality in Prisons: The Role of the Race Relations Liaison Officer*. London: Prison Reform Trust.

Jackson, K. and McGregor, R. (2000) *Control of Immigration: Statistics United Kingdom, First Half 2000*, Home Office Statistical Bulletin 22/00. London: Home Office.

Jacobs, J.B. (1979) 'Race Relations and the Prisoner Subculture', in N. Morris and M. Tonry (eds), *Crime and Justice: An Annual Review of Research*, Vol I. Chicago, CO: The University of Chicago Press.

James, C.L.R. (1938) *The Black Jacobins: Toussaint L'Ouverture and the San Domingo Revolution*. London: Secker & Warburg.

James, W. And Harris, C. (1993) *Inside Babylon*. London: Verso.

Jasper, L. (1998) 'Black Deaths in Custody: A Human Rights Perspective', in A. Liebling (ed.), *Deaths of Offenders: The Hidden Side of Justice*. Winchester: Waterside Press.

Jefferson, T. (1988) 'Race, Crime and Policing: Empirical, Theoretical and Methodological Issues', *International Journal of the Sociology of Law*, 16, 521–39.

Jefferson, T. (1991) 'Discrimination, Disadvantage, and Police Work', in E. Cashmore and E. McLaughlin (eds), *Out of Order? Policing Black People*. London: Routledge.

Jefferson, T. (1997) 'Masculinities and Crimes', in M. Maguire, R. Morgan and

R. Reiner (eds), *The Oxford Handbook of Criminology* (2nd edn). Oxford: Oxford University Press.

Jefferson, A. (1993) 'The Racism of Criminalization: Police and the Reproduction of the Criminal Other', in L.R. Gelsthorpe (ed.), *Minority Ethnic Groups in the Criminal Justice System*, Papers Presented to 21st Cropwood Roundtable Conference 1992. Cambridge: Cambridge Institute of Criminology.

Jefferson, T. and Walker, M.A. (1992) 'Ethnic Minorities in the Criminal Justice System', *Criminal Law Review*, 81, 140, 83–95.

Jefferson, T. and Walker, M.A. (1993) 'Attitudes to the Police of Ethnic Minorities in a Provincial City', *British Journal of Criminology*, 33, 2, 251–66.

Jenkinson, J. (1996) 'The 1919 Riots', in P. Panayi (ed.), *Racial Violence in Britain* (2nd ed). London: Leicester University Press/Pinter.

Jensen, A. (1969) 'How Much Can We Boost IQ and Scholastic Achievement?', *Harvard Educational Review*, 39, 1–123.

Jensen, E. (1993) 'International Nazi Cooperation: A Terrorist-Oriented Network', in T. Bjørgo and R. Witte (eds), *Racist Violence in Europe*, London: Macmillan.

John, G. (1970) *Race in the Inner City*. London: Runnymede Trust.

Joint Council for the Welfare of Immigrants (1995).

Jones, T. (1993) *Britain's Ethnic Minorities*. London: Policy Studies Institute.

Jones, T., Maclean, B. and Young, J. (1986) *The Islington Crime Survey: Crime, Victimisation and Policing in Inner-City London*. Aldershot: Gower.

Jones, T. and Newburn, T. (1997) *Policing After the Act*. London: Policy Studies Institute.

Jowitt, S. (2000) 'Interviews with Young People Convicted of Robbery under s.53 of the Children and Young Persons Act', Paper presented at the Police Staff College Bramshill.

Junger, M. (1989) 'Discrepancies between Police and Self-Report Data for Dutch Racial Minorities', *British Journal of Criminology*, 29, 3, Summer, 273–84.

Junger, M. (1990) 'Studying Ethnic Minorities in Relation to Crime and Police Discrimination: Answer to Bowling', *British Journal of Criminology*, 30, 4, 493–502.

Junger Tas J., Terlouw, J.G. and Klein, M. (eds), (1994) *Delinquent Behaviour Among Young People in the Western World: First Results of the International Self-Report Delinquency Survey*. Amsterdam: Kugler.

Justice (1999) *Under Surveillance*. London: Justice.

Justices' Clerks' Society (1995) *Black People in Magistrates' Courts*. Yeovil: Justices' Clerks' Society.

Kalunta-Crumpton, A. (1996) 'The Influence of Race and Unemployment upon Prosecution in Drug Trafficking Trials', *Probation Journal*, 43, 4, 182–6.

Kalunta-Crumpton, A. (1999) *Race and Drug Trials: The Social Construction of Guilt and Innocence*. Aldershot: Avebury.

Kaplan, J. and Bjørgo, T. (1998) *Nation and Race: The Developing Euro-American Racist Subculture*. New York: New York University Press.

Kappeler, V.E., Sluder, R.D., and Alpert, G.P. (1994) *Forces of Deviance: Understanding the Dark Side of Policing.* Prospect Heights, Ill: Waveland Press.

Keith, M. (1988) 'Squaring Circles?: Consultation and "Inner City" Policing', *New Community*, 15, 1, 63–77.

Keith, M. (1993) *Race, Riots and Policing: Lore and Disorder in a Multi-Racist Society.* London: UCL Press.

Keith, M. and Murji, K. (1993) 'Reifying Crime, Legitimising Racism: Left Realism and the Local Politics of Policing' in W. Ball and J. Solomos (eds), *Race and Local Politics.* London: Macmillan.

Kelly, L. (1987) 'The Continuum of Sexual Violence', in J. Hanmer and M. Maynard (eds), *Women, Violence and Social Control.* London: Macmillan, pp. 46–60.

Kershaw, C., Budd, T., Kinshott, G., Mattinson, J., Mayhew, P. and Myhill A. (2000) *The 2000 British Crime Survey,* Home Office Statistical Bulletin 18/00. London: Home Office.

Kettle, M. and Hodges, L. (1992) *Uprising!: The Police, the People and the Riots in Britain's Cities.* London: Pan.

King, M. and Israel, M. (1989) 'The Pursuit of Excellence, or How Solicitors Maintain Racial Inequality', *New Community*, 16, 1, 107–20.

King, M. and May, C. (1985) *Black Magistrates.* London: Cobden Trust.

Kirk, B.M. (1996) *Negative Images: A Simple Matter of Black and White? An Examination of 'Race' and the Juvenile Justice System.* Aldershot: Avebury.

Kleg, M. (1993) *Hate Prejudice and Racism.* Albany: State University of New York Press.

Klier, J.D. (1993) 'The Pogrom Tradition in Eastern Europe', in T. Bjørgo and R. Witte (eds), *Racist Violence in Europe.* London: Macmillan.

Knox, R. (1852) *The Races of Men: A Philosophical Enquiry into the Influence of Race over the Destinies of Nations* (second edition). London. Henry Renshaw. pp (v), 243–4, 246.

Landau, S.F. (1981) 'Juveniles and the Police', *British Journal of Criminology*, 21, 1, 27–46.

Landau, S.F. and Nathan, G. (1983) 'Selecting Delinquents for Cautioning in the London Metropolitan Area', *British Journal of Criminology*, 23, 2, 128–49.

Langan, P.A. (1985) 'Racism on Trial: New Evidence to Explain the Racial Composition of Prisons in the United States', *Journal of Criminal Law and Criminology*, 76, 3, 666–83.

Law Society (1993) 'What is the ACA?', *ACA Student Handbook.* London: Law Society.

Lawrence, D. (1996) 'Race, Culture and the Probation Service: Groupwork Programme Design', in McIvor, G. (ed.), *Working with Offenders. Research Highlights in Social Work 26.* London: Jessica Kingsley.

Lea, J. (1987) 'Police Racism: Some Theories and their Policy Implications', in R. Mathews and J. Young (eds), *Confronting Crime.* London: Sage.

Lea, J., and Young, J. (1984) *What is to be Done about Law and Order?* Harmondsworth: Penguin.

Bibliography

Leitner, M., Shapland, J., and Wiles, P. (1993) *Drug Usage and Drugs Prevention: The Views and Habits of the General Public*. London: Home Office.

Lemert, E. (1951) *Social Pathology*. New York, NY: McGraw Hill.

Lewis, H., and Mair, G. (1988) *Bail and Probation Work II: The Use of London Probation/Bail Hostels for Bailees*, Home Office Research and Planning Unit Paper 50. London: Home Office.

Lombroso, C. (1876) *L'Uomo Delinquente* [Criminal Man]. Turin: Fratelli Bocca.

Lööw, H. (1993) 'The Cult of Violence: The Swedish Racist Counterculture', in T. Bjørgo and R. Witte (eds), *Racist Violence in Europe*. London: Macmillan.

Lustgarten, L. (1986) *The Governance of the Police*. London: Sweet & Maxwell.

Mac an Ghaill, M. (1999) *Contemporary Racisms and Ethnicities: Social and Cultural Transformations*. Milton Keynes: Open University Press.

Macey, M. (1999) 'Class Gender and Religious Influences on Changing Patterns of Pakisani Muslim Male Violence in Bradford', *Ethnic and Racial Studies*, 22, 5, September, 845–66.

MacIver, R.M. (1948) *The More Perfect Union*. New York: Macmillan.

MacLean, B. and Milovanovic, D. (eds), (1990) *Racism, Empiricism and Criminal Justice*. Vancouver: The Collective Press.

Macpherson, W. (1999) *The Stephen Lawrence Inquiry, Report of an Inquiry by Sir William Macpherson of Cluny. Advised by Tom Cook, The Right Reverend Dr John Sentamu and Dr Richard Stone*. Cm 4262–1. London: Home Office.

Maden, A., Swinton, M., and Gunn, J. (1992) 'The Ethnic Origin of Women Serving a Prison Sentence', *British Journal of Criminology*, 32, 2, 218–21.

Magrath, P. (1997) 'Direction Sufficient to Deal With Jury Bias', *Independent*, 5 March.

Maguire, M., Morgan, R. and Reiner, R. (eds), (1997) *The Oxford Handbook of Criminology* (2nd edn). Oxford: Oxford University Press.

Mair, G. (1986) 'Ethnic Minorities, Probation and the Magistrates' Courts', *British Journal of Criminology*, 26, 2, 147–55.

Malik, K. (1996) *The Meaning of Race*. London: Macmillan.

Malik, M. (1999) 'Racist Crime: Racially Aggravated Offences in the Crime and Disorder Act 1998 Part II', *Modern Law Review*, 62, 3, May, 409–24.

Malleson, K. and Banda, F. (2000) 'Factors Affecting the Decision to Apply for Silk and Judicial Office', www.open.gov.uk/lcd/research/2000/200es.htm

Mama, A. (1984/1997) 'Black Women, the Economic Crisis and the British State', in H. Mirza (ed.), *Black British Feminism: A Reader*. London: Routledge.

Mama, A. (1995) *Beyond the Mask: Race, Gender and Subjectivity*. London: Routledge.

Mama, A. (1996) *The Hidden Struggle*. (2nd edn). London: Whiting & Birch.

Mann, C.R. (1993) *Unequal Justice: A Question of Colour*. Bloomington, IN: Indiana University Press.

Mannheim, H. (1965) *Comparative Criminology: A Text Book*. Vols I and II. London: Routledge & Kegan Paul.

Marshall, I.H. (1997) *Minorities, Migrants, and Crime: Diversity and Similarity Across Europe and the United States*. Thousand Oaks, CA: Sage.

Marx, K. (1961) *Selected Writings in Sociology and Social Philosophy*, edited by T.B. Bottomore and Maximilien Rubel. London: Watts.

Mason, D. (1995) *Race and Ethnicity in Modern Britain*. Oxford: Oxford University Press.

Matthews, R. and Francis, P. (1996) *Prisons 2000: An International Perspective on the Current State and Future of Imprisonment*. London: Macmillan.

Mauer, M., (1990) 'Young Black Americans and the Criminal Justice System', Sentencing Project, Washington, DC.

Mavunga, P. (1993) 'Probation: A Basically Racist Service', in L.R. Gelsthorpe (ed.), *Minority Ethnic Groups in the Criminal Justice System*. Papers Presented to 21st Cropwood Roundtable Conference 1992. Cambridge: Cambridge, Institute of Criminology.

Mawby, R.I. (1979) *Policing the City*. Farnborough: Saxon House.

Mawby, B.I. and Batta, I.D. (1980) *Asians and Crime: The Bradford Experience*. Middlesex: Scope Communications.

May, R. and Cohen, R. (1974), 'The Interaction between Race and Colonialism: A Case Study of the Liverpool Race Riots of 1919', *Race and Class*, 16, 2, 111–26.

Mayhew, P., Aye Maung, N. and Mirrlees-Black, C. (1993) *The 1992 British Crime Survey*, Home Office Research Study 132. London: Home Office.

Mayhew, P., Elliott, D. and Dowds, L. (1989) *The 1988 British Crime Survey*, Home Office Research Study 111. London: Home Office.

Maynard, W. and Read, T. (1997) *Policing Racially Motivated Incidents*, Police Research Group Crime Detection and Prevention Series 59, London: Home Office.

McClintock, F.H. and Gibson, E. (1961) *Robbery in London. Cambridge Series in Criminology XIV*. London: Macmillan.

McConville, M. and Baldwin, J. (1982) 'The Influence of Race on Sentencing in England', *Criminal Law Review*, October, 652–8.

McConville, M. and Shepherd, D. (1992) *Watching Police Watching Communities*. London: Routledge.

McCrudden, C., Smith, D.J. and Brown, C. (1991) *Racial Justice at Work: The Enforcement of the 1976 Race Relations Act in Employment*. London: Policy Studies Institute.

McDermott, K. (1990) 'We Have No Problem: the Experience of Racism in Prison', *New Community*, 16, 2, 213–28.

McLaughlin, E. (1991) 'Police Accountability and Black People: Into the 1990s', in E. Casmore and E. McLaughlin (eds), *Out of Order?: Policing Black People*. London: Routledge.

McLaughlin, E. (1994) *Community, Policing and Accountability: The Politics of Policing in Manchester in the 1980s*. Aldershot: Avebury.

McLaughlin, E. and Murji, K. (1999) 'After the Stephen Lawrence Report', *Critical Social Policy*, 60, 19, 3, 371–85.

Bibliography

McLaughlin, E. and Murji, K. (2001) 'Ways of Seeing: The Media and the Problem of Racial Violence', in M. May *et al.* (eds), *Social Problems and Social Policy*. Oxford: Blackwell.

Merton, R.K. (1963) (1938) 'Social Structure and Anomie', *American Sociological Review*, 3, 672–82; rep. in *Social Theory and Social Structure*. Glencoe: Free Press, 1957; rev. edn 1963.

Metropolitan Police (various years) Annual Report. London.

Mhlanga, B. (1997) *The Colour of English Justice: A Multivariate Analysis*. Aldershot: Avebury.

Mhlanga, B. (1999) *Race and Crown Prosecution Service Decisions*. London: The Stationery Office.

Miles, R. (1989) *Racism*. London: Routledge.

Miles, R. and Phizacklea, A. (1984) *White Man's Country*. London: Pluto.

Miller, J. (1996) *Search and Destroy*. Cambridge: Cambridge University Press.

Mills, H. (1993) 'Swastika Displayed by Prison Officers in Reception Area', *Independent*, 15 November.

Mills, H. (1997) 'Driver Pulled up 34 Times Sues Police', *Observer*, 8 June.

Miller, J., Bland, N. and Quinton, P. (2000) *The Impact of Stops and Searches on Crime and the Community*, Police Research Series Paper 127. London: Home Office.

Miller, J.G. (1997) *Search and Destroy: African–American Males in the Criminal Justice System*. Cambridge: Cambridge University Press.

Mirrlees-Black, C. (2001) *Confidence in the Criminal Justice System: Findings from the 2000 British Crime Survey*, Home Office Research Findings 137. London: Home Office.

Mirrlees-Black, C., Mayhew, P. and Percy, A. (1996) *The 1996 British Crime Survey: England and Wales*, Home Office Statistical Bulletin 19/96. London: Home Office.

Mirza, H. (1997) (ed.) *Black British Feminism: A Reader*. London: Routledge.

Mistry, T. (1993) 'Working with Young Black Women', in D. Woodhill and P. Senior (eds), *Justice for Black Young People*. Sheffield: Panic Publications.

Modood, T. (1988) '"Black", Racial Equality and Asian Identity', *New Community*, 14, 397–404.

Modood, T. (1992) *Not Easy Being British: Colour, Culture and Citizenship*. Runnymede Trust and Trentham Books.

Modood, T. and Berthoud, R., with the assistance of Lakey, J., Nazroo, J., Smith, P., Virdee, S. and Beishon, S. (1997) *Ethnic Minorities in Britain: Diversity and Disadvantage*. London: Policy Studies Institute.

Montagu, A. (1997) *Man's Most Dangerous Myth: The Fallacy of Race* (6th edn). Walnut Creek, London: AltaMira Press.

Morgan, R. (1989) 'Policing by Consent: Legitimating the Doctrine', in R. Morgan and D.J. Smith (eds), *Coming to Terms with Policing: Perspectives on Policy*. London: Routledge.

MORI (1993) *The Rising Tide of Exclusions* (written by Bob Gosschalk). MORI.

Bibliography 293

Morris, T. (1958) *The Criminal Area: A Study in Social Ecology*. London: Routledge & Kegan Paul.

Mott, J. and Mirrlees-Black, C. (1995) *Self-Reported Drug Misuse in England and Wales: Findings from the 1992 British Crime Survey*, Research and Planning Unit Paper 89. London: Home Office.

Moxon, D. (1988) *Sentencing Practice in the Crown Court*, Home Office Research Study 103. London: Home Office.

Muncie, J. (1999) *Youth and Crime*. London: Sage.

Muncie, J. And MacLaughlin, E. (eds), (1998) *Criminological Perspectives: A Reader*. London: Sage.

Murji, K. (1999) 'Wild Life: Representations and Constructions of Yardies', in J. Ferrell and N. Websdale (eds), *Make Trouble: Cultural Representations of Crime, Deviance and Control*. New York: Aldine de Gruyter.

Murray, C. (1990) *The Emerging British Underclass*. London: Institute for Economic Affairs.

MVA and Joel Miller (2000) *Profiling Populations Available for Stops and Searches*, Police Research Series Paper 131. London: Home Office.

NAAPS (1997) *The National Association of Asian Probation Staff*, Leaflet. London.

NACRO (1991) *Black Communities and the Probation Service: Working Together for Change*. London.

NACRO (1997) *Policing Local Communities: The Tottenham Experiment*. London.

National Statistics (2000) *Census News*. London: National Statistics.

Newburn, T. and Stanko, E.A. (eds) (1994) *Just Boys Doing Business?: Men, Masculinities and Crime*. London: Routledge.

Newham Monitoring Project (1988, 1990, 1993) *Annual Reports*. London: NMP.

Newham Monitoring Project (1991) 'Forging a Black Community: Asian and Afro-Caribbean Struggles in Newham', London: NMP/CARF.

Norris, C., Fielding, N., Kemp, C. and Fielding, J. (1992) 'Black and Blue: An Analysis of the Influence of Race on Being Stopped by the Police', *British Journal of Sociology*, 43, 2, 207–23.

Norton-Taylor, R. (1999) (ed.) *Colour of Justice*. London: Theatre Communication Group.

Nuffield Foundation (1993) *Access to Justice: Non-English Speakers in the Legal System*. London: Nuffield Interpreter Project/Nuffield Foundation.

OFSTED (1999) 'Raising the Attainment of Ethnic Minority Pupils: School and LEA Responses', A Report from the office of Her Majesty's Chief Inspector of Schools. London: Office for Standards in Education.

Office of Population Censuses and Surveys (1983, 1984) 'Labour Force Survey'. London: Home Office.

Office of Population Censuses and Surveys (1991) Census.

Office of Population Censuses and Surveys (1992) *The National Prison Survey 1991*. London: Home Office.

Office of Population and Censuses Survey (1993) *1991 Census: Ethnic Group and Country of Birth (Great Britain)*. London: Home Office.

Bibliography

Painter, K. *et al.* (1989) *The Hammersmith and Fulham Crime and Policing Survey, 1988: Final Report*, London: Middlesex Polytechnic.

Palmer, C. Moon, G. and Cox, S. (1997) 'Discrimination at Work'. London: Legal Action Group.

Panayi, P. (1996) *Racial Violence in Britain* (2nd edn). London: Leicester University Press/Pinter.

Patel, P. (1997) 'Third wave feminism and black women's activism', in H. Mirza (ed.), *Black British Feminism: A Reader*. London: Routledge.

Pathak, S. (2000) 'Race Research for the Future: Ethnicity in Education, Training and the Labour Market', Research Topic Paper 01. London: Department for Education and Employment.

Paxman, J. (1999) *The English: A Portrait of a People*. London: Penguin.

Peach, C. and Byron, M. ((1993) 'Caribbean tenants in council housing: "race", class and gender'. *New Community* 19(3) 407–23.

Pearson, G. (1983) *Hooligan: A History of Respectable Fears*. London: Macmillan.

Pearson, G., Sampson, A., Blagg, H., Stubbs, P. and Smith, D.J. (1989) 'Policing Racism', in R. Morgan and D.J. Smith (eds), *Coming to Terms with Policing: Perspectives on Policy*. London: Routledge.

Percy, A. (1998) 'Ethnicity and Victimisation: Findings from the 1996 British Crime Survey', Home Office Statistical Bulletin. 6/98. 3 April. London: Home Office.

Phillips, C. and Bowling, B. (1997) 'Racism, ethnicity and criminology: developing minority perspectives'. Paper presented to the British Criminology Conference, Queen's University Belfast.

Phillips, C. and Brown, D. (1997) 'Observational Studies in Police Custody Areas: Some Hethodological and Ethical Issues Considered', *Policing and Society*, 7, 191–205.

Phillips, C. and Brown, D. (1998) 'Entry into the Criminal Justice System: A Survey of Police Arrests and Their Outcomes', Home Office Research Study 185. London: Home Office.

Phillips, C. and Sampson, A. (1998) 'Preventing Repeated Victimization: An Action Research Project', *British Journal of Criminology*, 38, 1, Winter, 124–44.

Phoenix, A. (1994) 'Narrow Definitions of Culture: the Case of Early Motherhood', in M. Evans (ed.), *The Woman Question* (2nd edn). London: Sage.

Pinkney, A. (1994) *White Hate Crimes: Howard Beach and Other Racial Atrocities*. Chicago: Third World Press.

Pitts, J. (1993) 'Thereotyping: Anti-Racism, Criminology and Black Young People', in D. Cook and B. Hudson (eds), *Racism and Criminology*. London: Sage.

Police Complaints Authority (1997) 'Report by the Police Complaints Authority on the Investigation of a Complaint against the Metropolitan Police Service by Mr N and Mrs D Lawrence: Presented to Parliament by the Secretary of State for the Home Department by Command of Her Majesty December 1997', London: Home Office.

Police Complaints Authority (2000) *Annual Report*. London: PCA.

Police (1999) 'The Buck Stops Where?', Editorial comment, *Police: The Voice of Service*, 31, 3, March.

Pope, D. (1976) *Community Relations – the Police Response*. London: Runnymede Trust.

Poulter, S. (1998) *Ethnicity Law and Human Rights: The English Experience*. Oxford: Oxford University Press.

Povey, D., Cotton, J. and Sisson, S. (2000) 'Recorded Crime Statistics: England and Wales, April 1999 to March 2000'. Home Office Statistical Bulletin 12/00. London: Home Office.

Pratt, M. (1981) *Mugging as a Social Problem*. London: Routledge.

Price, K. (1979) *Endless Pressure*. Harmondsworth: Penguin.

Prime, J., White, S., Livrano, S. and Patel, K. (2001) *Criminal Careers of those Born Between 1953 and 1978*. England and Wales. Home Office Statistical Bulletin 4/01. London: Home Office.

Prins, H. (1999) 'Report of the committee of inquiry into the death in Broadmoor Hospital of Orville Blackwood and a review of the deaths of two other Afro-Caribbean patients: "Big, Black and Dangerous?"' London: Special Hospitals Health Services Authority.

Prisons Ombudsman (2000) 'Annual Report 1999–2000: Independent Investigation of Prisoners' Complaints', Cm 4730. London: Home Office.

Prison Reform Trust (1998) 'Prisoner Unlawfully Killed by UKDS Staff', Prison Privatisation Report International No. 19. London: Prison Reform Trust.

Quinton, P., Bland, N. and Miller, J. (2000) 'Police Stops, Decision-Making and Practice', Police Research Series Paper 130. London: Home Office.

Ramsay, M. and Percy, A. (1996) 'Drug Misuse Declared: Results of the 1994 British Crime Survey', Home Office Research Study ISI. London: Home Office.

Ramsey, M. and Spiller, A. (1997) 'Drug Misuse Declared in 1996: Latest Results from the British Crime Survey', Home Office Research Study 172. London: Home Office.

Ray, L., Smith, D. and Wastell, L. (2000) 'Understanding Racist Violence', *Criminal Justice Matters*, 42 (Winter), 30–1.

Reardon, D. (1993) 'The Reality of Life for Black Professionals in the Criminal Justice System', in D. Woodhill and P. Senior (eds), *Justice for Black Young People*. Sheffield: Panic Publications.

Rein, M. (1983) *From Policy to Practice*. London: Macmillan.

Reiner, R. (1989) 'Race and Criminal Justice', *New Community*, 16, 1, 5–21.

Reiner, R. (1991) *Chief Constables*. Oxford: Oxford University Press.

Reiner, R. (1992) *The Politics of the Police* (2nd edn). London: Harvester Wheatsheaf.

Reiner, R. (1993) 'Race, Crime and Justice: Models of Interpretation', in L.R. Gelsthorpe (ed.), *Minority Ethnic Groups in the Criminal Justice System*. Cambridge: Cambridge Institute of Criminology.

Reiner, R. (2000) *The Politics of the Police* (3rd edn). London: Harvester Wheatsheaf.

Rex, J. and Moore, R. (1967) *Race, Community and Conflict*. London: Oxford University Press.

Bibliography

Rex, J. and Tomlinson, S. (1979) *Colonial Immigrants in a British City*. London: Routledge.

Rice, M. (1990) 'Challenging Orthodoxies in Feminist Theory: A Black Feminist Critique', in L. Gelsthorpe and A. Morris, *Feminist Perspectives in Criminology*. Milton Keynes: Open University Press.

Richards, M., McWilliams, B., Batten, N., Cameron, C., and Cutler, J. (1995a) 'Foreign Nationals in English Prisons: I. Family Ties and their Maintenance', *Howard Journal*, 34, 2, 158–75.

Richards, M., McWilliams, B., Batten, N., Cameron, C., and Cutler, J. (1995b) 'Foreign Nationals in English Prisons: II. Some Policy Issues', *Howard Journal*, 34, 3, 195–208.

Roach, J. (1978) *Social Reform in England 1780–1880*. London: Batsford.

Roach Family Support Committee (1989) *Policing in Hackney: 1945–1984: Report Produced by an Independent Committee of Inquiry for the Roach Family Support Committee*. Foreword by Professor Stuart Hall. London: Karia Press/RFSC.

Root, M. (ed) (1992) *Racially Mixed People in America*. London: Sage.

Rose, D. (1996) *In the Name of the Law: The Collapse of Criminal Justice*. London: Vintage.

The Rotterdam Charter (1996) *Policing for a Multi-Ethnic Society*, Rotterdam: Rotterdam Conference.

Royal Commission on Criminal Procedure (1981) *The Investigation and Prosecution of Criminal Offences in England and Wales: Law and Procedure*, Chairman, Sir Cyril Philips. Report. Cmnd 8092. London: Home Office.

Runnymede Trust (2000) *The Future of Multi-Ethnic Britain: The Parekh Report*. London: Profile Books.

Rushdie, S. (1989) *The Satanic Verses*. London: Viking.

Russell, K. (1998) *The Color of Crime*. New York: New York University Press.

Sampson, A. and Phillips, C. (1992) *Multiple Victimisation: Racial Attacks on an East London Estate*., Police Research Group Crime Prevention Unit Series Paper 36. London: Home Office.

Sampson, A. and Phillips, C. (1996) *Reducing Repeat Victimisation on an East London Estate*, Police Research Group Crime Prevention Unit Crime Prevention and Detection Paper 67. London: Home Office.

Sarwar, K. (1989) 'Working with Asian Women and the Police', in C. Dunhill, *The Boys in Blue*. London: Virago.

Saulsbury, W.E. and Bowling, B. (1991), *The Multi-Agency Approach in Practice: The North Plaistow Racial Harassment Project*, Home Office Research Study No. 64. London: Home Office.

Savill J. (1994) *Towards Understanding the Offender Profile of a Young Mugger. A Comparison of Young Offenders in the London Boroughs of Lambeth and Lewisham*, Unpublished thesis, University of Exeter.

Scarman, L. (1981) *The Scarman Report*. London: Home Office.

Scarman, L. (1986) *The Scarman Report* (revised edn). Harmondsworth: Penguin.

Schneider-Ross (1999) www.diversity-whatworks.gov.uk/resources.htm.

Scrap Sus Campaign (1979) 'A Fair Deal for All: Evidence and

Recommendations to the Royal Commission on Criminal Procedure',
London: Scrap Sus Campaign, Steering Committee.

Scraton, P. (1987) *Law, Order and the Authoritarian State: Readings in Critical Criminology*. Milton Keynes: Open University Press.

Seagrave, J. (1989) 'Racially Motivated Incidents Reported to the Police', Home Office Research and Planning Unit 54, London: Home Office.

Sewell, T. (1997) *Black Masculinities and Schooling: How Black Boys Survive Modern Schooling*, London: Trentham Books.

Shah, R. and Pease, K. (1992) 'Crime, Race and Reporting to the Police', *Howard Journal*, 31, 3, 192–9.

Shallice, A. and Gordon, P. (1990) *Black People, White Justice? Race and the Criminal Justice System*. London: Runnymede Trust.

Sharma, S., Hutnyk, J. and Sharma, A. (eds) (1996) *Dis-Orienting Rhythms – The Politics of the New Asian Dance Music*. London: Zed Books.

Shaw, C. (1994) Changing Lives 3 – the Third of a Series of Surveys Providing Information About the Education, Training and Work Experience of Young People From Britain's Inner Cities. London: Policy Studies Institute.

Shaw, C. and McKay, H. (1942) *Juvenile Delinquency and Urban Areas*. Chicago: University of Chicago Press.

Shaw, J.W. (1990) 'Institutional Racial Discrimination, Strategic Planning and Training in the Prison Department', *New Community*, 16, 4, 533–50.

Shiner, M. (1997) 'Entry into the Legal Professions: The Law Student Cohort Study Year 4', Law Society Research and Policy Planning Unit No. 25. London: Law Society.

Shiner, M. (1999) 'Entry into the Legal Professions: The Law Student Cohort Study Year 5', Law Society Research and Policy Planning Unit No. 33. London: Law Society.

Sibbitt, R. (1997) 'The Perpetrators of Racial Harassment and Racial Violence', Home Office Research Study 176. London: Home Office.

Sims, L. and Myhill, A. (2001) 'Policing and the Public: Findings from the 2000 British Crime Survey', Home Office Research Findings No. 136. London: Home Office.

Sivanandan, A. (1982) *A Different Hunger: Writings on Black Resistance*. London: Pluto.

Sivanandan, A. (1983) 'Challenging Racism: Strategies for the Eighties', *Race and Class*, 25, 1–2.

Skellington, R. (1996) *'Race' in Britain Today*. London: Sage.

Skogan, W.G. (1990) 'The Police and the Public in England and Wales: A British Crime Survey Report', Home Office Research Study 117. London: Home Office.

Skogan, W.G. (1994) 'Contacts Between Police and Public: Findings from the 1992 British Crime Survey', Home Office Research Study 134. London: Home Office.

Small, S. (1991) 'Racialised Relations in Liverpool: A Contemporary Anomaly', *New Community*, 17, 4, July.

Small, S. (1994) *Racialised Barriers: The Black Experience in the United States and England in the 1980s*. London, New York: Routledge.

Smith D.A., Visher, C.A. and Davidson, L.A. (1984) 'Equity and Discretionary Justice: the Influence of Race on Police Arrest Decisions', *Journal of Criminal Law and Criminology*, 75, 1, 234–49.

Smith, D.J. (1977) *Racial Disadvantage in Britain*. Harmondsworth: Penguin.

Smith, D.J. (1994) 'Race, Crime and Criminal Justice', in M. Maguire, R. Morgan and R. Reiner (eds), *The Oxford Handbook of Criminology*. Oxford: Clarendon Press.

Smith, D.J. (1997a) 'Ethnic Origins, Crime, and Criminal Justice in England and Wales', in M. Tonry (ed.), *Ethnicity, Crime, and Immigration: Comparative and Cross-National Perspectives. Crime and Justice: A Review of Research, Vol XXI*. Chicago, CO: The University of Chicago Press.

Smith, D.J. (1997b) 'Ethnic Origins, Crime, and Criminal Justice', in M. Maguire, R. Morgan and R. Reiner (eds), *The Oxford Handbook of Criminology* (2nd edn). Oxford: Clarendon.

Smith, D.J. and Gray, J. (1983) 'The Police in Action' (Police and People in London Vol. 4) London: Policy Studies Insitute.

Smith, D.J. and Gray, J. (1985) *People and Police in London*. London: Gower.

Smith, S.J. (1989) *The Politics of 'Race' and Residence: Citizenship, Segregation and White Supremacy in Britain*. Cambridge: Polity.

Solomos, J. (1988) *Black Youth, Racism and the State*. Cambridge: Cambridge University Press.

Solomos, J. (1993) *Race and Racism in Contemporary Britain*. London: Macmillan.

Solomos, J. and Back, L. (1994) *Race, Politics and Social Change*. London: Routledge.

Solomos, J. and Back, L. (1996) *Racism and Society*. London: Macmillan.

Southall Black Sisters (1989) 'Two Struggles: Challenging Male Violence and the Police', in C. Dunhill (ed.), *The Boys in Blue: Women's Challenge to the Police*. London: Virago.

Southgate, P. and Crisp, D. (1992) 'Public Satisfaction with Police Services', Home Office Research and Planning Unit Paper 73. London: Home Office.

Southgate, P. and Ekblom, P. (1984) 'Contacts between Police and Public: Findings from the British Crime Survey'. London: Home Office.

Sparks, R., Bottoms, A.E. and Hay, W. (1996) *Prisons and the Problem of Order*. Oxford: Oxford University Press.

Spencer, A.J. and Hough, M. (2000) *Policing Diversity: Lessons from Lambeth*, Policing and Reducing Crime Unit Paper 121. London: Home Office.

Stanko, E. (1990) *Everyday Violence*. London: Pandora.

Staples, R. (1975) 'White Racism, Black Crime and American Justice: An Application of the Colonial Model to Explain Race and Crime'. *Phylon*, 36: 14–22.

Steer, D. (1980) 'Uncovering Crime: The Police Role', Royal Commission on Criminal Procedure Research Study 7. London: Home Office.

Stevens, P. and Willis, C.F. (1979) 'Race, Crime and Arrests', Home Office Research Study 58. London: Home Office.

Stevens, P. and Willis, C.F. (1981) 'Ethnic Minorities and Complaints against the Police', Home Office Research and Planning Unit Paper 5. London: Home Office.

Stone, V. and Pettigrew, N. (2000) 'The Views of the Public on Stops and Searches', Police Research Series Paper 129. London: Home Office.

Stone, V. and Tuffin, R. (2000) 'Attitudes of People from Minority Ethnic Communities towards a Career in the Police Service', Police Research Series Paper 136. London: Home Office.

Sulton, A. (ed.) (1996) *African American Perspectives on Crime Causation, Criminal Justice Administration and Crime Prevention.* Oxford: Butterworth/Heinemann.

Tajfel, H. (1969) 'Cognitive Aspects of Prejudice' *Journal of Social Issues* 25, no 4: 79–97.

Tarling, R. and Dowds, L. (1995) *Perceptions of Criminal Justice* in British Social Attitudes Survey.

Tarling, R. and Dowds, L. (1997) 'Crime and Punishment', in R. Jowel, J. Curtice, A. Park, L. Brook, K. Thomson and C. Bryson, *British Social Attitudes: The End of Conservative Values*, the 14th report. Aldershot: Ashgate.

Tatum, B. (1996) 'The colonial model as a theoretical explanation of crime and delinquency, in A. Sulton (ed.) *African American Perspectives on Crime Causation, Criminal Justice Administration and Crime Prevention.* Oxford: Butterworth/Heinemann.

Tatum, B. (2000) *Crime, Violence and Minority Youths.* Aldershot: Ashgate.

Taylor, I.R., Walton, P. and Young, J. (1973) *The New Criminology: For a Social Theory of Deviance.* London: Routledge & Kegan Paul.

Thomas, R. (2000) 'Responding to perpetrators of racist violence', *Criminal Justice Matters*, 42 (Winter), 32–3.

Tipler, J. (1989) 'Is Justice Colour Blind: Race and Juvenile Justice', *Research, Policy and Planning*, 7, 1, 18–23.

Todd, M. (1996) *Opening Doors: An Evaluation of the Cultural Sensitivity of Offender Hostel Provision in Greater Manchester.* Manchester: Greater Manchester Probation Service.

Tompson, K. (1988) *Under Siege: Racial Violence in Britain Today.* Harmondsworth: Penguin.

Tonry, M. (1994) Racial Disproportion in US Prisons, *British Journal of Criminology*, 34, 97–115.

Tonry, M. (1995) *Malign Neglect: Race, Crime, and Punishment in America.* New York: Oxford University Press.

Tonry, M. (ed.) (1997) 'Ethnicity, Crime and Immigration', *Crime and Justice*, 21. London: University of Chicago Press.

Torkington, K. and Protaxia, N. (1991) *Black Heath: A Political Issue.* Liverpool: Catholic Association for Racial Justice.

Tuck, M. (1989) *Drinking and Disorder: A Study of Non-Metropolitan Violence*, Home Office Research Study 108. London: Home Office.

Bibliography

Tuck, M. and Southgate, P. (1981) *Ethnic Minorities, Crime and Policing: A Survey of the Experiences of West Indians and Whites*, Home Office Research Study 70. London: Home Office.

Tuttle, L. (1997) *Encyclopedia of Feminism*. London: Arrow Books.

Tyler, T. (1990) *Why People Obey the Law*. London: Yale University Press.

Uglow, S. (1998) *Policing Liberal Society*. Oxford: Oxford University Press.

Virdee, S. (1995) *Racial Violence and Harassment*. London: Policy Studies Institute.

Vold, G.B., Bernard, T.J. and Snipes, J.B. (1998) *Theoretical Criminology*. New York: Fourth Edition, Oxford: Oxford University Press.

Von Hirsch, A. (1993) *Censure and Sanction*. New York: Oxford University Press.

Von Hirsch, A. (1999) *Criminal Deterrence and Sentence Severity*. Oxford: Hart.

von Hirsch, A., Bottoms, A.E., Burney, E. and Wikstrom, P-O. (1999) *Criminal Deterrence and Sentence Severity*. Oxford: Hart.

Von Hirsch, A. and Roberts, J.V. 'Racial Disparity in Sentencing: Reflections on the Hood Study', *Howard Journal*, 36, 3, 227–36.

Vorhaus, G. (1984) 'The Stop and Search Effect: How Juveniles Respond to Police Stop and Search Procedures', Hayes Middlesex: Juveniles and the Law Research Project.

Walker, M.A. (1987) 'Interpreting Race and Crime Statistics', *Journal of the Royal Statistical Society, A*, 150, part 1, 39–56.

Walker, M.A. (1988) 'The Court Disposal of Young Males, by Race, in London in 1983', *British Journal of Criminology*, 28, 4, 441–60.

Walker, M.A. (1989) 'The Court Disposal and Remands of White, Afro-Caribbean, and Asian Men (London, 1983)', *British Journal of Criminology*, 29, 4, 353–67.

Walker, S., Spohn, C. and DeLone, M. (1996) *The Color of Justice: Race, Ethnicity, and Crime in America*. Belmont, CA: Wadsworth.

Walklate, S. (2001) *Gender, Crime and Criminal Justice*. Cullompton: Willan.

Walmsley, R., Howard, L. and White, S. (1992) 'The National Prison Survey 1991 Main Findings', Home Office Research Study 128. London: Home Office.

Wardak, A. (2000) *Social Control and Deviance: A South Asian Community in Scotland*. Aldershot: Ashgate.

Waters, R. (1988) 'Race and the Criminal Justice Process: Two Empirical Studies on Social Inquiry Reports and Ethnic Minority Defendants', *British Journal of Criminology*, 28, 1, 82–94.

Watson-Smyth, K. (1998) 'Prison Boss Toughs It Out In "Racist" Dispute', *Independent*, 28 March.

Weatheritt, M. (1986) *Innovations in Policing*. London: Croom Helm.

Weber, M. (1949) *The Methodology of Social Sciences*, E.A. Shils and H.A. Finch, trans. New York: Free Press.

Weber, L. and Gelsthorpe, L. (2000) *Deciding to Detain: How Decisions to Detain Asylum Seekers are Made at Points of Entry*, Cambridge: Cambridge University Institute of Criminology.

Webster, C. (1997) *Local Heroes: Racial Violence among Asian and White Young People*. Leicester: Leicester University.

Webster, C. (1997) 'Inverting Racism: An Empirical Study of Perpetrators of Racial Violence', Paper Presented to the British Criminology Conference, Queen's University Belfast, July 1997.

Webster, C. (1997) 'The Construction of British 'Asian' Criminality', *International Journal of the Sociology of Law*, 25, 65–86

Webster C. (1998) *Local Heroes: Racial Violence, Localism and Spacism among Asian and White Young People.* unpublished PhD

Webster, C. (2001) 'Representing Race and Crime', *Criminal Justice Matters*, No. 43, Spring, 16–17.

Webster, C. (Forthcoming) *Understanding Race and Crime*. Milton Keynes: Open University Press.

West, C. (1991) 'Nihilism in Black America', *Dissent*, Spring; reprinted in M. Wallace, *Black Popular Culture*. Seatle: Bay Press, pp. 37–48.

West, C. (1993) *Race Matters*. New York: First Vintage Books.

White, P. and Woodbridge, J. (1997) 'The Prison Population in 1996', Home Office Statistical Bulletin 18/97. London: Home Office.

White, P. (1998) 'The Prison Population in 1997: A Statistical Review', Research Findings No. 76. London: Home Office Research and Statistics Directorate.

Whitehouse, P. (1983) 'Race, Bias and Social Enquiry Reports', *Probation Journal*, 30/2, 43–9.

Wilkins, G. and Addicott, C. (1997) 'Operation of Certain Police Powers Under PACE, England and Wales, 1996', Home Office Statistical Bulletin Issue 27/97. London: Home Office.

Wilkins, L.T. (1964) *Social Devience*. London: Tavistock.

Willbanks, W. (1987) *The Myth of a Racist Criminal Justice System*. Monterey: Brooks/Cole.

Willis, C.F. (1983) 'The Use, Effectiveness and Impact of Police Stop and Search Powers', Home Office Research and Planning Unit Paper 15. London: Home Office.

Willis, P. (1977) *Learning to Labour: How Working Class Kids Get Working Class Jobs*. Farnborough: Saxon House.

Wilson, A. (1978) 'Finding a Voice: Asian Women In Britain', reprinted in H. Mirza (ed.) (1997) *Black British Feminism: A Reader*. London: Routledge.

Wilson, D., Holdaway, S. and Spencer, C. (1984) 'Black Police in the United Kingdom', *Policing*, 1, 1, 20–30.

Wilson, J. (1997) 'Rastafarian Wigs for Men in Police ID Video', *Guardian*, 19 August, p. 8.

Wilson, J.Q. (1968) *Varieties of Police Behaviour*. Cambridge MA: Harvard University Press.

Wilson, J.Q. and Herrnstein, R.J. (1985) *Crime and Human Nature*. New York: Simon & Schuster.

Wilson, S. and Hartley, M. (1989) 'London Borough of Lewisham: a Study of

Young People Sentenced by the Courts 1st January–31st December 1988', Unpublished Report.

Witte, R. (1996) *Racist Violence and the State*. London: Longman.

Wolfgang, M., and Ferracuti, F. (1967) *The Subculture of Violence: Towards an Integrated Theory in Criminology*. London: Tavistock.

Wolfgang, M. and Ferracuti, F. (1981) *The Subculture of Violence*, Beverly Hills, CA: Sage.

Wright, C. (1994) *Race Relations in the Primary School*. London: David Fulton Publishers.

Wright, C. (1998) '"Caught in the Crossfire": Reflections of a Black Female Ethnographer', in P. Connonlly and B. Troyna (eds), *Researching Racism in Education: Politics, Theory and Practice*. Milton Keynes: Open University Press.

Yin, R.K. (1989) *Case Study Research*. London: Sage.

Young, J. (1994) 'Policing the Streets: Stops and Searches in North London', Centre for Criminology, Middlesex University.

Young, J. (1971) 'The Role of the Police as Amplifiers of Deviance, Negotiators of Reality and Translators of Fantasy', in S. Cohen (ed.), *Images of Deviance*. Harmondsworth: Penguin.

Young, J. (1999) *The Exclusive Society: Social Exclusion in Crime and Difference in Late Modernity*. London: Sage.

Subject Index

1990 Trust 135, 257

accountability 12, 14, 17, 42, 164, 225, 257
acquittals 172
Africa 2–3, 5
African 31, 86, 206
African–Asian 45, 47, 51
African, Caribbean and Asian Lawyers Group 223
African/Caribbean xii–xiv, xvii, 51, 205, 223, 226–8, 240, 241, 247, 261
age 38, 143, 194
alcohol 58, 60, 117, 124
Alexander v Home Office 199–200
Aliens Act 1905 5
Anglo-Saxon 28
anomie 66, 247
anthropology 2
anti-discrimination law 17, 51–3, 257–8
antilocution 38
anti-racism 120, 233
anti-Semitism 29
apartheid 4, 39, 117
arrest xiii, 84, 86, 103, 129,148, 239, 242
arson 14, 109, 117
Aryan 2, 22, 28
Aryan Nations 22
Asian (*see also* South Asian, Indian, Pakistani, Bangladeshi) xii–xiv, xvii, 31, 68, 78, 80–1, 86, 25–6, 228, 241
Asianness 26
assaults 70, 76, 112, 122
assimilation 6, 51
Association of Black Probation Officers 227
Association of Chief Police Officers 120
asylum-seekers 117, 208

attitudes, racist 36–8, 156, 158–9, 161–2, 238
attitudes, towards the police 135–8
Australia 4
avoidance 38

backlash xv, 258–9
bail 169–71, 260
Bangladeshi 51, 68, 80–1, 198–9, 241
barristers 220–3
biology 2, 57–8, 74
Birmingham 7, 8, 63, 98, 129
Black Justice Project 151
blackness 25, 30–1, 79
black-on-black violence 97, 108
bombs (nailbombs) 111
Bradford 11, 13, 101
Bristol 2, 8, 129, 153
British Crime Survey 14, 83, 90, 99, 104, 112–13, 122, 135, 143, 173, 235, 237
British National Party 13, 22, 111, 117, 119
British Nationality Act 1981 7, 116
Brixton Prison 204
brutality 8, 128–9, 131–5, 137–8, 208–9
burglary 76, 87, 140

cannabis, small trades 130, 235
cannabis, use 101, 235, 260
Cardiff 11
case termination 168–9
Caucasian 2, 28
Celtic 28
census 33, 198
charging practices 149–52, 242
Chicago School 61–2
children of prisoners 207–8
Children and Young Persons Act 1969 152

Subject index

Chinese 17, 31, 198–9, 206–7, 241
choice theories 56
Civil litigation 166
civil rights, civil liberties (*see also* human rights) 28, 129
civil service 227
class (*see* social class)
classical theories 56
colonial/post-colonial theories 71–4
colonialism 3–5, 22, 117
colour bar (*see also* segregation in employment) 7, 28, 39, 160
colour-blind policies 43, 210
'coloured' people 6, 78, 128, 130
Commission for Racial Equality 15, 46, 49, 52, 108, 153, 229, 257
Commonwealth Immigrants Act 1962 6–7
Commonwealth Immigrants Act 1968 7
community crime prevention 119
community safety 82
complaints against the police (*see* police, complaints against)
compliance 57, 248
consent 12, 17, 141
Conservative Party 6–7, 8–9
control theories 56–7
convictions, and previous convictions 172, 187, 240
court clerks 220–3
courts 176–80, 220–3, 240–3
  Crown Courts 180–88
  Magistrates Courts 176–80
Crime (Sentences Act) 1997 253
Crime and Disorder Act 1998 121–2, 124, 253
crime, definitions of 82–3
crime, fear of 88, 113, 121
crime, ethnic differences in 83–107
criminal biology 57–60
criminal damage 122
Criminal Justice Act 1991 52, 176
Criminal Justice Act 1993 176
Criminal Justice and Public Order Act 1994 142, 154, 253
criminal justice process xv, 12, 44, 70, 83, 86, 169, 234, 237–8, 243, 255–6,
criminal justice policy xv, xvi, 260
criminal justice system 17, 39, 228, 241
criminalisation xv, 12, 242–3, 245, 247–8
criminality, social construction of 29, 77–82, 245
criminology xiii, xiv, xv, 55–75
Crown Prosecution Service 133, 152, 168, 173, 220–1, 228, 239–40, 242–3
cultural theories 60–1, 63, 116, 117, 249

culture 20, 38, 60, 63–4, 73, 161, 216–7
cumulative discrimination (*see* discrimination, cumulative effects of)
custodial sentences xii, 44, 176–87, 197–9
Cypriot 28

Darwinism 3–4, 58
deaths in custody 16, 131–135, 208–9
defamation 38
demoralisation 64, 73–4, 93, 249–50
deprivation 8, 48, 49, 67, 73, 104, 115, 194
  absolute 67, 247
  relative 67–8
detention centres 208
deterrence 56–7, 246
deviancy amplification 68, 243
deviancy theories 61–2, 66–8, 203, 243
difference 25, 26, 51, 203
disadvantage 9, 44–55, 194, 242
discretion 42, 82–3, 87, 141, 241
discrimination xiii, xiv, xv, xvii, 12, 14, 16, 19, 29, 36, 38, 40, 51, 105–6, 186, 252
  cumulative (effects of) xvi, 180, 241–2
  direct 39, 51, 144, 176, 231, 241–2
  indirect 39, 51, 53, 170, 176, 231, 240, 258
  systemic xvi
  contextual xvi, 41–2, 160–1, 183–5, 190, 243
disorder (*see also* riots) xiii
disparities 44, 212
disproportionate, disproportionality 43–4, 85, 88
diversity 51
domestic violence xvi, 81–2, 91–2, 250
drug supply 259
drug use 100, 130, 235

economic conditions 9, 65–8
education 41, 47, 48, 124, 194–5, 242
Elimination of All Forms of Racial Discrimination (1965) (international convention on) 51
empiricism xvi–xvii
employment 41, 48, 105, 194, 242
  in criminal justice agencies xiv, 213–32
England 4, 29
Englishness 29–30, 159
Enlightenment, Age of 1, 56
equal opportunities 43, 218–19, 229
Equal Opportunities Commission 49
Equality, definitions of 43–4, 252
equality of service 229, 252
essentialism xvii, 24, 26, 29, 31, 74, 246
ethnic categories xvii, 33–5
ethnic minority, definition of 24

Subject index   305

Ethnic Minority Network (in Home Office) 228
ethnic monitoring 52, 192
ethnicity xiii, 18, 24–5, 34–5, 38, 233
  definition of 24, 34–5
ethnocentricity 36, 48, 63
ethnology 4–5
eugenics 4–5, 58
Europe 1
European Convention on Human Rights 51, 52
exclusion 12, 38, 71, 116, 247, 252
exclusion, from school 47–8
extermination 3, 38, 74

fairness (*see also* justice, equality) 14, 16, 173
falsehood (*see also* defamation, prejudice, stereotypes) 36
family background/circumstances 50, 80
femininity 32, 69–70
feminist perspectives 69–70
final warning (*see also* police caution) 253
folk devils 8–9
force, excessive (*see also* brutality) 132

gender (*see also* women, men, femininity, masculinity) 24, 32, 38, 69
genetics 23, 58, 249
genocide (*see* extermination, holocaust)
Germany 2, 4–5, 33, 77, 116–17
Glasgow 13
governance (*see* police governance)
Greater London Council 120
Greek 28

harassment 13, 38, 120, 122–23, 157
Her Majesty's Inspectorate of Constabulary 162, 215–19, 231
Her Majesty's Inspectorate of Prisons 204, 208
Her Majesty's Inspectorate of Probation 210–11
heredity (*see also* genetics) 4–5
hierarchy 57
holocaust 116–17
Home Office 120, 124, 138, 140, 160, 199–200, 214, 228, 230–1
Home Secretary xv, 16–18, 218, 228
homelessness (*see also* housing) 46
homicide 76, 95–98, 244–5, 251
homophobia 111, 117
hooliganism 29, 93, 117
housing 10, 19, 38, 41, 44, 105, 119, 124, 240, 242, 251

human rights (*see also* civil rights) 233
Human Rights Act 1998 51, 53, 256
human variability 22–3
hybrid/hybridity 27, 31

identity 20, 25–7, 30, 130
immigration 4–7, 8, 19, 120, 122, 208
  internal controls 131
  legislation 4, 6–7, 40, 65, 130–1
  policing 130, 139, 163
Immigration Act 1971 7, 130–1, 139, 207
Immigration Service 258
imprisonment (*see also* prison) 86, 240, 248, 260
incapacitation 56, 74
income inequality (*see* deprivation) 49, 66–7
Indian 31, 47, 241
Indian sub-continent 5–7
individual theories
  of racism 36–8
  of crime 57–60
industrial tribunals 213, 231
inequality (*see also* equality) 11, 14, 46
inferiority 1, 24–5
inquests 135
Institute of Race Relations xvii, 108, 114, 122, 129–30, 132–3, 138
integration 6–7, 120
internet, racism on 118
interpreters 179
intersectionality 32, 70
intimidation 28, 201
Irish, Irishness 4, 29–30, 77
Islam, Islamophobia 26, 82
Italian 28–9, 117

Jews, Jewish 4–5, 28–9, 33, 77, 116
Jim Crow (*see also* segregation) 4, 160, 177, 178
judges, judiciary xv, 168–87, 220
juries 187–8
justice (*see also* fairness, equality) 14, 19, 255
juveniles (*see* children, young offenders)

Ku Klux Klan 22, 117

labelling theories 68
Labour Party 6–7, 16, 253–4, 256–7
language 16, 24, 38
Lawrence Family Campaign 15
Lawrence Inquiry xv, 14–16, 17–18, 40, 53, 124, 138, 145, 160, 218, 256, 258
Leeds 78, 98, 136–8, 144, 171

legal advice 151, 191
legal factors 175
liberty xv, 135, 255
Liverpool 2, 8
London 2, 6, 8, 13–15, 78–9, 98, 101, 111–12, 114–15, 119, 129, 132, 138, 144, 146, 245
  Brick Lane 111
  Brixton 9, 204
  Newham 13, 114
  Tottenham 129
lynching 174

magistrates 178, 180, 220–2
Maltese 28, 77
managerialism 164, 254–5
Manchester 8, 81, 98, 129
marginalisation 10, 22, 26, 226, 248, 252
Marxist theories 20, 63–6, 71–2, 93
masculinity 32, 69, 71
media 79, 93
Mediterranean 28
men (*see* masculinity)
mentally disordered offenders 170–71
Metropolitan Police Service, London 78, 120, 257
migration (*see also* immigration) 5–7, 29, 120
miscarriages of justice 173
misdiagnosis 47
Misuse of Drugs Act 1971 139
mixed race (*see also* hybridity) 4, 28, 31–2
Mode of Trial Bill 254
monitoring groups 120
moral panics 7–9, 131
Moroccan 102, 103
mouth restraints 131
mugging (*see* robbery)
multi-agency juvenile panels 152
multi-agency partnerships 120, 123
multivariate analysis 183, 189
murder (*see* homicide)
Muslim (*see also* Islam) 82
myths 79

National Association of Asian Probation Staff 227
National Black Police Association 217–18
National Front 8–9, 13, 117, 120, 199
National Socialism (*see* Nazi)
Nationality Act 1948 6, 116
Nationality Act 1980 116
Nazi 4–5, 28, 32–3
Negro 1–3, 28
neoclassical theories 56, 245, 248–9, 254

neopositivist theories 127, 246, 249
Netherlands, The 102, 120
New Cross fire 14
New Labour (*see* Labour Party)
nigger 1, 6, 13, 15, 128
nihilism 73–4
non-conformity 47
North Africa 26
not guilty pleas 183
Nottingham 6, 115

Oi-music 119
otherness 143
over-charging 183, 248
over-generalisation (*see* stereotypes)
over-policing 128
over-representation 12, 30, 86, 140, 149, 185, 194–9, 203, 241–2
Oxford 11

Pacific Islands 35
Pakistani 51, 80, 82, 198–9, 241
parole 199, 206–207, 225
partnerships (*see* multi-agency partnerships)
passport checks (*see* immigration policing)
pathology 69
perpetrators, racist 114–19
philosophy 1–2
phrenology 2–4
physiology 1
pogroms 5–6, 117
police 122, 128–167, 219, 230
  accountability 9, 125, 163–6
  cautions by 150, 152, 154, 168, 242
  complaints against 9, 18, 123, 135–8, 164–5, 205, 257
  confidence in 135–8
  culture 157–9, 230
  intelligence 129, 144
  prejudice 9, 224
  racism 156–7
  response 122–3, 136
  suspiciousness 140–1, 145, 238
  special operations 129, 139
  targeting 128
Police Complaints Authority 133, 165, 257
Police and Criminal Evidence Act 1994 139–141, 151, 163, 165
policing 8, 14, 29, 128–67
  proactive 128, 237
policy 40, 230
Policy Studies Institute 45
politics 20, 125
population 37, 115, 223

Subject index

positional asphyxia 134, 209
positive action 231
positivism/positivist theories 57–8, 249
poverty 49–50, 58, 66
practitioners 213
prejudice xv, xvi, 2fnl, 9, 19, 36, 38, 251
pre-sentence reports 176, 209
Prevention of Terrorism (Temporary Provisions) Act 1989 139, 247
prison (*see also* imprisonment) 192–212
  foreign nationals in 86, 197–9, 207–8
  officers 223
  work 202
probation 174, 209–12
  officers 192, 209–12, 220, 226
  policy 210–11
promotion 216, 218, 225
proportionality (*see also* disproportionality) 43, 56, 256
prosecution 168–91
protection 255
provocation 48
psychology 57–8

race xii, xiii,1–8, 12, 18, 38, 108, 260
Race Relations (Amendment) Act 2000 53, 257–8
Race Relations Act 1965 51, 120–1
Race Relations Act 1968 51, 120–1
Race Relations Act 1976 xv, 15, 46, 52, 120, 213
Race Relations Liaison Officers 207
racial
  aggravation 120–2
  degeneration 2–3
  harassment 48
  hoaxes 90
  hygienists 4, 74
  others 77
  purity 1–5
  science (*see also* Eugenics) 4–5
  supremacy 251
  superiority 3
  typologies xvii,1–4
racialisation 22
racially aggravated offences 120–2
raciology (*see* racial science, Eugenics)
racism xii, xvii, 19–22, 40, 132, 212, 229
  as ideology 21
  contextual 161–2
  cultural 41, 125–6
  institutional xv, 17, 40, 53, 125, 159–60, 242, 252, 257–8
  scientific 1
  state 41, 65–6

violent (*see* racist violence)
  abuse 205, 241
  aggravation 122, 126
  crime 120
racist
  ideology xvii, 29, 119
  insignia 13
  murder 15, 108–9, 111, 121
  offenders 114–19
  victimisation 109–114, 205–6, 250–1
  violence xv-xvi, 6, 13–15, 17, 26, 108–27, 113, 251
recruitment 215, 230
rehabilitation 227
religion 5, 38
remand 154, 169–70, 240, 242, 260
repatriation 7, 23
reprimand (*see also* final warning, police caution) 253
RESPECT 225
RESPOND 200, 204
retention 217
right to silence 151, 253
riots 8–10, 116, 119, 129
robbery 11, 76, 93–5, 102, 140, 251
Rotterdam Charter 231
Royal Commission on Criminal Procedure 129, 140
Runnymede Trust xvii, 27, 30
Russians 77

safety xv, xvi, 255
Scandinavia 117
scapegoating 38, 115
Scarman Inquiry 10, 14, 160, 215
Schools (*see* education)
Scotland, Scottish xiv fn1, 29
Scrap Sus Campaign 140
segregation (*see also apartheid*) 4–5, 74, 92
segregation, occupational 48, 213–14, 219
segregation, residential 45–46
self-defence 119
self-report studies (*see also* surveys, self report) 98, 102, 235, 244
sentencing 121, 172, 175–187, 240, 242
sexism 216
skin colour1–2, 77
slavery 2, 117
Smethwick 6–7
social class 8, 24, 38, 143, 194, 231, 260
social constructionism xvii, 29, 74, 77–82, 245–6
social disorganisation 61, 247
social exclusion (*see* exclusion)
social services 41

Subject index

Society of Black Lawyers 135, 222–3
socio-economics 48, 260
solicitors 220–3
South Africa 4, 32, 39
Spanish 28
statistics
   crime 78, 83–4
   prison 83–4, 86
   victimisation 87–8
stereotypes xv, 36–8, 40, 114, 123, 155, 158, 166, 169, 203, 241, 249
sterilisation policies 4–5, 74
stop and search xvi, 10, 16, 129–30, 135, 138, 166, 242, 257
   as a performance indicator 238
   discrimination in 10, 140, 143, 237
   statistics 148
   socio-demographic factors and 143
   'sus' 139
   suspect availability 144
   intelligence-gathering 144
   public attitudes towards 143
   supervision of 9
   reasonable suspicion in 140–1, 145, 148, 238
   Tottenham Experiment 146–8
   reduction in 145, 148, 166, 239
Stormfront 22
structural theories 20–22, 64–7, 73–4, 76, 161–2, 246
subculture (*see* culture)
surveys 244
   of experiences of policing 134, 138
   of drug use 101
   of racial disadvantage 44–5
   of racist violence 14, 110, 112
   of xenophobic attitudes 5, 37
   of public attitudes 136
   of self-reported offending 99–107
   of victimisation (*see also* British Crime Survey) 87–8, 89–91, 135
sus laws (*see also* stop and search, Scrap Sus Campaign) 130, 139
Sweden 5, 116
Switzerland 39

targets 43, 149
territorialism 116
theft 76, 95, 140, 149, 251
theories of crime 55–74, 114–18, 243–52
theories of racism 1–4, 17, 19–41, 65, 155–62
tolerance (*see also* intolerance, zero tolerance) 30, 255
Turkish 28, 77, 102–3
Tyneside 11

underclass 60, 80, 143, 249
under-protection 251
under-representation 203
unemployment 8, 10, 48, 68
urbanisation 45
United States of America 2, 4, 102, 108, 117–18
Universal Declaration of Human Rights (1948)

victimistation xiii, xiv, xv, xvi, xvii, 44, 70, 76, 89, 121
   in prisons 205
   repeat, racist 109, 113, 244, 251
violence (*see also* domestic violence, racist violence) 18, 62, 67, 72, 82, 113, 118

Wales, Welsh xiv, 29
welfare dependency 60
West Indian 63, 78, 206–7
White xii–xiv, xvii, 27–30
Whiteness 1, 27–8, 30
Women 32, 39, 44, 47, 69–70, 227, 229

xenophobia 15, 36

Yardies 98, fn.
young offenders 152–4
Young Offenders' Institutions xvii, 193, 204

zero tolerance 166, 233, 248
Zionist Occupational Government (ZOG) 21, 117

Names Index

Adler, Freda 69–70
Albrecht, H-J. 77
Alexander, Claire 80, 245, 265
Alfred, R. 223–5, 229, 268
Allaker, J. 211, 267
Allport, G.W. 36, 38
Al-Shahi, A. 258
Anthias, Floya 24, 26
Arslan, family 109
Atkinson, G. 116
Austin, Peter 209
Aye Maung, N. 14, 89, 91–2, 104, 112, 115, 135–6

Back, Les 1, 4, 19–20, 22, 27, 31–2, 263
Bagilhole, B. 230
Baldwin, J. 182, 187
Ball, Caroline 254
Banton, Michael 19, 36, 51, 263
Barclay, Gordon 169–70, 172, 176, 181, 267
Barker, Martin 21
Barker, Mary 94
Barron, A. 216–17, 223, 229, 268
Batta, I. D. 80
Bayne-Smith, M. 230
Beackon, Derek 22
Beccaria, Cesar 56
Beck, E.M. 119
Becker, Howard x, 68
Beishan, S 50
Bentham, Jeremy x, 56
Benyon, J. 266
Bernard, T.J. 58–9, 264
Berry, Shawn 108–9
Berthoud, R. 26–7, 31, 47–50, 92, 105, 145, 176
Bierne, P. 64, 69, 264

Bittner, E. 131
Bjorgo, Tore 109, 115–18, 265
Blackwood, Orville 208
Blakelock, Keith 10
Bland, N. 140–1, 144–5, 147, 217–19, 266, 268
Blom-Cooper, L. 149–50
Blumenbach, Johann Fredrich 2
Blumstein, A. 233, 238
Bonnet, A. 263
Bottomley, Keith 83, 141, 149
Bourgois, P.I. 71
Bourne, Jenny 47, 145
Bowling, Ben xvii, 12, 13, 43, 91, 99–103, 108–15, 119–124, 145, 159, 237–9, 250–3, 259, 264–5
Box, Stephen 66–7
Bratton, W. 254
Brennan, P.A. 58
Brewer, Lawrence 108–9
Bridges, Lee 10, 14, 47, 145, 164, 239, 254
Briggs, C 211
Brooks, Dwayne 16, 123, 160
Brown, B. 69
Brown, C. 39, 45, 160
Brown, David 139, 141–2, 149, 150–2, 154–5, 162, 169, 178–9, 181, 189, 228–31, 239–40, 266–7
Brown, I. 171
Brown, J. 43, 112
Browne, Deryck 170–1
Bucke, Tom 142–3, 151, 155, 266
Bufford, Bill 114, 265
Bundey, Ruth 74
Burke, Edmund 3
Burleigh, M. 4, 74
Burnett, R. 204

Names index

Burney, Elizabeth 93–4
Burrows, J.N 155
Butler, Gerald QC 133
Byrd, James 108

Caddle, D. 207
Cain, M. 130
Caine, Michael 28, 29
Campbell, Alex 118
Campbell, B. 11
Campbell, Duncan 98
Cao, L. 62
Carmichael, S. 40
Carter, B. 6
Cashmore, Ellis 2, 21, 40, 219, 263, 265
Cathcart, Brian 15, 16, 109, 156, 252, 257, 267
Chahal, Kusminder 113, 250, 265
Chambliss, W.J. 83
Chan, Janet 230, 266
Chaudhary, Vivek 98
Cheney, D. 207
Chesney-Lind, 69
Chigwada-Bailey, R. 32–3, 70, 131, 133, 136, 172, 200–2, 227, 249
Choong, S. 158
Choudry, 81
Clarke, R.V. 56
Clements, J. 204
Cloward, R.A. 62
Cohen, A. 61–2, 71
Cohen, S. 77
Coleman, A. 83, 102, 109, 141, 149, 156–7
Collinson, M. 71
Condon, Sir Paul 15, 239, 256
Cook, Dee xiv, 262, 265
Copeland, David 110–11, 126–7, 251
Corkery, J. 235, 254
Cornish, D.A. 56
Corsellis, A. 179
Cotton, J. 134, 149
Cove, J. 177–8
Crawford, A. 124
Crisp, D. 135, 169, 207
Cross, I 11

Daley, K. 69
Darwin, Charles 4, 58
DeLone, M. 41, 148, 219
Denney, D. 210, 211, 267
Dennis, Norman 238, 258, 267
Desai, Philly 80–2
Devenport, Justin 98
Dixon, D. 141
Dominelli, L. 226–7, 229

Douglas, Brian 134
Douglas, Wayne 134
Dowds, L. 37, 88, 165, 173–4
Downes, D.M. 62
Drabble, R. 149–50
Duff, E. 222
Dulaney, M.W. 219, 266
Dunhill, Christine 266
Durkheim, Emile x, 66
Dyer, R. 27
Dykes, Andrea 111

Ekblom, P. 105, 135
Ekwe-Ekwe, H. 171
Elkins, M. 254
Elliot, D.S. 87, 115
Engels, Friedrich 64
Erdos, G. 258
Evans, R. 152
Everitt, Richard 81
Ewing, Keith 59
Eze, E. 1

Fanon, Franz 71–2
Farrakhan, Louis 26
Farrall, S. 204
Farrington, D.P. 59
Faulkener, D.E.R. 220
Feagin, J.R. 113
Ferguson, Ivan 172
Ferracuti, F. 62
Ferri, E. 57
Field, S. 115, 117
Fielding, N. 157
Fionda, J. 253
FitzGerald, Marian xiv, 42, 87, 89–90, 112, 140, 142–6, 148, 153–4, 175, 194, 198, 229, 237–8, 266–7
Fitzpatrick, B. 52
Flood-Page, Claire 99, 264
Foster, Janet 41, 125, 132, 157, 251
Foucalt, Michel 56
Francis-Spence, M. 226
Fryer, Peter 1–3, 7–8, 108, 119, 263

Gabbidon, Shaun 264
Galton, Francis 4, 58
Gardner, Joy 131
Garland, David 269
Garvey, Marcus 26
Gelsthorpe, Loraine xiv, 69,131, 177, 208, 262, 264
Genders, Elaine 200–3, 267
Genn, Hazel 113
Gibson, E. 93–4

Names index

Gilroy, Paul 1, 8, 10, 24, 26, 30, 63–5, 77–9, 82, 91, 163, 265–6
Gobineau, Joseph Arthur 2
Goffman, Erving x
Goldberg, D.T. 22
Goldhagen, D.J. 5, 116
Gordon, Paul xiv, xv, 65–6, 126, 128, 130, 138, 172, 174, 176–8, 180–1, 192, 194, 199–200, 203, 224, 229, 262, 267
Gordon, Robert 59
Gordon-Walker, Patrick 6
Goring, C.B. 58
Gorman, L. 156–7
Gottfredson, M. R. 56
Graef, Roger 117, 132, 157–8, 238, 252
Graham, J. 99, 100–1, 264
Grant, Bernie 139
Gray, Jeremy 136, 149, 158, 160–2, 214, 238, 252, 254, 266
Green, Helen Taylor 210, 264
Griffiths, Peter 6
Grimshaw, R. 163
Gunn, J. 198
Gutzmore, C. 33, 79
Guze, S.B. 59

Hague, William 258
Hale, Chris 87, 89–90, 112, 237
Hall, Stuart 8, 25, 27, 30, 38, 64–5, 77–8, 161–2, 249–50, 254, 264–6
Hall, Trevor 139
Hamilton, Stokely 40
Hamm, Mark 108, 265
Harris, Clive 5, 6, 263
Harrison, M. 230
Hartley, M. 188
Hattersley, Roy 6, 9
Hawkins, Darnell 264
Hedderman, Carol 180, 183
Hegarty, P. 52
Hegel, G. 1–2
Herbert, D.P. 188, 239
Herrenstein, Richard 58, 59
Hesse, Barnor 111, 113–14, 116, 125, 251
Hindelang, M. 59, 102
Hiro, Dilip 7, 13, 263
Hirschi, T. 56, 59, 102
Hobbs, Dick 157
Hodges, Lucy 9, 266
Holdaway, Simon 157–8, 163, 211, 215–17, 219, 223, 229, 231, 238, 252, 265–8
Holmes, C. 5, 13
Hood, Roger 41, 130, 141, 151, 170–1, 181, 183–7, 190, 240, 267
Hough, Mike 134, 136, 138, 251

Howard, L. 30, 202
Howe, Darcus 8, 10, 17, 139, 266
Hudson, Barbara xiv, 170, 176, 178, 180, 185, 194, 262, 265
Hullin, R. 171, 178, 181
Hume, David 1
Hunte, J. 128
Husbands, C. 115–16, 125, 251
Hutnyk, J. 25

Israel, Mark 222

Jackson, K. 131, 205
James, W. 5, 32, 263
Jarrett, Cynthia 133
Jefferson, Tony 67, 71, 136–8, 143, 163, 179, 181
Jenkinson, J. 12, 116
Jensen, Erik 119
Jensin, V. 62
Johnson, Claude 213, 224
Jones, Trevor 48, 112, 136, 163–4, 176
Jowitt, S. 94
Julienne, Louise 250, 265
Junger, M. 99, 102–3
Junger-Tas, J. 99

Kalunta-Crumpton, Anita 172, 237, 267
Kant, Emmanuel 1–2
Kaplan, Jeffery 118, 265
Kappeler, V.E. 133
Keith, Michael 8, 11, 65, 91, 104, 106, 118, 129, 140, 156–7, 164, 245, 252, 266
Kelly, L. 113
Kershaw, C. 87–8
Kettle, Martin 9, 266
King, John, William 108–9
King, M. 220–22
King, Martin Luther 98
Kirk, B.M. 189
Kleg, Milton 2, 21, 23–4, 28, 36, 38, 263
Klein, M. 99
Klier, J.D. 6, 117
Knox, Dr Robert 3
Kwesi Johnson, Linton, 132

Lacey, M. 268
Lambert, J. 158
Landau, S.F. 152, 153
Langan, P.A. 233, 238
Lapite, Oluwasijibomi 133
Lawrence, D. 211
Lawrence, Doreen 15–16
Lawrence, Neville 15–16, 139

Names index

Lawrence, Stephen 14–16, 109, 111, 113–14, 123–25, 160, 256
Lea, John 40, 62–4, 67–8
Leitner, M. 101
Lembert, E. 68
Lewis, George 173
Lewis, H. 171
Light, John 111
Linne (Linnaeus), Carl 1
Lippmann, Walter 36
Lloyd, Peter 15
Lombroso, Cesare x, 57, 58, 74
Loow, H. 117
Lopez, Haney 28
Lumumba, Omasase 208
Lustgarten, L. 42, 163

Macey, M. 82
MacIver, R.M. 36
MacLean, Brian 112, 136, 138, 262
Macpherson, Sir William xv, 15–16, 18, 41, 53, 109, 114, 122, 125, 161, 239
Mac an Ghaill, Mairtin 29, 263
McBarnette, D. 230
McClintock, F.H. 93–4
McConville, Mike 91–2, 182, 187, 237, 266
McCrudden, C. 43
McCurbin, Clinton 133
McDermott, K. 203, 224
McKay, H. 61
McLaughlin, Eugene 132, 163, 243, 264–5
McNee, David 9
Macka B 132
Maden, A. 198
Maguire, M. 264
Mahony, Anthony 208
Mair, G. 171, 176–8
Major, John 15
Malik, Maleiha 1, 122, 265
Malleson, K. 222
Mama, Amina 32, 72, 92
Mann, Coramae, Richey 262
Mannheim, Hermann 57
Manning, Alton 209
Marshall, Ineke xiv, 175, 194, 198, 262–3, 267
Martin, Michael, 208
Marx, Karl 64
Mason, David 46, 48–9, 105
Mavunga, P. 210, 226
Mawby, R.I. 81, 149
Maxwell, A. 52
May, R. 220–22
Mayhew, Pat 87, 89, 91–2, 104, 115, 135
Maynard, W. 14, 110–11

Mednick, S. A. 58
Menson, Michael 95
Merton, Robert x, 66
Messerschmidt, J. 64, 69, 264
Mhlanga, Bonny 169, 172,181, 183, 189–90, 267
Miles, R. xv, 5, 20, 40, 65, 263
Miller, Jerome. G. 58, 74, 140–1, 144–5, 147, 259, 266, 269
Milovanovic, D. 262
Mirlees-Black, Catriona 14, 89, 91–2, 101, 104–5, 112, 115, 135, 174
Mirza, Heidi 32
Modood, Tariq 26–7, 31, 47–50, 91–2, 105, 145, 176, 263
Montagu, A. 33
Moore, R. 19–20, 29, 61
Moore, Nick 111
Morgan, Rodney 132, 155, 163–64
Morris, Alison, 264
Morris, Stephen 98
Morris, Terence 61, 69, 188
Mott, Joy 101
Moxon, D. 169, 180, 182–3
Moynihan, J. 83, 102, 109
Mubarek, Zahid 127
Muir, David 16, 157, 242
Muncie, John 3, 264
Murji, Karim 98, 104, 243, 245
Murray, Charles 59, 60, 249

Nagasawa, R.H. 83
Nathan, G. 153
Natt, Malkjitt 162
Newburn, Tim 71, 163–4
Newing, John 160
Norris, Clive 143–5
Norton-Taylor, R. 109
Nzegwu, F. 171

O'Brien, Richard 133
Ohlin, Lloyd 62
Oluwale, David 132
Ouseley, Herman 15

Panayi, Panikos 12, 108, 251, 265
Patel, P. 81, 92
Pathak, S. 47
Patten, John 171
Paxman, Jeremy 29–30
Pearson, Geoffrey 3, 4, 29, 77, 108, 113, 117, 248, 264
Pease, Ken 83, 90, 237
Percy, Andy 87–8, 100–1, 113, 123, 235
Pettigrew, N. 145, 148

Names index

Phillips, Coretta xvii, 111, 113, 124, 149–52, 154–5, 162, 169, 181, 189, 239–4, 266–7
Phizacklea, A. xv, 5, 65, 263
Pitts, John 18, 114, 264
Player, Elaine 200–1, 204, 267
Pope, D. 164
Poulter, Sebastian 263
Povey, D. 134, 149
Powell, Enoch 7–8
Pratt, M. 93–4
Price, K. 8
Prime, J. 247
Prins, H. 208

Quinton, P. 141, 144, 145, 147, 266

Ramsay, M. 100–1, 235, 264
Ray, L. 251
Read, Tm 14, 110–11
Read, John, Kingsley 13
Reardon, D. 226
Reel, Ricky 95
Rein, M. 124
Reiner, Robert 56, 143, 157–9, 163, 238, 252, 264
Rex, John 19–20, 29, 61
Rhodes, Cecil 3
Rice, Marcia 33, 70, 264
Richards, M. 207
Roach, J. 164
Roberts, J. 56, 260
Root, Maria 31–2, 35
Rose, David 114, 126, 265
Ross, A. 99
Rushdie, Salman 26–7
Russell, Kathryn 90, 108, 269

Sadigh, S. 130
Sampson, A. 111, 113, 124
Saulsbury, W.E. 112, 124
Savill, J. 94, 95
Scarman, Lord Leslie 9, 10–11, 17–18, 79, 156, 159–60, 164, 215, 257
Scraton, Phil 65
Seagrave, J. 14
Searle, C. 47, 145
Sentamu, Rev. Dr. John 139
Sewell, T. 93
Shah, R. 90, 237
Shallice, A. 172, 176–8, 180
Shapland, Joanna 101
Sharma, S. 25
Shaw, Clifford 61, 200, 267
Shepherd, Dan 91, 92, 94, 237, 266

Shiner, Mike 222, 268
Shockley, William 59
Sibbitt, Rae 110, 115, 142, 144–6, 149, 153–4, 229, 238, 251, 265
Simon, F. 105
Simon, Rita James 69–70
Sims, L. 137, 163
Sivandan, A. 8, 25, 65, 120,130, 132, 263
Skellington, R. 46, 48–50
Skogan, Wesley 135, 143, 237, 251, 266
Skolnick, Jerome 157
Small, Stephen 31
Smith, Benjamin 118
Smith, David xiv, 7, 11, 40–3, 45, 76, 86, 89–90, 149, 158, 160–2 , 166, 183, 214, 233, 238, 242, 252, 260, 262, 265–6
Smith, Susan J. 24–5, 40, 45–6, 106, 111, 116,138
Smith, Susan 90
Snipes, J.B. 58, 59, 264
Solomos, John 1, 4, 6–8, 10, 13, 19–20, 22, 27, 31–2, 51, 65, 79, 92, 118, 120, 263, 265–6
Southgate, P. 135
Spencer, A.J. 134, 136, 138, 215, 251
Spiller, A. 101
Spohn, C. 41, 148, 219
Stanko, E. 71, 113
Staples, 72
Steer, D. 149
Stevens, P. 85, 90, 130, 149, 165, 266
Stewart, Robert, 126–7
Stone, V. 145, 148, 216, 231
Straw, Jack 16, 18, 125, 245, 257
Sultan, Anne 264
Swinton, M. 198
Sylvester, Roger 134

Tajfel, H. 37

Tarling, R. 165, 173–4
Tatum, B.L. 72
Taylor, Laurie 60
Taylor, Lord John 139
Terlouw, G-J 99
Thatcher, Margaret 8
Tilt, Richard 209
Tipler, J. 153, 189
Todd, M. 171
Tolnay, S.E. 119
Tomlinson, S. 19–20
Tonry, Michael xiv, 56, 259–60, 267, 269
Torkington, K. 230
Tuck, Mary 117
Tuffin, Rachel 216, 230

Tuttle, L. 69
Tyler, Tom 57, 248

Uglow, S. 132

Virdee, Satnam 250, 265
Vold, G.B. 58–9, 61, 69–70
Von Hirsch, A. 56, 260

Walker, M.A. 136–7, 154–5, 170–2, 178–9, 181, 183, 189, 194, 219, 262
Walker, Sam 41
Walmsley, R. 30, 202
Walton, P. 57
Ward, D. 268
Wardak, Ali 80, 265
Watts, Joseph 208
Weatheritt, Mollie 124
Weber, Max 131, 208
Webster, Colin 80, 94, 114, 251, 265
Weis, J. 102

West, Cornel 72, 73
White, P. 30, 202, 263
Whitelaw, William 9, 14
Wiles, Paul 101
Wilkins, L. 68
Wilkinson, C. 152
Willbanks, William 262
Willis, Carole 71, 80, 85, 130, 149, 165
Wilson, A. 32, 157, 188, 215
Wilson, Harold 6
Wilson, J.Q. 59
Wipperman, W. 4, 74
Witte, Rob 109, 115–17, 120, 265
Wolfgang, M. 62
Wright, Ian 245, 250

Yin, R.K. 174
Young, Hugo 259
Young, Jock 37, 57, 62–4, 67–8, 112, 136, 138, 141, 146
Yuval-Davis, A. 26